GANGS
IN AMERICA
III

*To Pat, my wife and best friend for the past 33 years
and to our loving daughters, Tamara and Tiffany—
young women of whom we are very proud*

—CRH

GANGS IN AMERICA III

C. RONALD HUFF EDITOR
University of California, Irvine

Sage Publications
International Educational and Professional Publisher
Thousand Oaks ▪ London ▪ New Delhi

For information:

Sage Publications, Inc.
2455 Teller Road
Thousand Oaks, California 91320
E-mail: order@sagepub.com

Sage Publications Ltd.
6 Bonhill Street
London EC2A 4PU
United Kingdom

Sage Publications India Pvt. Ltd.
M-32 Market
Greater Kailash I
New Delhi 110 048 India

Printed in the United States of America

Library of Congress Cataloging-in-Publication Data

Main entry under title:

Gangs in America III / edited by C. Ronald Huff.
    p. cm.
Rev. ed. of: Gangs in America. 2nd ed. c1996.
Includes bibliographical references and index.
  ISBN 0-7619-2423-X (cloth: acid-free paper)
  ISBN 0-7619-2424-8 (pbk.: acid-free paper)
  1. Gangs—United States. I. Title: Gangs in America
II. Huff, C. Ronald.
  HV6439.U5 G36 2001
  364.1'06'0973—dc21   2001004076

01 02 03 04 05 06 10 9 8 7 6 5 4 3 2 1

Acquiring Editor:	Jerry Westby
Editorial Assistant:	Vonessa Vondera
Production Editor:	Denise Santoyo
Typesetter/Designer:	Janelle LeMaster
Indexer:	Kathy Paparchontis

Contents

Foreword

What Is Past Is Prelude:
Gangs in America and Elsewhere

JAMES F. SHORT, JR.

It is no longer the case that current issues in criminology, especially gang issues, are primarily "new urgencies to old issues" (Short, 1990, p. 223). Although many old issues remain unresolved and controversial, important developments since the appearance of the second edition of *Gangs in America (GIA)* warrant this third edition. New methodological approaches are explored (Howell, Moore, & Egley, Chapter 1; Meeker & Vila, Chapter 10; Fleisher, Chapter 13; Klein, Chapter 15), and new insights into female gangs and ganging (Maxson & Whitlock, Chapter 2; Miller, Chapter 12; Fleisher, Chapter 13), as well as ethnic diversity (Vigil & Yun, Chapter 11; Zhang, Chapter 14) are presented. New insights into old issues of economic, neighborhood, and school contexts of gang behavior are discussed (Bursik, Chapter 5; Cureton, Chapter 6; Hagedorn, Chapter 7; Trump, Chapter 8), as are gang, gun, and drug relationships (Esbensen, Peterson, Freng, & Taylor, Chapter 3; Hagedorn, Chapter 7); evaluations of approaches to the prevention of violence and the role of gangs in violence round out this edition (Decker & Lauritsen, Chapter 4; Huff & Shafer, Chapter 9; Geis, Chapter 16; Braga, Kennedy, & Tita, Chapter 17; Huff, Chapter 18). Although theoretical advances in the study of gangs continue to lag behind empirical descriptions, here also, this edition of *GIA* offers new insights and possibilities.

Here my focus is on three of these developments: (a) the distribution of gangs, in this country and elsewhere; (b) gangs and gender; and (c) gangs and age, race, and ethnicity. Finally, I attempt to assess the significance of these relationships for the state of knowledge about gangs and crime, and what they portend for the control of crime. Although the empirical picture is far from clear, it is clear that gangs are extremely diverse in virtually every dimension: their composition, structure, and behavior. The theoretical picture is even less clear, but among the chapters to follow, significant challenges are to be found. Indeed, observed changes here reported have important implications for much of social and behavioral science, as well as criminology.

The Distribution of Gangs

Youth, or street, gangs—however they are defined (still an important issue; see Klein, Chapter 15; Short, 1998)—are more prevalent in more places in the United States than ever before. Trends that were only beginning to be documented in 1996 (Curry, Ball, & Decker, 1996; Klein, 1995) have been confirmed or altered by more recent data (Howell et al., Chapter 1). Since 1996, the National Youth Gang Center (NYGC) has conducted annual surveys focused on the prevalence, composition, and behavior of youth gangs in local jurisdictions across the country. The most recent surveys gather data from more than 3,000 local law enforcement agencies. Howell and his colleagues summarize a great deal of the information that has been gleaned from these surveys and other sources.

The NYGC surveys have been refined each year and are becoming an increasingly valuable source of data. These and other studies suggest that street gangs remain predominantly a large city phenomenon, but that smaller jurisdictions also report a good deal of youth gang activity. Reports from cities serving populations of 100,000 or more suggest little change in numbers of gangs and gang members between 1996 and 1999, but smaller jurisdictions report modest declines in both figures over this period. Smaller jurisdictions also report that the prevalence of gangs is a more recent phenomenon than is the case in larger jurisdictions.

Although this period is too brief to constitute much of a trend, it does suggest a sort of ebb and flow of gang culture in many parts of the United States, the exception being very large cities in which gangs have a much longer history.[1] Gang culture is widely diffused here and, it appears, increasingly so in other countries. Gang culture, in turn, is related to youth culture, with influences going both ways. Fads and fashions that begin among the ghetto poor diffuse to middle- and upper-class young people, and vice versa. Styles of music, dance, and dress diffuse widely. Artifacts of affluence, such as shoes and gold chains, become symbols of status among the less affluent, often contributing to violent confrontations (Anderson & Short, in press; Klein, Chapter 15; Short, 1998; Sullivan, 1989).

Klein's Chapter 15 in this volume is an excellent summary of what is known about the prevalence and the nature of street gangs in countries other than the United States, as well as a review of pioneer work in which he and his colleagues are engaged in the Eurogang project (Klein, Kerner, Maxson, & Weitekamp, 2001). The chapter also discusses several of the most debated features of street gangs, such as definitions and research strategies, the composition of street gangs, their structure, cohesiveness and its consequences for behavior—all important and still controversial issues (see also Decker & Lauritsen, Chapter 4).

Gangs and Gender

Editions of *GIA* after the first devote increasing attention to female gangs and ganging. Reviews of that literature and original research here reported by Jody Miller (Chapter 12) and by Cheryl Maxson and Monica Whitlock (Chapter 2) present a somewhat confusing array of findings, suggesting that there is a great deal of variation in the extent to which young females participate in gangs and in the nature of their joining and participation. Risk factors for gang affiliation appear to be somewhat different for boys than for girls, but data from different studies conducted in different places are inconsistent. In view of the observed extreme diversity of gangs, the extent to which such inconsistencies reflect real differences in the groups and locations studied (and when they were studied) is an important issue, as yet quite unclear. Such differences notwithstanding, several observers conclude that "group processes, conflicts and rivalries provoke girls' participation in confrontations with rival gang members in ways similar to that of young men" (quoting Jody Miller, Chapter 12; see also Fleisher, 1998; Klein, 1995).

Mark Fleisher's Chapter 13 yields a somewhat different picture of female gang members and their gangs than has been portrayed in other gang research. Although some of these differences may be artifacts of methodology and unique to his research settings, it is quite possible—indeed, I think it is likely—that his research methods reveal some differences that have not been discovered by traditional survey and interviewing methods.

Using a combination of ethnographic and network methods, Fleisher focuses on the Fremont Hustlers, a Kansas City, Missouri, gang about which he has written extensively (Fleisher, 1998), and on female members of several gangs located in North Champaign, Illinois. Among the Fremont Hustlers, gender, race, and ethnicity—which are associated with gang affiliation and activities in most studies—were not important *either interpersonally or with respect to access to drug markets*. Moreover, the gang's location was due to "the fact that a female member's mother owned a house" at a particular corner, rather than based on neighborhood identity —also unlike many gangs. Most important, "so-called membership was identical with friendship," rather than being based on group-defined criteria other than friendship. The Fremont Hustlers, described more fully in Fleisher's (1998) book, *Dead End Kids: Gang Girls and the Boys They Know*, appear to be atypical of street gangs in a number of ways. " 'Membership,' " he reports, "is a peculiar idea" (p. 39), and their "boundaries" are extraordinarily fluid. Internal group relations appear to be based more on interpersonal and family relationships and problems than on gang affiliation. Group structure, norms, behavior, and artifacts are even less well defined than is reported in other empirical studies. The "gang label," he reports, was marked by toleration of one another, rather than bonding. They "never acted as a unit"[2] but as "small networks of adolescents who 'hated' other members."

Gang boundaries were also extremely fluid among the women in North Champaign, a racially isolated black community that Fleisher describes as "emerging." The women he is studying belong to black gangs with familiar names: Vice Lords, Gangster Disciples, Black P-Stones, and Black Disciples. Friendships that precede "joining a gang" continue after gang affiliation but, unlike the Fremont Hustlers, gang membership *promotes bonding*. Fleisher's theoretical construct—"ego-gang network"—seeks to measure "the total set of social relations of a gang member." Identification of gang membership based on self(ego)-identification, and identification of their friends (and *their* gang affiliations) yielded some surprising results. "No ego knew all members of her gang" and "the central-most Vice Lords (i.e., the Vice Lords who knew the highest number of Vice Lords and were known to the highest number) knew less than 10% of all Vice Lords listed as alters in the sample." Fleisher's wry observation is a challenge to us all: Given this circumstance, "the notion of the gang as a 'group' (a type of network) is extremely suspicious."

Gang researchers have long rejected stereotypical images of street gangs as tightly organized, rigidly controlled by group norms, and the like; but Fleisher's portrayal appears to represent an extreme case. Method effects and local contexts are important for all research, but they are especially so when methods are applied for the first time and in contexts that differ significantly from the sorts of settings in which most gang research has been carried out. One can only applaud Fleisher's recognition of the importance of replicating network methods and of studying gangs in other settings. The smaller size of minority populations in the two Kansas Cities (Missouri and Kansas), compared to larger metropolitan areas, may be a factor in the lack of racial or ethnic significance among the Fremont Hustlers. Black neighborhood poverty rates in the Kansas City metropolitan area in 1990 stood at 9.9%, somewhat below the rate in other midwestern cities (Jargowsky, 1998). And, although every community is in some sense unique, the "emerging" black community in North Champaign, Illinois, differs in many ways from large inner-city black ghettos. Fleisher's research is suggestive, nevertheless. The relationships found among North Champaign gang members may reflect the emergence of gang membership as a type of institutional affiliation similar to that which occurs throughout society, as people join a variety of organizations and groups with varied interests. That is, gangs in this instance become more like social clubs, service clubs, and other special interest groups. To the extent that this occurs, gangs become less "deviant" and more an aspect of "normal" association.

Age, Race and Ethnicity, and Gangs

Age is an especially telling characteristic of gangs; and here, again, definitions, methods effects, and contexts are important. Howell et al. (Chapter 1) note that National Youth Gang Center data suggest that in 1999 nearly two thirds (63%) of gang members were young adults, and that this represents a significant change from 1996 survey data when the numbers of young adults and juveniles were approximately equal. They also note, however, that police intelligence and record keeping systems may fail to purge *former gang members* from their records, thus overcounting older members and undercounting younger members of whom they are not yet aware. Because it is in the job description of the police to fight crime, intelligence about past behavior and gang affiliation is valued information, and this surmise is reasonable.[3] Surveys of high school students have the advantage that they can secure important information on self-reports of gang membership and behavior, but they are unlikely to reach many "young adults." Self-report studies have yielded much valuable information—for example, that gang membership is associated with increased delinquent and criminal behavior, and that when young people drop out of gangs they also report less involvement in such behavior (Thornberry, Krohn, Lizotte, & Chard-Wierschem, 1993).

Field studies are also more revealing of changes in the age structure of gangs and in differences among racial and ethnic categories. Sanchez-Jankowski's (1991) study of some 37 gangs in New York, Los Angeles, and Boston found significant variations among ethnic groups in the *upper age bounds* of gang members. Ages of his Latino gangs ranged from 12 to 42 years; among black gangs this range was from 14 to 37 years; and among white gangs, 14 to 26 years (pp. 323-324; data reported in the appendix). The *average* (mean) age span among these gangs was, for Latino gangs, 12.5 years; for black gangs, 12.3; for white gangs, 7.6 years.[4]

Before assessing the significance of these findings, a historical note is in order. Although Frederic Thrasher's somewhat awkward classification of the age ranges of the gangs he studied makes precise comparison impossible, it is useful to note that nearly one half (47%) of the gangs on which he presented data were said to range in age between 11 and 17; an additional 31% were listed as ranging in age between 16 and 25; and 38 (4%) between 21 and 50. An even wider, but unspecified, classification accounted for 16% (154) of the distribution (Thrasher, 1963, p. 60).[5] Clearly, older gangs were around early in the past century.

So were ethnic groups, of course, but that picture has changed enormously since Thrasher's day and in even more recent years (see Sanchez-Jankowski, 1991; Sanders, 1994; Suttles, 1968). Thrasher (1963) secured data on the race and nationality of the gangs he studied and then classified them into four categories: "American (native white parentage)" (45; 5.26%); Negro (63; 7.37%—footnoted, "The twenty-five gangs of mixed negroes and whites are necessarily omitted"); Foreign extraction (747; 87.37%; and "Other races than white or Negro (none—footnoted, "A number of Chicago Chinese are members of tongs, which are very similar to gangs. The number of such groups is not known"; p. 132).[6]

Howell et al. (Chapter 1) note that early in the 19th century, youth gangs were "composed of youth of various European backgrounds"—Thrasher's "foreign extraction" category. "By the late 1970s," however, black and Hispanic gangs made up "about four fifths of all gang members reported by law enforcement agencies," and this percentage "increased to 90% in the early 1990s" (see Curry, Fox, Ball, & Stone, 1992; Klein, 1995; Miller, 1992). The 1999 National Youth Gang Survey and self-report studies suggest that somewhat higher percentages of gang members are white and that the numbers of "Asian" gangs and gang members have increased (to about 7%). Black and Hispanic gangs and gang members still make up three quarters of those reported by law enforcement personnel; and self-reports confirm higher percentages of those categories claiming gang membership at some point in their lives.

Bridging Theoretical Gaps

The theoretical flowering that took place in the early- to mid-20th century (Shaw & McKay, and Thrasher, followed by Cohen, Walter Miller, and Cloward & Ohlin) continues to guide much research to this day. William Julius Wilson's work on the "ghetto poor" (the preferred term, rather than the "underclass"; Wilson, 1987, 1996) provided gang researchers and other criminologists with a theoretical frame that has led to modification of social disorganization and social control approaches (Sampson & Wilson, 1995; Sampson, Morenoff, & Earls, 1999; Sampson, Raudenbush, & Earls, 1997). Chapters in this volume reflect these developments and help to bridge both empirical and theoretical gaps in knowledge.

Advocating cross-cultural study of "multiple marginalities," Vigil and Yun (Chapter 11) stress the importance of "appreciation of each group's experiences, as that group understands them." Vigil, a long-time student of gangs, and Yun—his frequent collaborator—emphasize the importance of the histories of ethnic groups in their countries of origin, as well as in the United States; and of their unique cultural heritages. Based on Vigil's forthcoming book, *A Rainbow of Gangs,* African American, Chicano, Salvadoran, and Vietnamese experiences are contrasted, and resulting gang differences described. They note, however, that "street socialization," under circumstances in which "other institutions have become undermined, fragmented, made fragile and largely ineffective," exerts itself, blurring ethnic lines. Among all four groups, the result of such common experiences is that "remarkably similar things are learned on the streets where fear and vulnerability generate the need for protection, friendship, loyalty, and other routines and rhythms provided by the gang." Among those "similar things" are group processes and other types of collective behaviors about which we still know far too little.

Cureton (Chapter 6) observed and carried out ethnographic interviews with older members ("Original Gangsters") of the Hoovers, a South Central Los Angeles gang formerly known as the Hoover Crips. The interviews dramatically portray life in that community—and in the larger society—for these young men *as they experience it,* and as they perceive life for younger gang members. The Hoovers in this portrayal are an important community institution, with the power to impose and enforce restrictions on movement and hanging out on the streets.

From the interviews, vastly different perspectives on violence and criminal activity emerge, compared to the perspectives of younger "bangers" and compared to some portrayals of gangs. These men are weary of banging and of the necessity of skirting the law in order to make ends meet. Survival, status, and respect require such behavior among the young, and they recognize those same motivations in their own younger years. They reject the idea that violence and crime stem from black men's value systems, as well as the idea that black men are inherently violent, and recognize the importance of the lack of legitimate opportunities and the power of the "Code of the Street" (Anderson, 1999) to produce such behavior.

Marginalization has emerged as an important theoretical construct for understanding the manner in which ethnicity, immigration, social, political, and economic circumstances relate to crime and youth violence (Tonry, 1997; Tonry & Moore, 1998). The notion of "multiple marginalities," indicating marginalization with respect to more than a single institution or social domain—with additive and cumulative consequences—resonates in much research, and in several of the chapters to follow.

Theory that will tie together these and other strands of observation, insight, and experience is badly needed. Any such theory must include realities and constructs such as multiple cultural contexts and marginalization, group processes, and social capital. Most important, the changing nature of the macrosocial environments that shape these phenomena must be understood.

Bursik's Chapter 5 advances this agenda by reconsidering his earlier (with Grasmick) influential systemic model of gang behavior (Bursik & Grasmick, 1993). Drawing on a variety of studies and theoretical frames, Bursik emphasizes the complex and reciprocal impact of public/private relationships on the nature and effectiveness of social control at the local level. Ethnographic observations suggest, for example, that under certain conditions gangs become "*community* actors" (Venkatesh, 1996) that perform recognized economic and social control functions. Bursik also notes that the systemic model failed to give adequate attention to networks of power that effectively preserve elements in the industrial and occupational structure that perpetuate the association of poverty, crime, and gangs.

Hagedorn (Chapter 7; see also Hagedorn, 1998c) adds to this theoretical perspective with his discussion of the impact on gangs of the "postindustrial" economic era. As others have argued, as well, these conditions account in large measure for the changing age, racial, and ethnic distribution of gangs. For young men and women whose lives are bounded in communities of the ghetto poor, "growing out of" gangs by getting legitimate jobs, marrying, and having families often is not an alternative. Good jobs are no longer available, and they become *Locked in the Poorhouse,* the felicitous title of the book edited by former U.S. Senator Fred R. Harris and Milton S. Eisenhower Foundation President Lynn A. Curtis. The book documents the extent to which the ghetto poor have become a permanent part of American society (Harris & Curtis, 1998; see also Anderson, 1999; Short, 1997). Much less appreciated, or applied in criminology, is research by Manuel Castells, Alejandro Portes, Saskia Sassen-Koob, and others that documents *the transformation of economies and societies on a global scale* (Castells, 2000; Sassen-Koob, 1998). A major consequence of these developments is that informal economies have come to play an increasing role in societies throughout the world (Portes, Castells, & Benton, 1989b).

Hagedorn ties these developments to changes he has observed among gangs in Milwaukee and in Chicago. His study of drug "small businesses" in two inner-city Milwaukee neighborhoods—one primarily Hispanic, the other African American—suggests that 1 in 10 of the young men in both neighborhoods was in some way employed in selling drugs. Elsewhere, Hagedorn notes that the consequences for gangs are likely to differ in cities that adapt successfully to the "information age" and those that do not (Hagedorn, 1998; Hagedorn & Goldstein, 1999).

We know all too little about these matters, and more and better research is badly needed. Study of young adults in a variety of settings, however, suggests that the minority (African American and Hispanic) gangs that came into prominence during the last few decades of the 20th century have become institutionalized in much the same way as occurred among white gangs of European descent decades earlier. The blurring of legitimate and illegitimate economic opportunities that occurred with the advent of Prohibition is similar in some respects to the informal segment of current economies and the hustling adaptations that have long been a part of lower-class life (Anderson, 1999; Drake & Cayton, 1962; Valentine, 1978).

Social Capital

James Coleman invoked social capital as a theoretical construct that helped to explain the superior performance of parochial school children compared with their public school counterparts (Coleman, 1988; Coleman & Hoffer, 1987). Subsequently the notion has been explicated, elaborated, and applied to many social domains, including crime (Lin, 1999; Portes, 1998; Sampson & Laub, 1993; Sampson et al., 1999; Short, 1990).

Coleman stressed the quality of intergenerational relationships, especially in the family, as the most important locus of social capital. Beyond the family, however, important intergenerational relationships shape young people and their opportunities. Although we did not conceptualize our findings in terms of social capital, findings from our Chicago gang research "make sense" in terms of social capital. Measures of relationships with the adult world demonstrated the superior quality and quantity of such relationships among boys who did not belong to gangs, compared to gang members, as well as the advantages of middle-class compared to lower-class boys, and whites compared to blacks (see, e.g., Rivera & Short, 1967; Short, Rivera, & Marshal, 1964). Similarly, Sullivan (1989) found that superior personal networks, rather than "human capital in the form of either education or work experience" (p. 103), gave his white young men greater access to jobs. Anderson's (1999) discussion of the dilemma faced by "decent" parents as they try to help their children negotiate the demands and constraints imposed by the "code of the street" is a dramatic illustration of the complex relationships that are associated with social capital.

Fleisher's chapter emphasizes the variable qualities of relationships that he subsumes under the rubric of social capital. Bonds among the Fremont Hustlers, for example, were detrimental to the intergenerational relationships with mainstream society that Coleman emphasized—which Fleisher refers to as "bridging social capital." The *"valence"* of social capital —that is, its relationship to mainstream and other value systems—is an important dimension of socialization that, with few exceptions, has been neglected in the scholarly literature (cf. Pattillo-McCoy, 1999; Sampson et al., 1999). The networks that produce social capital vary not only in the types of social skills and contacts that they provide, but in the manner in which they relate to ambition, expectations, employment in conventional or illicit occupational pursuits, and so on.

Issues of Crime Control

Understanding diversity in *local contexts of violence*—including law enforcement contexts—is of critical importance to understanding gangs and to the success of crime control efforts. In some locations, gangs may lie at the heart of youth violence. In others, gangs and gang affiliation may be less important than is the identification of chronic offenders and the groups with which they are affiliated, some of which may be gangs, whereas others are not. In either case it is important to understand "the dynamics between and within these groups" (Braga, Kennedy, & Tita, Chapter 17).

The "gang question" may not be the most important issue with respect to those dynamics, Braga and colleagues observe (Chapter 17). The "strategic prevention of gang and group-involved violence" program developed in Boston, and adapted elsewhere, targets groups whose members include "chronic offenders" by delivering the message that violence will no longer be tolerated and promising to "pull every lever" legally available to stop it. The program is a cooperative effort between law enforcement agencies and community groups offering services to gang members, thus taking advantage of the "experiences, observations, local knowledge, and historical perspectives of police officers, streetworkers, and others with routine contact with offenders, communities, and criminal networks" (for another example, see Chapter 9 by Ronald Huff and Kent Shafer on community-oriented policing).

The "pulling-levers" approach to deterring chronic violent offenders may help to resolve a seeming gang paradox that is based on two observations: (a) violent events often serve to strengthen group solidarity; but (b) former gang members frequently report that the experience of violence plays a role in decisions to leave the gang (Decker & Lauritsen, Chapter 4). Threats of pulling levers, when combined with the reality of experience with violence and community services, may prove to be an effective intervention strategy with gangs and other young people.

Communities and law enforcement agencies are also diverse, of course. James Meeker and Bryan Vila's description (Chapter 10) of the regional Gang Incident Tracking System in Orange County (California) is a sobering reminder, not only of the difficulty of developing and maintaining data systems that involve multiple organizations and communities, but of professional, bureaucratic, and ethical considerations that accompany their development and application (see also Huff & Shafer, Chapter 9; Braga et al., Chapter 17). Community-oriented policing is a promising strategy for overcoming such impediments, as well as for reducing crime and promoting healthy, functional communities.

The Meeker/Vila chapter is a cautionary tale against reading too much into findings from data reporting systems about gangs. In the few years since the National Youth Gang Center began conducting annual surveys of law enforcement agencies, improvements have been made in sample coverage, question wording, definitions, and follow-up procedures to check the reliability of the reports. Analyses of the data have contributed to a variety of issues concerning the distribution, composition, and behavior of gangs, and to theoretical issues such as the efficacy of gang typologies (see citations in Howell et al., Chapter 1 in this volume). Still, questions regarding the reliability—and more important, the validity—of the data suggest that caution should be exercised in drawing conclusions based on these data and analyses. The NYGC system is perhaps in about the same stage of development as the FBI's Uniform Crime Reporting System in the mid-1930s, a few short years after the system began collecting data from local law enforcement agencies. The Eurogang Program (see Klein, Chapter 15) is at an even earlier stage of development. Much the same criticism can be leveled about any data collection system, of course, and about all record keeping systems. With a lot of hard work and repetition, greater confidence in the distributions and trends based on such data may be achieved.

Gilbert Geis (Chapter 16) also invokes ethical considerations in his discussion of constitutional and other legal issues related to the large number of "anti-gang" laws that have passed in this country in recent years. There is profound irony in the fact that such laws often are couched in much the same "child-saving" language as accompanied the juvenile court and "asylum" movements in the 19th century (see Platt, 1969; Rothman, 1971). The sometimes delicate balance between individual freedoms and the protection of society is not an easy one to accommodate. As a final note on crime control, the significance of prison gangs should not be ignored. Disagreements concerning research methods, data and what they mean, and the struggle for theoretical development notwithstanding, scholars surely can agree that prison gangs are an important aspect—only one of many—of the problem of overreliance on incarceration as a means of crime control (Howell et al., Chapter 1).

Conclusion

There is much food for thought in the pages that follow—and many challenges to scholars of gangs and of crime, and their students. I am already looking forward to *Gangs in America IV!*

Notes

1. Note, however, that historians of crime find that cities once built walls around themselves in order to protect themselves from criminals as well as armies. Johnson and Monkkonen (1996) observe that, "Gangs were in the countryside. Today, at least in the suburbs and rural parts of the United States, many people would like to wall cities to keep criminals and gangs in" (p. 1; see also Lane, 1997).

2. In this respect, except for very small groups, the Fremont Hustlers were similar to most other gangs (see my exchange with Paul Lerman: Short, 1968a; Klein, 1995).

3. Howell et al. also note that "commits crimes together" was the most important descriptive criterion chosen by law enforcement respondents to characterize gangs in their jurisdictions, and that this criterion was chosen by 50% of respondents. This finding is particularly interesting in view of the continuing controversy over gang definitions.

4. The average age span for four gangs classified as black/Latino was 22.25 years; for five gangs classified as Latino/black, 13.2 years.

5. Eighteen gangs (2%) were listed as being composed of 6- to 12-year-olds. Thrasher presented age data on 1,213 of his 1,313 gangs, but I have excluded from these calculations 243 gangs that he classified as "Athletic or social clubs," which Thrasher had included under other categories of "later adolescent" (aged 16-25), "adult" (aged 21-50), and "mixed" ("Wider range").

6. Thrasher listed nine "nationalities," including "Jewish," and an "Others" category. Polish, Italian, and Irish gangs predominate, accounting for more than 80% of the gangs on which such data are presented.

Acknowledgments

As I contemplated whether to undertake this project, it seemed to me that I had to address several key questions: Was there a need for a third edition of *Gangs in America (GIA)*? Was there a sufficient amount of high-quality new scholarship to justify a new edition? Would my colleagues agree to contribute to this project? Since you are reading this, you know that my answers to all three questions were positive. As suggested both by Short's Foreword and by Howell, Moore, and Egley's discussion in Chapter 1, much has changed with respect to gangs in the 6 years since the last edition of this book was published. The pages that follow will both document and explicate some of those changes and will, hopefully, be regarded as a valuable resource in updating our knowledge of the ever-changing landscape of gangs in America—and elsewhere, since this edition includes, for the first time, some discussion of gangs in other nations and the value of developing a cross-national perspective on gangs (see Klein, Chapter 15).

I want to acknowledge with sincere appreciation the contributions of the 29 colleagues whose work appears in these pages. The fact that 29 colleagues would take the time to develop chapters for this book, given their other commitments, underscores two things, in my judgment: (a) our collective interest in maintaining the current momentum of research and publication on gangs and gang members and (b) the impressive networking that has developed among gang researchers, as well as a significant group of policymakers and practitioners, who make concerted efforts to incorporate new findings into their own thinking. It is a stimulating group of colleagues, and within this network there is an impressive balance of scholarly criticism, on the one hand, and mutual support and sharing of information, on the other. This group of colleagues and contributing authors deserve much of the credit for this book.

Finally, I want to express my appreciation to Sage Publications, especially to Jerry Westby, with whom I worked most closely on this project from the beginning. Jerry has been extremely supportive and encouraging throughout the development of this book. Terry Hendrix has, as always, offered his encouragement and support as well, even though his duties did not bring him into direct contact with this project. Since the first edition of *GIA* more than a decade ago, it has been a continuing pleasure to work with Sage on this series of books, and I appreciate their continuing interest in and support of the *GIA* series. Will there be a *GIA IV*? Perhaps, if the three questions above can again be answered in the affirmative over the next 5 years or so.

Introduction

C. RONALD HUFF

In this third edition of *Gangs in America* I have sought to bring together a group of authors who could address gangs from a variety of academic and professional perspectives. These authors include academics who are experienced and well-known scholars and gang researchers; academics who have recently begun their careers and have been conducting valuable gang research; academics who are experienced scholars and researchers but whose work does not generally focus on gangs; and experienced practitioners who address gangs from the perspectives of both law enforcement and school safety and security. It is my hope that this broad approach to the subject of gangs will underscore the diversity of perspectives, as well as the diversity of issues. The gang is a complex and multifaceted phenomenon, and gang research, to be useful in either theoretical or policy applications, must take this complexity into account.

To address some of the major dimensions of gangs, the book is organized into four major parts. Part 1 provides an overview of gangs and some of the ways in which they have changed and continue to change, as well as discussions of issues involved in joining the gang, getting involved in "gang banging," and trying to leave the gang. Part 2 focuses our attention on some of the major "arenas" in which gangs operate: neighborhoods, communities, and schools; macrolevel and microlevel factors that affect gang formation and maintenance; as well as some of the efforts made by communities to improve the ways in which law enforcement, schools, and other agencies of social control attempt to address the challenges posed by gang-related crime. Part 3 includes a collection of chapters informing us about the ever-changing diversity of gangs, including cultural factors, the role of gender, the importance of cross-national research, and the implications of gang diversity for field research on gangs as social networks. Finally, Part 4 consists of several chapters that address public policy issues, such as the controversial use of civil injunctions to combat gangs, new strategies to prevent group (including gang) violence, and a discussion of public policy implications.

Part 1 begins with an overview of the changing nature of youth gangs in recent years. Howell, Moore, and Egley, who are affiliated with the National Youth Gang Center, focus especially on that Center's surveys since 1996. They argue that there is now more variety in types of gangs and that gangs are reported in more localities than ever before. Some of the factors they consider include age, gender, race and ethnicity, organization, initiation, duration, hybrid gangs, "late onset" versus "early onset" gang locations, migration, gangs and schools, and prison gangs. They underscore the importance of taking all of these—and other—complex factors into account when formulating and implementing policies and intervention strategies. In Chapter 2, Maxson and Whitlock discuss gender differences in risk factors for joining a gang. Their analysis focuses on four areas: prevalence, gang structures and female roles in gangs, criminal activity, and risk factors. They address such questions as whether the risk factors for joining gangs differ for females compared with males and, if so, what are the implications for programming aimed at prevention and intervention.

Once youths join gangs, their lives typically change in many ways. In Chapter 3, Esbensen, Peterson, Freng, and Taylor address the issue of whether youths who join gangs become involved in drug use, drug sales, and violence *after* they join or whether they engage in these behaviors either *prior* to joining or *simultaneously* with joining. Such information is important to inform both theory development and policies concerning prevention and intervention. Decker and Lauritsen (Chapter 4) address the next stage of gang life—trying to get out. Many gang members are unprepared for the violence that is often associated with gang life and often tire of living their lives while "looking over their shoulder." Popular wisdom has it that "once a gang member, always a gang member." Is that necessarily true? The discussion in Chapter 4 addresses some of these issues through interviews with both active and former gang members. The discussion places this issue in the broader context of desistance from crime, while also attempting to document what motivates gang members to leave the gang, the processes followed in leaving the gang, costs and benefits associated with leaving, and the complex role of violence in both promoting gang solidarity and providing motivation to leave the gang.

Bursik (Chapter 5) begins Part 2 by stating that the theoretical model he and Grasmick developed concerning neighborhood structures and dynamics must now be modified in several important respects in order to provide a more adequate framework for analyzing gangs in the neighborhood context. Recent scholarship has documented the importance of such variables as the relationship between private and public levels of social control, the relationship between social networks and informal social control, and the importance of public level networks developed with industry/occupational structures. Bursik argues that some of the predictions that would have been made based on the earlier Bursik/Grasmick model would not have held up due to these newer developments, thus requiring a reformulation of the theoretical model.

Cureton (Chapter 6) transports the reader from the world of theory to the streets of South Central Los Angeles, where he conducted a 2-year ethnographic study of the Hoover Crips. He provides insights that help us assess the extent to which our theories accurately capture some of the realities of "life in the 'hood," such as the importance of respect, the rationale for violence; the code of the street, the "gangster's mentality," survival, and the functional role of gangs in the 'hood. While acknowledging a strong sense of bonding with the "subjects" of his study, Cureton discusses the importance of objectivity in conducting such intensive, long-term field research as well. Chapter 7 keeps us in the field, where Hagedorn reports the results of a recent study he conducted in Milwaukee. He relates recent changes in postindustrial gangs to the radically changed economic conditions available to youth, including gang members, and the failure of modernization to provide formal economic opportunities in the United States and other nations. This failure, he argues, has fueled the development of an array of *informal* economic activities, including drug sales. He then analyzes the informal economy in two inner-city Milwaukee neighborhoods, comparing "retail drug businesses" with legitimate minority businesses on a number of dimensions (e.g., number of employees, income, startup business failures), and concluding that much of what we call crime is, in fact, work.

Another arena in which gangs have had an impact has been schools. In Chapter 8, Kenneth Trump, a nationally respected school safety and security expert, discusses the impact of gangs on schools, including such issues as the differing characteristics of gang and nongang school violence, the problem of denial by school officials, and the dangers of stereotyping gangs and gang members and of dismissing as unimportant the gang "wannabes." Trump emphasizes the importance of focusing on the *behavior* of students, the development of interagency collaboration between the schools and other community agencies, and the importance of a balanced approach that includes strong emphases on prevention and intervention, including a comprehensive "safe schools" plan.

In Chapter 9, I collaborate with a nationally respected and progressive law enforcement leader to discuss the community-oriented policing

(COP) model as it relates to the issue of gangs. We compare more traditional law enforcement gang control tactics with COP-oriented tactics, citing some examples of where the COP approach is being successfully applied. We argue that it is more productive for law enforcement agencies to collaborate with the community in a COP-oriented, community problem-solving approach, rather than relying on the more traditional paramilitary, suppression-oriented tactics. Although suppression remains a necessary and important component of law enforcement's attempts to address gang-related crime, it cannot be a sufficient response. Finally, we argue that the greatest challenge in making this transition is not the technical challenge but rather the challenge of changing the organizational culture of law enforcement agencies from "crime fighting" to community partnerships. We assert that making that change has significant longer-term benefits for communities.

Chapter 10 keeps our attention focused on law enforcement, but this time the issue is how a number of law enforcement jurisdictions might collaborate to document and track gang incidents across their jurisdictional boundaries. The answer, it turns out, is "with great difficulty." As in Chapter 9, part of the challenge involves changing traditional law enforcement organizational cultures. Meeker and Vila present a cogent discussion of the history, development, and issues associated with the Orange County, California, Gang Incident Tracking System (GITS). Because gang "turf" and gang-related crime cut across jurisdictional boundaries, many regions are interested in developing such a shared database, but there are multiple barriers to cooperating in such an enterprise. This chapter reports on one such effort, involving all 23 law enforcement agencies in a county of nearly 3 million residents. The discussion documents the steps that were taken to develop the system, the obstacles that were faced, the successes and limitations that resulted from this effort, legal barriers, incentives/disincentives for street officers, and the advantages and disadvantages of alternative models of developing such a shared database.

In Part 3, the focus shifts to the increasing diversity of gangs. Vigil and Yun (Chapter 11) keep us focused on Southern California but turn our attention to the cross-cultural factors involved in the breakdown of social control in four Los Angeles ethnic communities (African American, Chicano, Salvadoran, and Vietnamese). They apply the concept of "multiple marginality" (developed earlier by Vigil) to the breakdown of social control in families, schools, and law enforcement that has led to street socialization and, in turn, gang involvement for some youths in these communities. Vigil and Yun discuss the dynamics of the street socialization process and describe how that learning process actually blurs some of the distinctions among these four ethnic groups. Finally, they discuss the ecological, economic, and social psychological factors that affect minorities in ways that increase their risk for gang involvement and gang crime.

The past two decades have brought an increased interest in, and research on, female involvement in gangs. In Chapter 12, Miller discusses some of the historic stereotypes concerning girls' involvement in gangs and notes that some of these stereotypes have now been overcome through recent research. She then provides an updated appraisal of the status of our knowledge concerning girls in gangs, focusing her discussion on (a) the level of female gang involvement; (b) risk factors for gang membership and girls' pathways into gangs; (c) the level and character of gang girls' delinquency and its context in gang life for girls; and (d) the consequences of gang involvement for girls. Miller documents that girls join gangs in response to an array of problems in their lives, and although they often join gangs due to the promise (or perceived promise) of a better life, the reality is that gangs tend to exacerbate their problems, thus further constraining their options in life.

In Chapter 13, Fleisher discusses his extensive field research with gangs in Kansas City and in Champaign, Illinois. Employing anthropological ethnography, sociological theory with data analysis, and social network theory with data analysis, he analyzes gangs as *social networks*. His findings offer challenges to conventional wisdom and conceptualizations of gangs. He argues that although much gang research relies on respondents' self-declarations of gang affiliation as the sole test of gang membership, such self-declarations can be either an *attribute* of an individual or an *inference* about one's relations to others who are similarly self-motivated. By comparison, social network analysis focuses on the *nature* of relations as they affect gang life and the *attachments* among actors. Fleisher's analysis concludes with some advice to those who would design intervention programs: Focus on the longer-term development of human capital.

Zhang (Chapter 14) brings to our attention the fact that the stereotype of Chinese youth in the United States as hard-working, high achieving, well disciplined, and very bright is not always consistent with day-to-day reality in the community. Many cultural and structural barriers combine to challenge recent Chinese immigrants and their children. Zhang's focus in this chapter is on how Chinese parents deal with their children's delinquency in the context of the "new world" in which they live. He analyzes Chinese traditions and practices with respect to their social control influences and how these influences have broken down. Like Vigil and Yun's discussion in Chapter 11, Zhang's documents the breakdown in social control in the family as the demands and constraints of the new world, including the financial, linguistic, and cultural barriers it imposes, all combine to disrupt the social control mechanisms traditionally associated with Chinese culture, rendering Chinese youth more susceptible to delinquency and gang involvement.

Another type of diversity is addressed by Klein who, in Chapter 15, discusses the recent development of an interactive network of U.S. and European researchers interested in studying street gangs and developing principles for the prevention and control of gang activities. This Eurogang network began with Klein's survey of European cities where street gangs had emerged in the 1980s and 1990s. That survey was followed by the development of a steering committee, workshops, and, in short order, more than 100 participants, including both researchers and policymakers. Klein's cross-national and multimethod approach is essential since, as he notes, American research may well be culture-bound and certainly cannot simply be applied to other nations. Finally, Klein discusses the "Eurogang paradox" (denial that European gangs are like "typical" American gangs, while the image of a "typical" American gang does not square with the reality of American gangs). Klein also discusses a typology of gangs that has proved helpful in this cross-national context.

Part 4 begins with Geis (Chapter 16) tracing court decisions since 1936 that involved laws targeting gang members. The courts have noted the vague definitions of *gang* that have been employed in legislative attempts to target gangs. He then offers an analysis of recent legislation targeting gangs, such as the extension of RICO prosecutions to gangs. Geis argues that such legislation has been used in a discriminatory manner. He questions, for example, why it should be illegal for two or more gang members to interact but not illegal for two or more corporate executives (representing corporations known to be engaged in antitrust violations) to meet in order to engage in antitrust violations. He asserts that although gang-related crime poses threats, the new wave of laws targeting gangs may pose even greater threats—to our liberty and our constitutional rights. The element of *personal* culpability, with proof, is often overlooked in such laws, and he concludes by arguing that gangs have become the most recent focus of legislation that in the past was directed at vagrancy, loitering, and "public nuisances"—all disproportionately impacting the poor and minorities.

The Boston Gun Project and its Operation Ceasefire have received a great deal of national attention in recent years and have resulted in a number of recent experiments involving attempts to address gang-related and other group-related violence. In Chapter 17, Braga, Kennedy, and Tita discuss the development of some of these initiatives, compare their similarities and differences, and synthesize some key dimensions of prevention based on these examples. The authors discuss the key strategy, known as "pulling levers," involved in the successful Boston project. This involved a combination of "sticks and carrots" (pulling every lever of deterrence and combining them with positive support, community services, etc., whenever violence occurred). The idea is to break the cycle of violence–response. Communities have developed custom-designed strategies based on the Boston model but modified to fit their local circumstances. The authors argue that although most of these initiatives have not yet been rigorously evaluated, they do seem to show promise, based on preliminary results.

The book concludes with my attempt, in Chapter 18, to discuss some of the policy implications of the collective contributions to this volume. There is much to learn from the work of our contributing authors, so I attempt to address the question, "So what?" with respect to public policy, asking how the chapters in this volume might help inform our discussion of public policy. I argue for a balanced approach involving prevention, intervention, and suppression—all of which must be applied within the context of neighborhoods and communities and with the collaboration and partnership of the citizens who live there. The chapters in this volume provide valuable insights into the dynamics of gangs and implications for how we might improve our efforts to prevent and control gang-related crime and violence.

PART

The Gang:
Changing Boundaries, Joining,
"Banging," and Getting Out

The Changing Boundaries
of Youth Gangs

JAMES C. HOWELL
JOHN P. MOORE
ARLEN EGLEY, JR.

After studying more than 1,000 Chicago gangs, Thrasher (1963) observed that "no two gangs are just alike; [there is] an endless variety of forms" (p. 5). "[The gang] may vary as to membership, type of leaders, mode of organization, interests and activities, and finally as to its status in the community" (p. 36). Thrasher's "endless variety of forms" has been characteristic of youth gangs in the United States for more than a century (see Sante, 1991).

From the 1950s through the 1970s, researchers described many kinds of gang organizational forms. Spergel (1995, p. 79) documented 16 sets of dimensions developed by numerous researchers to classify gangs. Miller (1992) subsumed gangs of the late 1970s under a broad typology of 20 "law-violating youth groups" (p. 20). Some researchers described black and Hispanic gangs that began to predominate in the 1950s and 1960s as having a "vertical" or age-graded structure consisting of numerous cliques (Moore, 1978). Klein (1971, p. 66) favored a turnip-shaped structure, with fewer young gang members at the bottom and fewer older gang members at the top than in the middle.

In the 1980s and 1990s, some youth gangs were described as violent drug trafficking operations resembling adult criminal organizations. The most common stereotype of youth gangs conveyed by the print and broadcast media closely resembles an image portrayed more than a decade ago in a California study (Skolnick, Correl, Navarro, & Rabb, 1988). Entrepreneurial youth gangs were said to be the product of the crack cocaine epidemic (Skolnick, 1989) and economic restructuring that resulted from the deindustrialization of major cities (Fagan, 1996; Hagedorn, 1988; Skolnick, 1990; Taylor, 1990). Some of these gangs were said to be highly structured, much like military organizations, and to be operating criminal enterprises (see Klein, 1995, pp. 40-43, 112-135, for the history of this image, promulgated primarily by broadcast media). Empirical support for the popular image of youth gangs as instigated by Skolnick and his colleagues in the California studies is limited (Howell & Decker, 1999; Klein, 1995; Moore, 1993).

Nevertheless, different varieties of youth gangs continue to exist and evolve. The central theme of this chapter is that youth gang characteristics and operations have changed considerably during the past decade or so. These changes can be viewed from two contrasting perspectives—that of the empirical gang studies conducted earlier, and that of the stereotypes promulgated by the mass media and other sources. We use the term youth gang *boundaries* to refer to demographic characteristics of gang members, the level of gang organization, and selected forms of gang activity, such as drug trafficking. It appears that changing gang boundaries are most evident in newer gang problem localities, those in which gang problems have developed over the past 10 to 15 years.[1] A "hybrid gang culture" that characterizes some newer gangs represents a relatively new development. The role of school-linked gangs, gang member migration, and prison gangs in bringing about the expansion of youth gang boundaries is also discussed.

Our review begins with selected findings from the National Youth Gang Survey. We summarize some of the trend data reported in the survey, then follow with a presentation of evidence of recent gang boundary changes. We conclude with a brief discussion of policy and program issues suggested by these changing boundaries.

National Youth Gang Survey Trends

Since 1996, the National Youth Gang Center (NYGC) has conducted annual surveys of a nationally representative sample of more than 3,000 law enforcement agencies.[2] Forty-four percent of respondents reported active youth gangs in their jurisdiction in 1999, down 4% from the previous year and down 9% from 1996. The NYGC estimates that more than 26,000 gangs and 840,500 gang members were active in the United States in 1999 (Egley, 2000). This latter number represents an 8% increase since 1998 and approaches an estimated high of nearly 846,500 gang members in 1996.

The presence of gang activity varies markedly by the size of the jurisdiction served by law enforcement agencies. In 1999, gang activity was reported by 16% of those agencies serving a population of 9,999 and below and by 28% of the agencies serving populations of 10,000 to 24,999. Although this represents a decline of 8% and 12%, respectively, from 1996, it is apparent that even the smallest jurisdictions are not immune to gang activity. In addition, 50% of the agencies serving a population between 25,000 and 49,999 and nearly two thirds (65%) of those serving a population between 50,000 and 99,999 reported gang activity in 1999. This represents a 12% and 11% drop, respectively, from 1996, but shows that one half or more of our nation's medium-sized jurisdictions still experience gang activity.

At the other end of the spectrum are the largest jurisdictions. In 1999, 92% of agencies serving the largest populated areas (i.e., 250,000 and above) and 84% of those serving a population between 100,000 and 249,999 reported gang problems. Three important observations can be made here. First, almost all jurisdictions with large population bases report gang activity. Second, unlike the modest decline in the presence of gang activity in other areas (as reported above), the proportion of agencies with populations of 100,000 and above that reported gang activity remained virtually unchanged from 1996 through 1999. Third, agencies serving these areas consistently report substantially higher averages of both active gangs and gang members than do their counterparts (NYGC, 2000a). Taken together, these findings suggest that current gang problem localities are both concentrated, in that the largest populated jurisdictions retain a disproportionate share of gang activity, and widespread, in that gang activity continues to appear and remain in jurisdictions of differing population sizes (see also W. Miller, 2001).

Characteristics of Youth Gangs and Gang Members

Because researchers, practitioners, and law enforcement agencies cannot agree on a common definition of a "youth gang" (Horowitz, 1990; Miller, 1992; Needle & Stapleton, 1983; Spergel & Bobrowski, 1989), the NYGC surveys allow respondents to use their own definitions.[3] Each NYGC survey asks questions aimed at improving our understanding of the characteristics of contemporary youth gangs.

The 1998 NYGC survey asked respondents who reported gang problems to rank order six youth gang characteristics. These were definitional elements that law enforcement respondents (and other agency representatives) in previous gang surveys said are important gang characteristics (Miller, 1992; Needle & Stapleton, 1983): (a) "has a name"; (b) "commits crimes together"; (c) "has a leader or several leaders"; (d) "hangs out together"; (e) "displays or wears common colors or other insignia"; and (f) "claims a turf or territory." None of these criteria received an overwhelming majority of votes as most important (Howell, Egley, & Gleason, 2000). However, "commits crimes together" clearly was the most important criterion, receiving a first-place selection by 50% of the respondents. The next most popular characteristic, "has a name," was ranked most important by only 19% of the respondents. The remaining criteria received a smaller fraction of top selections as most important criterion. Thus, a common set of gang characteristics is not apparent in this analysis. Further analysis of the frequency and sequencing with which law enforcement agencies use the six criteria revealed that they use them in a variety of combinations (Howell et al., 2000).

Age

Contemporary youth gang members appear, on average, to be older than in the past. In 1996, law enforcement agencies estimated that approximately half of their gang members were juveniles (under age 18) and that half were young adults (18 and older; NYGC, 1999a). In 1999, 63% of the gang members were estimated to be young adults and only 37% juveniles (Egley, 2000). Between 1996 and 1999, the proportion of young adult gang members (ages 18-24) increased sharply, from 37% to 50% of all gang members (Egley, 2000).

What accounts for the increased prevalence of older gang members in the NYGC survey data? It's possible that law enforcement agencies tend to undercount younger gang members, a possibility discussed later in this chapter. Another possibility is that the evidence supporting the finding that there are more older gang members may be a product, at least in part, of improvements in records systems and the use of standardized gang indexing criteria. This seemingly oxymoronic hypothesis arises from two law enforcement trends that have accompanied growth in gangs over the past 20 years: (a) widespread adoption of criteria to be applied to subjects; and (b) rapid development of automated databases for criminal intelligence.

In the past 10 years, at least 20 states have passed laws defining *gang* and *gang member*,[4] chiefly to "enhance" or increase the severity of penalties for criminal offenses if committed by a gang member. Criteria for indexing individuals in gang intelligence databases are also set forth in a few states' laws. Whether established for penalty enhancement or police intelligence purposes, such criteria have been standardized in a number of states and are accepted by law enforcement personnel in those states. In other states, where uniform codification is lacking, many local police agencies have developed their own criteria for indexing gang members. Further, the National Crime Information Center (NCIC), the National Drug Intelligence Center (NDIC, 1995), and the National Alliance of Gang Investigators Associations (NAGIA) all have developed gang and gang member definitions. Almost universally, such definitions include illegal or criminal activity by the gang and several tests for membership.

With the advent of law enforcement database automation, agencies have developed stand-alone and shared gang intelligence systems. The extent and sophistication of these systems cannot be adequately described here because of space limitations. Some are pointer systems, containing only identifying data on suspected gang members, including photos, and "pointing" the inquiring agency to additional information. Others give direct access to extensive intelligence. It is increasingly common for officers to access central gang databases and intelligence-sharing networks with laptops while in the field. Having agreed upon indexing criteria, law enforcement personnel have steadily accumulated information on gangs and gang members. Therein lies the problem. Absent purging criteria, a youth meeting all of an agency's requirements at the time of indexing could fail to come to police attention again and remain a gang member forever, "aging" through the passage of time. The Code of Federal Regulations (28CFR Part 43) establishes, inter alia, that a subject can remain in an intelligence database for only 5 years without additional activity or other validation. This purge requirement applies, however, only to state and local law enforcement agency intelligence databases established with federal funds. Many local gang databases are not required to comply with 28CFR and may not otherwise have established retention periods. An informal query directed to NAGIA officers affirmed that such "aging in the system" is possible. In any event, according to NYGC survey data, the average youth gang member is now a young adult, between ages 18 and 24.

Gender

Gender is another youth gang characteristic that has changed. Youth gang membership among girls is much more common than in the past (see Curry, 1998; Moore & Hagedorn, 2001). Nationally, among 10- to 16-year-olds, the male to female ratio among youths who had ever belonged to a gang was 2:1 in 1997 (see Snyder & Sickmund, 1999, pp. 58-59). This proportion was exceeded slightly in an 11-site survey of eighth graders *in known gang problem localities* (Esbensen & Deschenes, 1998). About 14% of the boys and 8% of the girls were gang members; 38% of the students who said they were gang members were female (Esbensen & Osgood, 1997).[5] Other studies suggest that gender mixing is also common (Fleisher, 1998; J. Miller, 2001a). Girls appear to be most predominant among very young gang members (Bjerregaard & Smith, 1993), in part because they tend to leave gangs earlier than boys.

Gender-mixed gangs also are more common now than in the past. In Esbensen and colleagues' 11-site survey of eighth graders, 92% of gang youth said both boys and girls belonged to their gang (Esbensen, Deschenes, & Winfree, 1999, p. 42; see also Fleisher, 1998, and J. Miller, 2001a). Interestingly, 9 of the 11 sites from which Esbensen and colleagues drew their student sample reported fairly late onset of gang problems (1982-1994) in the 1996 National Youth Gang Survey (the importance of this observation is discussed later in this chapter).

Race and Ethnicity

Early in the history of youth gangs in the United States, large proportions of their members were white, composed of youth of various European backgrounds (Sante, 1991; Spergel, 1995). By the late 1970s, about four fifths of all gang members reported by law enforcement agencies were black or Hispanic (Miller, 1992). Their proportion increased to 90% in the early 1990s (Curry, Fox, Ball, & Stone, 1992). In the 1999 National Youth Gang Survey, respondents said 47% of their gang members are Hispanic; 31%, African American; 13%, Caucasian; 7%, Asian; and 2%, "other" (Egley, 2000). Thus white gang members have come to represent a larger share of gang members reported by law enforcement agencies. However, white youths represent a much larger share of gang members in self-report studies. In Esbensen and colleagues' 11-site study, 31% of the students who said they were gang members were black, but equal percentages (25%) were Hispanic or white, 5% were Asian, and 15% were of other racial and ethnic groups (Esbensen & Osgood, 1997). Nationwide, among 12- to 16-year-old males, 2% of white youths, 6% of black youths, and 5% of Hispanic youths reported ever having belonged to a gang (see Snyder & Sickmund, 1999, p. 60). The corresponding percentages for females were 1% white, 2% black, and 2% Hispanic.

Racial and Ethnic Mixed Gangs

Some racial/ethnic mixing in gangs was fairly common, according to the earliest gang descriptions. For example, 40% of 800 of the Chicago gangs Thrasher (1963) studied had such a mixture. Most of this mixture, however, was among nationalities, not racial and ethnic groups. Post-World War II youth gangs were racially and ethnically homogeneous (Spergel, 1995, pp. 58-69), and this remained a common pattern into the mid-1990s, at least in major American cities (Klein, 1995, pp. 106-107).

In contrast, almost half (46%) of all gangs in the United States were reported to be multiethnic/multiracial in the 1996 National Youth Gang Survey. To measure this occurrence more specifically, the 1998 National Youth Gang Survey asked respondents to estimate the percentage of youth gangs in their jurisdiction with a "significant mixture of two or more racial/ethnic groups." Respondents estimated that more than a third of their youth gangs consisted of a significant mixture of such members. The largest proportion of this type of hybrid gang was reported in small cities (54% of all gangs), and the smallest proportion was in large cities (32%; Howell, Egley,

& Gleason, in press). The earlier onset localities were significantly less likely than later ones to report multiethnic or multiracial gangs. About one third (32%) of the respondents in localities with an onset of gang problems before 1981 reported hybrid gangs. This percentage was much higher in the 1991-1992 gang problem onset group (56%).

Level of Gang Organization

A common media image of youth gangs is that they are "highly disciplined criminal organizations with elaborate networks of 'soldiers' under strict control from the top" (Moore, 1993, p. 28). Several studies challenge the notion that youth gangs are highly organized, particularly in emerging gang cities. Numerous studies have questioned the extent of youth gang organization in emerging gang cities such as Denver, Cleveland, and Columbus (Huff, 1996, 1998a; J. Miller, 2001a); Kansas City (Fleisher, 1998); Milwaukee (Hagedorn, 1988); Pittsburgh (Klein, 1995); San Francisco (Waldorf, 1993); San Diego (Decker, Bynum, & Weisel, 1998; Sanders, 1994); Seattle (Fleisher, 1995); St. Louis (Decker & Curry, 2000; Decker & Van Winkle, 1996; J. Miller, 2001a); and Las Vegas and Reno (Miethe & McCorkle, 1997). Decker and colleagues (1998) compared two gangs in Chicago and two in San Diego that police reported were most highly organized. They found that the Chicago Gangster Disciples were far more organized than the Latin Kings from Chicago and the two San Diego gangs, but that none of the gangs exhibited the extremely high level of gang organization attributed to them by law enforcement. In St. Louis, an emerging gang city, Decker and Curry (2000) found "strong evidence that the gangs described by [their members] are not well organized" (p. 481).

Initiation, Duration, and Degree of Gang Membership

Best and Hutchinson (1996) debunk several myths promulgated in the media and popular discourse regarding gang initiation rites, such as "the slasher under the car," "the slasher in the back seat," "flicked headlights," and random acts of violence on innocent people as part of an initiation rite (see also Fernandez, 1998; Fleisher, 1995, pp. 130, 140-141). Other recent studies challenge certain stereotypes of gangs and gang members (see especially Decker et al., 1998; Fleisher, 1995, 1998; McCorkle & Miethe, 1998; Miethe & McCorkle, 1997). Studies also show that gang members (especially marginal members) typically can leave the gang without serious consequences (Decker et al., 1998; Decker & Lauritsen, 1996; Decker & Van Winkle, 1996; Fleisher, 1995). At least in emerging gang areas, most adolescents do not remain in gangs for long periods of time. Studies in Denver; Rochester, NY; and Seattle show that from one half to two thirds of adolescents stayed in a gang for 1 year or less; from 9% to 21% maintained membership for 3 or more years in the respective cities (Thornberry, 1998). Intergenerational gang membership is far more common in cities with longstanding gang problems, such as Chicago (Horowitz, 1983) and Los Angeles (Moore, 1978).

Few gang members are "core" members of the gang. In an ingenious study using gradations of gang definitions to categorize gang members, Esbensen, Winfree, He, and Taylor (2001) classified gang members according to five levels of gang involvement. Of some 6,000 eighth graders who were surveyed, 17% had "ever been" a gang member, 9% were "current" gang members, 8% were members of a "delinquent" gang, 5% were members of an "organized" delinquent gang, and only 2% were "core" members of an organized delinquent gang. Thus, less than a third of the current members considered themselves "core" members of an organized delinquent gang.

Hybrid Gangs That Do Not Fit the Stereotypical Gang Mold

Sergeant David Starbuck, formerly of the Kansas City Police Department's gang unit, characterizes many newer gangs as having a "hybrid gang culture" (Starbuck, Howell, & Lindquist, 2001). By this he means that many of the newer gangs that have sprung up throughout the country may not follow the established rules or methods of operation carried out by their predecessors from Los Angeles or Chicago. Although Kansas City and other midwest areas experienced gang migration during the 1980s and early 1990s, most of the region's larger collectives continue to be locally based "hybrids." These homegrown gangs consider themselves to be distinct gangster entities with no alliance to groups such as the Blood/Crip or Folk/People. Other law enforcement gang investigators have reported hybrid or "mutant" gangs (see Valdez, 2000),[6] but there is no gang research literature on this form of variation in gang culture.[7]

Over the past decade, Kansas City's hybrid gang members have adopted some characteristics of established gang culture (Starbuck et al., 2001), but Sgt. Starbuck and his fellow officers began to see that midwest gangs had modified established gang culture with personal interpretations and agendas. They often "cut and paste" bits of Hollywood's media images and big-city gang lore into a local version of a nationally known gang. For example, these "hybrid culture" gangs may adopt a mixture of symbols from both Chicago- and Los Angeles-based gangs. They may not have an allegiance to a traditional "color"; they may change the name of their gang; members may change their affiliation from one gang to another or belong to more than one gang; and two or more gangs may suddenly merge and form a new gang. Sgt. Starbuck contends that this "hybrid gang culture" is one of the dominant gang types found in communities that had no gangs prior to the 1980s or 1990s.

Sgt. Starbuck gives an example (Starbuck et al., 2001). In separate sections of Kansas City, Missouri, two different gangs operate as the "Athens Park Boys." These groups share the name with the original APBs, a well-established Blood set originating in Los Angeles County. Although both of the Kansas City APB gangs engage in criminal activities, there is no connection other than the shared name. One set consists of African American teens on the east side of the city, and the other consists of Caucasian teens, primarily from affluent families residing in the suburbs. In fact, it seems each group is unaware of its Kansas City counterpart. In addition, neither set is connected to the Athens Park Boys in California or any other jurisdiction with local versions of the APB.

A subsample of respondents that reported gang problems was queried regarding the prevalence of hybrid gang culture in a special survey NYGC conducted in conjunction with the 1999 National Youth Gang Survey. These gangs were described in the survey question as follows: "These gangs may have several of the following characteristics: a mixture of racial/ethnic groups, male and female members, display symbols and graffiti of different gangs, or have members who sometimes switch from one gang to another." Respondents were asked if they have gangs that fit this description. Six out of 10 respondents (61%) said they had such gangs. However, the average number of gangs (4) that "don't fit the mold" is small, and they are most prevalent in areas with large populations.

Gangs in Late Onset Localities

A new generation of youth gangs has emerged. The overwhelming majority of gang problem localities first experienced the emergence of gangs within the past 15 years. Nearly 9 out of 10 (87%) of the localities reporting gang problems in the 1996 National Youth Gang Survey (NYGC, 1999a) said that onset occurred during the 10-year period from 1986 to 1996 (Howell et al., in press). More than half (57%) of the responding law enforcement agencies said their gang problems began in the 1990s. The average year of gang problem onset was 1989 for large cities, 1990 for suburban counties, 1992 for small cities, and 1993 for rural counties (NYGC, 1999a). A cascading pattern also was evident in the population size of localities, with smaller and smaller jurisdictions reporting onset of gang problems over time. These newer gang problem localities are most likely to be found in rural counties, small cities, and suburban counties of less than 50,000 population. Our findings suggest a general pattern of cultural diffusion of gangs among young persons in the late 1980s and early 1990s with respect to population clusters.

An analysis of NYGC survey data in early versus late onset localities (Howell et al., in press) found that the youth gangs in the newer gang problem localities were distinctly different in their demographic characteristics from the gangs in the jurisdictions where gang problems began much earlier. The late onset localities had younger members, slightly more females, more Caucasians, and were more likely to have a racial/ethnic mixture. Surprisingly, Caucasians were the predominant racial/ethnic group in the latest onset localities (with onset in 1995-1996). The newer gangs (in localities where gang problems began in the past 10-15 years) also tend to have a much larger proportion of middle-class teens. Gang members in the late onset localities (during the 1990s) also were far less likely than gang members in the early onset jurisdictions (prior to the 1990s) to be involved in violent crimes (homicide, aggravated assault, robbery, and use of firearms) as well as property crimes and drug trafficking.

Research on youth gangs in late onset localities does not generally support the media image of a gangs-drug trafficking-violence connection (see Howell & Decker, 1999; Klein, 1995; and Moore, 1993, for reviews of previous research and stereotypes). An investigation of this connection using 1996 National Youth Gang Survey data (Howell & Gleason, 1999) found that both gang member drug sales and gang control of drug distribution are much less likely to be significant problems in jurisdictions where gang problems emerged in the past decade or so. Gang control of drug distribution also is less likely than gang member involvement in drug sales to be extensive in the newer gang problem localities. Jurisdictions reporting onset of gang problems between 1981 and 1985 show the highest level of gang member involvement in drug sales (Howell & Gleason, 1999). Jurisdictions in which gang problems emerged after 1985 show lower levels of gang member involvement in drug sales, and these levels decreased in each subsequent time period of onset through 1995-1996.

Gang Member Migration

Migrating gang members appear to have contributed to changes in the characteristics of youth gangs in newer gang problem localities in the past 10 to 15 years. The dispersion of the urban population to less populated areas contributed to the proliferation of gangs in suburban areas, small towns, and rural areas. Migrant gang members may act as cultural carriers of the folkways, mythologies, and other trappings of more sophisticated urban gangs (Maxson, 1998, p. 3). Gang member migration (movement of gang members from one city to another) increased over the past decade or more, but the character of their relocation is quite different from the stereotype of youth gangs that suggested they were expanding their drug trafficking operations to markets in distant cities (Skolnick et al., 1988). A nationwide gang migration study (Maxson, 1998; see also Maxson, Woods, &

Klein, 1996) found that slightly more than two thirds of some 1,000 responding cities' law enforcement agencies said they had experienced gang migration by 1992. "The sheer number of cities with migrant gang members and the widespread geographic distribution of these cities across the country is dramatic, but the volume of gang migration presents a far less alarming picture" (Maxson, 1999, p. 6). Almost half (47%) of the cities providing an estimate reported the arrival of no more than 10 migrants in the prior year. Only one fifth of cities reporting gang migration attributed the genesis of their gang problem to this development. The most common reasons to migrate are social considerations (57% of cities), including family moves to improve the quality of life and to be near relatives and friends. Drug market expansion was a distant second most frequently cited motivation (20%). Migrants usually arrive individually rather than with gang companions. Most of the gang migration was regional, within about 100 miles of the city of origin.

The existence of local gangs generally preceded migrating gang members (Maxson, 1999). The exception is cities with gang onset after 1985. These were less likely to report that their local gangs preceded gang migration. A number of local studies of individual gangs question their ties to larger gangs in distant cities such as the Crips and Bloods (Decker & Van Winkle, 1996; Hagedorn, 1988; Huff, 1989; Rosenbaum & Grant, 1983; Waldorf, 1993; Zevitz & Takata, 1992). In the 1999 National Youth Gang Survey, respondents estimated that 18% of their gang members were migrants. This survey raises questions regarding the motives of the migrating gang members, however. More than 8 out of 10 (83%) respondents agreed that the appearance of gang members in the suburbs, small cities, and rural areas is because of population shifts from central cities into these areas (Egley, 2000). However, cities reporting gang migration said local crime rates or patterns generally were affected by migrants, primarily through increases in theft, robbery, and other violent crimes. Gang migrants were generally not perceived as having a substantial impact on the local drug market, probably because of their relatively low numbers (Maxson et al., 1996, p. 27). Most youth gang problems are "homegrown" (Klein, 1995).

School-Linked Youth Gangs

Youth gangs have been rather prevalent in schools in large cities since the 1970s (Miller, 1992). However, they have become more prevalent in schools in the recent past. In the 1995 National Crime Victimization Survey of students ages 12 to 19 (Chandler, Chapman, Rand, & Taylor, 1998), more than one third (37%) of the students reported gangs at their schools (Howell & Lynch, 2000),[8] and the percentage of students reporting the presence of gangs at their schools nearly doubled between 1989 and 1995. About two thirds of the surveyed students reported that gangs at school were involved in one or more of three types of illegal activity (violence, drug sales, or gun carrying). However, just 8% of the students said gangs were involved in all three types of activity. About one in five students (21%) said gangs were involved in two of the measured activities, and 40% of the students said gangs were involved in only one of these three types of activity. Thus, only a small fraction of the surveyed students said gangs were highly active in all three types of serious crimes.[9]

It is not clear how well school-linked gangs are represented in the youth gangs that law enforcement agencies report in the National Youth Gang Survey. Because only a small fraction of student-affiliated youth gangs may be involved in multiple types of serious and violent crimes, law enforcement agencies may be reporting only a small portion of gangs and gang members who are actually present in schools. This undercount could be significant. An 11-site survey of some 6,000 eighth graders (in known gang problem localities) found that 11% were currently members of a gang and 17% said they had belonged to a gang at some point in their young lives (Esbensen & Deschenes, 1998).

Curry's (2000) 5-year follow-up study of self-reported gang members among young students (Grades 6-8) suggests that law enforcement agencies may not enumerate young student gang members for several years. Curry found a great deal of continuity between gang membership at young ages and police records examined 5 years later. Most of the self-identified gang-involved youth who also were self-identified delinquents eventually were identified as offenders by police in at least one delinquent incident. Conversely, among the police-identified gang offenders, the majority were self-identified earlier as gang involved and delinquent in the middle school survey. Thus, Curry argues, gangs and gang members identified in student surveys are not a separate gang problem from that indicated in law enforcement data. But law enforcement agencies are far less likely to count young gang members who do not yet appear in their arrest records. Based on Curry's study, it seems safe to say that law enforcement undercounts young gang members, particularly students.

Prison Gangs

The growth of prison gangs appears to be affecting the boundaries of youth gangs in adjacent communities. Although there are no reliable national data on the prevalence and membership of prison gangs, in the first collection of research articles published on prison gangs (Fleisher, Decker, & Curry, 2001b), experts agree that prison gangs got bigger and more entrenched in the 1980s and 1990s (see Jacobs, 2001).[10] Whereas prior discussions of prison gangs centered on the major ones (Fleisher, Decker, & Curry, 2001a), a distinction is now made between these gangs and youth gangs imported into prisons, or prison equivalents of youth gangs (Fleisher et al., 2001a).

Because of the dearth of prison gang studies, the relationship between prison gangs and gangs on the street is not well understood. Jacobs (2001) contends that "the worst-case scenario is that prison gangs serve to strengthen gangs on the street. There is fluid communication between the gang members outside and inside prison. Criminal schemes are hatched in prison and carried out on the streets and vice versa" (p. vi). In one study that researched the dynamic relationship between prison gangs and youth gangs (Valdez, Alvarado, & Arcos, 2000), Mexican American prison gangs gradually came to dominate and dissolve the local gangs in a large southwestern city. In another study (Curtis, 1999), middle-aged returnees who attached themselves to street-corner groups found themselves challenged by youngsters eager to make a reputation on the street. These youngsters soon had stitches and broken bones to prove their lack of respect for returning elders.

Policy and Program Implications

Youth gang policy in the United States has been dominated by law enforcement suppression approaches for nearly two decades (Klein, 1995; Spergel & Curry, 1990). With but a few exceptions (Fritsch, Caeti, & Taylor, 1999; Orange County Chiefs' and Sheriff's Association, 1999; Vogel & Torres, 1998; Wiebe, 1998), this policy has not succeeded in dismantling gangs, and the long-term success of these suppression effects is not known. Most communities that begin with a singular police suppression approach shift to more comprehensive approaches within a few years (Weisel & Painter, 1997). A number of factors strongly suggest that comprehensive approaches are needed to produce a lasting impact on youth gangs. These include the integration of youth gangs within the social fabric of our society and communities (Bursik & Grasmick, 1993; Miller, 1990; Short, 1974); their attractiveness to adolescents (Curry & Decker, 1998); the degree of adolescent bonding to them (Esbensen et al., 2001); the multiple problems of inner-city gang members (Hill, Howell, Hawkins, & Battin, 1999); the basic necessities of life that gang membership affords to some disadvantaged youngsters (Fleisher, 1998); and the negative life-course impact of gang membership (Thornberry, Krohn, Lizotte, Smith, & Tobin, in press). Thus, youth gang policies that integrate prevention, social intervention, and suppression approaches are most likely to be successful.

These and other dimensions of youth gangs need to be taken into account in formulating program responses to youth gangs. For one thing, gangs in later onset localities do not fit the stereotype of gangs in chronic gang problem cities. All jurisdictions experiencing a gang problem need to assess carefully their gang problem in light of the gang characteristics reviewed in this chapter and others in this section. The National Youth Gang Center (2001a) has developed a protocol that communities can use to guide the assessment of their gang problem. This assessment protocol is applicable in communities of all sizes and characteristics.

Over the past few years, the federal Office of Juvenile Justice and Delinquency Prevention (Burch & Kane, 1999) has invested considerable resources in the development and testing of a Comprehensive Community-Wide Approach to Gang Prevention, Intervention, and Suppression (Spergel, Chance, et al., 1994; Spergel, Curry, et al., 1994). This model, based on a national assessment of youth gang policies and programs (Spergel & Curry, 1990, 1993), is a general framework that addresses the youth gang problem through five interrelated strategies:

- Community mobilization
- Social intervention, including prevention and street outreach
- Opportunities provision
- Suppression/social control
- Organizational change and development

In practice, this comprehensive model is a flexible format for responding to gang problems at the community level (Curry & Decker, 1997). It "is intended to be tailored to the special needs of each individual community, to take advantage of local agency strengths, and provide a framework that facilitates interagency cooperation and minimizes inter-agency conflict" (p. 528). The comprehensive model is being implemented and tested in a number of sites with OJJDP support, with promising preliminary results. It also is being implemented and evaluated in St. Louis (Curry & Decker, 1997; Fearn, Decker, & Curry, 2000). The National Youth Gang Center (2001b) has prepared a planning guide to assist communities in developing a plan to implement the comprehensive gang model.

Conclusion

More than half of the contemporary youth gang problems are relatively new, having emerged in the past 10 to 15 years. The youth gangs in these newer gang problem localities are distinctly different from the gangs that emerged in other jurisdictions before the mid-1980s. The newer gangs in the suburbs, small cities and towns, and rural areas are not highly organized and have younger members, more females, more Caucasians, and tend to have more mixed gender and race/ethnicity membership than gangs in cities with more long-standing gang problems. The newer gangs also are less involved in criminal activity, including drug trafficking, than their earlier counterparts. These are changes in degree rather than in kind of gang activity and gang characteristics. The most entrenched youth gang problems remain in the largest cities.

Contemporary youth gangs differ in several important respects from enduring stereotypical broadcast media images of them. They are less organized, not extensively involved in setting up and operating drug trafficking enterprises in distant cities, not as ritualized in initiating and controlling members, and most of them are not extensively involved in organized drug trafficking and associated violence.

The criteria that traditionally have been used to define youth gangs do not appear to apply well to gangs in the newer gang problem localities, or to gangs exhibiting "hybrid gang culture." More explicit youth gang criteria also are needed for practical utility, especially in counting and assessing adolescent gangs and their members. It appears that law enforcement agencies seriously undercount these adolescent gangs and their members.

An unresolved issue concerns the link between membership in adolescent gangs (e.g., school linked) and older ones observed by law enforcement. Youth gang participation is mainly an adolescent phenomenon, yet the gangs reported by law enforcement agencies have a preponderance of adult members. Curry's (2000) pioneering research suggests considerable continuity in membership over time during the adolescent period. However, little research has been done on the childhood characteristics of gang members who continue gang membership into late adolescence. One longitudinal study (Battin-Pearson, Guo, Hill, Abbott, & Hawkins, 1999) found that, once in a gang, those youths who were most behaviorally and socially maladjusted in childhood (at ages 10-12) are most likely to remain in the gang for multiple years.

Gang researchers were cautioned a decade ago that the parameters of youth gangs could not easily be described and that the effort to do so is probably a futile exercise because "agreement likely will never be achieved, and definitions often obscure problematic areas and may not encourage the development of new questions" (Horowitz, 1990, p. 38). Horowitz's advice is well taken. Contemporary gangs that emerged in the past 10 to 15 years in many respects do not fit the mold of stereotypical youth gangs and thus are very difficult to define.

Thrasher's (1963) observation that "no two gangs are just alike" may well apply more surely today than ever before. It appears that the changing youth gang boundaries have generated a wider variety of gang forms in more localities than have previously existed. More than 30 years ago the eminent gang researcher Jim Short (1968b) said, "the universe of gang members is one of largely unknown dimensions, and no census of gangs is likely to be complete for any length of time, so variable are the definitions and so shifting in character are these phenomena" (p. 10). His words were prophetic of contemporary youth gangs.

Notes

1. Youth gangs in places where gang problems are a fairly recent development tend not to have the characteristics of gangs in entrenched or "chronic" gang cities, particularly larger ones such as Chicago (Block, Christakos, Jacob, & Przybylski, 1996; Spergel, 1995) and Los Angeles (Hutson, Anglin, Kyriacou, Hart, & Spears, 1995; Klein, 1995). Excellent descriptions of the most organized gangs in Chicago are available (Decker et al., 1998; Perkins, 1987).

2. The sample consists of 3,018 police and sheriff departments that are surveyed each year. This sample consists of four subsamples: (a) all police departments serving cities with populations over 25,000; (b) a randomly selected sample of police departments serving cities with populations between 2,500 and 25,000; (c) all "suburban county" police and sheriff departments; and (d) a randomly selected sample of "rural county" police and sheriff departments. Of 3,018 recipients, 2,603 (86%) responded to the 1999 survey (Egley, 2000). Annual reports have been published on the 1996 (NYGC, 1999a), 1997 (NYGC, 1999b), and 1998 (NYGC, 2000a) surveys. The next full report will cover the 1999, 2000, and 2001 surveys. In the interim, "fact sheets" will be published by the federal Office of Juvenile Justice and Delinquency Prevention (see Egley, 2000, for results of the 1999 survey).

3. For purposes of the NYGC surveys, a *youth gang* is defined as "a group of youths or young adults in (the respondent's) jurisdiction that (the respondent) or other responsible persons in (the respondent's) agency or community are willing to identify or classify as a 'gang.' Do not include motorcycle gangs, hate or ideology groups, prison gangs, or other exclusively adult gangs."

4. The NYGC maintains a database of state-by-state gang legislation that can be accessed at its Web site: www.iir.com/nygc.

5. Gang membership in this study was determined by self-reports of ever having been in a gang that engaged in at least one type of delinquent behavior (fighting with other gangs, general stealing, auto theft, or robbing people).

6. Al Valdez, an Orange County, California, gang investigator, reports that hybrid or mutant gangs first appeared in that county in about 1990 (Valdez, 2000). He describes them as being less territorial than other gangs, wearing nontraditional gang colors and a variety of tattoos, having members from outside the area, and of mixed gender and mixed race/ethnicity.

7. Researchers have noted more ethnic mixing of gangs than in the past (see Klein, 1995, pp. 36, 107; Spergel, 1995, p. 64), but the closest they come to describing gangs with a hybrid culture is exemplified in Spergel's (1995) reference to the "bewildering array, complexity, and variability of structures, purposes, and behavioral characteristics of gangs" (p. 79).

8. This study analyzed data collected in the 1995 School Crime Supplement to the National Crime Victim Survey. The supplement was distributed in 1995 to a nationally representative sample of approximately 10,000 students.

9. The survey did not measure involvement in other kinds of illegal activities.

10. In the past, inmate involvement in prison gangs was linked with the five major adult prison gangs: the Mexican Mafia (La Eme), the Aryan Brotherhood (a white supremacist group), La Nuestra Familia ("our family"), the Texas Syndicate, and Mexikanemi (known also as the Texas Mexican Mafia) (Fleisher, Decker, & and Curry, 2001a). A sixth one, the Netas, a major concern to federal investigative agencies, recently moved into the U.S. prison system from Puerto Rican prisons.

Joining the Gang

Gender Differences in Risk Factors for Gang Membership

CHERYL MAXSON
MONICA L. WHITLOCK

The participation of girls in street gangs is an intriguing issue to researchers, law enforcement, community youth practitioners, and journalists. It seems to surprise many that girls would be attracted to such street-focused activities as gangs. This interest has resulted in a growing amount of research from scholars who have investigated the extent of involvement of girls in gangs.[1] Whether female activity in gangs has increased in the past decade or simply the attention paid to it, the concern for developing preventive strategies nevertheless has become apparent. To whatever extent that girls in gangs could be characterized as "invisible" in much of the older gang research (Chesney-Lind, Shelden, & Joe, 1996), that is certainly not the case today.

Despite the recent contributions to our understanding of female gang involvement, we have not yet reached a level of knowledge to permit *gen-*

AUTHORS' NOTE: This chapter was originally presented as "Gender Differences in Risk Factors for Gang Membership" at the 1998 annual meeting of the American Sociological Association. The research was conducted with the support of Grant #94-19 from The California Wellness Foundation. Points of view expressed herein are those of the authors and do not necessarily represent TCWF. Malcolm Klein, a co-investigator on the grant, contributed to the study's design and analysis.

eralized descriptions of female gang members or to compare them with male gang members. We are only beginning to amass a body of literature that allows us to make sense of the various findings across locations, ethnic groups, and study designs. Given the variations in study designs, it is not surprising that there is considerable debate among researchers about the prevalence of female gang membership, gang structures, and the roles of females in gangs. This lack of consensus extends to the nature and extent of girl gang members' involvement in criminal and, especially, violent activity and in levels of victimization.

It is nearly impossible to address questions about whether or not female gang involvement has changed over the past several decades. Regardless of whether we are reacting to an actual increase in female gang involvement, or we are just now paying attention to a phenomenon that has escaped our interest for decades, it is clear that girls are joining gangs and committing sufficient crime to be of concern. Gang membership increases the risk of victimization and reduces life opportunities for these young women and perhaps their offspring (see Moore, 1991; J. Miller, 2001b). Clearly, the process of aggregating information about the scope, nature, and consequences of female gang involvement is important and timely.

Our research contributes to this investigation by examining the risk factors associated with joining gangs for both males and females. We ask how the characteristics of females who join gangs differ from those of girls who don't join gangs, and how these differ from the risk factors for males. A primary interest is to consider the implications of our study findings, along with those of other gang researchers, for the development of prevention and intervention programs for girls.

Contemporary Research on Female Gang Involvement

Gang researchers have used various methodological approaches, different sampling techniques, different or nonexistent comparison groups, different age group samples, and different locales (see Esbensen, Deschenes, & Winfree, 1999), making the search for general patterns difficult. The ambiguity in the definition of gang membership also confounds the ability to draw comparative conclusions. We simply do not know whether the diversity in the findings of gang research reflects different characteristics of gangs and gang members in different places or is an artifact of research method. Because thorough reviews of the contemporary female gang literature are available elsewhere (see Curry, 1998; J. Miller, 2001b), we will summarize here the range in four topical areas: prevalence, gang structures and female roles in gangs, criminal activity, and risk factors.

Prevalence

Studies of representative samples of youth in selected cities report that between 10% and 20% claim to be gang members (Bjerregaard & Smith, 1993; Esbensen & Deschenes, 1998; Huizinga, 1997). The proportion of girls who join gangs varies by study. For example, the Rochester Youth Development Study found that 22% of all girls and 18% of all boys ages 13 to 15 report being gang members (Bjerregaard & Smith, 1993). Researchers in Denver interviewed youth in high-risk neighborhoods and reported lower prevalence rates for females (9%) than for males (18%) (Huizinga, 1997). A recent survey of eighth graders in 11 sites with the Gang Resistance Education and Training (G.R.E.A.T.) found that 8% of girls and 14% of boys reported gang membership (Esbensen & Deschenes, 1998).

A second approach to estimating female gang prevalence is to examine the proportion of gang members who are female. One survey of a nonrepresentative sample in New York (Campbell, 1991) suggests that approximately 10% of gang members were females. A survey in Los Angeles, Chicago, and San Diego (Fagan, 1990), and a survey of Latino gangs in East Los Angeles (Moore, 1991) both reported that females constituted about one third of all gang members. The female proportion of gang membership reported in the representative samples cited above was 46% in Denver (Esbensen & Huizinga, 1993), 30% in Rochester (Bjerregaard & Smith, 1993), and 38% across the G.R.E.A.T. sites (Esbensen & Winfree, 1998). Jody Miller (2001b) describes the varying sex ratios *within gangs* reported by the girls she interviewed in St. Louis and Columbus:

> Girls were as few as seven percent or as many as 75 percent of the membership in mixed-gender gangs, and of course, 100 percent of the members in autonomous female gangs. Despite this variation, by and large, girls were in the numeric minority in their gangs: half (24 of 48) were in gangs with a third or fewer female members, and two thirds (32 of 48) were in gangs in which females were less than half of the members. (p. 116)

If girls tend to join gangs at younger ages than do boys, and to exit gangs at younger ages as well, then prevalence estimates may differ considerably with the age of the study sample. Studies that interview younger adolescents would produce higher female prevalence estimates than studies that focus on mid-teens or young adults. An example of this relationship among age, gender, and gang joining is evidenced in the Denver study where Esbensen and Huizinga (1993) reported that 46% of the gang members were females when the youth were 11 to 15 years of age, but the proportion decreased to 20% when the sample matured to between 13 and 19 years of age.

Surveys of law enforcement agencies generally produce lower estimates of female gang involvement. A 1992 survey that included agencies from primarily large cities yielded an estimate of about 4% females among those agencies that reported any female gang members (Curry, 1998). A survey of all agencies in cities with populations over 25,000 residents found that in 1998, 8% of gang members known to the police were females (National Youth Gang Center [NYGC], 2000b). Curry (1998) suggests that a lower probability of detection, inaccurate identification of gang members, or differential patterns in police labeling practices by gender might explain the lower levels of female gang participation found in police, as compared with youth, surveys.

Despite the variations we have found in the estimates of female gang prevalence, it is reasonable to conclude that girls represent a substantial proportion of gang members, probably somewhere between one fourth and one third of all gang members. If for no other reason, the magnitude of female gang involvement warrants considerable attention by gang researchers.

Female Gang Structures

One holdover from earlier gang research is the tendency to categorize female gangs as (a) auxiliary subgroups affiliated with larger male structures, (b) independent/autonomous, or (c) part of integrated, mixed-gender gangs (Miller, 1975). Although Hagedorn and Devitt (1999) quite correctly term this approach as sexist because the gender structure of male gangs is rarely at issue, no researchers to date have advanced an alternative typology. There is consensus in the current literature that autonomous female gangs are unusual (Curry, 1998; Lauderback, Hansen, & Waldorf, 1992). Earlier research found most female gangs to be of the auxiliary type (Miller, 1975). However, such descriptions are far less common in current research. Curry (1998) reported that just over one third of the 110 female gang members he studied were in female auxiliaries of male gangs. The girls interviewed by Jody Miller (1998a) in Columbus described their membership in predominantly male gangs, which she termed "male-dominated, integrated mixed gender groups."[2]

Peterson, Miller, and Esbensen (2001) report that 64% of girls in their eighth-grade sample described their gangs as mixed (i.e., neither sex exceeded two thirds of the gang membership), 30% belonged to majority male gangs, and 13% participated in majority female gangs. In this sample, just 16% of males were in all-male gangs. These authors examined whether youths' descriptions of the organizational characteristics (initiation rites, leadership, meetings, rules, and symbols) varied across gang types by sex composition and found that, with few exceptions (i.e., regular meetings and specific rules), girls described similar characteristics across all gang types. However, the pattern among boys differed by gang type. Males in all-male gangs described the lowest levels of organization and those in mixed gangs reported the highest levels.

Hagedorn and Devitt (1999) are somewhat vague about gender composition of the groups to which their female respondents belong. These are referred to as female gangs, but they appear to have substantial male membership. Hagedorn and Devitt report that African American females emphatically deny that their gangs are auxiliaries to male gangs, but Hispanic females display more variability in their reports of female decision making and separate meetings among female gang members. These authors argue that perceptions of autonomy are tied to differing conceptions of gender:

> The social construction of the gang experience varied not just between and within ethnic groups, but even within the "same" gang. The boundaries, membership, and structure of the gang itself were socially constructed and this construction was related to various conceptions of gender. (Hagedorn & Devitt, 1999, p. 269)

These current investigations of gang structures find the gender composition of gangs to be much more complex than is reflected in the typology proposed by Walter Miller (1975). Recent literature suggests that the totally subservient, auxiliary female subgroup; the fully integrated, gender-blind mixed-sex gang; and the fully independent, autonomous female gang are probably very uncommon. Nevertheless, Miller's typology continues to serve a purpose for current researchers who might take up the challenge to suggest an alternative framework that more accurately reflects the structural elements emerging among female gang participants (see also Curry, 1998).

Criminal Activity

Gang members are far more active in crime than are other youth (see summaries in Curry & Decker, 1998; Huizinga, 1997; Klein, 1995; Spergel, 1995; Thornberry, 1998). Gang females commit significantly more crime than comparable nongang females, and their crime levels also exceed those of nongang males (Bjerregaard & Smith, 1993; Esbensen & Winfree, 1998). Gang girls may equal or exceed the serious, violent activity of gang boys (Huizinga, 1997), but most research finds their participation rates to be lower than that of male gang members (Chesney-Lind et al., 1996; Esbensen et al., 1990; Miller, 1998a).

Female gang members are victims as well as perpetrators of violence (Hagedorn & Devitt, 1999; Miller, 1998a; Moore, 1991). Researchers have described a variety of negative consequences or "social injury" (Curry, 1998) associated with gang membership. For example, Joan Moore (1991) discusses the enhanced risks borne by female gang members for mental health, drug, and other social problems as they reach middle age.

Risk Factors

The gang literature is replete with speculations as to why youth join gangs, and several recent accounts examine the social characteristics of gang versus nongang youth (see Howell, 1998, for summary). Comparisons of gender differences in characteristics are less common. Bjerregaard and Smith (1993) used multivariate logistic regression to examine eight characteristics hypothesized to increase the chances of gang joining.[3] They found engaging in sexual activity and having delinquent peers to be significant factors in gang joining for both males and females, although sexual activity was a significantly stronger factor for females. Low school expectations (i.e., whether subjects believe they will graduate from high school) was the only variable uniquely associated with gang membership for females. Measures of social disorganization, poverty, parental attachment, parental supervision, and self-esteem did not influence the probability of joining gangs for either males or females.

The Bjerregaard and Smith analysis utilized measures of gang membership and the independent variables during the same time period. A later article by Thornberry (1998) tested 26 risk factors on the probability of gang joining as reported by Rochester Youth Development Study subjects in nine successive interview waves. Unlike the Bjerregaard and Smith analysis, Thornberry tested each variable separately. Eighteen risk factors were identified for males and 11 for females. Eight of the 11 risk factors for females also surfaced for males. These included four measures of poor attitudes toward school, access to and positive values about drugs, delinquent involvement, and neighborhood integration. It is noteworthy that integration was positively associated with gang joining for females, but negatively associated for males. Risk factors unique to female gang involvement were neighborhood disorganization, neighborhood violence, and low parental involvement.

These two reports from the same study identified different sets of factors associated with joining gangs and differed also in the assessment of which factors are associated for males and females. The Thornberry analysis suggests that male gang members may be somewhat more distinct from their nongang counterparts than are females, based upon the higher number of distinguishing factors. Of the eight variables examined by Bjerregaard and Smith, just one produced a different effect for males than females. Although the longitudinal approach adopted by Thornberry is superior for addressing issues of prediction, his bivariate analysis approach precludes the identification of variables that are independent predictors of gang joining.

Esbensen and Deschenes (1998) used multivariate logistic regression to test variables derived from social control theory and social learning theory, separately.[4] After controlling for demographic variables, Esbensen and Deschenes found major differences in the contribution of social control factors for male and female gang membership. Only low parental monitoring was significant for both males and females. Risk seeking and low school commitment predicted female, but not male, gang involvement. Maternal attachment and low social isolation predicted male, but not female, gang involvement.

The models including the social learning variables were far more similar for males and females. Guilt, neutralization, negative peer commitment, and low school safety predicted gang membership for both genders. Only the lack of prosocial peers predicted female, but not male, gang involvement.

Overall, both models were a better fit for males than for females, suggesting again that male gang members may be more distinctive than their nongang counterparts than is true for females. However, we can't discount the concern that the characteristics that explain female gang joining have not been adequately measured.

In both the Rochester and G.R.E.A.T. data sets, the majority of characteristics that distinguish girl gang members from girls who don't join gangs also differentiated gang involvement among boys, but all three studies found factors that were unique to females. Unfortunately, the nature of the factors unique to girl gang membership varied from one study to the next. This lack of stable, unique predictors does not bode well for the development of effective gender-specific programs.

Current Study

Our research adds to this literature on characteristics associated with female gang membership and also adds variation in method, sample, and location. Our data are cross-sectional and derived from interviews conducted in 1995 and 1996 with 221 gang and nongang girls and boys aged between 13 and 15 years. The subjects resided in two neighborhoods in San Diego, neighborhoods selected because they had the highest gang activity levels in the city. Thus the neighborhoods are not representative of the city (Maxson, Whitlock, & Klein, 1997, 1998).

Nor are our subjects representative of neighborhood youth. Subjects were selected from service agencies and school environments that focused on gang members and youth at credible risk for gang membership. These agency samples were supplemented with snowball referrals and street contacts. In other words, we attempted to select the highest-risk kids in the highest-risk neighborhoods to see if we could determine why such youths don't join gangs by comparing them to similarly situated youth who do join. Although the study sample is not representative of a defined population, we use standard tests of statistical significance as an indicator of meaningful distinctions between the subgroups of interest.

The sample design called for an equal number of gang and nongang youth, one fourth of whom were to be females (Maxson et al., 1997). As much as possible, gang and nongang samples were drawn from similar sources. Interviews were conducted with 103 youth (26 females) who identified themselves as current or previous gang members and with 118 youth (30 females) who did not report gang membership. This study focused exclusively on African American youth.

In addition to the important question of etiology—that is, whether or not the motivations and social processes of joining gangs differ for girls and boys—our primary interest is whether gang prevention and intervention programs should be gender specific. Therefore, in these analyses, we pay less attention to gang activities (and not at all to prevalence or structure) than to the characteristics that distinguish gang from nongang males and females, and what these suggest for policy and programmatic interventions.

Findings

The findings of this study are presented in several steps. First, we examine the characteristics that differentiate gang from nongang males and females within the broad and sometimes arbitrarily defined categories of individual, family, peer, school, and neighborhood variables. These are comparisons of each separate variable with gang status. This does not control for the possibility that these measurements might be tapping into the same underlying dimension of differences between gang and nongang members. Multivariate analysis techniques are required to sort out that issue. The multivariate strategy identifies the most important variables in differentiating gang and nongang members and whether the variables in this model operate differently for boys and girls.

Data from interviews with gang and nongang boys and girls were analyzed by first examining bivariate logistic regression equations of each independent variable with the dichotomous dependent variable, gang membership (data not tabled). Eighteen variables representing the highest partial correlation coefficients within each domain were selected for model fitting. Decisions about variable selection were somewhat arbitrary, a result of evaluating the conceptual validity of the items and their potential for differentiating either male or female gang and nongang members. These variables, along with means and percentages, are listed in Table 2.1.

Every variable tested in this model differentiated gang and nongang boys and girls in the predicted directions. In every domain, among each

Table 2.1   Means, Standard Deviations, Percentages, and Ns for Independent Variables by Gender and Gang Status

Variable Description	Female		Male	
	Gang (n = 26)	Nongang (n = 30)	Gang (n = 77)	Nongang (n = 88)
Individual				
Positive conflict resolution	2.28 (.75)	2.82 (.77)	2.17 (.77)	2.70 (.63)
Critical events	1.55 (.24)	1.46 (.21)	1.58 (.22)	1.34 (.24)
Barriers to success	2.43 (.57)	2.19 (.61)	2.50 (.61)	2.24 (.56)
Participation in community sports	15% (4)	40% (12)	60% (46)	65% (57)
Family				
Positive self-esteem derived from home environment	3.11 (.45)	3.18 (.48)	2.96 (.34)	3.22 (.46)
Parental monitoring	2.31 (.44)	2.49 (.41)	2.33 (.37)	2.50 (.33)
Parental inconsistency	2.32 (.75)	1.97 (.77)	2.01 (.65)	1.78 (.67)
Family deviance	2.23 (1.1)	1.77 (1.3)	2.39 (1.2)	1.41 (1.1)
Peer				
Likes to hang on the corner with friends	50% (13)	7% (2)	52% (40)	13% (11)
Friends handle conflict by threatening	3.50 (.86)	2.93 (.94)	3.32 (.80)	2.65 (1.1)
Does things that get others in trouble	1.73 (.78)	1.43 (.68)	2.12 (.69)	1.35 (.50)
School				
Receive honor or award at school	35% (9)	70% (21)	44% (34)	58% (51)
Positive educational attitudes	3.20 (.40)	3.18 (.43)	2.94 (.47)	3.21 (.40)
Teachers' perceptions of youth as delinquent or in poor mental health	2.66 (.83)	2.21 (.66)	2.94 (.72)	2.49 (.64)
Miss more than one day of school per month	62% (16)	43% (17)	70% (54)	50% (44)
Number of teachers liked (1 = none . . . 3 = all)	1.73 (.87)	2.33 (.84)	1.77 (.84)	1.99 (.91)
Neighborhood				
Police treat people unfairly	50% (13)	33% (10)	64% (49)	36% (32)
Exposure to violence	1.54 (.26)	1.43 (.18)	1.61 (.20)	1.41 (.18)

variable tested, gang members reported fewer prosocial attitudes and experiences than did the nongang members. For example, female nongang members were more likely to resolve conflict nonaggressively, to participate in community sports, and to report liking more teachers. Girls who claimed gang membership reported their friends were more likely to handle conflict by threatening, and they experienced more exposure to violence in the neighborhood. A glance at these data suggests that the magnitude of the differences appears to be greater for males than for females. This comparison and the statistical importance of each of these variables were tested in the next analytic step.

Table 2.2   Bivariate Logistic *R*s for Gang Joining by Gender

Domain	Variable Description	Bivariate Regression	
		Male (n = 165)	Female (n = 56)
Individual			
	Positive conflict resolution	−.27***	−.22*
	Critical events	.34***	.00
	Barriers to success	.16**	.05
	Participation in community sports	.00	-.16*
Family			
	Positive self-esteem derived from home environment	−.23***	.00
	Parental monitoring	−.17**	−.06
	Parental inconsistency	.11*	.10
	Family deviance	.30***	.00
Peer			
	Likes to hang on the corner with friends	.33***	.32**
	Friends handle conflict by threatening	.25***	.19*
	Does things that get others in trouble	.39***	.06
School			
	Receive honor or award at school	−.07	−.25**
	Educational attitudes	−.22***	.00
	Teachers' perceptions of youth as delinquent or in poor mental health	.24***	.18*
	Missed more than one day of school per month	.14**	.00
	Number of teachers liked (1 = none . . . 3 = all)	−.05	−.23**
Neighborhood			
	Police treat people unfairly	.21***	.00
	Exposure to violence	.35***	.12

*p < .05; **p < .01; ***p < .001

Bivariate Regressions

Table 2.2 presents the bivariate regression coefficients for males and for females. Among the 18 variables included in this model, 7 are statistically significant for girls, and all but 3 are significant for boys. This preliminary examination suggests that this model may fit better for males than for females. Of the 7 significant coefficients for females, 3 are unique to females: participation in community sports, receiving an honor or award at school, and liking more teachers than did gang girls. These positive school and community attachments are associated with a reduced probability of joining gangs.

Four of the variables that significantly distinguish female gang and nongang youth are also significant for males. Gang members enjoy hanging on the corner with friends, report that their friends handle conflict by threatening, and believe that their teachers perceive them as bad or in poor mental health. For both males and females, a nonaggressive conflict style (handling conflict by talking it out, compromising, or walking away) is associated with lower odds of gang joining. It appears that conflict resolution tactics have armed some youth with skills to help them avoid joining gangs. In contrast, both male and female gang members enjoy spending unstructured time with their peers—"hanging out"—more than do nongang members. Teachers' negative perceptions of youth (as reported by the youth) also are related to a youth's likelihood of joining a gang. It is possible that the teachers' negative perceptions of the youth are a response to gang membership rather than a precursor. Our cross-sectional data cannot address this distinction.

It is striking that none of the family variables distinguished gang from nongang females, and all four did so for males. Male gang members report lower self-esteem in the family context, more parental inconsistency (as measured by the youth's ability to talk parents out of punishment), and less parental monitoring. Male gang members are more likely than nongang members to have families with drug and alcohol abuse and criminal involvement. None of these variables were significant for the girls, indicating that for these girls, family environment did not affect the likelihood of joining a gang. It could be that at-risk girls are less affected by family milieu because they are strengthened by successes at school that are not shared by the boys. This chapter does not address these and other possible interactions, but it is an area that should be addressed in future research.

Multivariate Regression

To evaluate the strength of each of the variables in relation to all other variables in the model, and to assess the relative strength of the model in predicting gang membership by gender, all 18 variables were entered into separate logistic regression equations for males and females. The results are presented in Table 2.3. As expected, the model predicts gang membership more accurately for males than for females (males: BIC = –14.89; classification success 85%; females: BIC = 30.00; classification success 80%). The model for females does predict well above chance, but only 2 variables significantly contribute to the model. These variables are (a) hanging on the corner with friends and (b) receiving an honor or award at school. A girl who reports enjoying hanging on the corner with her friends is 18 times more likely to join a gang (data not shown). Receiving school recognition lowers the risk of joining gangs for girls but not for boys. Six variables emerged as significant independent predictors for the boys in the multivariate model. Only one of these variables (hanging on the corner with friends) also significantly differentiated gang from nongang girls.

Table 2.3   Multivariate Logistic Rs for Gang Joining by Gender

Domain	Variable Description	Multiple Regression	
		Male	Female
Individual			
	Positive conflict resolution	−.05	.00
	Critical events	.12*	.00
	Barriers to success	−.02	.00
	Participation in community sports	−.05	−.08
Family			
	Positive self-esteem derived from home environment	.00	.00
	Parental monitoring	.00	.00
	Parental inconsistency	.11*	.00
	Family deviance	.14**	.00
Peer			
	Likes to hang on the corner with friends	.12*	.17*
	Friends handle conflict by threatening	.00	.09
	Does things that get others in trouble	.25***	.00
School			
	Receive honor or award at school	.00	−.18*
	Educational attitudes	.00	.00
	Teachers' perceptions of youth as delinquent or in poor mental health	.00	.00
	Missed more than one day of school per month	.00	.07
	Number of teachers liked (1 = none . . . 3 = all)	.00	.00
Neighborhood			
	Police treat people unfairly	.13*	.00
	Exposure to violence	.00	.00
N		163	55
	−2 log likelihood	106.577	42.132
	Goodness of fit	196.531	45.742
	Model chi-square	118.351	33.659
	Significance	< .001	.0139
	Degrees of freedom	18	18
	Classification success—total	90%	84%
	Classification success for gang	85%	80%
	Classification success for nongang	93%	87%
	BIC statistic	−14.89	30.00

NOTES: The BIC statistic takes into account the sample n, the number of variables in the model, and the −2 log likelihood in order to assess how well the model fits the data. The lower the BIC, the better the model.
*$p < .05$; **$p < .01$; ***$p < .001$.

Discussion

The analyses we have presented indicate that the risk factors for gang joining differ for males and females and that applying a model or program designed to address risk for boys would not benefit girls. The bivariate regressions revealed different constellations of risk factors for boys and girls. However, the supplemental multivariate regression models failed to produce a pattern of risk factors for females. These data do not successfully capture risk factors for girls; most of the variables measured did not distinguish gang from nongang girls. Thus, the current study cannot suggest specific programming strategies with the exception of decreasing unstructured time and increasing school competence and recognition. What can be said with certainty is that girls require different programming than boys. Our findings are consistent with Thornberry's, who argued for different programmatic interventions for males and females. Conversely, the Bjerregaard and Smith findings suggest only the school domain as a source for different program content.

Our findings raise several questions about the sample and the research design. We wondered whether our methods (self-report) for identifying gang members may have been less appropriate for girls, or perhaps our sampling techniques generated less "gangy" girls. We were able to examine these issues using data gathered during the course of the interviews. First, we compared the reasons gang and nongang youth offered for joining friendship groups. Second, we examined the sources from which each sample group was derived. Next, we compared the self-reported delinquent activity of the subsamples. Finally, we assessed the level and visibility of gang activity in these neighborhoods as reported in the interviews.

Reasons for Joining

One indication of how distinct our gang and nongang groups really are focuses on the reasons gang members offered for joining a gang, compared to the reasons only at-risk youth joined the groups to which they belong. If the motivations for joining gangs are very different for girls than for boys, this might suggest the need for special programming for girls. Table 2.4 presents the primary reasons for joining a gang or group by gender and by gang status. As expected, nongang youth joined groups for (quite obviously) nongang and prosocial reasons: to make friends (male and female); fill up empty time (female); keep out of trouble (male and female); share secrets (female); and participate in group activities (male). Conversely, gang youth indicated that they joined their groups for very different reasons, and these differed by gender. Boys reported joining gangs for excitement, to have a territory of their own, and for protection and belonging. Girls joined because family and friends were involved and to get a reputation.

Girls join gangs for different reasons than do boys. Girls cited the socialization and associational aspects of gang joining, whereas boys reported joining for protection, for a sense of excitement, and to belong. Esbensen and colleagues (1999) reported only one significant difference between

Table 2.4   Reasons for Joining Gang or Group by Gender

	Females		
Gang	*(% yes)*	*Nongang*	*(% yes)*
Family members were involved	73	Make friends	77
Friends were involved	62	Fill up empty time	69
Get a reputation	58	Keep out of trouble/Share secrets*	65
	Males		
Gang	*(% yes)*	*Nongang*	*(% yes)*
Excitement	78	Make friends	77
To have a territory of one's own/Protection*	71	Participate in group activities	76
Belonging	61	Keep out of trouble	67

*Indicates the same percentage of subjects responded for each separate item.

boys and girls in their reasons for joining gangs: Boys were more likely to report joining for money. In their sample, protection was the most common reason cited for joining among both boys and girls. J. Miller (1998a, 2001a) also provides a useful discussion of what girls expect to get out of gang participation.

Prevention and intervention efforts might be modeled for these different sources of attraction to gangs. For the girls, efforts might focus on strengthening decision-making skills to help them stay out of a gang while recognizing the intense associational ties drawing them in. These data also support the distinctness of our sample of gang members. The reasons for joining gangs and groups are markedly different for gang and nongang youth, and these are consistent with expectations for gang/nongang differences.

Sample Sources

Another concern was whether boys and girls or gang and nongang youths were sampled from different sources, thereby making comparisons between these categories suspect. As shown in Table 2.5, a lower proportion of gang girls came from community-based agencies than did nongang girls or either type of boy. Furthermore, more gang girls were obtained from probation, suggesting that they may have been more seriously involved in criminal offending. This slight difference in sampling should have resulted in larger differences between gang and nongang girls, relative to boys. Because this did not occur, we cannot attribute findings to different sample sources.

Table 2.5   Percentage and N of Respondents by Source, Gender, and Gang Status

	Female		Male	
	Gang (n = 26)	Nongang (n = 30)	Gang (n = 77)	Nongang (n = 88)
Agencies	27% (7)	50% (15)	53% (41)	51% (45)
Fortuitous contacts	35% (9)	50% (15)	34% (26)	42% (37)
Probation	39% (10)	0% (0)	13% (10)	7% (6)

NOTE: $\chi^2 < .001$ for females; however, expected cell frequencies were low, so caution must be taken in interpretation; $\chi^2 = .30$ for males.

Involvement in Delinquency

An additional question was whether the sampled girls (both gang and nongang) were less involved in offending than were the boys and, thus, were an inappropriately low risk sample for purposes of comparison. It is possible that there is a lower threshold of tolerance for delinquent behavior for girls that net them into social agencies. If so, gang girl offending patterns would not differ much from nongang girls. Examining self-report data by gang status and gender, however, suggests the opposite. Judged by their criminal activity, the nongang girls in this sample represent a high-risk population. Table 2.6 presents the 6-month prevalence rates for scales of general delinquency, serious property offenses, and violence. As expected, gang membership is associated with increased offending for both girls and boys. An alarming 90% of the nongang girls have committed a general delinquent offense, and all of the gang girls had done so. This difference was not statistically significant. In fact, the nongang girls in this sample were just as involved in (general) offending, serious property crime, and violence as were the nongang boys. We can conclude from these data that we did not sample "lightweight" girls, which would have hindered the ability of the data to show differences. In fact, our gang and nongang girls look very similar in their patterns of offending. A possible explanation could be that for girls, joining a gang does not exert the same impact on one's identity that it does for the boys. Perhaps involvement in delinquency alone is sufficient to alter the girl's self-concept and change her behavior, but for boys, delinquent misbehavior does not influence a change in identity and behavior as much as gang joining does. This lack of differences in offending for girls would explain the lack of a distinct constellation of risk factors among gang girls in the analyses reported earlier.

Gang Activity in the Neighborhood

A final test of gang/nongang differences in the level of gang activity in the neighborhood revealed a similar lack of differences between gang and

Table 2.6   Six-Month Delinquency Prevalence Rates by Gender and Gang Status

	Female		Male	
	Gang (n = 26)	Nongang (n = 30)	Gang (n = 77)	Nongang (n = 88)
General delinquency	100%	90%	95%	77%,***
Serious property	46%	30%	58%	23%***
Violence	81%	57%*	79%	44%***

NOTE: Statistical tests represent comparisons within gender. Gang and nongang tests for differences across gender were all nonsignificant.
*p < .05; **p < .01; ***p < .001

nongang girls. Gang girls did not report any greater presence of gang activity in their neighborhoods than did nongang girls, with the exception of gang rivalries, where 81% of gang members reported gang rivalries nearby, whereas 57% of nongang girls did so (data not shown). On the other hand, male gang members reported more talk about gangs, more gang activity, more rivalries, more gang members on their streets, and greater importance attached to being in a gang. Gang girls did not differ from gang boys, however, on any of the measures of the presence of gang activity. Interestingly, more nongang girls perceived pressure in their neighborhoods to join gangs than did the gang girls (67% of nongang girls and 46% of gang girls), although this difference was not statistically significant. Nongang girls even reported more pressure to join than did the nongang boys. So, by no means are these girls at low risk for gang membership. In fact, the nongang girls respond quite similarly to the gang girls and also the gang boys. This pattern was also evident in the examination of involvement in delinquency discussed above.

Conclusion

The study findings on female gang participation present a further challenge to youth service providers. The minimal differences between girl gang members and other girls suggest that gang status may be less important than the broader constellation of factors that foster involvement in delinquent behavior. Differential expectations and social norms for acceptable behavior in girls may mean that at-risk females cross the major threshold for norm violation when they engage in criminal activity; gang participation does not appear to aggravate the already risk-laden circumstances of the girls in this sample. We might have better understood this issue if we had included low-risk girls in this study.

The dynamics of criminal offending and gang participation among females is an area of research eliciting much interest among scholars of gender issues. The processes that encourage or inhibit involvement in young girls are not yet well understood. The selection of variables to investigate in this study relied on a theoretic and research literature that focused overwhelmingly on male delinquency and gang issues. We may have omitted consideration of important features unique to female involvement, although the sheer volume of variables in the study makes this unlikely. Empirical assessment of female gang processes would benefit enormously from the development of conceptual frameworks concerned with females on their own merit. Given these limitations, our findings argue against the implementation of gang prevention or intervention programs for girls, especially if these programs have been based on assumptions about the relevance to females of male gang-joining issues. Instead, programming for girls should focus on delinquency prevention until the distinct patterns of risk factors for female gang joining can be elucidated.

Notes

1. Evidence of a renewed interest in this decade can be found in ethnographic studies that focus on female gang issues (J. Miller, 1998a, 2001a; Moore & Hagedorn, 1996; Joe & Chesney-Lind, 1995; Moore, 1991), in analyses of survey data that compare male and female gang members (Bjerregaard & Smith, 1993; Esbensen & Deschenes, 1998; Esbensen, Deschenes, & Winfree, 1999; Esbensen & Huizinga, 1993; Esbensen & Winfree, 1998; Thornberry, 1998), and in the increased frequency of gender-specific gang panels at conferences. There is sufficient new research on female gang members to generate review articles (Curry, 1998) and an edited volume (Chesney-Lind & Hagedorn, 1999).

2. The variability in the degree to which female gang structures are dominated by, or are subservient to, male gang members is echoed in other ethnographic work by Quicker (1983), Moore (1991), and Harris (1988). Work by Miller and her colleagues (J. Miller, 2001b; Miller & Brunson, 2000; Peterson, Miller, & Esbensen, 2001) suggests that both girls' and boys' perceptions of the delinquent and social aspects of gang life may be influenced by the sex composition of gangs.

3. Their data are from interview waves 2 and 3 (youth ages 13-15) in the Rochester Youth Development Study. Samples were weighted to reproduce a random sample of the eighth- and ninth-grade population of the Rochester public schools.

4. Their cross-sectional study included nearly 6,000 eighth grade students from 42 schools in 11 states.

Initiation of Drug Use, Drug Sales, and Violent Offending Among a Sample of Gang and Nongang Youth

FINN-AAGE ESBENSEN
DANA PETERSON
ADRIENNE FRENG
TERRANCE J. TAYLOR

Drug use, drug sales, and violent offending are often considered the domain of gangs and their members, and the co-occurrence of these behaviors has been widely documented. Less attention, however, has been given to the temporal sequencing of these criminal events. That is, do youths join gangs and then begin their involvement in drug use, drug sales, and violent offending? Do youths already engage in these activities prior to joining the gang? Or, are these events that occur simultaneously? And importantly, why is this issue of interest? We believe that there are three main reasons for pursuing this line of inquiry: to provide a description of adolescent offending, to advance ideas for theory development and testing, and

AUTHORS' NOTE: An earlier version of this chapter was presented at the 2000 annual meeting of the Western Society of Criminology. This research is supported under award #94-IJ-CX-0058 from the National Institute of Justice, Office of Justice Programs, U.S. Department of Justice. Points of view in this document are those of the authors and do not necessarily represent the official position of the U.S. Department of Justice.

to inform gang prevention and intervention policy. Of some concern is simply the accuracy of the stereotype that after youths join gangs they become involved in drug use, drug sales, and violent offending. Is this media image borne out in research? From a theoretical perspective, do gangs attract youths who are already quite delinquent or do gangs facilitate initiation of delinquency, especially drug trafficking and violence? These competing questions pit social control theory against social learning theory. Or, is it that a combination of these two perspectives best explains the relationship between gang affiliation and involvement in illegal activities? From a policy perspective, knowledge of the initiation patterns may also be of some value. Depending on the transition pattern, prevention or intervention strategies may be the more suitable approach for addressing the gang problem.

In this chapter we utilize two samples of students to describe typologies of offenders and to disentangle the initiation patterns of these activities. A cross-sectional study of students provides the basis for describing typologies of offenders. For the latter objective, we use 4 years of data from the National Evaluation of the Gang Resistance Education and Training (G.R.E.A.T.) program to examine whether gang membership precedes involvement in drug use, drug sales, and violent offending or whether these activities are already part of the future gang members' behavioral repertoire prior to joining the gang.

Literature Review

There is a considerable body of research that has noted the co-occurrence of drug use and/or drug sales with other forms of delinquency, including gang membership (e.g., Elliott, Huizinga, & Menard, 1989; Fagan, Weis, & Cheng, 1990; Huizinga, Loeber, Thornberry, & Cothern, 2000; van Kammen, Maguin, & Loeber, 1994). Case studies of gangs have documented the prevalence of drug use, drug trafficking, and/or violent offending among gang members (e.g., Decker & Van Winkle, 1996; Hagedorn, 1988; Moore, 1990). General survey samples have also produced data sets that confirm the co-occurrence of these behaviors among a larger population of adolescents. Investigation of the relationship among gang membership, drug use, drug sales, and violence has become increasingly important given the "proliferation of U.S. cities with street gang activity" (Maxson & Klein, 2001, p. 173).

Representative of the general survey approach, in 1986, the Office of Juvenile Justice and Delinquency Prevention (OJJDP) funded three projects collectively known as the Program of Research on the Causes and Correlates of Delinquency. Researchers from three universities collaborated on this project, conducting general surveys of "high-risk" youth in Denver, Colorado; Pittsburgh, Pennsylvania; and Rochester, New York. The Denver Youth Survey (DYS) and the Rochester Youth Development Study (RYDS) both contained survey information about gang involvement, and both of these studies are ongoing as of 2001. The DYS is a household probability sample consisting of 1,530 youth aged 7 to 15 during the first year of data collection. These youth completed annual face-to-face interviews that lasted between 50 and 90 minutes. The RYDS is a school-based sample composed of approximately 1,000 students who completed one-hour interviews every 6 months. Although the sampling procedures and frequency of interviews varied, the two projects used comparable questions to measure a variety of factors, including gang affiliation, self-reported delinquency, and drug use. These two studies have produced several important investigations of the role of gangs in violence, examining changes across time (Bjerregaard & Smith, 1993; Esbensen & Huizinga, 1993; Thornberry, Krohn, Lizotte, & Chard-Wierschem, 1993). Another school-based study, the Seattle Social Development Project, recently has contributed to this emerging body of gang literature derived from a general youth sample (e.g., Battin, Hill, Abbott, Catalano, & Hawkins, 1998; Hill, Howell, Hawkins, & Battin-Pearson, 1999). Of particular relevance to the current inquiry is the finding from these studies that self-reported delinquency increases substantially after a youth has joined a gang. These studies, however, relied upon more global measures of delinquency and rates of offending rather than individual initiation. As such, they did not address the issue of whether the individual youths were involved specifically in violence and drug sales prior to joining the gang.

On the basis of decades of gang research, whether utilizing law enforcement data, case studies or ethnographic studies, qualitative interviews, or general surveys, there is very little question concerning the heightened levels of delinquency and drug use among gang members. Representative of the extent to which gang members are involved in delinquency, estimates from the RYDS and the DYS are that gang members account for well over one half of the self-reported delinquency among youths in those studies. Thornberry and Burch (1997), for instance, reported that gang members accounted for 86% of serious delinquent acts, 69% of the violent offenses, and 70% of drug sales over a 4-year period, although gang youths (youths who were gang members at some time during the study period) represented only 30% of the sample. Similar results were reported for the Denver Youth Survey (Esbensen & Huizinga, 1993), the Seattle Social Development Project (Battin-Pearson, Thornberry, Hawkins, & Krohn, 1998), the G.R.E.A.T. Evaluation (Esbensen & Winfree, 1998), and in Huff's (1998) four-city study.

Drug trafficking has been widely attributed to gangs, and there is considerable agreement that gang youths are significantly more active in this arena than are nongang youths. There remains a question, however, concerning the extent to which gangs control drug sales. Some researchers maintain that the organizational structure of the typical youth gang is not conducive to organized drug trafficking. That is, youth gangs tend to be loosely organized with ephemeral leadership and to lack financial resources and cohesiveness; all traits deemed necessary for organized drug distribution (e.g., Klein, 1995; Moore, 1990; Spergel, 1995). In contrast, others have identified a subset of gangs that are primarily drug-selling gangs (Fagan, 1989; Taylor, 1989). In other research conducted in St. Louis and Kansas City, Decker and Van Winkle (1996) and Fleisher (1998), respectively, reported that profits from drug sales were generally kept by individuals and were not produced as a collective activity by the gang and subsequently not seen as gang property. Thus, these authors suggest that although gang members may be involved in drug selling, it is not common for the gangs themselves to be organized for that purpose. Whether drug sales are an organized gang activity or not, the consensus is that, "Drug use, drug trafficking, and violence overlap considerably in gangs" (Howell, 1998, p. 11).

In their review of the literature examining the co-occurrence of youth gangs, drug use, drug sales, and violence, Howell and Decker (1999) focused their attention more on general societal trends. In that report they examined such relationships as the introduction of crack cocaine and the rise in youth violence and homicides, and the increase in gang violence and drug trafficking across time. In this chapter, our focus is on the extent to which individuals are involved in these activities and whether there is a specific pattern of initiation into these activities; that is, we examine the within-individual change across time.

Prior gang research has, for the most part, not addressed the issue of whether drug use, drug sales, and violent offending precede gang involvement, whether they co-occur, or whether they are a product of joining the gang. There is a small body of research that has examined transition from one type of drug use to another or the transition from drug use to delinquency (e.g., Clayton, 1992; Elliott et al., 1989; van Kammen & Loeber, 1994; van Kammen et al., 1994; Yamaguchi & Kandel, 1984). These questions of initiation patterns are of both theoretical and practical importance. If we can identify a pattern or sequencing of behavior, we are better able to target interventions that may inhibit progression from one behavior to another.

Some longitudinal researchers have addressed the question of whether gangs recruit already delinquent youth (a "selection" model) or whether the gangs socialize new members into delinquent activity (a "social facilitation" model). Thornberry and colleagues (1993) and Esbensen and Huizinga (1993) found support for a facilitation and an "enhancement model" that incorporates both processes: Gang members appear to be active in delinquent activity prior to joining the gang, but their level of delinquency increases greatly during their period of membership and declines after leaving the gang, although it does remain at levels more elevated than for those who were never in a gang.

With respect to policy, considerable attention has been paid to prevention, intervention, and suppression approaches of responding to gang proliferation. If the selection model were the dominant pattern, it would seem logical to employ a general delinquency prevention program coupled with a targeted gang intervention. If the social facilitation model were dominant, targeted interventions with gang members would be recommended.

In this chapter, we explore two questions: (a) What are the prevalence rates for drug use, drug sales, and violent offending for gang and nongang youth? Is there offense specialization or as Klein (1995) argues, "cafeteria-style" delinquency? And importantly, (b) What is the temporal sequencing of these behaviors? Is there a selection, a social facilitation, or an enhancement effect?

Current Study

The analyses reported in this chapter are based upon two separate studies, one cross-sectional and one longitudinal, that were part of the National Evaluation of the Gang Resistance Education and Training (G.R.E.A.T.) program. The cross-sectional study was conducted during the spring semester of 1995. Approximately 6,000 eighth-grade students enrolled in 42 different public schools in 11 cities across the continental United States completed anonymous group-administered questionnaires. From fall 1995 through fall 1999, a longitudinal study of slightly more than 2,000 students who were surveyed each year was conducted in six different cities (the analyses in this chapter utilize the 1995-1998 data). At the outset of this investigation, these students were enrolled in seventh grade (sixth in one site), representing 22 schools. The same questions were included in both studies so that we could replicate the analyses with the two samples.

In both studies, cities were purposively selected to allow for evaluation of the G.R.E.A.T. program. Clearly, only those cities with the program were included. A second consideration for site selection was geographical location. Even with a relatively small number of cities, we sought sites that would provide geographical diversity and varying levels of urbanization. A third criterion was the cooperation of the school districts and the police departments in each site. The cross-sectional cities were: Kansas City, Missouri; Las Cruces, New Mexico; Milwaukee, Wisconsin; Omaha, Nebraska; Orlando, Florida; Philadelphia, Pennsylvania; Phoenix, Arizona; Pocatello, Idaho; Providence, Rhode Island; Torrance, California; and Will County, Illinois. The longitudinal cities included the following: an east coast city (Philadelphia, Pennsylvania); a west coast location (Portland,

Oregon); the site of the G.R.E.A.T. program's inception (Phoenix, Arizona); a midwest city (Omaha, Nebraska); a small city and home of the research project (Lincoln, Nebraska); and a small "border town" with a chronic gang problem (Las Cruces, New Mexico).

Active Consent Procedures

When conducting research with minors, a more restrictive code of ethics is applied than that guiding research involving adults. In addition to providing the standard information to potential respondents (i.e., information on the potential benefits and risks, the voluntariness of their participation, the purposes of the research, the procedures to be followed, the degree of confidentiality), researchers must also secure consent from the parents of the minors. Two different types of parental consent may be used by researchers: active parental consent and passive parental consent. Passive parental consent requires the researcher to inform parents or legal guardians about the research and to provide them with the opportunity to refuse to allow their child's participation in the research. Under this provision, absent a refusal, parental consent is implied and the child is included in the research. Active parental consent is more rigorous and more difficult to attain. Under this standard, the researcher must obtain a signed consent form from the parent or legal guardian providing permission for the child to participate in the study. Absent a signed consent form, it is assumed that the parent has withheld permission and the child is excluded from study participation.

Passive consent procedures were used in 10 of the 11 cross-sectional sites (one school district required active parental consent procedures), but active parental consent was used in the longitudinal study. In no school did more than 2% of parents return refusal forms under the passive consent procedures; in fact, no refusals was the norm at most schools. Under the active consent procedures, many students were excluded from participation, in spite of concerted efforts to obtain the parental permission.

In all the longitudinal sites, the same active consent procedures were followed. Prior to the planned surveys, three direct mailings were made to parents of potential survey participants. Included in the mailings were a cover letter, two copies of the parent consent form for student participation, and a business reply envelope. With substantial Spanish-speaking populations in Phoenix and Las Cruces, mailings to parents in these cities included Spanish versions of the cover letter and the consent form. In addition to the mailings, all parents not responding after the second mailing were contacted by telephone. School personnel also cooperated by distributing consent forms and cover letters at school. Teachers in all classrooms involved in the evaluation assisted with this process, rewarding students with a new pencil upon return of the forms. Some teachers agreed to allow us to offer incentives such as pizza parties for classrooms in which a minimum of 70% of students returned a completed consent form. Other teachers offered incentives of their own, including earlier lunch passes and extra credit points.

These procedures resulted in an overall response rate of 67% (57% providing affirmative consent and 10% withholding consent), with 33% of parents failing to return the consent forms. For a more detailed discussion of the active consent process and examination of the effects of active consent procedures on the representativeness of the sample, consult Esbensen, Miller, Taylor, He, and Freng (1999).

Questionnaire Completion Rates

The completion rates for the longitudinal student surveys were excellent. Of the 2,045 students for whom active parental consent was obtained, 1,761 (86%) students completed surveys during the second year of data collection. For the third- and fourth-year surveys, retention rates were 76% and 69%, respectively. Given the multisite, multischool sample, combined with the fact that respondents at five of the six sites made the transition from middle school to high school between the year-2 and year-3 surveys, this completion rate is commendable.

For the third- and fourth-year surveys, considerable difficulty was introduced into the retention of the student sample. As the cohort moved from middle school to high school, combined with normal mobility patterns, students were enrolled in more than 10 different high schools in each of four sites (Omaha, Phoenix, Portland, and Philadelphia), and by the last data collection effort, participating students were enrolled in more than 100 different schools. It was necessary to contact officials at these schools, whether fewer than 10 respondents or more than 100 were enrolled at the school. In some instances, these new schools were in different districts, which required approval from the necessary authorities to survey their students.

Measurement

Considerable debate surrounds the definition of gang membership (see, e.g., the writings of Curry & Decker, 1998; Decker & Kempf-Leonard, 1991; Klein, 1995; Winfree, Fuller, Backstrom, & Mays, 1992). Some self-report surveys have relied on a single item to determine gang status of respondents (e.g., Bjerregaard & Smith, 1993), whereas others have used multiple items to assess gang status (e.g., Esbensen & Huizinga, 1993; Esbensen & Winfree, 1998; Hill et al., 1999). In previous work with the cross-sectional data from this study, we examined the definitional issue in considerable detail. We investigated the effect of different definitions on the demographic composition of the resultant gangs and the attitudes and illegal involvement of gang members (Esbensen, Winfree, He, & Taylor, 2001). All respondents in that study answered the following two questions: "Have you ever been a gang member?" and "Are you now in a gang?" Those respondents indicating current gang membership were then asked to answer a number of questions about their gang, including organizational characteristics of the gang and the types of illegal activities in which gang members were involved. We then examined the demographic, attitudinal, and behavioral characteristics of "gang members" based on five increasingly more restrictive definitions (the most restrictive definition included only those youth who indicated that they were current and "core" gang members, that their gang was engaged in illegal activities, and that the gang had several types of organizational qualities). Clearly, the more restrictive definitions resulted in the identification of fewer gang members. Further, with each additional criterion, the remaining gang youth were more antisocial in their reported attitudes and behaviors. The largest change, however, remained the difference between those youth who had never been in a gang and those who acknowledged gang affiliation at some time. Based on this previous research, we chose in this chapter to use the single item reflecting current gang membership as our measure of gang status. Due to our interest in establishing the year of gang joining, use of the "ever" measure ("Have you ever been a member of a gang?") would have been inappropriate. This decision was also driven by practical considerations—maintaining as large a sample of gang members as possible in order to have an adequate sample size for any meaningful analyses.

Our dependent measures are drawn from respondents' self-reports of delinquency involvement. "Drug use" consisted of the reported use of three substances: marijuana, inhalants, and other illegal drugs. Although we initially had included alcohol and tobacco, we decided that these behaviors are too prevalent in the adolescent population to be of sufficient utility in this particular area of study. "Drug sales" consisted of two items: selling marijuana and selling other illegal drugs. The violence measure consisted of three items: attacking someone with a weapon, shooting at someone, and robbing someone. Initially we had included a fourth item, "hit someone with the idea of hurting them," but we found the prevalence rate of this behavior was such that it confounded the analyses. General delinquency is so prevalent in the sample that to better assess the relationship between gang affiliation and serious delinquency (those behaviors of most interest to public policy debates), we restricted our summary measures to what can be considered serious forms of drug use, drug sales, and violence. This high prevalence is demonstrated by the fact that by the fourth year of data collection, only 12% of the complete sample had *not* initiated general delinquent behavior (measured by a 17-item general delinquency scale). This is in sharp contrast to the finding that 57% of the nongang youth never initiated the three serious behaviors noted above.

Analysis Strategy

Our first objective was to provide a description of the two samples in terms of the extent to which they were nonoffenders, committed only one type of offense, or were involved in multiple types of offending. We classified respondents in the two samples into one of eight types of offenders. Excluding gang member status, respondents could be classified as: (a) nonoffenders, meaning that they reported no instances of drug use, drug sales, or violence; (b) single offenders, having initiated only one of the three activities (3 possibilities); (c) double offenders, engaging in two of the three behaviors (3 possible combinations); or (d) triple offenders, engaging in all three behaviors. Our primary interest in this chapter, however, is to determine which of these behaviors was initiated first. The cross-sectional data are not suitable for answering this question because we cannot establish the temporal ordering with only one data point. This question calls for within-individual change over time, so multiple data points for the same individuals are needed. Thus, to answer this question, longitudinal panel data are required.

Complicating the classification of respondents is what is referred to as a "left-hand censoring" problem—that is, some respondents already will have initiated two or more of the behaviors by the first data collection point and thus we cannot determine which occurred first. Depending on the research design, there may also be a "right-hand censoring" problem— that is, a respondent may initiate behaviors after the completion of the research, thus not allowing for assessment of the sequencing of events.

Results

The cross-sectional study consisted of 5,935 eighth-grade students. Sample demographics are as follows: 48% were male; 30% lived in single-parent households; 42% were white, 26% were African American, and 19% were Hispanic; their average age was 14; and the majority had parents who had some college education. After excluding incomplete surveys (i.e., those with missing data on one or more of the key variables), we were left with 5,485 (92.5%) usable questionnaires for the analyses reported in this chapter.

The longitudinal sample consisted of 2,045 students for whom active consent was obtained. The analyses reported in this chapter rely on ques-

Table 3.1   Typologies of Delinquent Behavior for Eighth Graders in the Cross-Sectional Data Set

	Total, Percentage (n = 5,485)	Nongang, Percentage (n = 4,935)	Gang, Percentage (n = 393)
Nonoffender	65	68	15
Drug use only	17	17	14
Violence only	4	4	4
Drug sales only	1	1	2
Use & violence	3	3	10
Use & sales	5	4	14
Sales & violence	0.4	0.3	2
Use, sales, & violence	6	3	40

NOTE: Percentages do not add to 100 due to rounding.

tionnaires completed during 4 years of the longitudinal study—1995 through 1998. These years encompass Grades 7 through 10 in five of the sites and Grades 6 through 9 at the sixth site. Based on demographic data provided during the first year of data collection, this sample is quite similar to the cross-sectional sample: 47% male; 52% white, 16% African American, 18% Hispanic; an average age of 12 at the study's outset; and 27% residing in single-parent households.

With respect to the offender types, the most common typology in the cross-sectional study was the nonoffender; fully 65% of the sample had not initiated any of the three behaviors (see Table 3.1). Another 22% reported participating in only one activity, with drug use being the most common. Only 14% of this large sample had initiated two or more behaviors at the time of data collection during spring semester of eighth grade. This figure is important to highlight; although general delinquency is quite rampant, serious offending (behaviors of specific interest in this study) is relatively infrequent. Examination of gang and nongang youth reveals the extent to which the gang youths are more highly involved in delinquency than are the nongang youths. Whereas slightly more than 10% of the nongang youth report initiation of two or more of these behaviors, this figure is in excess of 65% among the gang youths.

A similar classification of the longitudinal sample reflects stability across samples. In order to approximate the cross-sectional sample, we used data collected during the year in which this longitudinal sample was in eighth grade (the second-year data). As shown in Table 3.2, more than three fourths of the longitudinal sample had not yet initiated the three types of delinquency measured in these analyses and only 9% had initiated two or more activities. Among the gang and nongang youths, the pattern resembled that reported for the cross-sectional respondents.

Table 3.2   Typologies of Delinquent Behavior for Eighth Graders in the Longitudinal Data Set

	Total, Percentage (n = 1,684)	Nongang, Percentage (n = 1,591)	Gang, Percentage (n = 66)
Nonoffender	77	79	15
Drug use only	11	11	14
Violence only	3	3	8
Drug sales only	0.4	0.3	2
Use & violence	2	1	12
Use & sales	3	3	18
Sales & violence	1	1	0
Use, sales, & violence	3	2	32

NOTE: Percentages do not add to 100 due to rounding.

Initiation Patterns

Examination of initiation patterns is limited to the longitudinal sample. Given our research interest, we had to restrict our analyses to those cases for which we had complete data across all four time points (1,091 or 53%). The left-hand censoring problem (i.e., youths who had already initiated two or more behaviors) further reduced our sample for the transition analyses to 883 youths (43% of the active consent sample). Of these youths, the issue then became one of identifying the year in which they initiated one or more of the four behaviors in question. With four variables (drug use, drug sales, violent offending, and gang membership) measured at four points in time, there are a total of 64 possible patterns of initiation (e.g., drug use and gang membership in the same year followed by drug sales the next year and no violence initiation represents one possible pattern of initiation).

To facilitate discussion of the initiation patterns, we first report the overall prevalence of the behaviors for the restricted sample. During the 4-year data collection period, 42% of the youths had initiated drug use, 16% had initiated drug sales, 16% had initiated serious violence, and 7% reported joining a gang. These prevalence rates suggest that it is a small subset of the sample that will have initiated multiple types of offenses.

The next step in the analysis was to identify the initiation patterns. Table 3.3 reveals that for the vast majority of survey participants, no initiation pattern could be determined. For fully 89% of the restricted sample, the youths had either not initiated any of the behaviors, had initiated only one of the behaviors, or had initiated two or more behaviors in the same year with no subsequent initiations. Among the gang youths, 14% reported only joining a gang; 6% initiated only one of the other delinquency types; and 35% co-initiated two or more delinquency types in the first year. We are thus left with a small sample of youths to test our main point of inquiry —the role of gangs in drug use, drug sales, and violence.

Table 3.3   Initiation of Behaviors for the Longitudinal Sample

	Total, Percentage (n = 883)	Nongang, Percentage (n = 832)	Gang, Percentage (n = 51)
No pattern discernible	89	92	55
Nonoffender	54	57	14
One behavior only	27	28	6
Two or more behaviors co-initiated in same year	9	7	35
Pattern discernible	11	8	45

Table 3.4   Bivariate Initiation Sequences Among Gang Members, $n = 51$

	Drug Use, Percentage	Drug Sales, Percentage	Violence, Percentage
Never initiate behavior	18	37	35
Behavior before gang	22	10	16
Gang before behavior	14	18	14

We now turn our attention to the transition patterns for the sample of gang youths (see Table 3.4). It is important to note that even with our large sample of youths, we are restricted to examining the actual initiation patterns of only 51 gang youths. For parsimony, we examine three bivariate transitional possibilities—whether gang membership preceded, followed, or occurred simultaneously with drug use, drug sales, and violent offending. When the gang youth initiated the behavior in question, the most common pattern was for the behavior in question to be initiated during the same year the youth reported joining the gang. For example, 47% reported joining a gang the same year they started using drugs. Similarly, 35% initiated violence and drug sales the same year of gang joining. Interestingly, more than one third of the gang youth did not initiate violent offending or drug sales during the 4-year study period. No clear pattern emerged for the remaining youths with regard to the initiation of the behavior, either before or after joining the gang. Clearly, there is no conclusive evidence that joining a gang causes drug use, drug sales, or violence among gang members or that youths who are already involved in these activities join gangs.

Conclusion

Our purpose in pursuing this particular line of inquiry was to explore the two questions posed at the outset of this chapter: (a) What are the prevalence rates for drug use, drug sales, and violent offending for gang and nongang youth? Is there offense specialization or, as Klein (1995) argues, cafeteria-style delinquency; and, importantly, (b) What is the temporal sequencing of these behaviors? Is there a selection, a social facilitation, or an enhancement effect?

With respect to the first question, these analyses confirm what others have reported: Gang members are disproportionately involved in drug use, drug sales, and violent offending. Furthermore, it appears that the gang members participate in a more diverse range of illegal activities than do the nongang youth. Whereas more than 90% of nongang youth in both samples indicated that they were either nonoffenders or involved in only one of the three types of illegal behaviors, more than 60% of gang members in each sample indicated that they engaged in two or more of the activities. We realize that our focus on serious forms of delinquency may well underestimate prevalence rates and subsequently the observed co-occurrence of delinquent activities. Therefore, the fact that the majority of gang youth reported involvement in two or more of these forms of delinquency is quite noteworthy, especially given the relatively young age of the cross-sectional sample and the longitudinal sample used in the typology analyses.

With respect to the second question, these analyses suggest that an enhancement model best fits the data. The most common pattern of initiation into drug use, drug sales, violent offending, and gang membership was for the delinquent activity to be initiated during the same year as joining the gang. These analyses do not allow us to conclude that joining a gang is a precursor to involvement in drug use, drug sales, or violent offending, or that delinquency is a precursor to gang joining. Although participation in these activities is considerably more common among gang members, a sizable minority of the gang members does not report engaging in drug selling or violence, although we acknowledge that we may have a right-hand censoring problem. That is, some of these gang members may simply not have initiated the behaviors prior to the conclusion of the current study period.

Several limitations to the study reported here should be discussed. First, to assess initiation patterns from one behavior to another, it may be desirable to have more frequent data collection points, or to ask respondents specific questions to determine at what point during the year an event occurred. The annual data upon which our analyses relied provide only a crude estimate of initiation; that is, it is difficult to disentangle the actual initiation pattern accurately. With weekly or monthly recording of illegal activity, it would be possible (perhaps) to determine the initiation patterns for those gang members who co-initiate in the same year.

Second, we chose to restrict our measures of offending to what can be considered serious criminal activity. This meant excluding more common types of delinquency (minor assault) and drug use (alcohol and tobacco). Our concern here was not the transition in offending from minor to serious, but rather the extent to which joining a gang is associated with involvement in serious forms of delinquency. One consequence of this decision to restrict the analyses to serious offending is that it made our task more difficult. That is, the prevalence of the selected behaviors is relatively low. Therefore, there are few individuals who have actually engaged in two or more of the offenses, making it difficult to assess initiation patterns.

The fact that there is a low prevalence rate of involvement in these behaviors, although posing a problem for these analyses, is encouraging news. Involvement in delinquent activities may be quite common in a general sample of adolescents, but serious offending is relatively rare. For research purposes, it is worth noting how difficult it is to examine low prevalence behaviors in a general sample. From the active consent sample of 2,045 youths, we were ultimately limited to a sample of 51 gang members to conduct the necessary analyses. It is difficult to examine the effects of gang membership with so few cases.

Where does this leave us? Although these analyses are exploratory in nature, they do provide a descriptive picture of within-individual change in offending across 4 years. Several policy-related suggestions seem relevant. First, even with this young sample, a sizable proportion of youths is already engaged in drug use by eighth grade. Thus, it is clear that drug prevention efforts need to target youth prior to eighth grade. To date, many school-based drug prevention programs have targeted elementary school-aged youth, without much apparent success. Recently, one of the more popular programs (DARE) announced plans to implement the program in middle schools, thereby focusing their efforts on the age at which drug use initiation generally occurs. It will be interesting to see if this strategy will be more successful. There is also evidence in these analyses for general delinquency prevention efforts. Whereas the prevalence rates are low for violent offending and joining a gang, the fact remains that youth aged 13, 14, and 15 are getting involved in serious forms of offending. With respect to the effect of gangs on behavior, the analyses reported in this chapter, although limited by the data, are supportive of the enhancement model. It appears that delinquent youth are attracted to gangs and that gangs facilitate involvement in delinquency. For gang policy, this suggests that it is feasible to promote both prevention strategies and targeted intervention. Programs such as the Comprehensive Community-Wide Approach promoted by the Office of Juvenile Justice and Delinquency Prevention (OJJDP), though difficult to implement and evaluate, find support in the analyses reported here (see Howell, 2000, for an overview of programs and strategies).

4

Leaving the Gang

SCOTT H. DECKER
JANET L. LAURITSEN

Early studies of gangs found that adult membership in gangs was a rare phenomenon, and more recent surveys of high-risk youth confirm the importance of studying gang membership as a transitory affiliation. For instance, Thrasher (1927/1963) argued that gangs were overwhelmingly composed of adolescent boys, and Thornberry, Krohn, Lizotte, and Chard-Wierschem (1993) and Esbensen and Huizinga (1993) found that the vast majority of youth who reported gang membership also reported that affiliation to be of short duration. Despite findings that leaving the gang appears to be associated with reductions in criminal involvement (e.g., Rand, 1987), most analyses of gang involvement focus on becoming a gang member rather than discontinuing those affiliations.

The more general topic of desistance from crime has also been given less attention than other aspects of criminal activity. Recently, however, interest in desistance processes has been renewed, spurred in part by the availability of longitudinal data sources describing individuals' lives (Sampson & Laub, 1993). The findings from this literature highlight the significance of social ties, such as marriage, employment, military service, and parenthood, and broader emotional and psychological processes of maturational reform. Using a phenomenological approach, Maruna (2001) describes the fluidity of the desistance process and encourages researchers to approach the study of "going straight" as a process rather than an outcome with discrete properties.

In this chapter, we describe how gang members in St. Louis leave their gangs, using data from a field study of gang and ex-gang members. We draw conclusions about these findings in the context of the existing research on gangs and the broader literature on desistance. Finally, we discuss the need to resolve complex definitional issues, and the need for additional information for theoretical and programmatic purposes.

What Is Known About Leaving the Gang?

In 1971, Klein noted that there had been no study of the progression of gang members to adulthood. Although Moore (1991) and Vigil (1988a) have sketched out some of the details of this progression, it remains a topic about which too little is known. Sanchez-Jankowski (1991, p. 61) speculated that there were six ways gang members could exit from their gang: (a) age out, (b) die, (c) go to prison, (d) get jobs, (e) join other organizations, and (f) leave as the gang subdivides. His research found no systematic pattern in the way individual gang members left their gangs, and he underscored the diversity of reasons that individual gang members provided when asked how they came to disassociate themselves from the gang.

Additional insight about leaving the gang has been gleaned from studies of prison gangs. Based on a series of prisoner interviews, Skolnick (1988) reported that the only way to leave the gang was to "fade out" by gradually withdrawing from the activities of the group (p. 4). Despite this observation, he reported that prison gang members believed that membership was permanent—that is, they believed that gang members had no way out of their gang other than death. Similarly, Fong, Vogel, and Buentello (1995) studied data from the Texas prison system and found that inmates who left their prison gangs experienced greater consequences than those leaving street gangs, since the prison constituted a closed system in which gang members could not move, hide, or enmesh themselves in alternative networks. Nonetheless, Fong et al. reported that a substantial number of prison gang members left their gangs each year, generally without consequence.

Of course, findings based on prison gangs may not be generalizable to life outside the walls. Prison gangs often include the most hardened and criminally involved inmates, some of whom were gang members before their imprisonment, and there is evidence to suggest that the prison experience itself may increase solidarity among gang members (Fleisher & Decker, 2001). But even in such an extreme environment, leaving a gang may occur more often than has generally been assumed. Moreover, gang members themselves may be especially likely to overstate the consequences of leaving the gang.

Vigil (1988a) presents one of the most detailed discussions of the process of exiting the gang. In his analysis of Chicano gangs in Los Angeles, he found that there was a "succession quality" to leaving the gang—that is, most gang members left the gang through a process not dissimilar to that which they used in entering the gang—a gradual series of steps and commitments. The social process underlying this transition is important to underscore. Most life changes do not occur in a sudden manner. Just as getting married or growing enmeshed in a job does not typically occur overnight, severing ties with friends in a gang is unlikely to occur instantaneously.

Unlike the findings from other research, Vigil reports that exiting the gang was frequently accompanied by the ritual of being "beaten out." This process involves either running a line or being in a circle to absorb the blows of fellow gang members to prove one's worth. Thus, in his research, leaving the gang also involved a symbolic process that announced to fellow gang members that the tie between the group and the individual had been severed.

Vigil also found that members who left the gang typically had developed increased ties to social institutions, most often prison, but also with jobs and family. He characterizes the process of leaving the gang as more difficult than joining, in part because leaving the group means rejecting one's friends and peers. He argues that because the gang provides a source of support and friendship, members do not leave until a suitable substitute has been found. Vigil emphasizes how difficult this may be for adolescents, for whom peer associations are particularly important.

Hagedorn (1994a) conducted a series of interviews with Milwaukee gang members that consisted of 47 interviews in 1987 and 101 interviews in 1992. Most of the latter set of interviews was with adults (median age = 26), and 23 of these gang members had also been interviewed in 1987. From these interviews Hagedorn developed a four-category typology of adult gang members, based largely on their relationships to drug sales and employment in the legitimate economy. Two of these categories—"Legits" and "Homeboys"—are relevant for the current discussion.

Despite strong commitments to the goals of legitimate society, few of the African American and Latino gang members from the original sample had become Legits—that is, individuals who had reported that they left the gang, were not involved in drug sales, and were involved in jobs or school. The Legits were most easily classified as ex-gang members using their behaviors, attachments, and identification as criteria. However, identification of the gang member status of Homeboys was more difficult. The typical Homeboy was in his mid-20s, past the peak age of offending, and generally worked in the legitimate economy. But Homeboys often found themselves unable to fulfill their conventional aspirations and moved between the legitimate and the illegal economy quite frequently. Thus, Homeboys represented a middle category of gang member, falling somewhere between Legits and active gang members. As such, they reinforce the notion that leaving the gang is a gradual process, often involving increasing commitments to conventional institutions. What remains unclear, however, is whether the impetus to leave the gang is the result or the cause of conventional affiliations.

Much of the gang literature suggests that gang members age out of the gang (Horowitz, 1983; Klein, 1971), and recent research on high-risk youth confirms this description. Battin, Hill, Abbott, Catalano, and Hawkins (1998) and Thornberry, Lizotte, Krohn, Farnworth, and Jang (1994) note that gang membership among teenagers typically averages 2 years or less. Thus gang membership is most often short-lived, characterized as much by leaving as by joining. However, aging out does not appear to be uniformly experienced by all gang members. Horowitz (1983) reports that "peripheral" or "fringe" members found it easier to leave the gang than did "core" members, due to lesser involvement in gang activities and reduced dependence on the gang for social or instrumental support.

Individuals may encounter a variety of problems when leaving the gang, some of which stem from the gang itself, but many have their focus outside the gang. For instance, despite announcing a decision to leave the gang, ex-gang members may continue to be seen as gang members by their own gang, rival gangs, the police, and the community. Gang identities often remain fixed well after the decision to leave the gang has been made and acted on. Some acts committed while a gang member transcend the period of membership. For instance, the announcement of a decision to leave the gang would not necessarily reduce the incentive for rival gang members to redress a previous act of violence, nor would such information reduce the efforts of police to make arrests for criminal activities committed while a gang member. Past gang activity may also hinder an individual's ability to gain employment, making it more difficult for the labor market to produce conformity.

Under these conditions it is easy to imagine that some gang members may decide that leaving the gang is not worth the effort. After all, what incentive is there to leave the gang when it is the source of friendships and when past activities as a gang member cause others to continue to treat them as if they were still gang members? Even though adolescence is a period in life when many affiliations are tried and rejected, the dilemma surrounding gang membership is that it has a more enduring external character than many other affiliations.

Our reading of the literature surrounding the process of leaving the gang found that most of this research is descriptive. We found no research designed to assess systematically the conditions under which members choose to leave the gang or the factors that account for the length of time one remains a gang member. However, gang members do report that they see themselves and others leaving for a variety of reasons and in numerous ways. These accounts can guide researchers' efforts in determining whether the decision to leave the gang is driven by individual characteris-

tics, experiences within the gang, external ties such as investments in social institutions or attachments to prosocial persons, or some other set of
unknown factors. In order to examine the significance of these factors,
many definitional issues need to be addressed. These issues became apparent in our investigation of gang and ex-gang members in St. Louis.

_____ **The Data**

To structure our investigation of leaving the gang, we rely on data from a
3-year field study of gangs in St. Louis conducted between October 1990
and September 1993, and follow-up data for approximately half of the
sample through 1998. The city of St. Louis experienced dramatic economic
and population losses similar to those that plagued many other midwestern industrialized cities in the 1970s and 1980s. Gangs in St. Louis grew in
number and membership during the mid-1980s (Decker & Van Winkle,
1996).

For this project, *gangs* were defined as age-graded peer groups that exhibited permanence, engaged in criminal activity, and had symbolic repre-
sentations of membership. A street ethnographer who verified membership and observed gang activity in neighborhoods made contacts with
active and ex-gang members. This person, an ex-offender himself, had
built a reputation as "solid" on the street through his work with the community and previous research work. Using snowball sampling procedures, initial field contacts were made and the sample was built to include
more subjects (Biernacki & Waldorf, 1981; Decker & Van Winkle, 1996).

Individuals who admitted current or past membership and agreed to an
interview became part of our sample. Current and past membership was
also verified by information from field observation or other subjects, and
individuals were considered "ex-gang members" based on self-reports.
Subjects had to have been ex-gang members for at least 3 months to be classified as such. We also sought to include family members of gang members
in our interviews.

Three features distinguish this work from most studies of gangs. First,
no criminal justice contacts were used to gain access to the members of the
sample. Using criminal justice channels (police, courts, probation, and social service agencies) may result in a different type of subject than one
found in the field. For example, police and criminal justice samples may be
more involved in law breaking. Second, the gang members themselves
told their story. Although an interview instrument was used, ample opportunity was provided in open-ended questions for the subjects to elaborate on questions and add new insights. Third, this was a field study of
gangs, not conducted in the offices of a social service or youth agency. All
participants in the study were initially contacted in the neighborhoods
where they lived and acted out their gang activities. This enabled project

personnel to observe a number of gang activities, including violent encounters between gangs. It is our belief that a sample recruited in this way enhances the validity of responses.

The data for this analysis consist of interviews with 99 active gang members and 24 ex-gang members. We look at data from both sets of subjects so that active members' perceptions of what leaving the gang would entail could be compared to the experiences of ex-members. As expected, the ex-gang members were somewhat older (mean = 19 years of age) than the currently active gang members (mean = 17). Twenty-two of the ex-gang members were black males and 2 were black females. The sample of active gang members included 4 white males, 7 black females, and 88 black males. Half of the ex-gang members had left the gang for a period of less than a year at the time of the interview.

The past gangs of ex-gang members were each classified according to the level of organization (Decker, Bynum, & Weisel, 1998). Eleven of the ex-gang members came from gangs with a "loose" organizational structure, lacking leadership and having few group goals and infrequent group associations. Five ex-members came from gangs with a high level of organization, and five came from gangs that were organized in moderate fashion.

Reasons for Leaving

Ex-Gang Member Reports

We begin by examining the reasons ex-members offered for leaving the gang, as well as the way in which they left their gangs. When asked why they left their gangs, the majority (16 ex-gang members, or two thirds of this group) offered a specific reason: They left because of the level of violence. Many of these individuals left because of personal experiences of violence.

EX003:   Well, after I got shot, I got shot in my leg. You know how your life just flash? I was walking to my father's house, he stay on the westside. I was walking and then I saw, see I don't like the color red, I hate the color red, and it was like a whole corner full of Bloods. It was like, what's up, Blood? I said no. They said, "What you claim?" And then we had a fight and I hit a few of them. It was like ten of them and then I ran and then all I heard was pow, I was still running. I had on some white jogging pants and I saw blood running down the back of my leg and I just ran over to my father's house. It [the bullet] didn't go in, it was like grazing me. It just scared me cause I ended up being shot at. I had a gun put to my head before but I never been shot at.

INT:[1]   Why did you quit being in the gang?

EX014:   Because I was put in the hospital.

INT: You were hospitalized?

EX014:   Yeah, for four days.

INT: What were you hospitalized for?

EX014:   I got beat in the back of the head with a bat.

INT: By other gang members, some Bloods or something?

EX014:   Hoover. [Crips]

INT: Why did you get out?

EX011:   Because I got to realizing it wasn't my type of life. I didn't want to live that type of life. One time, I got seriously stabbed and I was in the hospital for like three months.

INT: Where did you get it?

EX011:   Right in my back. Close to the kidney. I was in the hospital for like three months. After I got out of the hospital, I tried to cope with it a little more, but I just faded away from it.

In other cases, the *threat or fear of personal violence* was offered by the individual as a reason for leaving the gang.

INT: Why did you quit?

EX001:   Because we might get shot. Somebody in our hood got shot last night and the day before that. They killing for no reason.

EX013:   I didn't want to die. Just one day I got out.

Some left because *family members were the victims of violence* or violence was threatened against family members. For these individuals, this single event was reported as the reason for leaving the gang.

INT: Why did you leave?

EX018:   My cousin got shot.

The majority of ex-members who cited violence as the reason they left their gangs underscored the vicarious nature of violence that had occurred against other members of their gangs.

EX016:   Yeah, that really came to me because when one of my friends got killed and you look at his face, it was hard. It could have been me. His parents were at the point. . . . It was just hard on me because the reason why he got in was because of me. It was hard for me to go up to his parents. At that point, I was saying that it wasn't my fault. When I really woke up was when my friend died because we got in there together. He said I'm gonna get in if you get in.

INT: Can you tell me why did you decide to leave the gang?

EX002: Because all my friends were getting killed that I used to hang with and because the 'hood I'm staying in there's a lot of Bloods, which I didn't want to be.

INT: Why did you leave?

EX009: Because people was dying. It wasn't about nothing to me no more.

INT: Why did you leave?

EX012: My best friend, he got killed. We was in the eighth grade together [and] freshman year.

The remaining eight individuals offered diverse reasons why they left their gangs. Three said that they had moved out of town, severing ties with the gangs in their former cities of residence. Two additional ex-members could not offer a reason why they left. Three individuals cited family ties, including caring for children or other obligations to family.

INT: Why did you quit?

EX021: Because I've got two children to live for.

INT: Why did you leave?

EX013: Because of my loved ones. I just couldn't keep neglecting them.

EX011: When I was in the gang I wasn't spending time with my daughter, I wasn't taking care of her, I wasn't doing, that's mainly why me and my baby's mother broke up because stuff I was getting in. She didn't want to be around me, the kind of person that I was then. Now, I have got me a job, I was getting locked up before.

In some of these cases, gang members reported a single event (especially violence) for leaving their gangs; in others an accumulation of events and attachments preceded the decision. Thus, a combination of maturational reform, aging, and proximity to violence produced the motivation for leaving the gang for a number of individuals. Similar to other studies (e.g., Hagedorn, 1994a), we found that participation declined with age and was associated with involvement in activities in postadolescent stages of the life course (job, family, concern about one's future). Familial ties and victimization experiences were cited far more often than institutional affiliations as reasons to terminate ties to the gang.

Next, we describe the specific method or route by which ex-members left their gang. Once again, a single answer dominated the responses. Fifteen of the 24 ex-gang members (63%) told us that they simply quit their gangs and that this did not involve a specific method or technique. While others have noted gang rituals for leaving, this was not observed among St. Louis gang members. This may be due to the fact that the gangs were characterized by loose ties among members, few formal rules, few strong leaders, and little articulated structure. Also, subgroups within St. Louis gangs claimed stronger allegiances than did the larger gang (Decker & Van Winkle, 1996). It was in those subgroups that most illegal activity, especially drug sales, but also robberies and burglaries, took place. It is also possible that the strength of friendship ties within the subgroup protected ex-gang members from retaliation for leaving the gang. Perhaps ironically, the peer group that facilitated gang membership later served to mitigate the consequences of leaving the gang, particularly when an ex-member maintained associations with gang members after leaving.

EX001:   I just quit. I stopped hanging out with them. There was about three of us that quit, we just stopped hanging out with them and everything.

INT: How did you leave? Did you have to announce something, did you get beat out?

EX008:   Just stopped claiming.

INT: So when guys would ask you if you were claiming, you would say no, I'm out of that now?

EX008:   Yeah.

INT: Did people respect that?

EX008:   No.

INT: What did they do when you told them you weren't claiming any more?

EX008:   Most of them started talking stuff. Once you in, you in it for life and all that stuff.

INT: How did you get out?

EX011:   Some of them be funning saying they got to kill they mother but some of the stuff is true. How I really got out of it, I just got me a little job, stopped hanging out with them.

INT: How did you leave?

EX019:   I just walked away.

INT: It was that easy? They didn't. . . .

EX019:   No, they didn't fuck with me.

A small number of ex-gang members told us they were threatened after they left the gang.

INT: How did you leave?

EX016:   I just stopped socializing with them. I was threatened to get killed after I left but it really didn't faze me.

Interestingly, only a small number of ex-members report having to fight a member to formally leave the gang.

EX004:   If you want to get out you get beat down.

INT: So you get out the same way you get in?

EX004:   Right. There's more dudes on you. About six dudes on you.

INT: How did you leave the gang?

EX024:   Moved out of there.

INT: You had to beat up on other members to get out?

EX024:   Yeah.

While this was reported to have happened to only a few ex-gang members, it was the predominant myth among gang members. As Klein (1971) and Decker and Van Winkle (1996) have noted, such myths among gangs have served to dominate the public's views of gangs. If so, these false perceptions should not serve as the basis of gang intervention policy.

A final group of five ex-members reported that they left their gangs by moving. One, who had moved to St. Louis from California, told us that one could never really leave the gang, but that moving out of state was the way he severed ties with his gang.

INT: When did you quit the gang?

EX006:   I never did quit. You can never get out of the gang. Only way you can quit is to stop hanging around them or move to another state.

INT: How long [since] you moved from California?

EX006:   Four years, really three and a half.

INT: So [the] gang consider[s] you in the gang until you die, right?

EX006:   You can get out of the gang if you really wanted to. But in California you have to kill somebody to get out of the gang. You got to kill your mother or somebody like that to get out of it. I can't get out of it. I ain't killing my mother.

Overall, most members of our ex-gang sample indicated they left the gang because of concerns over violence targeted directly at them or at members of their gang. Many commentators (Klein, 1971; Sanchez-

Jankowski, 1991; Short & Strodtbeck, 1965/1974; Vigil, 1988a; Yablonsky, 1973) identify violence as a defining feature of gang life. A large body of research indicates that gang violence (real or mythic) provides much of the solidarity that keeps gangs together (Klein, 1971; Moore, 1978; Short & Strodtbeck, 1965/1974; Thrasher, 1927/1963; Vigil, 1988a). Our findings suggest that violence may have contradictory consequences: The very activity that may keep gangs together appears to have provided the impetus for the majority of this sample to leave the gang. This paradox is certainly worth more detailed exploration.

Active Gang Member Reports

We now turn to data from the 99 active gang members—first to their reports during the 3-year field study, and then to the results of a follow-up search for these members approximately 5 years later. Some have argued that status as a gang member is a "master status," one that influences most behavior and is not shed easily (Sanchez-Jankowski, 1991). Active gang members have a stake in maintaining such a view of gang membership because the viability of their gang depends on the ability of active gang members to maintain the perception that leaving the gang is nearly impossible. This may, in part, explain the efforts of active gang members to foster the belief that drastic steps (such as killing your mother) are the only means by which individuals can leave the gang.

Although most active gang members strongly expressed the belief that one can never leave the gang, a majority of the active gang members knew individuals who had left their gang. Indeed, 55 of the 81 active gang members who responded to this question (68%) told us they knew individuals who had left. This apparent contradiction may be the result of close associations that remained beyond the gang identification. We also found that the reasons that individuals left the gang were essentially the same among gang and ex-gang members. In rank order, violence, family, and just stopping were the three categories identified most often by active gang members. Again, gang experiences and social processes, rather than institutional commitments, were the core reasons for leaving the gang.

Almost half of the active gang members who knew individuals who left their gang identified violence as the primary reason. Being shot or beaten up was the reason offered most frequently.

INT: Why did they decide to leave, do you know?
036:     Got shot in the head.

INT: Why did he get out of it?
048:     Cause he was getting beat up too much.

INT: Why did they leave the gang?

083:     They got beat up bad.

Other gang members left because they knew members of their own gang who had been the victims of violence.

INT: How did they decide to leave?

004:     One of they friends got killed.

INT: Why did they leave?

035:     Death in they family.

INT: You mean somebody was killed?

035:     Somebody that was real close to them and they figured they had to leave.

Often, the victims were relatives of a gang member, making the violence more salient to them.

INT: Do you know why he decided to leave?

075:     One person left because his brother got shot so he just went out.

INT: His brother didn't die, did he?

075:     Yeah, he did.

Or in other cases, gang members grew weary of threats against their families.

INT: Do you know why he decided to leave?

087:     Same reason I left from where I was at.

INT: Too much heat and static?

087:     Yeah, cause it would get so far as they will harass your family, like shoot your house up or something.

The second-largest category of active gang members who knew a fellow gang member who had left the gang identified family and job concerns as the primary reason for breaking ties with the gang.

INT: Do you know why he left?

093:     This white boy Gary used to be with us, he use to be a Blood and stuff like that but he got this gal pregnant and he got his own house and he told us he didn't want to be in the gang any more.

INT: Do you know anybody who used to be in a gang but isn't any more?

021:     My brother used to be in a gang but he don't claim no more.

INT: How come?

021:     He was with the gang but he got serious with his girlfriend and got her pregnant and he said fuck that shit [the gang]. I'm just going to lay low with my gal, I ain't got time for that. He don't got time for that [gang] stuff.

037:     My big brother [left the gang]. He was in the 38s. They say to get out of the 38s you got to kill your parents, kill one of your parents. My brother was making good grades, got him a scholarship and everything and he was like, I'm leaving this alone. They tried to make him kill my mother. He was like, you must be crazy, and I was on his side.

A number of gang members also told us they knew gang members who had simply stopped being in the gang.

INT: Are there people who used to be in your gang but aren't any more?

003:     Well, we did have a few people who left but they had talked to us about it and said they didn't want to be in the gang any more. We said all right man, that's cool. We a gang; if you just want out, you want out, you out of here.

INT: Do you know why they decided to leave?

011:     Cause it don't prove anything cause everybody splitting up slowly cause it don't really prove nothing. If we need their help they will come back and help.

INT: Do you know anybody who used to be in a gang but isn't any more?

086:     Yeah.

INT: Do you know why they decided to leave?

086:     They just stopped. They not in it but they still a gang member.

These observations confirm the view that leaving the gang is not a process that requires taking exceptional steps, and most ex-gang members report gradually severing the bonds between themselves and the gang. Indeed, in many instances active gang members saw the logic of such decisions made by their peers.

Active Gang Member Reports: Five Years Later

Perhaps the most striking finding we can report is the number of deaths that had occurred to the original sample of active gang members approximately 5 years after they were interviewed. The salience of violence for life in the gang has been reported for a variety of contexts (Decker & Van Winkle, 1996; Klein, 1995; Sanders, 1994), and our follow-up study of the initial sample reaffirms this view. The search for the original 99 gang members through December 1998 yielded 51 subjects, of whom 19 had died, 2 were in state prison, and 4 were in vocational rehabilitation (wheelchairs). While we could track only about half of the initial sample (51 out of 99), these grim outcomes occurred to approximately half of those who could be located (i.e., approximately one quarter of the initial sample). It is difficult to predict whether those who could not be found experienced similar fates.

Defining an Ex-Gang Member

These interviews also illustrate some of the difficulties in determining when gang membership ceases and how that may influence future interactions and affiliations with active gang members. What some subjects describe as a rather simple experience, in fact draws attention to important definitional issues. For instance, the last two subjects (011 and 086) indicate that ex-gang members could still be designated as a gang member, because they report emotional ties (086) or see themselves as individuals who can be counted on for involvement in certain gang activities (011). We address this complexity below.

The answer to the question, "Is this subject still a gang member?" is explicitly tied to the definitions of both a *gang* and a *member*, and there is still considerable debate over these terms (see, e.g., Ball & Curry, 1995; Covey, Menard, & Franzese, 1992; Decker & Kempf, 1991). Most studies rely on self-report questions (e.g., "Are you a member of a street or youth gang?") and require that the group to which the youth belongs engage in some illegal activity (see, e.g., Esbensen & Huizinga, 1993). If we use these criteria for gang membership, it also seems reasonable to rely on self-reports for determining ex-gang member status as well.

Although each of the "ex-gang members" reported that he or she was no longer a member of a gang, a considerable proportion claimed that they continued to participate in both criminal and noncriminal activities with members of the gang, and others reported emotional ties to gang members. Using these two dimensions—activities and attachments—we display in Table 4.1 a typology for describing an ex-member's relationship with the gang.

Persons who fall into Category A are most easily classified as ex-gang members. These individuals no longer have attachments to members of

Table 4.1   Typology of Self-Reported Ex-Gang Membership Status

	Emotional Ties With Members of Previous Gang Network	
	NO	*YES*
NO	A	B
YES	C	D

Engage in Activities With Members of Previous Gang Network

their former gangs and no longer engage in activities (criminal or noncriminal) with those members. Ex-members who have moved to new towns, and those who report new families and jobs and no current ties to the gang, would be easily placed in this category. Ex-gang members who said that they no longer associated with members of their gangs but still had friendships that were strong enough to elicit "helping out" their old associates if there was "trouble" fall into Category B. Ex-gang members falling into Category C are those who no longer report emotional ties to the gang but still engage in activities with persons still in the gang. These ex-members seek out former associates for activities such as drug sales or hanging out, but they eschew the affiliation as a member of the gang and their relationships appear to be more instrumental. In the St. Louis data, these were individuals who most likely left for family or employment reasons and who no longer define themselves as gang members because their primary commitments lie elsewhere. Although an argument could be made that these individuals are still active gang members (despite their own protests), to do so would require changing the working definition of membership to include only activity and attachments, and to disregard self-reported status. Finally, we also uncovered ex-gang members who claimed to be involved in activities with their gang and committed to emotional aspects of the gang (Category D), yet no longer considered themselves to be gang members. The primary difference between these persons and those in Category C is the degree to which these friendships are valued.

As the above categories suggest, determining when a person is an "ex-gang member" was found to be more difficult than initially expected because self-described ex-gang members continue to report varying degrees of attachments and activities with others in the gang, and the process of disengagement is often gradual. This conceptual difficulty parallels some of the obstacles highlighted in the more general literature on recidivism. For instance, Maruna (2001) discusses the tendency for desistance to be viewed by criminologists as an event or voluntary decision in the lives of offenders. Yet few subjects who report that they no longer engage in criminal conduct made these decisions only once. Maruna reminds us that criminal behavior is sporadic, and as such "termination" or "desistance" takes place repeatedly (p. 23). He also reminds us that there is a vast difference between the decision to go straight and the actual process of doing so.

Conclusions

Leaving the gang is a more complex and variable process than suggested in previous research, and many parallels can be found in the research on desistance. In some instances, it appears that persons make an explicit decision to leave; others simply drift away. The St. Louis data suggest that the way in which individuals "leave" the gang may be related to the characteristics of both the group and the individual, but more likely reflects informal social processes than institutional involvement or incentives. Violent experiences also motivated some gang members to leave. A key area for gang research should be to investigate not only individual and group-level influences, but also to examine the role of potential "triggering events" in individual motivations and decision making. Unfortunately, these data do not permit us to determine what factors distinguish those who leave following violent experiences from those who stay.

Despite these complexities, do we have sufficient information for suggesting how the duration of gang membership might be shortened? One of the ironic findings noted above was that the majority of ex-gang members in this sample said that violence had played a role in their decision to leave the gang while at the same time the prior literature has found that violent events tend to strengthen group solidarity. Although our findings do not tell us how this process operates, they do suggest an opportunity for intervention. Seizing opportunities when gang members have been victimized by violence or have witnessed a close friend's victimization may offer promising avenues for reducing gang involvement.

Our findings suggest that the role of violence in discouraging membership or enhancing cohesion may have an important time dimension. In the short term, violence may cause some gang members to reflect on the risks of their participation in the gang and to question the viability of their membership. The extent to which they are physically separated from the gang will likely play a large role in determining how salient violent victimization will be for their decision to leave the gang. Over the longer term, enhanced by interaction with other gang members, violence can serve to enhance cohesion (Klein, 1971; Short & Strodtbeck, 1965/1974). The trick, then, is to intervene immediately following acts of violence, when gang members are separated from their gang, or at least when they are in small groups that are apart from the gang. Such opportunities are not likely to exist in the offices of social service agencies. Rather, they are likely to be found in hospital emergency rooms, at the police station, or in family settings. As Fearn, Decker, and Curry (2000) argue, gang intervention policies need to adopt strategies that address proximate and fundamental causes of gangs. Such intervention is likely to be successful to the extent that it (a) occurs very shortly after the victimization, and (b) occurs separate from the influence of the gang. Follow-up services may be necessary, particularly to counteract the socializing power of the gang in "reconstructing" the violence in a fashion that serves to reintegrate the gang member into the collective.

Note

1. INT stands for interviewer; the digit number stands for the number of the subject. Ex-gang members are denoted by EX before the subject number.

PART

2

The Arenas:
Neighborhoods, Communities,
and Schools

The Systemic Model
of Gang Behavior
A Reconsideration

ROBERT J. BURSIK, JR.

Although criminologists can confidently state that certain neighborhood characteristics are at least partial determinants of the geographic distribution of youth gangs, we have yet to develop a fully satisfactory explanation of this relationship. Rather, our understanding of these complex dynamics historically has reflected an ongoing process in which once-dominant orientations have been reconsidered in light of new evidence or theoretical insights and either discarded entirely or replaced by new frameworks that attempt to integrate the old and new perspectives parsimoniously. In turn, these synthesized models eventually are challenged in their own right.

We are at just such a cusp in the study of gangs and local communities. After an extended period in which it was moribund, the traditional theory of social disorganization was revitalized by systemic reformulations that attempted to resolve the logical and empirical difficulties that led to the decline of the original theory's popularity (see, e.g., Bellair, 1995, 1997, 2000; Bursik, 1988, 1999; Bursik & Grasmick, 1993, 1995b; Rountree & Warner, 1999; Sampson & Groves, 1989; Sampson, Raudenbush, & Earls, 1997; Sampson, Morenoff, & Earls, 1999; Taylor, 1997; Warner & Rountree, 1997). However, although these revisionist orientations have generated important new insights into the community factors that increase the likelihood of gang activity, recent applications of the model clearly indicate that some significant revisions are necessary. This chapter highlights the problems that I consider to be most critical and suggests some directions for their resolution.

The Intellectual Precursors
of the Systemic Model

Although the clustering of illegal behavior within particular urban neighborhoods has been recognized since Allison's (1840) ambitious study of early 19th century London, the earliest and most influential theoretically grounded explanation of such patterns is found in Thrasher's (1927/1963) investigation of Chicago's gangs. At the heart of his framework was the assumption that such groups "develop in definite and predictable ways, in accordance with a form of entelechy that is predetermined by characteristic internal processes and mechanisms, and have, in short, a nature and natural history" (p. 4). For the purposes of this chapter, the most important of these mechanisms were the dynamics of urban growth and differentiation that were emphasized by the human ecology model of Park and Burgess (1924; Burgess, 1925).

Park and Burgess argued that competition over the control of scarce but desirable space determined the parts of the city in which different populations could reside. Because newly arrived immigrant groups with few financial assets could afford only inexpensive housing, they tended to move into older, run-down sections in the "zone of transition" that surrounded the central business district. These areas were characterized by extreme poverty, deteriorated housing stock, rapid population turnover, and high levels of racial and ethnic heterogeneity. However, as they became assimilated into the occupational structure and had greater economic resources at their disposal, these groups moved progressively outward into increasingly expensive neighborhoods where more attractive housing was available.

Thrasher's (1927/1963) study indicated that most of the 1,313 gangs upon which he focused were located in this transitory "interstitial" zone (p. 20), and he concluded that they were "one manifestation of the economic, moral and cultural frontier" (p. 21) found in these sections of the city. Unfortunately, his presentation of the "Gangland" material was largely descriptive, and barely three pages are devoted to a discussion of the ecological processes associated with the spatial concentration of gang activity (pp. 20-22). Thus, while the consequential conceptual impact of Thrasher's work is undeniable, it represented a preliminary, suggestive perspective rather than a well-developed model of gangs and neighborhoods (see Short, 1963).

A more extensive specification of these processes was offered shortly thereafter by Clifford Shaw and Henry McKay, whose work had been strongly influenced not only by the research of Park and Burgess, and Thrasher, but also by the social disorganization theory of Thomas and Znaniecki (1920; see Shaw & McKay, 1931, 1942; Shaw, Zorbaugh, McKay, & Cottrell, 1929). Shaw and McKay's findings that delinquency rates in general tended to be highest in those impoverished areas that had been identified as Gangland provided a strong confirmation of Thrasher's results. Drawing from the work of Thomas and Znaniecki (1920), Shaw and McKay formalized and extended Thrasher's Park and Burgess-based interpretation by proposing that rapid population change and heterogeneity led to a condition of social disorganization in which the effectiveness of existing social institutions and rules of behavior becomes substantially weakened (Shaw et al., 1929, p. 6; see Bursik, 1988, 2000). Economic deprivation was considered to be related to crime only to the extent that it increased the likelihood that a community was characterized by elevated levels of residential instability and population heterogeneity.

Although Shaw and McKay did not attempt to account specifically for the distribution of gang behavior, they stressed the group nature of most delinquent and criminal activity throughout their writings, and emphasized the degree to which their framework complemented that of Thrasher (see Shaw, Zorbaugh, McKay, & Cotrell, 1929, chap. I, footnote 10). For example, they stated that, "The play group is a spontaneous form of primary relationship which reflects community life and is very significant in determining attitudes, habits, and standards of conduct in the juvenile. In certain areas of the city these groups become delinquent gangs" (p. 7). In fact, the Conclusion of *Juvenile Delinquency and Urban Areas* (Shaw & McKay, 1942) emphasized that, "Delinquency—particularly group delinquency, which constitutes a preponderance of all officially recorded offenses committed by boys and young men—has its roots in the dynamic life of the community" (p. 315). Thus, despite its general orientation, Shaw and McKay's social disorganization model unquestionably represents one of the most important theories of gang behavior published during the 20th century.

Although this framework was a central component of American criminology for many years, some serious reservations had been expressed by 1950, and by the mid-1970s most criminologists considered the social disorganization model to be historically interesting but theoretically irrelevant (see Bursik, 1988; Bursik & Grasmick, 1993). However, Shaw and McKay have re-emerged as important contemporary figures due to the influence of their perspective on recent systemic approaches to the neighborhood and gangs issue.

Systemic Models of Neighborhoods and Gang Activity

The hallmark of all systemic approaches is a focus on the regulatory capacities that are embedded in the affiliational, interactional, and communication ties of neighborhood residents. Nevertheless, there are important variants of this model, differing in the amount of emphasis that is placed on one or more of three complementary considerations (Bursik, 2000):

1. *Structural* approaches highlight the number of people who are bound together through formal or informal networks (size), the percentage of all possible network ties that actually exist (density), and the degree to which the networks link together the various groups residing in the area (breadth). Network characteristics that have been shown to be especially salient are intergenerational closure, reciprocal exchange, and shared child control (Sampson et al., 1999).

2. Some systemic work emphasizes the *functional differentiation* of networks. Drawing from the work of Hunter (1985), Bursik and Grasmick (1993) focused on three basic types. *Private* networks integrate residents into the intimate primary groups of a neighborhood, such as the family or friendship groups. *Parochial* networks represent relationships that do not have the same degree of intimacy as those at the private level, such as ties to casual acquaintances or participation in local clubs, associations, and institutions. *Public* networks connect local residents to noncommunity-based persons or agencies that control political, economic, and social resources that may be useful for regulatory purposes.

3. There is significant variation in the *content* of the interchanges among network members. Sampson and his colleagues (1997), in particular, have explored the nature of the social capital that may be transferred through these ties and the degree to which it affects a collective sense of efficacy pertaining to the control of local problems.

A systemic reformulation of Shaw and McKay's orientation makes it much easier to conceptually differentiate social disorganization from the ecological processes that make internal self-regulation problematic and from the rates of crime and delinquency that are expected to be the result (see Bursik, 1999). For example, because it is assumed that relational networks are difficult to establish and maintain when a neighborhood is characterized by rapid population turnover, high levels of residential instability are assumed to lead to low capacities for neighborhood regulation (see Bursik & Grasmick, 1993, p. 33). Likewise, Merry (1981) suggests that racial and ethnic heterogeneity can significantly decrease the degree to which relational networks span the various subgroups residing in a community since mutual distrust often exists among these groups.

However, the systemic model does not simply restate the Shaw and McKay propositions in terms of network properties. Most notably, the emphasis on public networks is an important departure from the traditional social disorganization perspective and represents an explicit attempt to account for a devastating empirical contradiction of their assumptions about the role of economic deprivation that first was reported in William F. Whyte's *Street Corner Society* (1943), and that subsequently has been observed many times (see, e.g., Suttles, 1968, or Moore, 1978): Some impoverished neighborhoods are characterized by relatively strong private and parochial linkages among local residents, yet nevertheless are the site of gang activity.

Bursik and Grasmick (1993, p. 17) argued that Shaw and McKay failed to appreciate sufficiently the degree to which factors external to a community (such as the provision of educational, law enforcement, and other social services, and the structure of occupational opportunities, etc.) could mediate the ability of local networks and institutions to control the threat of crime. Thus, as Finestone (1976) observed, Shaw and McKay gave the impression that the internal organization of urban neighborhoods is independent of the broader political and economic dynamics of the city. Bursik and Grasmick attempted to account for the findings reported by Whyte and others by maintaining that the relationship between economic composition and gang activity was indeed indirect, but that Shaw and McKay had not incorporated the key mediating mechanism into their theory; that is, the ability to solicit regulatory resources from outside of the community. It is interesting to note, by the way, that Thrasher *did* emphasize the importance of political indifference and the exclusion of local residents from high-paying occupations, although he did not formally pursue the theoretical implications (see Bursik & Grasmick, 1993, pp. 128-129).

A focus on the public level of control has led to some findings about the dynamics of gang formation and maintenance that could not be anticipated by the Shaw and McKay model. Zatz and Portillos (2000), for example, report that there are locally staffed programs in the South Phoenix neighborhood that provide tutoring and job-placement services for young residents, as well as voluntary block watch organizations that try to prevent violence, burglaries, graffiti, and drug sales in the area. Yet the long tradition of gang activity in this area has continued despite efforts to control it with the internal forms of social control that were emphasized by Shaw and McKay.

Zatz and Portillos (2000) attempt to explain this anomaly by focusing on the effectiveness of public control networks. For example, they note that local, Mexican-born men are not likely to know how to access public resources that might enable them to control their children and/or grandchildren better. Likewise, many residents are hesitant to ask the police to intercede on their behalf due to a long history of tense relationships with law enforcement agencies and the widespread perception that they cannot be counted on to provide protective services (p. 383). This attitude is part of a more general belief that decision makers with the power to make a difference in the community have abandoned the area. For example, many feel that state and local politicians and officials have reduced the community's resource base and placed it low on the priority list for revitalization, and that businesses take money from the area but do not invest in it. As a result, many gang members reported that it was necessary to engage in criminal activities because of their role as "protectors of their communities" (p. 382).

Although Zatz and Portillos provide important support for the systemic theory, that framework cannot yet account for other results. The dynamics emphasized by most systemic theorists are grounded in the basic assumption that neighborhood residents share a common goal of living in an area relatively free from the threat of serious crime (Bursik & Grasmick, 1993, p. 15; see also Bursik, 1988). Yet Zatz and Portillos (2000) present evidence of considerable variation in the willingness of residents to condemn gang activities outright. Rather, important differences are associated with gender, the degree of identification with traditional Mexican values, the length of residence in the United States, and educational achievement (pp. 384-385). Likewise, whereas Bursik and Grasmick assumed that the regulatory effects of private, parochial, and public control would be mutually complementary, Zatz and Portillos note the difficulty of engaging in effective private control when parents are incarcerated (i.e., subjected to a form of public control).

Given their focus on a single, disenfranchised neighborhood located in a somewhat unique urban area it might seem reasonable to regard these patterns very cautiously. Yet, as will be documented below, departures from the standard systemic predictions have been reported in a variety of areas, with a variety of populations, and using a variety of methodological techniques. Therefore, it has become increasingly apparent that such findings cannot be discounted as exceptions to the rule and that the theoretical specification of systemic processes is still consequentially incomplete. Unless the model can be modified to account for these empirical findings in a manner that is logically consistent with the rest of the framework, it is destined to share the fate of the Shaw and McKay theory and gradually fade from view. The remainder of this essay focuses on those issues that I consider to be most central to the disciplinary survival of this perspective.

Consensus and the Nature of Social Capital

A central assumption of Coleman's (1990) version of social capital theory is that the structural relationships that link actors into a network facilitate a wide range of expressive and instrumental exchanges, some of which are directly related to social control. For example, Coleman (1990, pp. 310-311) has noted that social capital can take the form of informal negative sanctions, such as avoidance, physical harm, gossip, and so forth (see Black,

1989). Although it is generally uncontested that a sensitivity to the opinion and potential reactions of significant others acts as a powerful constraint on criminal behavior, the basic question for the systemic model is the degree to which this form of social capital is transmitted through neighborhood-based associational structures.

Although this may appear to be a mundane issue, its resolution represents one of the key challenges to the viability of a systemic approach. As presented by Bursik and Grasmick, it is an explicitly control-theoretic perspective that assumes all people would engage in criminal activities to obtain scarce resources unless there are effective constraints on such behavior (Hirschi, 1969). A key element of such control is the transferal of capital that socializes individuals into a conventional, law-abiding value system. Whereas such socialization may be more or less successful, it is presumed that the content of this socialization is not in competition with other cultural messages that encourage people to approve of violence (see Hagedorn, 1998b, pp. 179-180). While early systemic statements such as those of Bursik and Grasmick made this assumption a priori, it now is clear that an alternative "code of the street" may be especially relevant to gang behavior.

Most residents of extremely impoverished neighborhoods deplore violence and strongly disapprove of local gang activities. Nevertheless, Anderson (1999) argues that such belief systems typically coexist with "oppositional cultures" that reject many traditional middle-class values, including those pertaining to the "rightness or wrongness" of certain crimes, because they are irrelevant to daily life. In fact, when multiple generations of family members have belonged to the same gang, youthful continuation of that tradition can be a source of pride to the elders (Zatz & Portillos, 2000). Even when there is no participatory history, gang membership may be perceived as an unfortunate but understandable fact of life because it provides "protection from real and apparent threats of physical violence and revenge or retaliation for real or perceived injuries and insults" (Decker & Van Winkle, 1996, p. 172). The strongest of bonds to conventional significant others may not be able to insulate a youth from such temptations for, as Anderson (1999) eloquently states, "Children from even the most decent homes must come to terms with the various influences of the street" (p. 67). In such situations, young family members may be taught to avoid trouble if at all possible, but to "stand their ground" if necessary. Gang membership is an effective means of resolving this problem for it sends a public message that a person can take care of him- or herself and will resort to violence to do so if necessary (Anderson, 1999, p. 72).

The critical question is whether oppositional cultures are an intrinsic and persistent part of the lower class experience, as suggested by Miller (1958), or whether they represent mutable adaptations to the structural dislocations of the neighborhoods in which members of this group are likely to reside. Most systemic theorists subscribe to the latter explanation, arguing that these cultures arise largely in response to the occupational marginalization of the residents of impoverished areas (see, e.g., Bankston, 1998, or Sampson & Lauritsen, 1997).

Messner and Rosenfeld (1994) have persuasively argued that economic institutions dominate the social life of the United States and that participation in others, such as those associated with educational attainment, is valued only insofar as it leads to financial rewards. Unfortunately, structural blockages severely restrict the degree to which residents of extremely poor neighborhoods can penetrate and rise within the occupational structure. When people do not have a history of conventional accomplishments that establish a claim to deference, respect, and honor on the basis of the core value of economic success, the only recourse is to develop one's "juice" on the basis of ongoing demonstrations that such respect is merited (Anderson, 1999, pp. 72-76; Horowitz, 1983, p. 81). Involvement in violent activities often is the only perceived avenue for the immediate establishment of such an "honor-worthy" identity.

The implication, of course, is that the salience of oppositional subcultures eventually should decline once meaningful occupational resources are channeled on a sustained basis into neighborhoods with gang problems. In fact, this was the experience of many white ethnic groups as they became progressively integrated into the American occupational structure (see Martinez & Lee, 2000). However, the processes have unfolded much differently for persons of color who reside in areas of concentrated disadvantage. Johnson, Farrell, and Stoloff (2000), for example, have shown that the economic situation of inner-city African American males has steadily deteriorated over the past quarter century (see also Wilson, Quane, & Rankin, 1998). As a result, the dynamics associated with "cultures of poverty" and weak systemic public control are highly confounded. However, indirect evidence can be offered in support of the systemic interpretation. Chicago statistics indicate that the three highest group-specific arrest rates in 1929 were for African Americans, persons of Greek nativity, and persons of Lithuanian nativity (Abbott, 1931). One would be hard put in contemporary times to find a sizeable number of people who consider the second and third groups to be intrinsically criminogenic, although such stereotypes were common at the time that Abbott's report was published (see Simon, 1985). The systemic model predicts that a similar change in criminal activity would have occurred for African Americans if it were not for the unique constraints faced by this population (see Johnson et al., 2000). Yet other evidence undermines such a purely structural perspective. Vigil (1988a) has argued that although the initial emergence of oppositional values in the barrios of Southern California was due to the economic marginality of these communities, they eventually became a persistent cultural feature that was transmitted from one generation to the next. Likewise,

Pattillo (1998) has shown that gang behavior exists in a middle-class,politically connected black community in Chicago (see also Fagan, 1990). Unfortunately, we do not yet have the data that are necessary to definitively resolve the cultural heterogeneity/consensus controversy (see Hagedorn, 1998b, pp. 179-180).

_____ **Networks as Sources of Effective Control**

Due to the influence of control theory on the development of the initial systemic models, it was expected that the effectiveness of informal social control would be a linear (or at least monotonic) function of the size, strength, and density of local social networks. Unfortunately, research conducted during the past 15 years has shown that such an assumption is naïve (Warner & Rountree, 1997). A major shortcoming of the Bursik and Grasmick specification was a failure to recognize that extensive ties to family members, fictive kin, and other neighbors could tie individuals simultaneously to law-abiding citizens and gang members (Pattillo, 1998). For example, a sizeable number of Decker and Van Winkle's (1996) respondents reported that their neighbors had nothing but contempt for the gang to which they belonged, but did tend to like them as individuals. A similar pattern has been observed by Pattillo (1998), who demonstrates how the presence of gang members and drug dealers in otherwise conventional networks complicates the processes of social control. In particular, due to personal ties to gang members, some residents are reluctant to solicit police intervention into what are perceived as essentially local matters. This tendency may be heightened by a general cynicism about the legal process (Sampson & Bartusch, 1998), a distrust of the police (Reisig & Parks, 2000), and the recognition that the gangs are providing services to the community that would not be otherwise available (Sanchez-Jankowski, 1991; Venkatesh, 1997). Therefore, the matter is not nearly as straightforward as Bursik and Grasmick's emphasis on the _inability_ of impoverished areas to set the processes of public control into motion would suggest. Rather, disadvantaged neighborhoods with a dense set of relational networks also may be _unwilling_ to do so.

There are further complications. Hirschi's (1969) presentation of control theory argues that constraints on illegal behavior are strongest when there are strong bonds to significant others. Given the intensely personal interactions that characterize private networks, one would assume that the social control that is exercised within such relationships would have much stronger effects on behavior than that which occurs during more impersonal interactions (see Bursik, 2000). However, Bursik (1999) presents evidence that the residents of Oklahoma City are as concerned about sanctions imposed by parochial network members as they are when the source of those sanctions is a member of one's private network; Bellair's (1997)

findings have similar implications. Thus, the systemic control that ema-
nates from nonintimate relationships may be at least as effective in the control of gang activities as that which is derived from primary groups. In addition, there are significant gender differences in the manner in which
these processes operate (Hagedorn, 1998b; Rountree & Warner, 1999;
Warner & Rountree, 1997; Zatz & Portillos, 2000).

These findings indicate that many current systemic models tend to have
an underdeveloped appreciation for the complicated nature of these network dynamics. What is needed is a major reformulation of the standard
decision-making model of control theory that assumes that the motivation
to engage in criminal and deviant behavior is essentially constant across
individuals. As such, work in this tradition assumes that the key considerations for a potential offender are the potential costs of involvement in
these activities. That is, the "perceived benefits of involvement" have been
eliminated from the equation and only the reactions of conventional audiences are considered. Given the dual embeddedness of many gang members in both licit and illicit networks, this is a critical oversight.

Nonrecursive Aspects of the Systemic Model

Although Bursik and Grasmick (1993, pp. 57-59) emphasized the potential
importance of reciprocal relationships between crime and systemic forms
of control, they did not explore the issue in great detail because there had
been few formal examinations of this association at the time of their monograph. Although this literature still is scarce, there has been at least partial
support for their contention that crime rates can directly affect neighborhood systemic capacities (see, e.g., Bellair, 1995; Sampson & Raudenbush,
1999). Perhaps the most intriguing findings in this regard were reported by
Decker and Van Winkle (1996), although the theoretical implications were
not explored in detail. As the standard systemic model would predict,
most of the gang members that they interviewed did not have strong ties to
conventional society. However, for a sizeable number of these respondents, existing relational ties were dissolved only *after* joining a gang.

Other research has explored the nonrecursive associations among the
three forms of systemic control, a question that was not addressed by
Bursik and Grasmick. These dynamics, for example, are reflected in the reluctance of residents who have personal relationships with gang members
to utilize public control mechanisms, as noted previously. The effects of
such decisions on the neighborhood have been explored most extensively
by Rose and Clear (1998; Rose, Clear, & Ryder, 2000), who argue that the incarceration of local offenders can have a debilitating impact on the human
capital of residents and the transferal of social capital through informal
networks of social control. That is, the effective exercise of systemic control
at one level may decrease the effectiveness of control at another. In addi-

tion to indicating that our current models may be significantly underspecified through our failure to consider and account for these interactions, the policy implications are enormous. As such, this question deserves intensive scrutiny.

Conclusions

This chapter has highlighted a number of theoretical challenges that need to be resolved before the systemic version of social disorganization can provide a comprehensive neighborhood-based theory of gang activity. Although I believe that these modifications can be made in a manner that maintains the logical integrity of the framework, it will necessitate a much broader specification of these processes than currently is the case, drawing from the literature in a wide range of disciplines. Otherwise, the theory will provide only a crude, general model of how neighborhoods shape gang behavior without being able to account for much of the rich complexity of that relationship.

6

Introducing Hoover
I'll Ride for You, Gangsta'

STEVEN R. CURETON

For the past 2 years I have been conducting interviews and ethnographic research on the Hoover Crips from South Central Los Angeles. For 2 weeks in May 1999 and 10 days in August 2000 I walked "Hoover Bricks" and talked with Original Gangsters in their alleys, homes, and Manchester Park, affectionately termed "the green within the ghetto" or "our shit." When I am not there, my race brothers are my eyes and ears as they continue to inform me of the happenings in the 'hood. They have all become my teachers, and it is an extraordinary relationship producing a wealth of information that will no doubt be hard for some gang scholars to accept because it may not fit neatly into well-accepted traditional gang perspectives.

My main interest in South Central Los Angeles's Hoover Crips was fueled by a desire to study black gang members in their natural environment. Ethnographic research forces the observer to describe social constructions

AUTHOR'S NOTE: I wish to express my deep gratitude and appreciation to all of the Hoovers who continue to support my research efforts. I appreciate their honesty, hospitality, and patience. I am indebted to Chris Moton for his initial involvement. I am extremely thankful to Mann for spending many hours ushering me around the streets of Hoover. I remain forever grateful to Duc, Mad Dog, Big Frog, and Alli. I can't say enough about the "respect" that was given to me and the security of those "ghetto passes." My deep appreciation goes to Jim Short for helping me secure the necessary funds from The National Consortium On Violence Research (NCOVR). Thank you, NCOVR, for providing the funds to go to South Central Los Angeles. I can't express enough gratitude to Charles Tittle and Jim Short for continuing to make sure that I maintain balance and objectivity.

by returning to the origins of phenomena. Closeness to "authentic truisms" concerning gangs will come only from a concentrated return to the old "Chicago" style of research, which incorporated social ecological themes in its research style (Liska, 1987).

Now, after 2 years of intense personal interaction, I feel a sense of connectedness with my gangster brothers. I call them my brothers because that ascription is given us by virtue of our skin color and common heritage. Walking the Hoover Bricks was, for me, a highly emotional experience, because the culture is so overwhelmingly gripping. I soon realized that the streets' pavement often was the only cushion for fallen comrades. Indeed, the walls came alive and the alleys revealed stories of past and present "ghetto super-stars." During my visits the temperature was consistently hot enough to agitate and promote hostility, and the air reeked with the smell of death. My ears burned with the undeniable reality of gang wars.

Having stated this, I'm fully aware that critics may suggest that I have so crossed the line that I cannot be objective when it comes to Hoover Gang members. Some may suggest that I am "in too deep" to distinguish truth from fiction. Furthermore, characterizing Hoovers as race brothers may be regarded as proof that I have lost the ability to be objective. I can only respond that I have been taught "disciplined thinking," which I endeavor to employ at all times. My mentors continue to caution me against the possibility of losing objectivity, sensationalizing, and generalizing. Nevertheless, I argue that the social construction of Hoover is real for the gangsters, with life and death consequences, and I suspect that there are many streets just like Hoover in socially disorganized urban areas across the United States. My goal is to portray the reality of the Hoovers *as they see it* and to provide a sociological interpretation.

It is no secret (at least among my mentors) that I am very critical of gang studies based too long in the past when they are now used to address contemporary issues concerning black gangs. Too many studies of black gangs and black gangsters are based on secondhand data, often from persons who are strangers to the streets and to the everyday life of gangsters. Too many are misguided, misdirected, and misunderstood reflections embedded in traditional stereotypes and conditioned by fear. Such unacknowledged fear keeps many researchers at a safe distance from the streets and the gangs they profess to explain. Some research that passes as ethnographic consists primarily of surveys of individual gang members in safe settings far away from the gangsters' environment. Under such circumstances, vital contextual information inevitably is lost (see Dawley, 1992).

Moreover, although it is often seen as appropriate to study young white males' collective responses to deprivation in order to understand their group responses to blocked life chances, it is often thought inappropriate to use the principles derived in this way to standardize measures, scales, or surveys to study young black males' collective responses to deprivation. A large body of research demonstrates that black males do not encounter the same types of deprivation as their white counterparts. The deprivation evident in the natural habitat of African American males is far more institutional, systemic, and generational than that of whites. Moreover, black males are responding to economic, social, cultural, and spiritual deprivation coupled with structural and social isolation not only from whites, but from other blacks as well. These differences produce a different type of gang and/or gangbanger. Perhaps because of their fears and their failure to spend time in the ghettos, slums, 'hoods, jungles, and bottoms of black America, and dealing with the reality that America is not the land of equal opportunity, some researchers conclude that the black male and the black gangster are a different "animal" altogether and that his potential for brutal violence is a manifestation of some "innate pre-disposition" (Wilson & Herrnstein, 1985, p. 69). Research at a distance is less labor- and emotionally intensive, but without evidence produced by witnessing attempts at "survival" in an American environment that "damn sure ain't a part of America," gang banging cannot be fully understood.

During my most recent visit to South Central Los Angeles (in August 2000), I had the privilege of interviewing and interacting with more than a dozen gangsters from Hoover. As part of my larger project, these interviews are the data for this chapter. It was a hot summer and the OGs (Original Gangsters) had grown weary of the many lives lost to gang warfare for that summer. To decrease the probability of losing another homie to gun violence, the OGs had recently imposed (and enforced via patrol) a street code that restricted movement and prohibited hanging out. It was strange to witness inactive streets and watch most of the gangsters interacting within the confines of their own yards. Driving through (Mann was the driver and I the passenger in his four-door burgundy Tahoe) what appeared to be, and felt like, a cease-fire zone was eerie. Watching an entire community move about with tension and limited freedom (self-imposed or not) is a testimony to the seriousness of the violence, and what a community will put up with to ensure its relative safety.

Three Original Gangsters agreed to do interviews at Manchester Park, a public park claimed by Hoover Crips. The fourth, Mann, talked as he drove me around the community. Let's hear from Mann (age 24), from Five Deuce, Mad Dog (age 32), and Big Frog (age 32), and from Seven Four and Alli (late 20s), formerly of Hoover, on issues concerning humiliation, doubt, rejection, the code of the street, endorsing the "bad ass" or the "I don't give a fuck" attitude, and violence. The interviews with Mann, Mad Dog, Big Frog, and Alli took place on different days and took the better part of 4 to 6 hours. I chose to interview older gangsters first in an effort to gain their respect and get their permission to talk to the younger gang members. Approaching young gang members first, without the consent of

Original Gangsters, is an offense to street protocol and could have resulted in personal injury. Original Gangsters were afforded the courtesy of speaking first, and going through the interview experience helped put their suspicions to rest. Moreover, returning to Hoover the second summer represented (to them) that I was not only serious but that I could be trusted with what they were telling me. Finally, I chose to record Original Gangsters' experiences because they have served time for their crimes and owe no further debt to society. This may not necessarily be the case for the younger bangers. Thus, I opted not to record their responses in an effort to avoid becoming involved in a legal quandary, particularly for unsolved crimes.

Jack Katz's (1988) street elite theory implies that potential gangsters are those who have been rejected or denied access to legitimate life chances. These potential street elites become humiliated or humbled by the lack of prospects for participating in conventional society. He suggests that these rejected gangsters feel cheated and resentful, which pushes them to create and participate in a local culture of control (subculture of the streets). Katz goes on to say that only those who embrace the controlling, hostile, and mean persona of the "bad ass" will seek the gang. In the course of my observations I have questioned many Hoovers about this presumption of humility, doubt, resentfulness, rejection, and hopelessness, and this is what these OGs had to say. The responses are reported as they were said. Any paraphrasing was cleared during the interviews by my restating their responses and then getting their reaction(s).

Question: *On occasion do you doubt your ability to succeed in life and obtain a part of the American Dream?*

The responses seem to indicate very little humility or doubt in their abilities to be successful in whatever they are attempting to do. In fact, the responses suggest that they are confident in their abilities to be successful in conventional society but believe that legitimate opportunities of the American Dream are not open to them. All four seem to agree that access to legitimate opportunities is blocked. One gangster explicitly implies that he is tired of gang banging and wants to earn a basic standard of living through legitimate means but, given that this does not seem possible, he and others in similar positions don't see any option other than to "gang bang."

Mann's Response

> When you are young, you are full of doubts but it was never about whether I could measure up to anything . . . you know, I've always been a confident person. But is opportunity really open to us? It's almost like you have to survive a bunch of shit first just to get a little chance at something legitimate and even then it's still hard. Just give me a chance and I can do whatever.

Mad Dog's Response

Man we don't give a fuck about the American Dream. . . . the white picket fence and dog . . . all that bullshit. That shit is for white people. All we want is to be comfortable, not have to struggle so damn much. I've never doubted my ability in nothing. Whatever I was doing I was going to do it the best I could. Man, I don't want to bang, rob and steal all the time. Nobody wants to do that shit for a living but if you look around here, what choice do we have? We know right from wrong but we know survival. I'm over thirty years old and I want to get my money the right way. Ain't nobody gonna put a black man like me to work, give me a try. I got a family to feed so I'm gonna go to work and work hard every day. There are lots of niggers around here just like me who want to work but ain't nobody hiring.

Big Frog's Response

I'm a grown man, a hell of a motherfucker. I ain't never doubted shit about myself but I'm all about that money, you know. I've lived in this 'hood and I am also over thirty but I'm surviving so I know, if given the same opportunity, I could handle this American Dream shit.

Alli's Response

The white man got us all chasing this diseased dollar bill, you know. But money changes quickly to dust, you know. We all caught up in this game and if we can't get it we turn on one another. With the Will of Allah, I'm never less deserving or there is no part of me that is weak or has doubt.

Question: *Do you sometimes feel resentful or cheated when you don't get your way?*

Mann, Mad Dog, Big Frog, and Alli suggest strongly that feelings are much deeper than feeling cheated or resentful. Each harbors a deep sense of frustration, anger, and hostility toward being rejected or seemingly teased with symbols of success that are out of their reach. They imply that their feelings are a reaction to perceived institutional rejection, denial, suppression, and oppression. The responses indicate that they are well aware of what success is supposed to look like and that their life chances (like so many others in the 'hood) don't even come close to what success is. Mann and Big Frog asked me how would I feel or act in similar surroundings, and I must admit that I would be extremely bitter and even hostile, too. Mad Dog argues the point that a person bringing opportunity to the 'hood will not face hostility or harm; in fact, those persons would be protected, just as I have been.

Mann's Response

If you mean some petty shit, no. But if you are talking about feeling like you are a part of America, of course any man would be or feel resentful. We got a lot of little homies, little kids, running around feeling frustrated at how they living, and who wouldn't? Look around you, man. What are little kids supposed to do? Of course they gonna feel like life has dealt them a raw deal because that is the truth. Don't think we don't know what success looks like; and then we look at what we have gone through or what we have.

Mad Dog's Response

Resentful is an understatement, homie! I am hot about the way shit works out for me and the homies in the 'hood. Opportunity never comes this way so we all pissed about that. People stay away from us like they are scared of us but if you are coming down here trying to help us out, we will look out for you. You never gonna harm the hand that provides you with opportunity. Look at how we treat you. We take care of you, make sure nobody fuck with you, because you down here doing something right.

Big Frog's Response

Shit is fucked up around here; you see that, don't you? How would you feel about this situation if you were in it? You would be pissed off just like we are, and along with that feeling will come some type of retaliation.

Alli's Response

You asking questions like you CIA or FBI or something. How does any brother feel when he is denied basic standard of living rights? Not getting my way sounds too simple, my brother. We have been denied things that are essential for living in harmony and if it was not for Allah my feelings would be misguided just like every other brother who has not come into this light.

Question: *Has society cast you aside, rejected you to the point of your feeling hopeless?*

All four respondents share the perception that mainstream society does not care about them and that this lack of care is demonstrated by the absence of opportunities. This perception that mainstream society has actively participated in their marginalization has contributed to alienation and intra-'hood collective deviance, crime, and violence. For Mann, suggesting that gang members feel hopeless may be too strong a statement, given that the gang itself represents hope for some type of success. For

Mad Dog, many young people have internalized society's apparent lack of concern about them. Big Frog implies that every waking day represents hope, but that too much frustration can limit one's perception of reality. Although Alli seems to continue along the lines of "spiritual enlightenment," his response implies that self-destruction (in this case, young black males in the 'hood) is inevitable, given that so many young brothers are chasing money instead of seeking the knowledge of Allah.

Mann's Response

Look, when you are young, you feel a lot of things but as you get older you try to change. But by that time you probably have a record or have been identified as a banger so society becomes more restrictive or oppressive towards you as you get older. But you still got to feed the family so you might take any type of job to pay your bills. Feeling hopeless may be too strong a word. We see what we want but we often times can't reach it. There is always hope, and ironically, that is what the gangs seem to offer—hope in an environment that is so far from America that it is mind-boggling.

Mad Dog's Response

It's obvious that not too many people care about us and it has even led to us not caring about ourselves. We know that we are destroying our own but that does not stop us. As you get older you try to do right but doing right is hard; and then you got the little homies who are just running around doing their own thing. I feel like society does not care about us and it seems they never will. It is a shame because you got niggers that want to do right but don't have the opportunity to always do what is right . . . you know what I mean?

Big Frog's Response

Really, it is obvious that nobody gives a fuck really. We got to look out for our own. Do I feel hopeless? No, but frustration makes you blind to a lot of things. I wake up every morning full of hope, hoping to live, pay my bills, feed the family, and survive. Do I hope that society will one day accept me? I'm not even worried about that.

Alli's Response

I used to be caught up in that paper chase without guidance from Allah, and my father was the same, as were men before him and the list goes on. Generations of young soldiers out here chasing the devil, and the devil will lead to mass destruction. One day it ain't gonna be no more of us if we keep this up and that ain't funny to me. Allah is the only hope provider. The white man is a deceiver of man, bent on total destruction of the black man. Just like money, which turns to dust and blows away; our lives are essentially becoming as thin as the money we pursue.

Cultural deviance theories imply that marginalized populations respond to isolation and alienation by creating subcultures with values, attitudes, and special norms of conduct. Similarly Katz (1988) and Anderson (1999) imply that local cultures of control and codes of the street provide a different set of contextual and situational circumstances, which leads to deviance, crime, and violence, especially for those who reside in or near socially disorganized communities. A local culture of control negates conventional values ("decent," in Anderson's phrasing), rendering them absurd by providing a proving ground for humiliated youth. Anderson goes a step farther by suggesting that African American youth, regardless of social class, must learn the code of the street for survival purposes, whereas boys from middle-class or functional families are afforded the luxury of "code switching" (abiding by a set of morals that are sensitive to mainstream society if the situation permits or abiding by ethics of survival on the streets if the situation involves a street oriented confrontation; Anderson, 1999, p. 36). The code of the street requires that earning respect and defending one's respectability by any means necessary, including fighting and violence, be given top priority. "Respect" is an essential form of "social capital" because it assures relative physical and social survival in inner cities. However, the code-of-the-street mentality is not limited to inner cities, because it is a "germ of masculinity" that is carried by most youth professing manhood or a respectable reputation (Anderson, 1999).

How would Mann, Mad Dog, Big Frog, and Alli respond to these presumptions of an existing local culture of control or code of the street mentality?

Question: *What are the rules of the 'hood and how early do young children learn them?*

The responses seem to support Elijah Anderson's "code of the street." Mann, Mad Dog, Big Frog, and Alli all appear to be in agreement that having a street mentality is essential for survival. In contrast, Katz's street elite perspective leaves room for speculation that young black gangsters are participating in a local culture of control only in order to get back at mainstream society or engaging in "bad ass" without regard for "self-preservation" (Katz, 1988, p. 81). The responses explicitly argue that this code-of-the-street mentality is a survival mechanism. Some have noted that the code-of-the-street mentality does not ensure survival; in fact, that it may promote death. This contradiction seems to imply an irrational logic for actively participating in code-of-the-street behavior. The message that is being overlooked or misunderstood is that survival means living with respectability and even facing death with respectability. It is better that one die like a man than live as a coward or an individual with no respect. Although physical death seems to be a highly probable consequence of attempting to earn and defend one's respect, it is still thought to be far better to die for respect than to live with a weak reputation. Living with a weak reputation or no respect leads to many "social deaths" as predators consistently confront you in attempts to "take your heart or bitch you" in front of social audiences. From a street perspective, that is no way to live.

Mann's Response

Always know where you are and who you are fucking with. It's hard to play because sometimes playing will get you killed. Banging is a job and you got to be on point at all times. Your enemy is recognizable at all times and you have to be able to protect yourself and be in battle mode at all times. Disrespect won't be tolerated because you are not an individual, you are a part of something bigger, the gang! Any disrespect towards you and that will fall on whatever you represent. So that is why you see so many young people out here trying to establish themselves in the 'hood . . . establish the fact that your young ass ain't no punk and you can throw your hands. The 'hood never forgets a face and has a long memory. So whatever you do, somebody will remember it and it will come back on you, and you have to be prepared for that. Young kids get introduced to this as soon as they are old enough to hang out. Their parents place them up for adoption, given they are not taking proper care of their own kids and the gang will be there to adopt them. Or the parents indirectly support gang activity and association because they do things in accordance to the 'hood politics too. Things like buy their kids clothes with colors that support Crip or Blood, depending on the 'hood, you know.

Mad Dog's Response

The rules used to be that you are down for the gang, the 'hood, and your homies in the gang. You rob, steal, bang or do whatever with the gang. And if something comes back and you got to take the fall for it legally in terms of the law, you handle your business. You don't drag the homies into that shit with you. But the way it is now, a nigger will snitch in a minute. Not that it means the gang is not down for one another. You have to look at what he is snitching for. You just have to be careful, especially with these young bangers. They are trying to reach a peak that can't be reached! If everybody is living by the code of the 'hood or trying to achieve ghetto superstar status, then you got potential enemies everywhere, which decreases the chances of you living long enough to claim that you are that nigger in the 'hood.

Big Frog's Response

The way of life around here is simple. Do onto others before they do onto you. If you want answers to why killing, banging, robbing, and all that is going on, then I would have to say that we are doing it to them because they are doing it to us. The real enemy is not even close to us, really, so we do those who are closest to us. It just happens to be our own kind. The little homies learn it from birth, really. And as soon as they can get from under their parents' wing, the 'hood will drive them right to the gang. The gang will offer them respect, status, prestige, freedom, and success on these hot ass streets. I agree with Mad Dog, banging and being in a gang used to be different, but now these young fools are for self above " all first."

Alli's Response

It's funny you should ask such a question. I mean, you seem to be searching for things. Of course the kids gonna learn whatever is offered to them when it is offered. They don't know no better way if their elders are not teaching it to them. Unfortunately, not every man standing here has Allah in him or even know of his teachings. If Allah is absent in their lives then [there's] no true solution to whatever ills this 'hood will ever develop. We will continue to respond to earthly deprivation, suffocation, oppression in earthly ways. Back us into a corner and we will Bust! You know, make that gun go boom and keep rolling. What you see in this 'hood is that these young black males are following the creed of the 'hood, which is to have a basic standard of living and even floss a little. This takes money and opportunities that you see for yourself are not available to them. So what happens is that these young brothers get caught up much the same way as I did and my father did. You know they used to call my father "Mac A Do" because he would do anything to feed his family and I do mean anything. But like I was saying, these young brothers are chasing a dream that is funded by the earthly bound "almighty dollar," and so the pursuit of such a dream as tainted as it is will reflect banging, robbing, stealing, raping other 'hoods and killing. In the absence of Allah, you have no guidance and understanding of self, so you can't possibly know others or understand the essence of what is really going on, so you live by the streets and you die by the streets.

Violence is a consequence of the code-of-the-street mentality, and the manifestation of violence is highly probable for those individuals with a gangster's mentality (the "I don't give a fuck" attitude). Again, the gangsters feel as though a certain level of violence substantiates the idea that they are not to be messed with or any part of their world threatened or challenged (i.e., their respect, money, territory, including their social and personal activities with women). Violent behavior, especially if it is committed while one is young, enhances a gangster's reputation and endows him with certain liberties and rights in the 'hood. For example, a gangbanger's violent tendencies will force people to fear and respect him so much that they will defer to him and take orders from him. Thus, a gangster's violent behavior elevates his status among his peers. Violence is also a method of settling disputes, even though it would seem to perpetuate further violence. In reality (as far as Hoover goes), the more extreme the violence, the less likely the recipients are to retaliate, because they think twice about the impending consequences of their actions. On the surface, it appears to be a never-ending cycle, but closer inspection reveals hesitation and even nonresponses to violence, depending on the seriousness of the violence and other situational factors.

Another critical point that Mann brings to light is the idea of controlled violence. How much violence depends on what the gangster wants to do, given that decisions to be violent depend so much on issues of perceived respectability. Violence dissipates when both parties feel they can walk away with their individual honor and their gang's dignity still intact. Gangbangers are not "heartless killers" or determined perpetrators of violence, as demonstrated by the fact that certain indiscretions committed by their enemies are pardoned (e.g., by allowing " 'hood passes").

Mad Dog states that violence is a "young" thing, given that so many young black males in the 'hood are out to prove that they are "hard." Mad Dog implies that if conditions were better, then these same young black males would express themselves in other ways. He feels that it will take more than "word campaigns" to resolve violence. Violence can be resolved through the elimination of the frustration that is created by deprived situational circumstances. Until better life chances are offered, violence will continue, because some gangsters don't perceive those similarly circumstanced as brothers. Indeed, some gangsters don't look at what they are doing to one another as black-on-black violence. They see one another as enemies.

Alli argues (with great religious conviction) that violence is the consequence of being in love with the devil. He also argues that violence is not limited to black males, because history has shown that America will demonstrate its strength when it is pushed to do so, and white men used violence and mass destruction to colonize America. Alli continues to suggest that America was settled on what he calls "one big gang banging philosophy." According to Alli, gang banging is not only the deprived black males' approach, but it is the "American way."

Question: *Why the violence? What is the fuel for all this violence?*

Mann's Response:

Violence is not without reason around here. There is a reason for violence; there are reasons young boys gang bang and kill. A lot of it has to do with respect. You know, wanting and needing to be respected by your peers so much that you will kill for it. Remember, these young kids are coming from situations where their home life and environment is probably not the best and respect is the one thing they feel they can have some control over. In South Central, fighting and violence is what gets you your reputation. A solid reputation for a young kid is essential for his survival, believe it or not. See, if you have respect and you gained it through fighting then people are not going to fuck with you as much, or they are going to think twice about it first. So put your time in when you are young and willing to throw some hands and it will get you a long ways. The more work you put in when you are young, the better your chances to possibly take a back seat and give orders to others when you get older.

So violence, fighting, gang banging is a necessary function of the 'hood. Often, there are going to be situations where you have choices and you could choose not to be violent, I mean the 'hood respects men but on the other hand there are consequences with every choice and men must be willing to deal with them. You might find yourself catching more hell if you don't go ahead and handle the initial situation with violence or fighting. You can't let it get back to the homies that you backed down. You don't want your peers thinking you are some bitch or mark. For instance when you are with me, I make sure that nothing will happen to you that won't happen to me. There is no way that I could understand myself if I were not to retaliate for any wrong doing that would come my homies' way or fools that I am down with. A lot of violent confrontations come from one fool somehow feeling disrespected by another, and even though it may be personal, it becomes gang related because those individuals are from 'hoods. See what I mean? If you live in a 'hood, then you are from a 'hood and you are a part of that 'hood, so you have to represent yourself, which also means you represent the 'hood. Violence goes in cycles too. There could be a lot of killing that happens in one month. Then there is peace for a minute, then it starts all over again. Believe it or not, the violence is controlled. These gangs know everything and dictate everything. Whenever they want it to stop, then it will and when they want shit to pop off then that will happen too. The shit is not as random as it is portrayed. Violence has a purpose, as I said before, and that purpose is to get points across when points need to be gotten across. If the other side is hard of hearing or does not understand, then the shit escalates. Resolution of violence rests with both sides feeling they can walk away from the situation without any disrespect. Still, sometimes homies will spare enemies—give them a pass—but they expect a return favor in the future. See, it happens. The violence is rationalized, it has a purpose and a reason. You have thinking individuals committing these acts. Some want to say that these young kids are heartless but they are not; they just demonstrate whatever needs to be done to get the job done. But the violence has a purpose, remember that. Also when there is too much peace you might have these phony ass cops starting shit up again. You would be surprised about how many killings were actually instigated by L.A.'s worst.

Mad Dog's Response

Man, it is like this, you do what needs to be done to show that you are not to be fucked with. You know, earn your respect so you can be comfortable walking these streets. A lot of niggers, young niggers, are on edge but somebody like me can go wherever I want and take another person with me and nobody will fuck with us because I'm respected like that in other 'hoods. We all represent different 'hoods but you usually know somebody from the other 'hood and ya'll probably kick it together. So it's those connections that work to calm things when these young fools start acting up. This violence shit is a young thing really. When you are young you are trying to prove so much and gang banging is the right way, given where you living. If these kids had better conditions then they would have better ways to express themselves, but unfortunately this is their play ground, right here in South Central, right here on Hoover! Just telling these kids to stop the violence is not enough.

So I don't care who you get to come down and talk with us, if they are not of us, then we ain't trying to hear it. We listen to people who have walked in our shoes and can offer a better way. Just saying stop the killing because you are hurting your own is not enough! It's not enough because you are asking people to internalize that frustration and that would lead to self-destruction. People are exploding with frustration and they take it out on the nigger that is closer to them. You might say we are killing our own, but most young kids are not thinking like that. They thinking more along the lines of "Fuck that fool, I don't know him." They not looking at him as a potential doctor, lawyer, judge. You know, somebody important or somebody that is loved. They just see enemy, somebody in the way, one less nigger I got to deal with in the future. Really, we all paranoid thinking some nigger is out to get us, so we bust without any hesitation. The shit is senseless and useless bullshit sometimes but what can you do, what can you tell these young niggers? Shit, I was doing the same thing, only we use to throw hands a little more. That way at least you lived to fight another day. Now with this generation there is no other day because your ass is dead. A lot of these young bangers probably don't know how to throw their hands because they have always been trigger-happy. If violence had one purpose it would be to achieve respect and if violence had one consequence it would be death. Either way you are dead, so people live with respect, which is gotten through violence.

Big Frog's Response

Man, violence is over respect, money, drugs, and especially bitches. All these things make the world go around and young niggers feel they need all this shit to survive. You can only get it one way though. All this shit is part of the game. The bitches love the gangster because they want to be with fools that can protect them. So if you want a female around here, you got to bang. Respect is given to the gangster first and foremost, so if you want respect you got to bang, and banging involves violence when necessary, especially when you come from a set like Hoover that don't get along with nobody. A lot of money around here is dirty money, so you got to work for that and drugs. Well, fools want to get high and some need to get high to change the reality of the hell they living in. Any of these necessary things requires use of violence just to be living, to survive, to hang out, to be cool, to be in, to be near the action and perhaps get the bitches too. A lot of talk does not go far, but knock a nigger upside his head and see how much he understands. Violence brings about an understanding that we all men and ain't no bitch-made niggers around, so lets handle our business—you know the game.

Alli's Response

Again without the knowledge of Allah and the true understanding of your righteous path, what do or can you really expect? Violence is the devil and some of us are in love with that devil because it brings us pleasure. Don't ask why the violence; like it's just us doing it. Look at what America does when other countries offend or threaten us. Look at what America does when they want to take control of some other country, enforce their way of living. Look at what America did to black folks. Look at what the white man has done to every population of people he wanted to colonize. Look at what America does when they want to flex. They send their Army, Navy, Marines, Air Force, Secret Service, CIA, whatever out to be as forceful as possible. That ain't nothing but gang banging. America was settled and developed on one big gang banging philosophy with mass death and mass violence, and mass destruction. So when you ask why the violence, I would have to say that violence happens down here for the same reason that it happens anywhere else. We want what we want and we need what we need and if somebody else is in the way, we flex and push him out of this lifetime. Now America has achieved all it has and now they send people around asking why we do this or that. So hypocritical you know. The fuel for violence is self respect, and just as white men and America continue to fight for it, we will too. America has always gone to war. Well, in South Central, young black men are in a Civil War—only this Civil War is funded by the country they live in. This should not be news to you, it is reality, a reality that folks keep dodging behind to make you think we are animals. There is nothing more animal-like than the Americans who profess to be Christians.

Jack Katz's (1988) perspective on "bad assing" and Miller's (1958) notion of lower-class males' concentration on certain focal concerns, which generate a gang subculture, imply that lower-class males accept these values and actively aspire to demonstrate these characteristics at all times. Although Miller states that individuals concentrating on trouble, toughness, smartness, excitement, and autonomy are not psychologically disturbed and are very capable individuals, the latter part of his message seems to lose its significance when referring to black male gangsters.

The responses reveal that Hoover gangsters are not hard-core, heartless individuals who continuously engage in deviant, criminal, or violent behavior. Instead, the responses suggest the possibility that black male gangsters have a compassionate side and are trying to do what is right. Mann implies that gangsters really look after you, especially when they see something positive in you. Mann speaks very candidly about a Big Homie who did his best to keep him from the gang. Mann continues, suggesting that the 'hood produces quite different types of gang members (e.g., the hard-core, always on point, gangbanger, the closet bangers, the affiliated athletic type—associated by virtue of living in the 'hood). Whereas the hard-core gangbanger seems to fit Katz's notion of the "bad ass" and Miller's lower-class gangster type, the closet banger and the athlete do not. In the next set of responses, Mann also introduces the notion that Hoover has a compassionate side, as it will not recruit and will protect those individuals "who have something going for them" (e.g., athletic ability or intelligence).

Mad Dog and Big Frog contend that the conditions of the 'hood produce mean, hostile, aggressive, and trouble-prone young black men. Both suggest that young people are socialized to be prepared for the situational circumstances that can occur in the 'hood. Some situations require hostility, anger, violence, and aggression, and others may require compassion. Hoovers are prepared to be whatever it takes. Alli's responses continue to be guided by his belief in Allah. He does not believe that intra-racial violence, hate, or aggression is ever appropriate. He suggests that living in deprived conditions will create a strict code of conduct where love and patience for another black man will be in short supply. According to Alli, real changes will bring about changes in people's emotional state.

Question: *Is it okay to be mean, hostile, tough, aggressive, and ready to cause trouble?*

Mann's Response

Man, it's not okay to be that way, really. I mean, some of these bangers are the nicest, most caring people you could ever run into. I mean, the way they look after you is truly amazing. For instance, one of my Big Homies would beat my ass to stay away from the gang. He saw that I had talent and that I could be somebody. He felt I was not meant to be a banger, you know. So he would constantly beat my ass to stop me from coming on the set. He sat me down and told me that I did not need to be dealing with this shit. When he went off to prison, his main thoughts were, did he do enough to keep Mann from 'banging?

Question: *Did it work?*

Mann's Response

To a certain extent, it really did. But I was out on my own at the age of fourteen. I was my own man so to speak. I had to survive, make a living, you know. So I did what was necessary to live. I loved that money, so dealing was my thing. I was a paid little fourteen-year-old and I was smart with my money. I gave back to the community in such a way that I can walk the streets and nobody fucks with Mann because they know. I mean, you see how I got it; people are doing things for you because you with me and they know I don't fuck around with no bullshit. Plus they know I went off to school, they know about the Ques. They see that same brand on your arm and they recognize that immediately. But getting back to the question, the 'hood produces all types of individuals really. You got your straight up hard-core types, the real soldiers, that will get dirty and do whatever. They the real bangers, always on point and will voluntarily get in your ass. That is their way. You got your bitches or females that try to ride the fence and then a few are really down with it. You don't see them out too much because fools are not discriminating anymore. If you are banging, they don't care if you are a female or not. Then you got your closet bangers who are only gonna bang when the situation is in their favor to. Their reputation rides on that group manhood, but if you find them alone or if they recognize an enemy they ain't gonna do shit really. Then you got your athletes, who we consider soft because they love sports so much that you know they will snitch on you in a minute. The gang really don't fuck with those good athletes too much. In fact, they would support them and try to keep them away from the gang. As I said before, if you got something going for you, the gang or the Big Homies will see to it that you stay clean and that you go on to represent the 'hood another way. Go off to school, get your education but give back. So as you see, the 'hood produces all types. It really depends on who you dealing with from the start.

Mad Dog's Response

No, you don't have to be that way all the time, but hard times automatically produce hard ass attitudes. Again, you would be surprised at what deprivation and oppression or just plain hard-ass conditions will do to your mentality. I mean, you can't even stare at niggers too long. And believe me, niggers will stare at your ass, forcing you to pick up on that shit and ride it for what it is worth. Staring at me too damn long is an offense to me and I have to ask, "Nigger, what the fuck is you looking at?"—then it goes from there. It is never really okay to be anything except a Man; but given what you are dealing with, you get knuckleheads and hard-core niggers, you know. It's not a value system though; nobody wants to voluntarily teach their kids to be that way. But the streets, the bricks, the 'hood will force you to teach your child survival. They got to know some hard shit too. I mean, you don't want them to grow up soft either but you already know that if they are going to survive with respectability then they gotta' have certain things instilled in them. Now surviving does not necessarily mean a long prosperous life; it means living with respectability for as long as the 'hood would allow.

Big Frog's Response

Man, I don't care what anybody say, you got to be that way because it is too much drama going on in the 'hood. Drama over other niggers, other 'hoods, and mainly bitches. Most of the violence takes place because of bitches. You might be dating some female that used to date another nigger and some shit will pop off over her dumb ass. If you are going to be well known or a hell of a motherfucker around here, you gotta be that nigger that will control all situations at all times, which means you gonna be hostile, mean, or a difficult person. But again all that goes with the situation and the moment. Whatever the situation requires, is what you are going to get. We can be whatever we need to be from hated, to feared, to respected, and loved, which means you got to be that hostile nigger, who is also there for the homies and the set.

Alli's Response

Look, it's like this. Hate directed towards another brother is never okay. I hope people don't believe that something like that is our value system, because it is not. We have always been an adapting people. We adapt to whatever conditions we are placed in. If we are forced into deprived conditions then we will have attitudes that will be short on love and patience for the other man. That is not just black people, but any people. So it is never okay to be that way; in fact, Allah teaches the opposite. And given Islam is the religion for us, then we know that something like that is not in our nature. But given where we are and how earthly and 'hood-bound our thinking is, what can you really expect until somebody shows or demonstrates a better way? It won't fall out [of] the air either. People have to witness real changes before they change their emotional state.

Closing Remarks

I conducted face-to-face interviews with other Hoover gangsters whose sentiments where similar to those presented in this chapter. A more detailed presentation of my research will appear in my forthcoming book, *Hoover: A Gangster's Perspective*. This chapter presents particularizations rather than generalizations. Although these social constructions are those of the Hoovers interviewed, I have a hunch that similar 'hoods with similar conditions would produce similar results regarding black gang members and black gangs, under similar circumstances. My intention is to demonstrate that there may be some things (e.g., the rationale for violence, the code of the street, the gangster's mentality, survival, the functional role of gangs, the compassionate characteristics of gang members) relative to black gangs that have not been captured by most current methodologies. Some portrayals of black gangs seem clearly to be inappropriate for contemporary black gangbangers such as those from Hoover. There is a richness of information out there waiting to be gathered and analyzed, and I am certain that a concentrated return to the field would produce a healthy discourse about the nature of gangs and gang members. Given the tense history of race relations, the worst we can do is to leave gaps in research that foster the inference that no matter what the condition, the black man and the black gangster will always be the more violent and aggressive because it is in their nature. This only enhances the perception that black men and black gangsters not only are symbolic, but innate, super-predators.

Gangs and the
Informal Economy

JOHN M. HAGEDORN

This chapter represents a departure from the "normal science" of industrial-era gang studies and focuses on the interaction of gangs and the "informal" economy. In the first edition of this book (Hagedorn, 1990, p. 257), I argued that field researchers should be "inventive" in developing methods to investigate what I suspected were new characteristics of contemporary gangs. Differing from Walter Miller's (1990) view that gangs are relatively unchanging products of stable lower-class cultural values, I suggested that economic restructuring was altering the prime functions and nature of gangs. Genuine, innovative fieldwork, I thought, would promote a reconceptualization of gangs in contemporary social science.

Although there has been a profusion of gang research over the past decade, there has not been a parallel rethinking of theory. This chapter reports on a study that was undertaken from a unique perspective and adds some data that may be helpful in rethinking the nature of gangs in poor communities.

Gangs and the Failure of
the Promise of Modernity

Gangs today are different in many ways from the delinquent peer groups described by the Chicago School (Thrasher, 1927). Many contemporary gangs still start as play groups, spontaneously integrated through conflict. But today, many more poor kids in cities like Milwaukee and Chicago grow up in neighborhoods with an institutionalized neighborhood-based gang structure (Hagedorn, 1998c). An adolescent joins a gang not only because local institutions are weak, but also because of the established presence of neighborhood gangs or street organizations that offer both social and economic benefits.

There have been many multigenerational gangs in the past, and in some areas, like East Los Angeles (Moore, 1978), gangs have been institutionalized for decades. But, at least in Chicago and Milwaukee, some contemporary urban gangs differ from their past cousins mainly by how they are responding to the new, globalized, information economy. In Thrasher's era and into the middle of the last century, as a gang member aged, even if he had not graduated from high school he could find work in the factories. Industrial work was hard and uncertain, but perseverance often paid off with union-scale wages, relative job security, and home ownership (see, e.g., Whyte, 1943, for Italians in Boston; Spergel, Turner, Pleas, & Brown, 1969, and Kornblum, 1974, for African Americans in Chicago). The gang, along with its ethnic group, was expected to assimilate, and its former members would eventually participate in the mainstream economy.

Today, access to entry-level industrial jobs and union wages is disappearing, with the globalization of production transporting "generic" working-class jobs to wherever wages and costs are lowest. To get a good job, 21st-century gang members, male or female, need to have far more education and skills than did their industrial-era counterparts. As I first described in *People and Folks* (1988), these postindustrial economic trends have forever altered the capacity of many youths to "mature out of the gang." As a result, gangs are no longer a primarily adolescent phenomenon as in the past (but note Whyte's Depression-era Italians and Chicago's ethnic "social athletic clubs"). In cities like Milwaukee and Chicago, gangs institutionalized as racial segregation and economic segmentation shattered the false promises of "integration" and the American Dream. Contrary to the expectations of the Chicago School, the ghetto did not disappear (Bernard, 1970; Clark, 1965; Park, 1969), and gangs became permanent social organizations within it.

But poor people, gangs among them, have not taken declining opportunities lying down. An "informal economy," or patterned work activities outside of the legal economy, flourishes around the world. For example, in Latin America and elsewhere, modernization has not had the anticipated effect of drawing people away from informal economic activities (Portes, Castells, & Benton, 1989a). Instead, an informal sector that is as large, if not larger, than the formal sector of many countries, persists (see de Soto, 1990, for Peru; Thoumi, 1995, for Colombia; and Jimenez, 1989, for Bolivia). This informal economy is also present in central cities in the United States (see, e.g., Duneier, 1999; Stepick, 1989).

Inner-city communities are dotted with backdoor beauty shops, curb-side auto repair, and street vending, among other informal enterprises. There also are off-the-books construction and domestic jobs; a variety of on-books and off-the-books service jobs; and sales of arts, crafts, and other goods in gentrifying areas. However, by far the most profitable of all informal economic activities is the sale of drugs. My previous studies described the transition of Milwaukee gangs into drug selling enterprises (Hagedorn, 1994a, 1994b). A more recent study (Hagedorn, 1998a) looks more carefully at the nature of all the drug businesses in two neighborhoods and how inner-city drug selling differs from suburban and downtown drug dealing.

What I'm arguing here is that gang persistence in Milwaukee is not the mechanical result of "community disorganization" as much as it is a conscious product of collective and individual actors (Touraine, 1995) faced with the prospect of permanent conditions of economic and social exclusion. The modern era has failed to deliver the goods to what Wilson (1987) called the underclass and Castells (1996) more accurately calls the "socially excluded." Male and female peer groups in U.S. cities have consciously or unconsciously grasped this situation and acted, often destructively, but almost always following economic self-interest. Rather than the withering away of gangs as their ethnic group assimilates and joins the middle class, gangs stabilize as different kinds of social, economic, and political structures within an immobile community. Gangs in late modernity don't go away; they become part of the landscape. In this chapter I suggest that gang drug enterprises resemble informal economic businesses of the Third World more than they do industrial-era gangs, organized crime, or traditional drug dealing.

Methods and Sponsorship

This most recent study is my fourth, and probably last, gang study in Milwaukee. I was assisted by several former gang members who have long worked with me as community researchers. I also was assisted by an assortment of key informants within the white youth culture. Due to problems in guaranteeing confidentiality, we recorded no names and did not tape responses. We basically conducted a small business survey of the entire population of drug businesses within two neighborhoods. We used the small business and minority entrepreneurship literature (e.g., Reynolds & White, 1993) both because it fit our perspective, and as a way for our recommendations to address the business community.

This study was commissioned in 1997 by a conservative, business-oriented think tank, the Wisconsin Policy Research Institute (WPRI). The full text of the report, and its methodology, can be retrieved from their website (http://www.wpri.org). The Institute asked me to do the study to investigate the extent of the informal economy in Milwaukee, in hopes of demonstrating that such off-the-books income was capable of compensating for the loss of welfare benefits. They did not interfere in any way with the study, nor censor any of my findings. They treated me and my research with the utmost respect.

The study was controversial in Milwaukee, with the mayor attacking me as "drug addled" and making a serious attempt to get the WPRI executive director fired. The principal finding of the study, that "much of what we call crime is in fact work," was blasted by the mayor so viciously that he effectively silenced other local voices. However, columnists Mary Mitchell and Eric Zorn of Chicago's *Sun-Times and Tribune*, as well as columnists from *Time, Reason,* and other national publications, praised the study and made fun of the mayor for being afraid of uncomfortable truths. What follows is based on the main body of that report, slightly edited and without its detailed description of Milwaukee's informal economy. Both this introduction and the conclusion were written especially for this volume, replacing the more Milwaukee-focused sections in the original report.

The Character of the Drug Business in Horatiotown and Algerville

The two inner-city neighborhoods we studied were 16 contiguous blocks for the Latino area (we'll call it Horatiotown), and 37 contiguous blocks in the African American neighborhood (Algerville). All but one of the Algerville drug businesses were contained in a smaller area of 27 blocks, with one drug selling business located on a corner that was outside that area. The Census reports that there were 1,611 people living in the Horatiotown neighborhood in 444 households. Of all residents, 764 reported themselves as being of Hispanic origin. In the predominantly African American Algerville neighborhood there were 6,869 persons from 3,112 households in the 37 blocks. There were 1,704 whites and 4,472 blacks residing in Algerville.

Each drug business in these areas, like typical new licit minority businesses, had few employees. None were large enterprises, with only two businesses having as many as 20 employees. Drug businesses, however, did employ, on average, more workers than did new licit white or minority entrepreneurial firms. Drug enterprises had a mean number of employees of 6.8 compared to 6.0 for all new Wisconsin licit entrepreneurial businesses with employees.

In the two neighborhoods we surveyed we compiled detailed descriptions of 28 drug selling businesses, 14 in each neighborhood. Although we believe we identified all retail drug businesses in the area, it is possible that our respondents may not have knowledge of some drug enterprises. Thus,

Table 7.1   Total Employed Selling Drugs in Horatiotown and Algerville

Number of Employees	Frequency	Valid Percentage	Cumulative Percentage
1	3	10.7	10.7
2	4	14.3	25.0
3	2	7.1	32.1
4	3	10.7	42.9
5	1	3.6	46.4
6	4	14.3	60.7
7	3	10.7	71.4
9	1	3.6	75.0
10	2	7.1	82.1
13	2	7.1	89.3
16	1	3.6	92.9
20	1	3.6	96.4
21	1	3.6	100.0
Total	28	100.0	100.0

Total Employees	191
Horatioville	86
Algerville	105
Mean number of employees	6.82
Standard Deviation	5.49
Minimum: 1 employee	Maximum: 21 employees

the data in Table 7.1 may underestimate actual drug business activity in these two neighborhoods.

Our data find that at least 10% of all young Hispanic men living in Horatiotown were employed in some way selling drugs. Here are our calculations: According to the Census, the total number of Hispanic origin males aged 18 to 29 in Horatiotown was 258. But simple division of 86 drug workers by 258 would be misleading. Some employees are older than 29 and a few younger than 18, though our informants insisted that most fit this age group. A few of the drug sellers in Horatiotown are not of Hispanic origin. A handful are female. Some, but not many, do not live in the neighborhood they "serve" (on the streets, someone who sells drugs is said to be "serving"). If we add to these qualifiers the possibility that there may be a serious undercount of Latino males due to illegal immigration, we might increase the Census's number of young males by as much as a third, giving us 344 males aged 18 to 29. Using these overly conservative assumptions, 344 divided by 43 yields an estimate that 12% of *all Horatiotown Latino males were employed in the drug game.*

In Algerville, our informants reported that all 105 drug employees were African American, nearly all male, and almost all lived in the neighborhood. Some are older than 29 and a few are under 18. Thus, out of a total of

Table 7.2   Numbers of "Runners" in Horatiotown and Algerville

Value	Frequency	Valid Percentage	Cumulative Percentage
0	7	25.0	25.9
1	1	3.6	29.6
2	4	14.3	44.4
3	3	10.7	55.6
4	4	14.3	70.4
5	3	10.7	81.5
6	1	3.6	85.2
8	1	3.6	88.9
10	1	3.6	92.6
15	1	3.6	96.3
20	1	3.6	100.0
Missing	1	3.6	
Total	28	100.0	100.0

Sum 108.00

626 African American males aged 18 to 29 living in Algerville, if only 60, or slightly more than half, were African Americans aged 18 to 29, then conservatively, *10% of African American males aged 18 to 29 living in Algerville were employed in the drug business.*

The employees of these "drug firms" had special characteristics. Although each "firm" had at least one owner or partner, the majority of employees were "runners," usually drug addicts or heavy cocaine users (often called "dope fiends") who make contact with customers and do the riskier job of selling (see Table 7.2). This method of drug sales has become more common in Milwaukee, largely replacing the older method of sales through "drug houses." We will discuss the innovative sales techniques later in this report.

In our earlier research (Hagedorn, 1994a, 1998b), which studied the first years of the cocaine business, we found that most drug sellers were also regular users of cocaine. In other words, in the early 1990s, even those who were wholesalers or dealers who sold to others also typically used cocaine. But times have changed, and there is a stigma on the streets for anyone who uses cocaine. The term *dope fiend* has become a dismissive epithet. The selling of cocaine is now much more a way to make money than it is part of the user lifestyle, especially in Algerville (see Table 7.3). Latino drug sellers in Horatiotown, however, were more likely still to be drug users, consistent with more regular drug use by Latinos in our earlier studies (Hagedorn, 1994b; Hagedorn, Torres, & Giglio 1998).

Most new African American and Latino licit entrepreneurial firms in Wisconsin have less than one paid employee and earn less than $50,000 in sales per year (Reynolds & White, 1993). By comparison, the drug busi-

Table 7.3   Are Horatiotown and Algerville Entrepreneurs Users of Cocaine?

	Horatiotown		Algerville		Row Totals	Percentage
User	8		3		11	42.3
Nonuser	4		11		15	57.7
Column totals	12	46.2%	14	53.8%	26	100.0

Table 7.4   Gross Receipts per Month in Horatiotown and Algerville Drug Businesses

Value Label	Value	Frequency	Valid Percentage	Cumulative Percentage
Less than $500	1	4	14.3	14.3
$500-$1,000	2	6	21.4	35.7
$1,000-$5,000	3	14	50.0	85.7
Over $5,000	4	4	14.3	100.0
Totals	—	28	100.0	100.0

Mean 2.643   Median 3.000   Mode 3.000

Valid cases 28   Missing cases 0

nesses in these two neighborhoods employ more workers, but three quarters of those employees were paid in drugs, rather than in cash (table not shown). Most of these drug businesses were rather small. As indicated in Table 7.4, only about one in seven reported receipts from drug sales of more $5,000 per month, or at least $60,000 per year. Thus, in purely economic terms, most could be categorized as "small businesses," comparable to most new licit businesses run by Latinos or African Americans.

Three of the four businesses making more than $5,000 per month were in the predominantly African American Algerville neighborhood. Only one Algerville business reported gross receipts of less than $12,000 per year, and 9 of 14 Horatiotown "stores" fell into the less profitable "under $12,000 per year" range (table not shown). In these two neighborhoods, Latinos were more likely to be users and to make less money selling drugs than were African Americans. The businesses that gross "over $5,000" per month include a few drug sellers who are wholesalers and not retailers. They sell to smaller local drug businessmen as well as to suburban dealers.

Although most minority, licit, entrepreneurial firms report serious start-up problems, and 10% of all new licit businesses fail each year, the drug firms we studied were among the majority of small companies that had "made it." Those interviewed reported that between a half dozen and a dozen drug businesses in their neighborhood went out of business or moved their operation in the last year, three times higher than the average

Table 7.5   How Long Have Horatiotown and Algerville Entrepreneurs
Been in Business?

Value Label	Frequency	Valid Percentage	Cumulative Percentage
6 mo to 1 year	5	17.9	17.9
1 to 2 years	10	35.7	53.6
More than 2 yrs	13	46.4	100.0
Totals	28	100.0	100.0
Mean 3.286	Median 3.000	Mode 4.000	
Valid cases 28	Missing cases 0		

10% failure rate of licit businesses. Importantly, almost half (13) of the 28 businesses that were selling drugs at the time of our study had been in operation for more than 2 years, as reported in Table 7.5.

Is the drug business a full-time job or something done on the side? For licit entrepreneurs, Reynolds and White (1993) report, more than three quarters will continue to hold a regular job as they begin the entrepreneurial process. This pattern is slightly different for most of the entrepreneurs who are selling drugs (Note: this discussion is about the entrepreneurs, not the runners). For most, the drug business is a full-time job, though a minority also hold a legitimate job, either using their licit job to supplement drug sales or using their drug sales to supplement their legitimate job. The majority of African American drug entrepreneurs in the Algerville neighborhood did not have a legitimate job, and as many Latinos in the Horatiotown area were holding a legitimate job as were working full-time selling drugs (see Table 7.6).

Most of those selling drugs were reported to be married or have a spouse. Yet more than three quarters of the spouses of our almost entirely male sample are not involved in the drug business (see Table 7.7). Many of these women have either been on welfare or working a legitimate job, and more than half (63.6%) are not in the labor market but may be raising their family full-time (table not shown). Our data do not support the beliefs by some that women are becoming significantly more involved with the drug economy, at least not in these neighborhoods. The impact of welfare reform, however, is too recent to draw any firm conclusions.

Innovation and Entrepreneurship in Drug Selling

When the cocaine business began in earnest on Milwaukee's northside in the late 1980s and early 1990s, drug sales largely took place either on corners or at drug houses. "Corner sales" mean just that: Drug sellers stand on corners and sell drugs to passersby, either neighborhood residents or peo-

Table 7.6   Does the Drug Entrepreneur Also Have a Legitimate Job?

	Horatiotown	Algerville	Total	Percentage
Mostly full-time	5	2	7	25.0
Mostly part-time	0	1	1	3.6
AFDC or welfare	4	2	6	21.4
No legitimate job	5	9	14	50.0
Totals	14	14	28	100.0

Number of missing observations: 0

Table 7.7   Does the Spouse of the Drug Entrepreneur Also Sell Drugs?

Spouse Sells Drugs . . .	Male Drug Seller		Female Drug Seller		Row Totals	Percentage
Full-time	1		2		3	13.6
Part-time	2		0		2	9.1
Not at all	14		3		17	77.3
Totals/Percentages	17	77.3%	5	22.7%	22	100.0

Number of missing observations: 6

ple who drive through the area to buy drugs. Corner sellers may hold the drugs in their pockets but more commonly keep drugs as a "dead man," or hidden in a crumbled up cigarette or potato chip package on the ground near them. Then, after a sale, the customer can be directed to get the rocks of cocaine from the package. This minimizes risk.

Before 1991, most cocaine sold in Milwaukee was sold as powder. Customers typically bought powder and then cooked it themselves into crack, adding adulterants like baking soda to the powder, then heating it on a spoon until it "cracks" and turns into "rock." By 1992, almost all northside street-side retail cocaine sales were taken over by the direct sales of crack. Crack cocaine is not necessarily more profitable. But crack, rather than powder, came to dominate inner-city markets because it is ready to use, especially by dope fiends who may not have the patience to heat it up or the skill to prepare it properly. Thus, one early Milwaukee name for crack was "ready rock." All Algerville retailers sold crack, not powder.

In Horatiotown, retail sales of cocaine were both powder and rock. Powder was sold more to the partying crowd, those who use it "fashionably" in bathrooms of nightclubs or at after-hours parties. Crack was sold mainly to dope fiends, or regular users. These users would typically buy "tens" or "twenties," a small number of rocks costing $10 or $20. In both

Table 7.8   Primary Location of Drug Selling Sites in Horatiotown and Algerville

Primary Location	Horatiotown	Algerville	Row Totals	Percentage
Private home	5	1	6	21.4
Bar	4	1	5	17.9
Other legitimate business	0	1	1	3.6
Follows seller	5	11	16	57.1
Totals	14	14	28	100.0

Algerville and Horatiotown, entrepreneurs most often bought an "eightball" of powder cocaine (3.5 grams of cocaine, or less than the weight of a nickel, costing around $150 wholesale) or an ounce, which wholesales for anywhere from $800 to $1,200. Drug entrepreneurs would then turn the powder into crack by adding baking soda and heating it. The crack is then packaged into small quantities for resale. The rule of thumb in cocaine sales is that a good businessman will double his money, or turn an investment of $1,000 (for an ounce) into $2,000 in sales, for a cool $1,000 in profit. Some "businessmen" can make as much as $2,500 on an ounce, and others say they try to make "double their money minus a $100" on the purchase of an ounce.

Crack is favored on the streets because dope fiends will return time and again to buy a "ten" or "twenty" to party on. Some Algerville businessmen sell "fives," or one or two small rocks for $5. The "high" may last a few minutes or longer, and within half an hour the user will return to buy more crack until his or her money runs out. Women whose money runs out often exchange sex for the drug. Crack is a quicker, more powerful high than powder cocaine, which is typically ingested intranasally. Smoking crack is believed on the streets to have a more potent, more addictive, effect.

In the first years of the expansion of cocaine sales, corner sales were complemented by sales in drug houses. There were two types of drug houses. One, a retail outlet, sold drugs "over the counter" for consumption by the customer at his or her home or elsewhere. "Smoke houses" were houses where crack parties took place and people gathered to use drugs and party. These drug houses were an innovative practice from earlier, more informal methods of drug dealing and the "shooting galleries" of the past—bleak apartments where addicts gathered to inject heroin.

Our data show that drug distributors have further innovated since the early 1990s. As indicated in Table 7.8, the modal way to sell drugs has ceased to be on a set corner or at a drug house, though both still occur. Most drug sellers, especially in Algerville, run their retail business "on the fly." They may have a beeper and hang out at a bar or at a friend's house from the late afternoon hours until early morning. Rather than making transactions themselves, they will deal only with "runners," or addicts who are employed as a means of obtaining cocaine for themselves. The runners will be contacted by customers and take their orders for small amounts of cocaine to the seller. The drug seller can be found by the runner by looking around the neighborhood. The runner pays for the drugs, is given the proper amount, and then returns to the buyer, sometimes taking a cut of the drugs for himself. Often a runner will be given an extra "ten" of cocaine for every four or five "tens" he sells.

This method of employing users as "salesmen" cuts overhead while keeping the seller secured from identification by customers and police. Several of the drug sellers we interviewed told us with pride that none of their customers had ever met them. Other drug sellers are known as Electronic Dealers because they make all transactions through a beeper and return calls only by cellular phone.

The seller may have a small amount of cocaine on him, or more likely have it at a nearby location. Thus the risk of arrest for the seller is quite low. "Buy and bust" tactics by police thus arrest a disproportionate number of runners who, if they are arrested, may or may not "flip" and give information about the seller to the police. Even if they do give information, arresting the seller with a large amount of cocaine is extremely difficult. Remember, the amount of sales in any given month for most sellers is quite low, and they are unlikely to possess more than an eightball (3.5 grams) or, at most, a few ounces of cocaine at any given time.

In this way, much modern drug selling fits Peter Drucker's definition of entrepreneurship as something more than a new venture. Drucker (1985) explains that a new mom-and-pop store would not be classified as entrepreneurial because it is just doing something that has already been done. But when a business applies new management techniques or appeals to a new market or new customers, or revises old ways of doing things, "that," Drucker (1985) says, "is entrepreneurship" (p. 22). By substantially reducing the risks of apprehension and nearly eliminating overhead, modern inner-city drug dealing is a good example of what Drucker would call entrepreneurship. Sixteen of the 28 drug businesses in Horatiotown and Algerville could easily fit this entrepreneurial description.

Licit Business, Gangs, and Violence

Licit businesses also participate in the drug trade. Bars not only became spots for contacts for drug sales, but meager profits in the tavern and restaurant business led their owners to underwrite drug buys and some began to sell cocaine, marijuana, and heroin directly. Many drug sellers had direct contact with area prostitutes who steer "johns" to the drug sellers for drugs to consume as they "party." Several drug dealers also had informal arrangements with nearby apartments where, for a charge, a drug cus-

Table 7.9   Open and Closed Drug Markets

	Horatiotown	Algerville	Row Totals	Percentage
Open	10	6	16	59.3
Closed	4	7	11	40.7
Totals	14	13		

Number of missing observations: 1

tomer could get drugs, a woman to party with, and a room for privacy and assorted sexual acts.

In Algerville, one busy corner was a high sales area with many drive-by customers. This corner, which was run by a gang, employed (using the lowest estimates of our informants) 20 individual entrepreneurs who bought drugs on consignment from a member of their gang and sold them as part of their gang activities. Concentrated areas of gang drug sales, like this one, are spread throughout Milwaukee, and we deliberately focused on areas where the gangs do not dominate drug trafficking. Still, gangs make their influence felt everywhere there is a drug trade. Ten drug dealers reported that their business was gang related, and 17 reported they sold "freelance" (table not shown). I have argued elsewhere (Hagedorn, 1998c) that many urban gangs today have transformed their nature and have adopted economic functions. Gangs have become a central part of many poor neighborhoods' informal economies.

How do drug sellers keep their customers? Are markets free and open to competition from others or are they "closed" to outsiders? Unlike many parts of Chicago and other cities, Milwaukee has maintained a tradition of "open markets," where anyone can sell as long as they don't try to steal customers from others. Gang drug dealers have differentiated Milwaukee from Chicago by describing Milwaukee as a city with "too much free enterprise" to become monopolized by a few gangs or other drug organizations (Hagedorn, 1998b, p. 104). Thus, competition between rival drug sellers is a standard feature of Milwaukee drug markets (see Table 7.9). This continuing competition may be one reason for only small declines in Milwaukee homicide rates. Today, most gang-dominated corners and neighborhoods are usually closed to any outside sellers, and violence in those neighborhoods may be more related to inter- and intra-gang and personal problems than exclusively to drug issues. Horatiotown, though near a gang-dominated area, was a largely nongang drug site. On the other hand, though Algerville had more gang selling sites, drug sellers in that neighborhood reported it was not exclusively gang dominated (table not shown).

One counterintuitive finding of this study was that the drug sellers reported few problems with violence and few problems with police. At the

Table 7.10   Incidence of Violence by Length of Time in Business

Violence Occurs . . .	Length of Time in Business			Row Totals	Percentage
	6 Months to 1 Year	1 to 2 Years	More Than 2 Years		
Weekly	0	0	3	3	11
Once a month or so	3	7	6	16	59
Not at all	2	3	3	8	30
Totals	5 18.5%	10 37.0%	12 44.4%	27	

Number of missing observations: 1

onset of the establishment of drug markets, Milwaukee's gangs waged a bloody war in neighborhoods across the northside (see Hagedorn, 1994b; Romenesko, 1990). Gang members and others with a violent history are likely to be disproportionately involved with drug sales, but while drug markets in many areas are still unstable, in areas like Horatiotown and Algerville, methods of business have been perfected that avoid violence.

It appears that the longer drug businesses persist, the fewer problems with violence occur. None of the drug entrepreneurs we surveyed reported "daily" problems with violence. This lends support to the notion that reductions in drug-related violence are a function of social learning by drug sellers and skill in running a business. Violence, as Cloward and Ohlin (1960) argued long ago, proves to be "bad for business." The more serious gang members become about making profits, the more they need to control violence. Violence may be inversely related to the "maturity" of drug markets (i.e., the developed relationships between retail sellers and their suppliers, between rival retail sellers, and between sellers and customers, in one area, over time).

In Horatiotown, a majority of the Latino drug sellers reported no problems with violence whatsoever, and the Algerville African American drug sellers generally reported violence occurring about once a month. Violence is usually related to problems with customers or rivals, but no data were gathered in this report on the nature of violence (see Hagedorn, 1998b). It is important, when viewing Table 7.10, to understand that most of the "violence" reported is not lethal and many "violent" events are fights or threats with drug addicts or other customers. Very few were drive-by shootings between drug rivals. What emerges is a very different picture from stereotypes of frequent drug-related violence, at least in established drug selling businesses.

Despite the saturation patrols by police in the areas we surveyed, drug sellers experienced few problems with police, as indicated in Table 7.11. Even though there is a high volume of daily drug activity, there appear to be few risks of arrest for the drug seller who knows what he is doing. In-

Table 7.11   Problems With Police by Length of Time in Business

Problems With Police Occur . . .	Length of Time in Business			Row Totals	Percentage
	6 Months to 1 Year	1 to 2 Years	More Than 2 Years		
Daily	—	—	1	1	3.7
Weekly	—	3	1	4	14.8
Once a month or so	4	5	6	15	55.6
Not at all	1	2	4	7	25.9
Totals	5 18.5%	10 37.0%	12 44.4%	27	

deed, almost all of those who were in business for more than 2 years experienced few or no problems with police. The site that reported "daily" problems with police was a high-volume corner where a gang sells openly to passersby, and police routinely "harass" gang members who are standing idly on the corner.

If these "successful" businessmen are avoiding problems with police and with violence, why do we have so many reports of shootings and so many arrests of small-time drug dealers? Although these data do not speak directly to the issue, it appears that violence is more likely as a "start-up" problem and contributes to the high failure rate of small drug businesses. It may be that drug sellers who rely on force are more likely to fail, and only the smart, innovative ones persist. There may be some variant of a Darwinian effect at work, "selecting" the street-smart over the practitioners of crude violence. As we have seen in established drug businesses, runners assume most of the risk in drug sales. Our sample consists of those drug businesses in neighborhoods of substantial drug activity that had been able to avoid problems and keep doing business. Those drug businesses that went "bankrupt" were probably less able to negotiate relations with neighbors, customers, rivals, and suppliers, which means they were not as adept at keeping their businesses discreet and hidden from police. This is an area of needed further research.

The Customers

Finally, who are the customers of drug dealers in these areas? Drug customers constitute what Peter Drucker calls a "specialty market" (Drucker, 1985, p. 240) with drug sales fitting in an "ecological niche" that can be exploited by relatively uneducated lower-class businessmen and women. Between one third and two thirds of the customers in both areas were women, consistent with our earlier study (Hagedorn, 1994a, 1994b) and other studies of the crack trade. Indeed, the most active time for drug sales was still around the first of the month when welfare and disability checks were received. Some drug sellers reported that they sold for only the first few days of any month, then returned to a regular job or did not sell for the rest of the month.

In the study neighborhoods, only a minority of all retail customers were from the immediate area and a large percentage were white, though this varied by dealer. In this regard, drug sellers seemed to have learned from the difficulties of small licit minority businesses that are trapped, selling only to a local ethnic market. Many drug sellers in these neighborhoods have learned the lesson of rap music that the only way to make money is to "cross over" and sell to a more prosperous white retail market or to become a wholesaler.

Most customers were regulars, meaning either that they were dope fiends or that they had a regular "safe" contact with a seller (or usually his runner) and maintained that contact as long as the seller had dope. Depending on the dealer, the regulars might come from either the neighborhood or the suburbs. In both neighborhoods there were specific locales that gave innovative drug sellers access to large white markets.

In Algerville, there were three areas where the customers were mainly white. First, a group of women worked a prostitute "stroll" on a nearby avenue. We interviewed them, and they reported most of their johns were white, and they regularly used rooms provided by area drug dealers. Second, the high-profile corner had a substantial number of white, drive-by customers, most of them regulars. These young white men and women often quickly "stopped and shopped" on their way home after work, with the drug corner a kind of drive-through service.

The most profitable area for sales to whites was located outside a local dance hall. Popular performances by national music acts attract large numbers of white youth to this hall, and runners employed by Algerville sellers hung around outside the hall and made contact with musicians and young whites who regularly attended concerts. They also were introduced to new buyers who wanted to "score some coke." Some of these new buyers were ripped off, as runners took the money, went to buy the coke, and never returned. Most often, runners bought coke for the youthful white customers and returned to party with them.

In Horatiotown, white customers were mainly drive-through traffic from the suburbs. Long-time white customers drove down a main street that crossed through Horatiotown, and stopped outside of licit businesses where they would meet drug sellers specializing in marijuana, cocaine, or heroin. They would make the buy and then quickly get back in their cars and return to work or to the suburbs.

The largest market for illegal drugs in Milwaukee is the white youth and suburban market, even though street-side minority drug sellers are by far the most common arrestees. Let's turn to a description of the white and suburban drug market.

The White Youth and Suburban Drug Markets

One remarkable aspect of the white youth and suburban drug market is that, unlike in the inner city, drug sales are not neighborhood based. Try as we could, we could not locate any suburban or white alternative culture neighborhoods that resembled inner-city drug markets like Horatiotown or Algerville. Though we didn't conduct a countywide survey of suburban drug dealers, it appears that the vast majority of drug dealers located in the suburbs and selling to white youth are themselves white. Suburban drug selling has not changed much over the years; it still is basically a word-of-mouth operation.

Although there are many dealers and a variety of methods of distribution of drugs in the suburbs and among white youth, there are not as many people employed in the drug game as in the inner city. Drugs are a recreational pastime for youth and a stress-relaxer for older white adults, just as among poor minorities. But although many youthful white dealers worked full-time selling drugs, other postteen whites who sold drugs had a job, and drug sales were a sideline. It was a "business" only in a limited sense, as added income. Drug selling by whites most resembled the old method of drug dealing by user/dealers in the past. One way that drug selling to whites most differed from the retail drug sales businesses in Horatiotown and Algerville was the primacy of networks at one's place of employment as a regular outlet for white and suburban drug sales, rather than neighborhood-based sales.

Our research among white and suburban drug users focused on two aspects of the white market, especially for cocaine: (a) the transformation of the white youth market from marijuana and hallucinogens to cocaine as white Milwaukee's primary climax (most serious) drug; and (b) the different ways drugs are sold in the suburbs.

The Transformation of the White
Alternative Youth Culture Drug Market

In the early 1990s, a number of young white marijuana and hallucinogen dealers began to branch out into selling cocaine. In interviews with participants in the white youth culture, as part of this study, we profiled a dozen well-known drug dealers and what happened to them as they began to deal more and more cocaine.

Most of these young men and women were users of the drugs they sold and active participants in the teenage youth culture, living a life of partying. They had a variety of family backgrounds, from working class to upper middle class, but their use of illicit substances and popularity in the party circuit seemed to describe them all. After the introduction of cocaine into the northside Milwaukee market in the late 1980s, a few of these mid-level dealers utilized nebulous connections to northside drug dealers to "score" cocaine.

The national publicity around the cocaine "epidemic" prompted curiosity among young, white, Milwaukee drug users, and many tried cocaine for the first time in the early 1990s. By 1993, cocaine had become the main climax drug in the white youth culture in Milwaukee. The stories of the original dozen or so dealers we profiled followed a path similar to African American and Latino cocaine users/dealers, as described in our earlier work (Hagedorn, 1994a). Some white dealers went from casual to heavy using of cocaine, and the drug led many to their ruin. At least one became a heroin user, and others lapsed into paranoia. The murder of two young people outside an east-side church in 1995 sent the message that the violence associated with cocaine use and markets had arrived in the white youth culture.

The methods of distribution of cocaine in the white youth culture were no different from how these dealers had sold marijuana and other drugs. Sales depended primarily on the word-of-mouth knowledge of who had what drug for sale. The youth culture shares music, events, concerts, and certain bars and places to congregate. Knowledge of who are drug dealers is widespread. Most white youth drug dealers have a supply at their home or at the home of a friend and sell to friends and acquaintances, often late at night as people prepare to party. Although big dealers and suppliers had smaller dealers working for them, there was no neighborhood, retail-drug business structure like that found in the two inner-city neighborhoods.

The description, by Algerville drug sellers, of a dance hall as a main source of customers for Algerville drug dealers was confirmed by our white informants. In fact, we were repeatedly told that the dance hall was "the place to go" to score coke and that many "raves" were thinly disguised excuses for cocaine parties among hundreds of white youth. In the past few years, cocaine and other hard drugs have become a regular part of the alternative culture party scene.

Methods of Suburban Drug Distribution

Recent highly publicized cocaine cases have described drug distribution in the parking lots of stores or in suburban churches. After not finding any neighborhood-based drug selling locales, we decided to question suburban drug dealers about some of the different ways drugs were dispensed to white professionals and suburbanites. What stands out in these descriptions is that nearly all drug transactions were at places of employment or at after-work leisure activities, very unlike the model of selling drugs as a business that we described in the section on Horatiotown and Algerville drug markets. The distribution of cocaine in the suburbs appears to have not changed much from the traditional word-of-mouth ways drugs have been sold in the past.

The most common method of distribution we found was at work places. In any large bureaucracy, public or private, there is almost always someone (usually male) who either deals drugs himself or has knowledge of a "safe" drug dealer for different substances. Word of mouth spreads among users, and contacts are discretely made. For example, when I was working at the Milwaukee County Department of Human Services, I quickly learned—by accident—who had access to what drugs. For workers, illicit drugs are often "medicinal" and used to relieve the stress of work.

The second most common method of drug distribution in the suburbs is at bars and taverns, especially among participants in athletic leagues or tavern activities. After-work relaxation at a bar is a long-standing Wisconsin tradition, but drugs often supplement the more common staples of beer and brandy. I have been present at bars on payday when groups of white youth gather to drink and score cocaine, often going to the bathroom to sniff, rather than smoking it. Working-class bars, in this sense, differ little from bars frequented by young people in the alternative youth culture, where similar patterns of sales occur, or bars in Horatiotown and Algerville.

A third method of distribution is through nightclubs and popular establishments whose employees or owners are regularly involved in the drug trade. Among middle-class partygoers, it is common knowledge which restaurants and bars sell drugs. At some establishments, certain employees sell while on the job. At other places, the owner is making extra profit on drug sales, or providing drugs for business contacts or friends. Some sales methods can be very creative. For example, at one popular pizza business frequented by many Milwaukee notables, cocaine was distributed in small packets under the crust of the pizza, and the customer paid for both the pizza and the cocaine at the same time.

A final spot for drug distribution is suburban high schools, and at after-school parties and activities. Every high school we looked at had identifiable drug dealers and people who could score whatever substance was requested. We did no detailed investigation of high school drug dealing and will leave that inquiry to another time.

Unlike Horatiotown and Algerville, there were no known drug selling neighborhoods where drug dealing could be observed (and objected to) by neighbors and could become a focus for law enforcement. The use of more hidden, non-neighborhood-based, sales techniques explains much of the difference in racial disparity in drug apprehensions.

To summarize, the main difference between white suburban and inner-city drug use is economics. Although drugs are used as a way to relieve stress and get thrills by people of all walks of life, in the inner city drugs are also a major employer of young minority males. White suburban drug users are workers or housewives who experience stress on the job or anxiety at home and use drugs to relieve anxiety. The method of distribution of drugs in the suburbs and to the white youth market is at places of work or entertainment and is more hidden from law enforcement. But, as we have shown, they are not very difficult to locate. Law enforcement has chosen to focus on neighborhood-based drug sales more than workplace or entertainment-based drug sales, thus disproportionately arresting poor minority runners who sell in the open.

A New Context for Gang Research, A New Policy Toward Gangs

Hernando de Soto (1990), in his study of the Peruvian informal economy, argues:

> The real remedy for violence and poverty is to recognize the property and labor of those whom formality today excludes, so that where there is rebellion there will be a sense of belonging and responsibility. When people develop a taste for independence and faith in their own efforts, they will be able to believe in themselves and in economic freedom. (p. 258)

This study frames the postindustrial gang within an informal economy that is consciously created by poor people who have lost confidence in the capacity of late capitalism to deliver the goods. It thus refocuses our attention from a one-sided law enforcement perspective to the effects of social exclusion on poor people responding to globalization. It suggests that the fundamental issue for our time is to ensure that the new economy does not reinforce old inequalities, but reduces them (Portes et al., 1989a).

In conclusion, this study has four implications for research and public policy. First, this study suggests that gangs can be productively studied as social actors within their communities, as one party among many, with their own legitimate interests. Although many gangs still resemble the delinquent peer groups of the past, more and more gangs have been consciously constructed as organizations and play an active social, political, and economic role within their communities (see, e.g., Venkatesh, 1996, 2000). That gang-related drug organizations did not differ in any significant respects from nongang drug enterprises suggests that the informal economy approach of this study may have some merit. The notion that gangs are either organized crime or merely a hodge-podge of defective youth is an empirical question, and in cities like Milwaukee or Chicago does not appear to be generally accurate. The information era may have sweeping implications for contemporary gangs.

Second, entrepreneurship within the new economy is positively valued, and this study suggests that approach may have merit in poor communities as well. Though I don't think this means we should legalize drugs, perhaps we should learn from de Soto and those studying the informal economy and advocate a "look the other way" policy for marginally legal or for many nonviolent illegal enterprises. We even can learn from U.S. foreign policy. The United States sponsors "crop substitution" for cocaine growers in Latin America; why shouldn't the government promote a similar policy domestically? Why can't we lure workers from the drug economy into other, more socially productive businesses? The success of Homeboyz Interactive (http://www.homeboyz.com), a Web design business of former gang members, is one such business that deserves emulation and investment. This study was directed at the business community, especially those segments that support investment in poor communities, less regulation of small business, and promotion of minority entrepreneurship (see Porter, 1995). We should continue those efforts.

Third, this study strongly implies that we need to call a halt to the war on drugs. This policy is a "war," not on drug users, who are mainly white and more affluent, but on those who see drugs as work, as a means of survival. Filling our prisons with low-level workers in the drug economy, many of them heavy users, is a poor way to compensate for our economy's failure to provide secure work and our government's failure to provide a realistic safety net. In fact, prison has seemed to reinforce, not weaken, gangs and is now a normal part of day-to-day gang experience (see, e.g., Jacobs, 1977; Thompkins, 2000; Wacquant, 2000).

This study found that 1 in 10 young minority males in Milwaukee is engaged in the drug trade, and more minority youth were employed selling drugs than in any other sector of Milwaukee's economy. When these findings are coupled with the fact that one third of all young African Americans without a high school diploma are currently incarcerated (Russell Sage, 2000), we have created gulag-like conditions. In my view, the war on drugs is the most racist U.S. policy since slavery. We need a second Emancipation Proclamation.

Finally, the study points out that there is still a need for genuine field research, especially innovative studies that challenge conventional thinking. Getting "back into the field again" has made me realize that new research needs new theory, and I've been looking for more productive literatures to explain what I'm finding. Gang research today needs to break out of the "official definitions of reality" of the mass media, law enforcement, *and* classical criminology. It's time to rethink the way we think about gangs. And it's past time to change our one-sided lock 'em up, war-on-our-youth, policies.

Gangs, Violence, and Safe Schools

KENNETH S. TRUMP

A series of school shootings and associated violent acts that captured American headlines beginning in 1997 placed school safety at the top of the agenda for most educators and communities across the nation. These high-profile incidents, combined with anecdotal information suggesting that gang activity leveled off or diminished in a number of school communities, also shifted discussions on school violence away from gangs and onto "targeted violence" typically perpetrated by single offenders. Although adequate attention to nongang school violence is warranted, school and community leaders should be aware of the impact of gang activity on school safety and be familiar with the importance of early gang prevention, intervention, and enforcement strategies in school settings.

Gang Versus Nongang School Violence

Gang-related incidents in schools differ from most nongang offenses. School gang incidents typically involve a larger number of students and potential participants from outside of the school. They also are generally more retaliatory in nature and escalate much more quickly than nongang, one-on-one conflicts.

Whereas a one-on-one fight may end after the first staff intervention, gang-related fights and assaults tend to escalate from the initial two-person conflict to a series of other related conflicts or, in some cases, to a large-scale riot. To address gang conflicts as separate isolated incidents without addressing the overall gang-related nature of the incidents increases the risks of continued disruptions and violence. Going to the root of the gang-related problem can help prevent further "spin-off" altercations and escalating warfare, although school officials must exercise caution not to enhance the credibility of gangs and gang activity in the process of doing so. Gangs are not clubs or social organizations and should not be recognized as legitimate student groups (Trump, 1998).

School gang conflict frequently involves intense violence, the use of weapons, or in many cases, both. The level of violence and the potential for weapon involvement in gang incidents is generally greater than in cases involving one-on-one student conflicts and nongang offenses. Although the targeted-violence incidents of school shootings present an exception with respect to intensity and weapons use, schools in general are more likely to encounter one-on-one conflicts and gang-related incidents than these other types of shootings during the course of a school year.

Educators must also recognize the evolving concept of "turf" as it relates to gangs in general and to schools specifically. In past decades, turf typically referred to a particular neighborhoods or geographical areas that would be claimed by gangs as their areas of dominance and control. Today, the mobility of youth has expanded the concept of turf to include neighborhoods, malls and shopping centers, recreation and community centers, and schools.

School officials therefore cannot dismiss gang activity as simply being a "community problem." Although the gangs may have started in the community, they can become a school problem—especially when one or more gangs claim the school as their turf. In some cases, especially in larger school districts, gang members have abused and manipulated open enrollment and student transfer procedures for the primary purpose of increasing their membership and domination at a particular school (Trump, 1998).

Gangs may not even need to claim the school as their turf, per se, in order for school officials to experience a gang problem. Many gang-related conflicts that begin in the community, such as those starting at parties or community events on weekends, often spill over into the school in the form of large altercations as soon as the school doors open on Monday morning. Unfortunately, the school becomes the point of contact and conflict because many gang members who may be more difficult to locate by their rival gangs can easily be found at school on the next school day.

Gang Development and Definitions

Gang formation has been attributed to a myriad of social and economic factors that extend far beyond the schoolhouse doors. These may include power, status, security, family substitution, friendship, love, poverty, un-employment, alcohol, drugs, and/or the failure of educational, criminal justice, and other social institutions, to name a few. It is safe to say that re-gardless of the causes one attributes to gang formation, schools alone do not create gang problems.

School administrators and safety officials must, however, take steps to prevent gang development in their schools and to detect gang activity in its early stages should it actually occur. The emergence of gangs in a school, just as in the broader community, is a process rather than an event. Although many gangs may begin as informal social groups with common interests and progress over a period of time to more disruptive and crimi-nally active gangs, the time for school and safety officials to intercede is at the onset of formation, not after a problem has become chronic and en-trenched (Trump, 1993a).

Academicians and other gang specialists continue to debate the formal definition of the word *gang,* and no common definition is accepted by po-lice, schools, the academic community, and others across our nation. Therefore, it is important for school officials to work with the local police, court, social service agencies, and youth-service providers to develop a common definition that is agreed upon *in their particular community.* In ad-dition, though issues such as *appearance* and dress codes often come into play, it is important for school officials to place the primary focus of their policies and discipline codes on disruptive and/or criminal student *be-havior.*

This does not preclude educators from addressing dress issues, how-ever. The wearing of items identified as being affiliated with a gang is often a form of intimidation to other gangs as well as to the majority of students who are not gang affiliated. Educators should exercise caution not to focus solely on the dress aspect, however, and should strive for a dress code that is not too narrow or too vague, since gang identifiers tend to change over a period of time.

Student handbooks should clearly outline student rules and conse-quences, including those associated with gang-related misconduct, crimi-nal activity, and dress code violations (Trump, 1993b).

Denial

School officials, like many elected and governmental appointees, have long been notorious for denying the presence of gangs and gang activity in schools. In his first study of Ohio gangs, Huff (1988) described the effect of denial on schools by noting that,

> It is probable that the official denial of gang problems actually facilitates vic-timization by gangs, especially in public schools. School principals in sev-

eral Ohio cities are reluctant to acknowledge "gang-related" assaults for fear that such "problems" may be interpreted as negative reflections of their management ability. This "paralysis" may actually encourage gang-related assaults and may send the wrong signals to gang members, implying that they can operate within the vacuum created by this "political paralysis." (p. 9)

Similar findings of nonreporting, underreporting, and the lack of data on school-based, gang-related crime in America reinforce Huff's finding (Kodluboy & Evenrud, 1993; Lal, Lal, & Achilles, 1993; Spergel, 1990; Taylor, 1988).

There are a number of reasons why school administrators deny having a gang presence in school. In addition to issues related to perceptions of their management abilities, such as those described by Huff (1988), administrators also fear adverse parental and media attention that could arise from community concerns about school gang activity. Ironically, the adverse attention that administrators fear *will* actually result from the denial itself if problems are allowed to worsen and the gang problem can no longer be denied or concealed, even by the best public relations spin doctors.

A more subtle form of denial can also occur when educators dismiss as wanna-bes those students claiming gang affiliation. Gang members do not have to be gang "transplants" from large, "gang-infested" cities in order to be gang members. Educators must understand that gang members cross all boundaries of age, sex, race, and economic status, and may include straight-A students as well as those who are more academically challenged.

In the end, school officials face a "pay now or pay later" option in how they deal with gang issues in their schools. To address both the problem and public relations concerns, wise school administrators will acknowledge the problem (or potential for a problem) early on and deal with these issues before a gang presence becomes entrenched in their schools.

Identifying Gangs in Schools

Gang members have used a number of methods in schools to identify themselves to others as being gang affiliated. I have previously noted that these identifiers may include one or more of the following:

- Graffiti: unusual signs, symbols, or writing on walls, notebooks, class assignments, or gang "literature" books
- Colors: obvious or subtle colors of clothing, a particular clothing brand, bandannas, jewelry, or haircuts
- Tattoos: symbols on arms, chest, or body

■ Initiations: suspicious bruises, wounds or injuries resulting from a "jumping in" (Gang initiations have taken place in school rest rooms, gyms, locker rooms, playgrounds, and even hallways!)

■ Hand signs: unusual hand signals or handshakes

■ Language: uncommon terms or phrases

■ Behavior: sudden changes in behavior or secret meetings (Trump, 1998, p. 15)

Recognizing gang identifiers helps educators detect a gang presence early on so that they can more effectively prevent the negative behavior typically associated with gang activity.

In past years, schools have worked cooperatively with school security and public safety officials to equip themselves better to identify a gang presence on campus by participating in training programs geared toward increasing the awareness of school officials of gang identifiers and gang activity. Although such an approach is typically one of the first steps to better recognizing and managing a gang presence on campus, the heightened awareness of gang identifiers by school and public safety officials, as well as by parents, typically drives gang members either to change their identifiers or perhaps even to eliminate them totally. As a result, gang identifiers tend to change constantly and, in many cases, may be so low profile that educators may mistakenly believe that gangs do not exist in their schools.

It is important for school staff to place the issue of gang identifiers in a broader context so that identifiers are not overemphasized to the point where the identifiers become the focal point of dealing with the gang issue in schools. Educators, especially those administering disciplinary action, must be sure that common sense prevails when viewing the above list and in dealing with gang identifiers. Though identifiers serve to help identify gang members, the primary focus should be on student *behavior* and not simply on the gang identifiers themselves.

Enforcement and Investigations

Gang activity may involve violations of school rules, violations of the law, or both. Whereas school administrators are responsible for administering disciplinary action in response to violations of school rules, law enforcement officials are responsible for enforcing the violations of criminal law. Gang members, like any other offenders, should face both administrative disciplinary action and police intervention when they have committed a crime at school.

Unfortunately, the phrase *zero tolerance* has become so politically and rhetorically abused that it has lost its original meaning, especially in school settings. In essence, the majority of school administrators around the country always strive for firm, fair, and consistent discipline that is administered using good common sense. Gangs offer kids order, structure, and discipline; schools should offer all students—gang member or otherwise—the same.

School and public safety officials should also work together to forge a close relationship in order to prevent and effectively manage school and community gang activity. Gang activity that occurs in the community often spills over into the schools, and gang activity in the schools also frequently spills over into the neighborhoods. School and police officials should work together to foster information sharing on gang activity, awareness programs for school personnel, and prioritized investigation and enforcement of gang crimes in schools and around school property.

In some larger districts, school security and police departments actually have their own specialized officers who deal exclusively with gang prevention, intervention, and investigation efforts. Successful school and police partnerships, whether they involve full-scale gang units or simply individuals from each agency, have demonstrated that meaningful relationships across agencies can reduce school and community gang violence. Interagency collaboration should include not only schools and police, but also probation, parole, social service, and other community agencies serving gang members and youth in general (Torok & Trump, 1994; Trump, 1996).

Prevention and Intervention

Most professionals agree that enforcement, investigation, security, and crisis preparedness strategies must be balanced with prevention and intervention programs. A number of prevention and intervention programs have been implemented over the years to tackle the gang problem. The effectiveness of these programs varies, and a number of programs have undergone formal evaluations that should be reviewed prior to a school's adapting a particular strategy to its unique setting and circumstances.

Goldstein and Kodluboy (1998) identify the "essential variables" of a successful program as including the following:

- Prevention, including enhanced supervision, enhanced academic or social skills, or other development, along with an instructional component on gang resistance with skills rehearsals and enhanced supervision and instruction during times of greatest risk
- Prosocial focus on the development and maintenance of affective and functional conventional social skills and beliefs
- Comprehensiveness, not narrow or piecemeal programs
- Coordination to include open communication and cooperation with affiliated persons and agencies

- Youth input
- Prescriptiveness, where a particular need is assessed and then met or exceeded
- Program integrity, where the program is observed and implemented completely and comprehensively
- Program intensity, where an adequate level or quantity of the program is received and sufficient resources are allocated to implement the program, and timely in terms of having a determinate length with a summative evaluation at the end
- Evaluation that includes specific measurements of success, monitoring of progress, and external review
- Specific outcomes rather than vague indicators
- Standards reflective of the community, of a profession, and of conventional values and behaviors; validity in that the program is socially valid in improving the conditions of the individuals being served; and inclusive of all stakeholders to avoid a cultural bias (pp. 129-132)

School leaders may pick several models that have been successfully implemented outside of their community to consider for application in their own schools. In addition to the variables identified by Goldstein and Kodluboy, the keys to the ultimate success of a program are likely to rest with how the program is tailored to each unique school and community, to the skills of those who are operating these programs, and to the financial and operational support provided to the program by school and community leaders.

_____ **Security, Crisis Preparedness, and Safe Schools Plans**

School officials should incorporate gang-specific strategies into their overall comprehensive safe schools plan. Elsewhere (Trump, 2000), I have stressed that school safety planning must consist of an overall plan that includes, but is not necessarily limited to:

- Proactive security measures;
- Crisis preparedness planning;
- Firm, fair, and consistent discipline;
- Effective prevention and intervention programs;
- Mental health support services;
- A school climate stressing respect, acceptance of diversity, belonging, trust, pride, ownership, involvement, peaceful resolution of conflicts, and related characteristics;

■ Strong and challenging academic programs supplemented by diverse extracurricular activities; and

■ Parental and community involvement, support, and networking. (pp. 73-74)

School officials have historically addressed school safety through discipline, school climate, mental health, academic and extracurricular programs, and parent and community involvement strategies. However, up until the school shooting tragedies of the late 1990s and early 2000s, the *proactive security* and *crisis preparedness* components for dealing with crimes and violence were frequently neglected or relegated to a minor role in overall safe school efforts.

Educators must be able to identify the steps they have taken to reduce the risks of crime and violence, including gang-related incidents. They must also be able to identify the steps they have taken in preparing to manage those incidents effectively that *cannot* be prevented. Proactive security measures and crisis preparedness planning are critical elements for doing both.

School officials should evaluate their policies and procedures related to security and crisis situations. Staff training programs should be ongoing to increase the awareness of school employees concerning crime prevention, security, crisis procedures, and best practices. *School security assessments* should be conducted by in-house school security officials and/or school police, school resource officers, police crime prevention specialists experienced with K-12 schools, or qualified and experienced (outside K-12) school safety consultants.

District- and building-level *crisis preparedness teams* should be formed for managing serious incidents that cannot be prevented. *Crisis preparedness guidelines* should be created for dealing with both natural and man-made crises. Guidelines should then be tested and simulations conducted in order to ensure that what is on paper will actually work in the event of a real crisis.

School design and architectural issues can also play a significant role in preventing school crime and violence. When effectively used, security equipment can contribute to reducing risks. Professional school security personnel and school resource officers (SROs) regularly prevent disruptions and school violence, and serve as the first line of prevention programming in many of our schools. (For information on SRO programs, visit the National Association of School Resource Officers' Web site at www.nasro. org.)

The school safety profession is increasingly complex and has grown into a separate and distinct profession for supporting traditional school operations. Educators and public safety officials should ensure that all components of a safe schools plan, including the security and crisis preparedness components, are in place to prevent and manage both gang and nongang incidents on their school campuses.

_____ **Future Trends**

American schools have experienced a wave of "new times, new crimes" at the turn of the century that is unlike anything they have ever experienced in the history of education. Earlier school security threats included aggressive and violent behavior, drugs, weapons, gang activity, and "stranger danger." Today's school security threats still include those challenges, along with new threats of homemade bombs and bomb threats, computer-related offenses, hostage taking, and even terrorist-like threats.

Gang trends, like other school violence trends, have also changed. These changes include the presence of lower-profile, more sophisticated, and more organized gang members. Changes in gang crime reporting, data collection limitations, and gang-specific official responses and programs are likely to impact gang growth and development further.

A cycle of gang denial, acknowledgment, and action, followed by a shift back to denial and "qualified admittance" in many schools and communities, can be expected until major incidents or shifts in juvenile crime trends force officials to put gang prevention, intervention, and enforcement back at the top of their agendas. The changing nature of gangs and the changing public policy responses to gangs will require school, public safety, and community officials to communicate and to act in a more coordinated, collaborative manner in the future than they have ever had to do in the past.

9

Gangs and Community-Oriented Policing

Transforming Organizational Culture

C. RONALD HUFF
KENT H. SHAFER

A recent report by the Bureau of Justice Statistics (BJS, 2001) indicates that the utilization of the "community policing" approach to law enforcement continues to grow in the United States, although the ways in which community policing is operationally defined and implemented varies, of course, across jurisdictions. According to data collected via BJS's Law Enforcement Management and Administrative Statistics (LEMAS) survey:

- State and local law enforcement agencies had nearly 113,000 community policing officers or their equivalents in 1999, compared with about 21,000 in 1997. This included 91,000 local police officers in 1999, compared with 16,000 only 2 years earlier

- Sixty-four percent of local police departments serving 86% of all residents had full-time officers engaged in community policing in 1999 (34% of departments serving 62% of residents in 1997)

- By 1999, 87% of local police officers were employed by a department that provided community policing training for some or all new recruits, and 85% by a department that provided it for at least some in-service officers

- In 1999, 63% of local police departments serving 85% of all residents used routine foot and/or bicycle patrol. *About half of all officers worked for a department*

that actively encouraged them to engage in problem-solving projects on their patrol
beats

- As of 1999, 79% of local police departments serving 96% of all residents had met with community groups within the past year and *40% of departments serving 71% of residents had formed a problem-solving partnership within the past 3 years*

- During 1999, 92% of residents were served by a local police department that provided them with routine access to crime statistics or crime maps, compared to 70% in 1997 (Bureau of Justice Statistics, 2001; emphasis added)

The formal concept of Community-Oriented Policing (COP) has been around since the 1970s, although some of its roots can be traced to the "ward and watch" system involving citizen responsibility for "patrols" in the early days of our nation's history and to more recent "team policing" experiments that were ahead of their time, in terms of the receptivity of policymakers. The operational definition of COP has been modified and changed over the years as police learn effective ways of integrating the priorities and concerns of citizens into the performance of their duties. Regardless of how it is defined, COP has always included strategies to improve relations between the community and the police. It could be argued that many early attempts to implement COP involved programs that served to improve police-citizen interaction and relations, with no real emphasis or expectation that these programs would affect crime.

In recent years, serious practitioners of COP have learned to use the benefits of collaboration with citizens to increase their effectiveness in addressing crime and safety problems. This broader definition of COP includes more than building and maintaining collaborative relationships with members of the community. Fyfe (1997) describes this broader version of COP as a concept of police and citizens working together, in creative ways, to solve crime, safety, and order problems. Still, there is a widely held belief in policing that the strategies of COP simply do not apply to some problems. Many police managers believe that violent crimes and dangerous places require the use of more traditional police "crime-fighting" tactics. Undercover investigations and tactical street enforcement are seen as the primary tools for dealing with these types of problems. Gangs and the problems associated with their presence in a community are often viewed as one of the dangerous situations for which only crime-fighting tactics will work.

Gangs and their violent criminal activities are pervasive problems in most communities. The 1998 National Youth Gang Survey reported that 48% of the jurisdictions (more than 2,600) responding to the survey reported the presence of active gangs in their jurisdiction (Office of Juvenile Justice and Delinquency Prevention, 2000). For cities over 100,000 in population, the rate increases to 93% and is 100% for cities over 250,000. This situation exists despite the widespread establishment of specialized police gang units; the availability of information technology for recording, analyzing, and sharing information; and the presence of considerable research regarding gangs that has been conducted and published in recent years. The good news is that many cities have had some success in dealing with gangs, in reducing the negative impact of gang activities on the community, and in working with gang-involved and at-risk youth. The collaborative approaches endorsed by COP have been applied successfully in some communities to the problem of gangs and violent youth. This chapter will examine how COP strategies and philosophies can be effective in responding to gangs and the problems associated with their presence in the community.

Gangs and the Police

Law enforcement is usually the community's primary response to the presence of gangs. When gangs commit acts of violence and turn neighborhoods into dangerous (or more dangerous) places, the police are expected to act. Suppression of criminal activities committed by gangs is a necessary, important, and appropriate response. However, overreliance on a reactive, punitive approach is both insufficient and counterproductive (see, e.g., Klein, 1995, pp. 159-186). One of the most recent—and tragic—examples of what can happen when an elite, ultra-suppression-oriented special enforcement unit runs amok occurred in the Los Angeles Police Department (LAPD), whose Rampart Division's anti-gang unit (CRASH) has been at the center of multiple investigations that have led to indictments and convictions of police officers for engaging in lawless tactics directed at known or suspected gang members. Referring to the subculture that can exist in such elite special units and the effects of such subcultures, *Los Angeles Times* writer Terry McDermott (2000) observed,[1]

> Cops in these units are, by definition, set apart—even from other police. For most of his career, [Rafael] Perez, the man at the center of the LAPD Rampart scandal, worked in two of these units: gang suppression and undercover narcotics. It is common, particularly among the hardest charging cops in these units, to come to believe they reign over secret domains, that they are governed by codes of behavior of their own devising, liberated from normal life and its bothersome rules. In this shadow world, they can come to feel like royalty, true princes of the city and masters of all they survey. (p. A1)

Even more compelling insight into the dangers of such subcultures can be seen in an excerpt from Perez's own testimony:

> Well, sir, make no bones about it, what we did was wrong—planting evidence . . . fabricating evidence, perjuring ourselves—but our mentality was

us against them. . . . We knew that Rampart's crime rate, murder rate, was the highest in the city. And people come, lieutenants, captains and everybody else would come to our roll calls and say this has to end and you guys are in charge of gangs. Do something about it. That's your responsibility. . . . And the mentality was, it was like a war, us against them, and they didn't play fair, and we went right along with it and didn't play fair. If they ran from us and discarded the narcotics in the gutter, it was no big deal to us. We'll just put dope on you. We know you had it. . . . You run and toss a gun in the gutter or throw it behind a tree and we can't find it, no big deal. We'll get you on our own. . . . They were not going to get away with it. We were going to make sure. (McDermott, 2000, p. A22)

In our view, the community policing approach can help prevent such subcultures from developing, since great emphasis is placed on regular and frequent interaction with the entire community and with the entire law enforcement organization, rather than an approach that leads to the kind of detachment and isolation that characterized the Rampart Division's anti-gang unit. The concept of community policing is antithetical to the view that police are the "crime experts" and should maintain their distance from citizens, whose duty is simply to call the police after a crime occurs.

Three generally accepted strategies have emerged as important components of an effective model for community response to gangs: suppression, intervention, and prevention. Suppression involves active law enforcement attention to investigating gang crime and dealing with the crime, as it occurs, through street enforcement. It also requires that the police properly gather information about the gangs, their members, and their activities. Intervention involves programs and activities designed to encourage and assist gang members in getting out of the gang and avoiding situations that might lead to re-involvement in the gang and gang-related crime. Prevention, of course, involves specific steps to help youths avoid initial involvement in gangs. Longitudinal studies indicate that intervention tactics can be successful in helping youths involved in crime with a gang avoid further criminal activity. The data also show that involvement with drugs, which often begins or increases with gang membership, is a more difficult behavior to change (Battin, Hill, Abbott, Catalano, & Hawkins, 1998). Prevention, therefore, seems to have the greatest potential for avoiding crime, drug use, and gang activity involving young persons and, ultimately, for decreasing the presence of criminal gangs in the community. According to Howell (2000), prevention is also the most cost-effective of all the responses, but effective prevention strategies have been elusive. Without prevention and intervention programs that work, the police and suppression activities have often emerged as the principal "default" method of addressing the gang problem. This one-sided approach is not effective in the long run, but it is the one for which the police often seem best equipped and the one that they are most often eager to embrace.

The Role of the Police

In most communities, law enforcement is the community's primary re-source for dealing with crime and violence. As such, it is often the first re-source that is brought to bear in addressing gang-related crime and vio-lence. The police regularly gather intelligence, conduct investigations, and engage in enforcement activities. These functions are applicable in dealing with gangs and gang crime, provided that the police employ them appro-priately. To do so, the police must do more than conduct "business as usual," treating gangs as simply another routine crime problem with which they must deal. The complex nature of motivations and the antiso-cial norms associated with many gangs and gang members, as well as the variability of gang crime patterns, require the police to tailor their activi-ties to contend with this unique phenomenon. Police need to have an un-derstanding of the issues in the community that influence the formation and maintenance of gangs. They need a method of identifying gang-re-lated problems as they emerge, developing effective strategies of response, acting quickly, and evaluating the effects of their response on the problem. Police personnel need to identify outside influences (such as gang member migration), as well as changing local trends, and adjust their tactics accord-ingly. Most important, the police need to develop accurate, timely infor-mation regarding gang members and gang activities and share that infor-mation with other agencies in the community. Information sharing and collaboration among police, other criminal justice agencies, community service organizations, and citizens can significantly enhance the ability of the police to accomplish their (and the community's) objectives. This infor-mation sharing and collaboration is a key component of COP.

The Problem With Gangs

Persons living in a community where gangs are active do not need to re-view the literature to be convinced that there is a correlation between gangs and crime. The literature, however, has provided empirical evi-dence that underscores the importance of dealing effectively with the problem. Battin et al. (1998) discovered, based on a longitudinal study of 808 youths, that persons who joined a gang were significantly more in-volved in criminal and antisocial activity than were nonmembers. This finding held up even when taking into consideration the effect of having delinquent friends. Gang members were found to be more criminally in-volved than nonmembers—even nonmembers with friends who were in-volved in crime.

Huff (1996), in comparing gang members with youths who were not gang members but had similar risk factors, found that the gang members were likely to exhibit greater involvement in illegal activities, especially violent and major property crimes, than were at-risk youth who were not gang members. Huff's findings also indicate that gang members are more likely to engage in drug crimes and to have access to highly lethal weapons than were nonmembers with similar risk factors. In addition, his analysis of a cohort of early Columbus (Ohio) gang leaders and core members demonstrated that their mortality rate was significantly higher than would be expected for young people, based on any insurance company's actuarial chart. Finally, he observed that a relatively small window of opportunity existed in which to prevent youth from joining a gang or to intervene to redirect a youth away from the gang. His findings revealed that the average gang member began associating with the gang around 13 years of age, joined within 6 months, and committed his first crime approximately 6 months after joining. These findings document the criminogenic nature of gangs and underscore the need for effective responses to gangs in the community. They also reinforce the importance of proactive prevention programs and intervention efforts in addition to reactive, suppression-oriented activities.

The above discussion is not meant to suggest that enforcement and suppression by the police is unimportant. Our experience in Columbus, Ohio (one as a researcher, the other as a police commander), has shown that targeted enforcement actions can have a positive impact on neighborhoods where gangs are active and can serve as a disincentive for gangs to engage in activities that will attract police attention (see also Kelling & Coles, 1996). Indeed, Braga et al. (1999) conclude that focused, community-based enforcement efforts can be effective against crime and violence and will not necessarily cause displacement of the problem to other areas (also see Braga, Kennedy, & Tita, Chapter 17 in this volume). Police action can make a dangerous place safe (or safer) again without creating a new dangerous place. Howell (2000) asserts that targeting serious, violent, and chronic juvenile offenders can reduce gang problems. As Howell also points out, however, the police should not be expected to assume the entire responsibility for gang problems. Suppression and law enforcement should be viewed as important components of a broad-based community approach to dealing with gangs.

Beyond Suppression

In addition to being involved in violence and crime in a community, gangs contribute to disorder and create fear in neighborhoods. Methods for addressing violence, property crime, fear, and disorder are essential for an effective response to gangs. Arresting gang members who commit crime is but one of many possible tactics for minimizing the effect of gangs on the neighborhood. If arrest and "aggressive" policing tactics are implemented in an overzealous manner and are not part of a balanced, integrated community approach, the problem may, in fact, worsen due to the oppositional nature of gang dynamics, "martyrdom" of gang leaders, and other factors that serve only to reinforce gang presence and status in the community.

In the Kennedy School of Government/National Research Council report, *Violence in America* (1994), conclusions from a major conference on urban violence are cited as supporting community policing as a high priority to address violent crime for four reasons. First, COP addresses the problems that underlie violent incidents. Second, COP encourages the police to take into account the interests and concerns of the community in deciding on anticrime priorities and strategies. Third, arrests should be viewed as only one approach in dealing with crime problems. Finally, COP makes the community a valuable partner with the police in preventing and responding to violence and other crimes.

Braga et al. (1999) found that using problem-oriented tactics that are focused on places where violent crime occurs can reduce crime and disorder. In addition to arrests, effective problem-oriented techniques include clean-up and order maintenance; increased lighting; housing code enforcement; signage; parking enforcement; graffiti removal; video surveillance; public education; and others. McGarrell, Giacomazzi, and Thurman (1997) examined the related concepts of victimization, disorder, community concern, and fear of crime. The findings of that study support the collaborative nature of COP, concluding that the responsiveness of city hall, the police, and neighborhood associations have a significant positive influence on reducing fear in neighborhoods.

Among other activities, many gangs commit violent crimes and threaten the peace of neighborhoods, creating disorder and fear (see, e.g., Skogan, 1990, for a detailed discussion of that subject). When the police use a community-oriented approach in dealing with gangs, their strategies become collaborative, information driven, problem oriented, and correlated with the concerns of citizens. These improvements enhance the ability of the police to address problems brought on by gangs in the community.

Assumptions

The challenge of applying the tenets of COP in developing a police response to gangs is not really a matter of identifying particular strategies or tactics, but rather one of understanding and integrating the underlying philosophy into the police functions of investigation, enforcement, and intelligence work. The application of COP will also introduce additional functions for the police to perform. The following assumptions were developed by the Columbus (OH) Division of Police as a foundation for its plan to apply COP to gang and street crime problems (based on Shafer, 1999, pp. 4-5):

Assumption #1 (COP vs. Traditional Policing)

Traditional policing activities and community policing objectives are not mutually exclusive. Law enforcement agencies must simultaneously deal with the concepts of public safety and public perceptions. Public safety involves the traditional concepts of protecting life and property, preventing crime, apprehending criminals, regulating traffic, and maintaining order. Public perceptions relate to the citizens' concerns regarding quality of life, fear of crime, and their opinion of the agency.

Assumption #2 (The Role of the Police)

Relying solely upon traditional enforcement responses to crime is insufficient and ineffective. It is also unrealistic for the police to attempt to solve all of society's problems. Police agencies must focus their efforts on the tasks for which they are best equipped. Generally, investigation, enforcement, and crime prevention are the functions used by law enforcement to deal with public safety. These efforts, however, must reflect the concerns and needs of the citizens whom the agency is obligated to serve and protect. The broad law enforcement mission involves three distinct categories of activities:

- Conventional law enforcement duties and responsibilities
- Police responses specific to community problems and needs
- Police input and support for community based programs to address [other] needs

Assumption #3 (The Relationship Between the Police and the Public)

Traditionally, law enforcement has maintained a somewhat *independent* relationship with the citizens. The police generally decide what crime problems are important and what to do about them. Some views of community policing would have police involved in a *dependent* relationship with the public where the police agency would be responsible for solving almost every community problem. From our perspective, the ideal is for the police and the public to be *interdependent,* where each understands the other's needs and concerns. The police, consistent with their mission, listen to and respond to the concerns of the citizens, and the community understands what the police mission is and the constraints under which the police operate. Building this type of relationship between officers and citizens involves an ongoing process of changing attitudes and developing skills, *especially within the police agency.*

Assumption #4 (Enhancing the Effectiveness of Special Tactics Units)

The police have traditionally relied upon a number of specialized units to address drug, gang, and other street crime problems. As problems change and new concerns emerge, police need the flexibility to adapt tactics to the needs at hand. These specialized operations can be improved by increasing their awareness of the specific concerns of the public and by using a problem-oriented approach to address these problems.

Assumption #5 (Emphasis on Gangs, Youth, and Violent Crime)

With respect to crime, the public, criminal justice professionals, and the media continue to express concerns that focus heavily on gangs, juvenile criminals, and violent crime. The persons who belong to gangs and commit violent street crimes also create fear and concern in communities. Police responses to community concerns and to street-level criminal activity are interrelated. The most effective approach to these problems will be a broad-based effort, capable of focusing on all aspects of the street crime problem rather than a number of specialized programs, each independently focused and operated. Focusing on gangs and related youth violence problems is a critical part of responding to street-level crime and community safety. Suppression alone will not adequately address the complex problems of juvenile crime and gangs. The police must work cooperatively with the entire community to provide the components of prevention, intervention, and suppression in order to respond to youth at risk and those involved in criminal activity and gangs.

Application

The above assumptions serve as conceptual guidelines for applying COP to problems associated with gangs. Practical application of the assumptions will require the police to tailor the traditional functions of investigation, enforcement, and intelligence work to be effective in addressing gang-related crime. Investigative activities must include not only those specifically targeting gang-motivated crime but also habitual and violent offenders who may be associated with the gangs. Investigative efforts, to be successful, will require collaboration among the police, federal law enforcement agencies, prosecutors, probation and parole authorities, and corrections. Intelligence activities need to be guided by well-established policies designed to ensure the accuracy of the information contained in police files. Huff and McBride (1993) identify the need for a comprehensive police gang database that includes intelligence on gangs' organizational structures, rituals, leadership, and cultural beliefs. Huff (1990) also points out the importance of avoiding overlabeling and prematurely classifying individuals as gang members.

Utilizing a COP approach to gangs will also require the police to engage in community liaison and crime prevention activities. The community liaison function involves building relationships with community groups and other citizens to help identify problems and exchange information. It will require officers to serve as conduits of citizen concerns to appropriate organizational components within the police agency, especially to specialized gang and anti-street crime units. Community liaison activities also include referral of non-law enforcement problems to other agencies in the community for resolution. Crime prevention activities are aimed at proactive prevention through public education, neighborhood improvement, and other strategies aimed at eliminating the opportunity for criminal acts to occur.

Collaboration and information sharing is an integral component of COP. One way to facilitate those processes effectively, as they relate to dealing with gangs, is a task force or coordinating committee. Although these groups sometimes consist of only law enforcement and criminal justice members, we strongly recommend that they include representatives from neighborhoods, schools, community service organizations, and other stakeholders. The committees meet to enhance the capabilities of all member agencies and citizens in addressing gang-related problems. Coordinating committees can improve the community's awareness of gangs and their activities by developing appropriate training and improving the gathering and use of gang intelligence. They can increase the exchange of information among member agencies. This function is especially crucial when various police units or departments are investigating different crimes (homicides, robberies, narcotics) that involve gang members. Investigators often focus only on solving the individual crime without paying attention to potential links to gangs. Much valuable information is lost if efforts are not made to foster discussion of cases and the exchange of pertinent information. Committees or task forces serve to enhance enforcement and investigative capabilities by breaking down organizational barriers, sharing strategies, and pooling resources. Such groups can also work to ensure that intervention, prevention, and treatment options exist in the community, rather than overreliance on suppression.

COP improves community awareness and involvement while also enhancing the suppression of gang related criminal activities, the investigation and prosecution of gang members for crimes committed, and the recording of accurate, timely information about gang activities. It also permits law enforcement to respond to citizen concerns regarding disorder and fear that may not be possible if only traditional law enforcement strategies are used. COP also increases the exchange of information among the police, other criminal justice agencies, and the public.

The Police and the Community: Making it Work

Several things need to happen if the police-community partnership is to work effectively. First, *the police need to enlist community support*. Asking citizens to support police efforts involves the police reaching out to engage community groups and neighborhood representatives in a discussion of the problem. This process should include a community/police education component, providing information that will help both citizens and the police understand the problem and what each can and cannot do in response to it. The police should offer suggestions regarding what citizens can do (and shouldn't do) to help the police and the community deal more effectively with gangs. The concerns and needs of the citizens should be an important part of the discussions, helping the police to understand citizen perceptions, fears, and priorities.

The next step in applying COP involves *a shift in police focus from individual gangs and crimes to neighborhoods.* Traditional police approaches usually involve investigative and enforcement pursuits of a particular gang and its members. Shifting the focus to neighborhoods expands the scope of police actions to include the disorder, fear, and declining quality of life that often result from (and help sustain) the presence of the gangs. This is a more holistic and problem-oriented approach. McGarrell et al. (1997) point out that community policing strategies have often been applied in some of the more organized neighborhoods, which usually are more homogeneous and have fewer crime problems. Poorer, more disorganized, crime-ridden, inner-city neighborhoods have been less amenable to COP efforts but are often those that are affected most severely by gangs. It is these neighborhoods that most need comprehensive police-community collaboration to address gang-related crime.

The third shift necessary for the police to apply COP with respect to gang-related crime is *recognition of the importance of strategies and tactics beyond what the police can provide.* The police must begin to see themselves as *part* of the solution rather than *the* solution. This understanding will produce new roles for the police. First, police officers assigned to gang details should be engaged in frequent conversations with gang members apart from arrest situations and investigative pursuits. Officers have the potential to assist youth in avoiding or disconnecting from gang involvement. Next, police officers can play an important role in supporting prevention and intervention programs in the community. Officers can provide support to schools, faith-based institutions, civic organizations, and others attempting to provide programming. This support can be in the form of supplying information regarding gangs, in identifying persons or neighborhoods in need of services, or in actual involvement in program service delivery. The National Crime Prevention Council (1994), in its bulletin, *Partnerships to Prevent Youth Violence,* identified four steps in partnering between law enforcement and others in the community to prevent youth violence. These steps apply to anti-gang programming as well. The steps are: (a) learning what the problems really are; (b) selecting strategies that will work; (c) enlisting others in the effort; and (d) involving young people in developing solutions. The insights, contacts, and information available from the police can be of invaluable assistance at each of these steps.

Success in applying COP to gang problems is not simply a matter of the police talking with the community. It should not be a situation where the police independently perform certain functions (enforcement and investigation) while others in the community independently perform other tasks (prevention and intervention). Instead, it involves an *integrated, collaborative* approach to providing all the important components of an effective community anti-gang strategy.

Programs That Work

Theory and research support the hypothesis that COP can be effective in addressing gangs and the problems associated with their presence. It is important to note some examples of successful application of this approach.

Dallas, Texas

In Dallas, police identified five areas of the city where seven of the most violent gangs were present. Police tactics included saturation patrols, along with aggressive truancy and curfew enforcement. What made this situation unique is that the police gang unit officers teamed with the community policing officers, and worked closely with school districts in carrying out their activities. This collaborative approach resulted in a 57% decline in gang-related violence in the targeted neighborhoods, compared to a 37% decrease in these crimes in control areas (Howell, 2000).

Chicago, Illinois

To address gang and drug offenses in multiple-unit housing communities, the City of Chicago implemented a program that involved collaboration between the police and other city agencies in a problem-oriented approach. Community policing teams, utilizing crime statistics and information from the community, teamed up with prosecutors and city inspectors to identify housing units where gang activity was occurring. Police officers worked with inspectors to visit and evaluate building sites. The teams looked for criminal or code violations, nuisance problems, gang graffiti, litter, and property damage to assess each location. Where significant problems were found, landlords were notified, were required to attend training, and in some cases faced civil sanctions. The result was a significant reduction in target offenses. During the study period, gang narcotics offenses declined 88% at the targeted locations (–32% in control areas); criminal damage to property decreased 20% (control = –2%); violent index crimes dropped 11% (control = +1%); and property index crimes declined 13% (control = +5%) (Higgins & Coldren, 2000).

Redlands, California

In Redlands, police began Risk-Focused Policing, a community-oriented policing program that targeted at-risk youth and their families. Police officers worked with school officials to measure community, family, school, and peer group risk factors. Police, housing, and recreation services were consolidated and focused on reducing risk factors for substance abuse, delinquency, and violence. Major crime in the community reportedly dropped 36% over 3 years ("Criminal Justice Innovations," 2000).

Columbus, Ohio

After several years of responding to gang violence primarily through a specialized gang detail, the Columbus Division of Police decided to take a more community-oriented approach to gang and other street crime. The police created the Strategic Response Bureau, where community liaison officers (CLOs) were teamed with investigators and enforcement personnel. CLOs work with neighborhoods to identify problems that are then passed on to investigators and street-crime officers. The Bureau's personnel are primarily assigned by geographic area so that teams can collaborate on neighborhood specific problems. Emphasis is placed on accurate, timely gang intelligence and on targeting habitual offenders. Working with federal law enforcement agencies, and with local and federal prosecutors, the Bureau recently successfully targeted those violent street gangs that were responsible for more than 25 gang-related homicides and numerous other violent crimes. Arrests and successful prosecutions have significantly reduced gang-related crime. These actions have also improved the quality of life in the neighborhoods, reduced fear, and established partnerships that continue to benefit the groups involved.

Tradeoffs

For all of the potential gain that COP offers in dealing with gangs, there are also some tradeoffs when comparing COP with traditional approaches, and these must be evaluated. These tradeoffs include human resource requirements, difficulty of task, sustaining community involvement, dealing with denial, and the need for consensus.

Human Resource Requirements

Additional roles for the police result when they decide to involve the community and others as partners in dealing with gangs and other crime problems. These new roles include community liaison duties and crime prevention activities. Others may include liaison functions with prosecutors, other city agencies, federal law enforcement groups, and as task force members. With limited human resources and the need to sustain previously established police units and functions, COP may require hiring new personnel, redeploying officers, and/or redirecting officers' time to accomplish the additional duties required. Effectively utilizing COP may be more "personnel intensive" than are traditional suppression strategies.

Difficulty of Task

The traditional police activities of investigation, enforcement, and intelligence gathering are fairly well established in most police departments. Taking a COP approach to gangs not only requires modifying some of these functions, but also necessitates improving intelligence capacities and sharing of previously guarded information. These changes, especially sharing of intelligence information, may be difficult for many police agencies. Finding alternatives to making arrests and taking enforcement actions to solve neighborhood problems can also prove challenging, given the organizational cultures that have been established in most law enforcement agencies. Innovative, effective problem-solving tactics are often difficult to conceive and apply, whereas making arrests and issuing summonses are routine activities, produce easily quantified results, and usually please superiors. Using COP approaches to gang problems complicates the task of the police and requires the development of new procedures, new skills, and new relationships.

Sustaining Community Involvement

Citizens in neighborhoods with gang problems are often ready and willing to work with the police to address their concerns. This new collaboration often produces positive results. Once the immediate problems are solved, however, citizens may no longer perceive the need to keep talking to and working with the police. For the police to maintain these relationships, they must identify methods to keep citizens involved, even when crime and gang activity in the neighborhood are no longer critical concerns.

Dealing With Denial

For the police to collaborate with other agencies in the community, those agencies must be willing to engage in the partnership. Schools and other stakeholders are often unwilling to formally acknowledge the presence of gangs and the reality of their activities. Before these groups can be working partners in dealing with gang problems, they must overcome denial of the problem and be willing to take steps to address it. Denial often results from fear that school officials or others will be blamed for the problem, from uncertainty about how to respond to it, or from concern over public image if the problem is acknowledged (see, e.g., Huff & Trump, 1996; Trump, Chapter 8 in this volume). With traditional police approaches the police would simply do what they felt needed to be done without concern for these other groups. To utilize COP effectively, however, the police need the other groups' involvement in the solutions, and must, therefore, deal with denial and help them overcome it to be successful. One approach that can help in overcoming denial is the formation of the above-recommended task force. A task force can *collectively and simultaneously* take responsibility for acknowledging gang-related crime and for coordinating a response, thus redirecting much of the community's focus (and blame) away from the schools, the police, or other individual entities, underscoring that this is a *community* problem that will require a community solution.

Need for Consensus

With traditional police strategies, the police decide upon both the problems and the solutions. Their actions are unilateral and independent of others. Decisions regarding strategy and tactics are made by police managers and carried out by line officers. For the police to apply COP, they must collaborate with other groups, some of which may have interests that are competing with those of the police. School officials may be concerned about their careers and their school's image in the community and may not want police officers taking actions at school. Community groups may have their own opinions about *which* crimes and *which* areas the police should prioritize. Other government agencies (code enforcement, licensing, etc.) may have different goals that do not coincide with the police emphasis on suppression. The police suddenly find themselves in the roles of negotiators and consensus builders. These new roles require new skills. Equally important, consensus building requires more time, thus slowing down responsive actions. The police are accustomed to reacting quickly. The need for consensus building may be the most difficult tradeoff for the police to make.

Conclusion

Empirical research has indicated that COP strategies can be effective in responding to violent crime and in addressing related issues, such as dangerous places, neighborhood disorder, and fear of crime. These problems are often associated with the presence of gangs in the community. Many police agencies are now applying the tenets of COP to increase their effectiveness in addressing gang-related crime and related problems. However, although the research findings and anecdotal evidence are promising, most law enforcement agencies have not made the organizational changes necessary to implement the COP model. When the police shift from traditional, suppression-only tactics to COP and a community-based problem-solving approach, they must develop new skills and approaches to police work and make decisions regarding tradeoffs between COP and the old methods. The police must begin to see themselves as a *part* of the solution to gang problems, rather than *the* solution. They must recognize the importance of prevention and intervention and must support efforts to provide that programming. Police organizations must become partners and team members with citizen groups, schools, and other government agencies. Applying COP in response to gangs changes in fundamental ways the manner in which police work and the ways in which they relate to the community. Most important, it improves their potential for long-term success in dealing with gangs and gang related crime and in helping build healthy, functional communities with low levels of crime and fear—communities in which children can be nurtured, socialized, and educated to be responsible and productive citizens who will ultimately contribute to the stability of their communities.

Note

1. Excerpts from "Perez's Bitter Saga of Lies, Regret, and Harm" by Terry McDermott courtesy of the *Los Angeles Times*. © 2000, *Los Angeles Times*. Used with permission.

10

Issues in Developing and Maintaining a Regional Gang Incident Tracking System

JAMES W. MEEKER
BRYAN VILA

During the 1990s, gangs began to gain a foothold in many suburban and rural areas (Klein, 1995). As a result, communities that previously had considered themselves insulated from inner-city problems were forced to acknowledge that they too could be vulnerable to gang violence (Curry, Ball, & Fox, 1994; Spergel & Curry, 1995). In suburban areas, gang-related problems created a jurisdictional nightmare because of the jigsaw nature of municipal boundaries—and because street gangs tended to ignore abstract political boundaries. Thus, even a small gang's home turf might extend into two or three contiguous suburban cities, and the gang's criminal activities might reach into many other jurisdictions. This meant that many different agencies had to cooperate in order to track or respond to street gang

AUTHORS' NOTE: Portions of the project reported here were supported by grants from NIJ (96-IJ-CS-0030, 98-IJ-CX-0072); COPS (96 CNSX 0019); University of California, Irvine; California Governor's Office; Orange County, California; and the Pacific Mutual Foundation. The authors wish to acknowledge the vital contributions of UC Irvine Focused Research Group on Orange County Street Gangs; research associates Thomas E. Fossati, Ph.D.; Jodi Lane, Ph.D.; Katie J. B. Parsons, Ph.D.; Douglas Wiebe, Ph.D.; and Darcy Purvis, as well as the support of the members of the Orange County Chiefs' and Sheriff's Association; the Juvenile Justice and Gang Strategy Steering Committee and its chair, Chief Paul Walters of Santa Ana, and past chair, Chief James Cook of Westminster; Ms. Marilyn MacDougall and the "Project No Gangs" staff; and David Hartl, Ph.D.

crime. But cooperation on this scale was difficult because of mistrust, conflicting goals, and lack of standardization. This chapter explores the strengths and weaknesses of a unique effort by all 23 law enforcement agencies in a large suburban region that cooperated with university researchers to track gang crime.

Historical Overview of Cross-Jurisdictional Problems

Historically, the gross decentralization of police among literally thousands of towns, cities, counties, states, Indian nations, and federal jurisdictions within the United States has made interagency cooperation a thorny problem for more than 150 years. As Vila and Morris (1999) detail in their documentary history, *The Role of Police in American Society*, the inability of conventional law enforcement agencies to deal with cross-jurisdictional problems led first to the establishment of private police, such as the Pinkertons, about the same time modern policing was first being adopted in the United States. Beginning in 1855, the Pinkertons and others were used to combat crimes such as thefts from railroads or the interstate depredations of desperados like Jesse James or Butch Cassidy and the Sundance Kid—sometimes on their own and at other times with the help of local authorities.

However, by the early 20th century public law enforcement agencies were forced to begin finding ways to cooperate when improved transportation and communication technologies increased the ease with which cross-jurisdictional crimes could be committed and their perpetrators could flee. Many European countries responded to these challenges by consolidating police powers at the national level. But calls for a strong national police agency in the United States (e.g., Vollmer, 1936/1969) ran counter to Americans' traditional distrust of national government. Instead, there was a concerted effort in the United States to nurture informal links between agencies. One of the primary mechanisms for accomplishing this was the national training school for police (later the National Police Academy) that the FBI established in 1935 with strong backing from the International Association of Chiefs of Police (IACP). In addition to providing sorely needed training for promising officers from around the country, the Academy-inspired camaraderie gave each graduate a network of personal contacts upon whom he or she could call for help (Hoover, 1937, pp. 9-10). Today, despite their inefficiencies, informal interagency arrangements such as those spawned by the FBI and the IACP continue to be the dominant mode for managing cross-jurisdictional law enforcement problems in the United States.

Orange County Gang Incident Tracking System (GITS)

Located 40 miles south of Los Angeles, Orange County is a highly hetero-geneous suburban county with 2.7 million people living in 31 cities and unincorporated areas. Twenty-two independent municipal police depart-ments and the county sheriff's office provide most of the local law enforce-ment. These agencies have a formal organization, the Orange County Chiefs' and Sheriff's Association (OCCSA), that is composed of the chief executive officer of each law enforcement agency. Consequently, when the need arose the county already had a formal cooperative organization of law enforcement policymakers that could propose and support a collabo-rative gang data collection and sharing effort. In response to increasing public concern about rising gang crime in nearby Los Angeles, the OCCSA established a Gang Strategy Steering Committee (GSSC) in 1992. This com-mittee created a Gang Incident Tracking System (GITS) to document the extent of gang-related crime in the county, establish a baseline against which to identify future trends in gang-related crime, determine regional variation in gang-related crime patterns, and provide information for stra-tegic planning and evaluation purposes (for a detailed history, see Vila & Meeker, 1997, 1999; Meeker, Vila, & Parsons, in press).

The GSSC set up a working group to design the database and grapple with problems such as different, and often incompatible, report forms and records management systems as well as the fact that few departments col-lected gang data in a systematic manner. Their solution to these problems was to develop a standardized form that each law enforcement agency would use to report gang incidents in their jurisdiction.

Although OCCSA laid the foundation for interagency cooperation and data collection, it lacked the analytical resources and expertise to evaluate and monitor fully the effectiveness of GITS. In addition, OCCSA's mem-bers were concerned about claims by ethnic minority activists that police data on gang crime and trends were invalid. They believed that involving independent university researchers in the data collection, reporting, and analysis would improve public confidence in the conclusions they drew about gang crime in the region.

Early in 1995, OCCSA asked the University of California, Irvine (UCI) to enter into a long-term partnership to enhance their ability to analyze gang incident data. UCI responded by establishing a Focused Research Group (FRG) on Orange County Street Gangs within the School of Social Ecol-ogy's Department of Criminology, Law and Society. In keeping with the School's tradition of using innovative research techniques to tackle impor-tant community problems in a holistic fashion, the FRG's mission was to work with OCCSA and the GSSC to resolve a number of previously intrac-table questions about gangs, gang crime, and their effects on the community and help them develop strategies to prevent and control illegal gang activity.

GITS became operative January 1, 1993, when county law enforcement agencies began reporting all gang-related incidents, based on police reports, to a centralized database run by the Sheriff's office. By the summer of 1995, UCI's FRG had taken over the centralized data collection, and had begun evaluating the reliability and validity of the data being collected, and enhancing the database itself. The foundation for this partnership was a Memorandum of Understanding between OCCSA's members and UCI.

Memorandum of Understanding (MOU)

A cross-jurisdictional database depends upon the full and consistent cooperation of all participating agencies. Before data can be shared effectively, all parties must agree on their roles and responsibilities, the database's goals, how data will be collected, and how they will be used and distributed (see Etten & Petrone, 1994; Medaris, Campbell, & James, 1997; Slayton, 2000). The following MOU was developed by the UCI Focused Research Group and OCCSA. It went into effect in May 1995:

I. Purpose:

The purpose of this Memorandum of Understanding (MOU) is to describe the mutual goals and responsibilities with regard to the Orange County Gang Incident Tracking Systems (GITS) of the Orange County Chiefs' and Sheriff's Association (OCCSA) and The Regents of the University of California, on behalf of its Irvine Campus (UNIVERSITY).

II. Background:

The Gang Incident Tracking System is a management research tool developed by OCCSA over the past two years to identify the extent of gang activity in the county and facilitate strategic planning and resource allocation by:

1. Establishing a centralized database into which all Orange County law enforcement agencies report gang-related activities;
2. Accurately identifying the extent of gang crime in Orange County by identifying gangs that operate within the county, their membership, and crime related to their activities;[1]
3. Establishing a baseline against which to compare future gang crime; and
4. Identifying gang-related crime patterns and trends.

Since December 1993, law enforcement agencies in all Orange County law enforcement jurisdictions have reported on gang-related crimes in their respective areas. Their combined jurisdictions include all areas in the county except those under federal government control. Extensive efforts have been undertaken to establish procedures for consistent reporting. Validity issues have been addressed by administrative, training, and audit procedures.

III. Mutual Goals:

Both the OCCSA and the UNIVERSITY desire to enter into a cooperative partnership in order to assure the continuation of GITS, enhance its reliability and validity, and improve its utility as a management and research tool. Although the foci of OCCSA and UNIVERSITY differ, both desire to reduce substantially the negative impact of street gangs on the quality of life in Orange County. In furtherance of these goals, both parties agree to make every reasonable effort to fulfill the responsibilities outlined below in section IV.

IV. Parties' Roles and Responsibilities:

OCCSA will:

1. Identify key representatives of participating law enforcement agencies and make them accessible to UNIVERSITY researchers;
2. Collect and input gang incident data;
3. Provide UNIVERSITY researchers with timely access to original individual agency report sheets, monthly reports of raw data, and monthly data reports;
4. Assist UNIVERSITY research efforts to evaluate the validity and reliability of GITS data collection and reporting;
5. Consider UNIVERSITY recommendations regarding the improvement of GITS data collection and reporting;
6. Process security clearance for anyone accessing GITS data to ensure that state-mandated requirements are met;
7. Maintain security of data and sole authority for release of original GITS data;
8. Duplicate and distribute all data reports and secondary analyses provided by the UNIVERSITY;
9. Support the publication of scholarly research by UNIVERSITY researchers based on Orange County-wide analysis of GITS data—agency specific research and reporting only will be conducted at the request of, and with the written authorization of, the agency head; and
10. Actively participate in identifying and acquiring potential grants, funding sources, or other resources to benefit the OCCSA and UNIVERSITY partnership.

UNIVERSITY will:

1. Designate a Professor from the Department of Criminology, Law & Society to serve as lead researcher and GITS facilitator;
2. Provide computer hardware and software to enable UNIVERSITY researchers to analyze GITS data in a manner that is empirically appropriate and meets the needs of OCCSA;

3. Analyze GITS data and provide OCCSA with assistance in preparing quarterly, semi-annual, and annual county-wide reports of regional and individual agency data, if authorized;

4. Advise OCCSA on the interpretation, analysis, and policy implications of GITS data;

5. Upon mutual agreement, develop the utility of GITS data by, for example, acquiring and applying geographical information system (GIS) analysis capabilities;

6. Make every effort consistent with accepted standards of scholarly and academic conduct to be sensitive to the practical and political vulnerabilities of OCCSA and further the goals stated above in section III;

7. Participate with OCCSA in release of GITS data analyses to the public; and

8. Actively participate in identifying and acquiring potential grants, funding sources or other resources to benefit the OCCSA and UNIVERSITY partnership.

9. The University representatives shall adhere to the applicable institutional policies and procedures throughout their participation in the OCCSA and UNIVERSITY partnership.

V. Voluntary Disassociation:

This MOU is a nonbinding agreement that both parties have entered into in good faith. Either party may disassociate from the effort without penalty or liability by so notifying the other in writing. Written notice shall be sent sixty (60) days prior to the disassociation.

VI. Term and Amendment:

This Memorandum shall be in effect for the period of one year beginning May 1, 1995. Both parties reserve the right to renegotiate this Memorandum upon the mutual consent of the other party. At the conclusion of the one-year period, this Memorandum may be extended by common written consent of both parties. This Memorandum represents the entire understanding of both parties with respect to this partnership. Any modification of this Memorandum must be in writing and signed by the parties.

Although the MOU helped stabilize the relationship among agencies participating in GITS, there still were problems associated with conflicting goals.

Conflicting Goals

Despite the MOU, there was conflict over control of project data almost from the start. Although many issues related to data control were resolved amicably, others continued as sources of friction throughout the project. Part of this conflict arose from dissimilarities between law enforcement and university organizations. But many problems also arose from conflicts between the demands of a cooperative, regional data-sharing effort and the traditional reluctance of law enforcement agencies to share data—even among themselves.

Many of the law enforcement agencies were concerned that gang crime data could damage their communities' public image. Some feared that summary tallies of gang crime statistics by jurisdiction or publication of incident maps would make it possible to compare levels of gang crime between cities and neighborhoods, and that such comparisons would harm tourism, real estate values, and retail business in their cities. Alternatively, many other chiefs, even in jurisdictions with substantial gang crime, argued that the only effective way to deal with public concerns about this serious problem was to be open about the extent of gang crime. They took the position that every available analytical tool should be used to understand the causes of gang crime and that making those analyses public would increase confidence that every effort was being made to combat gang crime.

To solve this problem the MOU adopted sections 7 and 9 under the OCCSA provisions of Part IV. Although this allowed each law enforcement agency latitude in how gang data for their jurisdiction were disseminated, it created difficulties within the University. Representatives of UCI's contracts and grants office at first refused to sign the MOU because it violated the campus policy that researchers have exclusive control over data generated by their research. The University took the position that in order to protect the interests of the researcher and to preserve the integrity of the research project, the campus policy requiring researcher control of the data should be written into the MOU. Some chiefs would not accept this position; others felt it would require an independent review by their city attorney. The prospect of having attorneys for 23 different organizations agree about the MOU threatened the entire cooperative effort. Eventually, faculty researchers succeeded in getting the University to relent by arguing that University protection was unnecessary because they were free to withdraw from the project if at any time they were concerned about the validity of the project or control of the data. In addition, they argued that section 9 specifically supported the publication of scholarly research generated by the cooperative effort.

To date, fears about inappropriate jurisdictional comparisons have not been realized. However, the inability to be more open with GITS data has diminished the utility of the database somewhat. For example, on one occasion two jurisdictions whose boundaries resemble a complex jigsaw puzzle refused to share data with one another. This problem surfaced during an election-year political controversy regarding police services. Eventually the conflict ended, the data were shared, and researchers were able to develop an accurate picture of gang crime in the disputed areas.

Differences in management style among the chiefs also limit the tactical utility of GITS data. Some chiefs allow their gang officers complete access to GITS data, and others guard the information closely. As a consequence, many officers and gang units don't use the database because of the bureaucratic delays and inefficiencies involved in seeking permission.

Another issue that created misunderstandings and potential collaborative barriers had to do with standards for ethical research. University researchers had to meet the strict requirements of human subjects research regulations. Because GITS research was based primarily on crime incident data, which is considered public data under California's Public Records Act (CPRA, Government Code §§ 6250-6270; see Meeker, 1999) the project initially was granted exempt status. However, when the collaboration between UCI and local law enforcement agencies was publicized in the media after being awarded a substantial grant from the U.S. Department of Justice's Office of Community-Oriented Policing Services (COPS), a community activist group objected to the project. Based on a misunderstanding about the project, the activists alleged that UCI researchers were assisting police with the exploitation of ethnic and racial minorities by analyzing data used to support illegal suppression activities—and by increasing the credibility of those activities. In a nutshell, the activists claimed that police were identifying young people as gang members simply because of their ethnicity or the way they dressed. As a result of complaint letters sent to the chancellor of UCI and the U.S. Attorney General, the project's exempt status was revoked, and it was subjected to an exhaustive human subjects review by UCI's Institutional Review Board (IRB).

The researchers eventually were able to convince the IRB that the crime incident data did not violate human subjects regulations because our data validation protocol involved training and testing police clerical staff that filled out data forms, and riding along with police to observe how accurately they applied gang definitions when filling out police reports. Unfortunately, additional human subjects issues were raised by the review—only this time they centered on the rights of police employees. The IRB was convinced that clerical staff and police officers had to meet informed consent guidelines before they could be evaluated. Their rationale was that researchers' evaluations of clerical staff and officers potentially could have a negative impact on their job performance ratings. The chiefs found the idea of obtaining informed consent from their staff before observing how well they performed their duties completely unacceptable. It took several months and several rewrites of the research protocol before the IRB was satisfied that the research project would not violate the rights of police employees.

A final example of goal conflict arose when expectations for the project evolved over time until they no longer reflected the original project goals. Originally, the GSSC developed the GITS database to provide *strategic* information that would enable law enforcement managers to plan and implement gang prevention, intervention, and suppression efforts more effectively. It did not seem possible to develop GITS as a *tactical* asset at that time because it could take months for a gang-related incident to find its way into GITS.[2] This delay has continued throughout the course of the project (see Meeker, Vila, & Parsons, in press; Vila & Meeker, 1999). The time delay issue, coupled with MOU provisions restricting any agency from accessing another's data directly, has prevented any tactical use of the database. Nonetheless, over time some members of OCCSA have come to see the lack of tactical utility as a major shortcoming of the project.

The only way to avoid these conflicts—or at least to limit their negative effects when they do occur—is to assure that all parties to the partnership communicate frequently and that their representatives have the power to make decisions (see Slayton, 2000). The success that GITS has enjoyed since 1993 is largely due to the active role played by the GSSC and its leaders. GITS faculty researchers have become active members of the GSSC, which meets on a monthly basis. They also make frequent presentations to the OCCSA and communicate regularly with law enforcement executives.

Alternative Models

There are at least two different ways to develop a shared interagency database like the Gang Incident Tracking System—top-down or bottom-up. The top-down approach begins with a cooperative agreement among the heads of the various law enforcement agencies. An alternative is to work from the bottom up, based on cooperative data sharing by the people in each law enforcement agency who are actually managing and/or analyzing the data. Such sharing arrangements often involve crime analysts, gang officers, or members of some other specialized detail. Both models have strengths as well as weaknesses. GITS was developed using the top-down approach, and the well-regarded Regional Crime Analysis System in the Baltimore area provides an illustrative example of the bottom-up approach.

When GITS was created, OCCSA already had a long history of interagency cooperation, and its regular meetings provided a forum for the heads of the different agencies to discuss shared interests. When OCCSA created GITS as a strategic tool to measure the level of gang crime in the county and to trace its variation over time, all members agreed that GITS would be a high priority.

Absent the clout of OCCSA, it is doubtful that all of the law enforcement agencies in Orange County would have agreed to cooperate to create a shared database. OCCSA's backing also helped GITS persist because peer pressure could be used to encourage cooperation from chiefs who otherwise might not have participated or whose interest in the project waned. Because most of the 23 departments used unique reporting forms and had idiosyncratic records management systems, GITS had to rely on their willingness to fill out standardized gang incident reporting forms and submit them each month. Only the police chiefs had the power to make this happen.

An additional benefit of the top-down approach was that OCCSA could speak on behalf of all law enforcement in the county. This gave greater clout when it came to lobbying for external funding or asking UCI to provide researcher support. In turn, using UCI to collect and analyze the data gave the database additional credibility and provided the departments with access to more sophisticated analytical capabilities. This was particularly important in the application of geographic information systems (GIS) technology. At the beginning of the project none of the departments had this advanced capability and even today, there is wide variation in their ability to use GIS.

However, the GITS example also shows some of the drawbacks of the top-down approach to developing cooperative interagency projects. Originally, GITS was supposed to be a strategic tool that would provide a countywide summary of gang crime. This reflected the concerns of police chiefs in the early 1990s about the lack of systematic and valid countywide data on gang crime. In practice, differences in management style, organizational priorities, and political environments have resulted in variation in how well various departments keep up their reporting responsibilities. So far, this has meant that only two full GITS reports can be issued each year. Although this has been sufficient to meet the original strategic goal, it has severely limited GITS's tactical utility. In turn, low tactical use means that the street cops who generate original GITS data have little stake in the database because they don't have direct access to timely GITS data. Although this doesn't appear to have weakened the validity and completeness of GITS data, it certainly has the potential to do so.

The Regional Crime Analysis System (RCAS) that was established in the Baltimore-Washington area is a good example of a bottom-up approach to developing an interagency crime-mapping program. According to a presentation made at the Second Annual Crime Mapping Research Conference sponsored by the National Institute of Justice's Crime Mapping Research Center in December 1998, the RCAS was started by crime analysts in contiguous jurisdictions that were trying to improve their ability to recognize and respond to evolving crime patterns. This cooperative effort involves fewer than 10 departments whose analysts share and update geocoded crime data that are formatted according to standards specified by an oversight committee. Although RCAS operates with the permission of the participating agencies' chiefs, it is designed and run by analysts. As a consequence, RCAS provides access to the kind of timely tactical data required to track crimes across jurisdictions.

Despite its advantages, the bottom-up approach also has several drawbacks. One is that the focus on tactical concerns may limit its strategic value. In addition, many of the agencies in the geographic area are unable to participate because they lack the analytical capability required to provide or analyze data according to RCAS standards. Without the clout associated with being backed by a regional chiefs' association, it has been more difficult for RCAS to obtain outside funding compared to the OCCSA/GITS effort. Finally, all of the RCAS analyses are done in-house, so the participating agencies miss the credibility and additional expertise that a law enforcement agency/university partnership can bring to this type of endeavor.

In sum, both types of interagency cooperation have advantages as well as drawbacks. Clearly, the utility, flexibility, and durability of cooperative efforts such as GITS and RCAS depend a great deal upon how they are structured and the nature of their original goals. We think that a hybrid regional approach that combines the advantages of both the top-down and the bottom-up models may be well worth considering.

Potential Legal Barriers

A number of legal barriers can arise when agencies form a data-sharing partnership. These barriers may become particularly problematic when dealing with gang crime data because of the likely presence of juveniles. GITS, however, has fewer legal ramifications because it collects crime incident data and avoids individual identifiers. Access to this type of data is governed by the Federal Freedom of Information Act (Title 5, United States Code § 552) and relevant state statutes; in California, this is the California Public Records Act. Because of the public nature of this type of information, there were no legal barriers associated with the University's maintaining the database (see Meeker, 1999).

Interagency cooperative databases involving individual intelligence generate increased legal complexity. A recent Police Executive Research Forum report (PERF, 1999) on the Northeast Gang Information System (NEGIS) stresses this point. NEGIS is a cooperative effort involving five northeastern states that share criminal intelligence data on mobile gangs. One of the issues stressed in the PERF report is the importance of complying with 28 Code of Federal Regulations § 23 *et seq.*, which sets out the federal requirements for protecting individual privacy for regional information sharing systems. In addition, provisions of the Federal Privacy Act (5 U.S.C. § 552(a); 1CFR § 425.1 *et seq.*) also must be considered. Slayton (2000) outlines a number of other federal statutes that could impact interagency cooperative efforts to share data and stresses the importance of addressing these barriers early in the design phase.

Lessons Learned

The activities of street gangs seldom conform to the abstract boundaries that divide cities, school districts, or other governmental entities. This means that effective measures to prevent, interdict, or suppress gang crime often must involve many different agencies, each with its own goals, political imperatives, and ways of doing business. Our experience with Orange County, California's Gang Incident Tracking System shows that interagency data-sharing efforts on a regional scale can be developed and maintained, but that doing so requires substantial forethought, commitment, and persistence on the part of all participants.

In particular, we think that the following contributed substantially to the success of the GITS project:

- The existence of a strong regional police chiefs' and sheriff's association that established clear goals and objectives for the data collection system
- The involvement of university researchers who provided analytical and data collection expertise to the project and gave it scientific credibility. Establishing the project within a formal organizational unit (the Focused Research Group) in the university also helped it withstand assaults by political activists and deal with unforeseen bureaucratic hurdles.
- OCCSA's delegation of primary responsibility for gang-related issues to a standing Gang Strategy Steering Committee that met regularly and included faculty researchers in its activities. These committee meetings strengthened personal relationships among participants, helped minimize miscommunication, and encouraged amicable resolution of problems as they arose.
- Development of a memorandum of understanding that clearly identified the mutual goals and responsibilities of all participants without forcing them into legally binding contracts
- Avoidance of individual-level data in the database in order to simplify human subjects and legal issues

Finally, we think that the success of GITS owes a great deal to the leadership and management skills of police executives in the region. There were many instances where the project might have dissolved in acrimony had it not been for their goodwill, professionalism, and maturity.

Notes

1. Despite this statement, GITS was implemented to track only incident-level crime related to gangs and never contained membership data. At the time GITS was started, gang membership was tracked statewide by a cooperative law enforcement intelligence database. In Orange County, this database, called G.R.E.A.T. (later CALGANGS), was managed by the district attorney's office. Because of G.R.E.A.T.'s existence, and the legal, ethical, and human subjects problems associated with involving a university in this type of intelligence database, GITS never tracked gang members.

2. Recall that GITS data were drawn from special gang incident reports submitted each month by the agencies. This was necessary because the agencies involved did not share a standardized data record management system.

PART 3

The Increasing Diversity of Gangs

A Cross-Cultural Framework
for Understanding Gangs
Multiple Marginality and Los Angeles

JAMES DIEGO VIGIL
STEVE C. YUN

Gang researchers have emphasized different theoretical or conceptual models in gathering and presenting information on street life (Covey, Menard, & Franzese, 1992; Hazlehurst & Hazlehurst, 1998; Klein, 1995; Miller, Maxson, & Klein, 2001; Moore, 1991; Vigil, 1987). Collectively, such works show that youths from a wide variety of ethnic groups have become involved in gangs and that there are multiple dimensional facets to the gang phenomenon itself. A comparative look at Los Angeles gang dynamics adds to this tradition.

In this chapter we take a cross-cultural approach to illustrate how the multiple marginality conceptual framework can be applied to the experiences of youths in four Los Angeles ethnic communities: African American, Chicano, Salvadoran, and Vietnamese. This facilitates our examination of the disruptions of social control within families, schools, and law enforcement, and of how that disruption leads to street socialization and gang involvement on the part of some low-income, ethnic minority youth. Taking a cross-cultural approach helps clarify the similarities and differences among groups, while the conceptual model, multiple marginality, specifically identifies the forces that additively and cumulatively shape gangs and gang members. It is a model that gauges the weight and sequence of factors that impinge upon and affect youth who grow up on the streets, and it aids our understanding of the breakdown of social control and how street socialization transpires.

As a growing megalopolis stretching in all directions from the civic center, Los Angeles has become the prototype of urban diversity with a large immigrant population. It is a city rich with contrasting languages and cultural traditions, but also a place with ethnic and class tensions that threaten to erupt at any moment, as occurred in the King Riots of 1992 (*Los Angeles Times*, 1992; Oliver, Johnson, & Farrell, 1993). The changes the city has undergone since the 1960s include white flight and suburbanization; economic restructuring; large-scale immigration, particularly from Mexico, Central America, and Asia; and, most important, the entrenchment of street gangs.

Gangs are a stark subset of youth subcultures in a complex society, making up a dark side of Los Angeles in particular and urban America generally. This is especially the case since the 1980s when diffusion of gang members and gang culture affected other regions and cities (Maxson, 1998; Maxson, Woods, & Klein, 1996). Street gangs are found primarily in low-income, ethnic minority neighborhoods, and emerge from situations and conditions of social neglect and ostracism, economic marginalization, and cultural repression. In Los Angeles, some of them can be traced from the 1930s, following several decades of urbanization and spottily planned change in the region.

Similar difficulties have also afflicted or are beginning to afflict other urban centers worldwide (Hazlehurst & Hazlehurst, 1998). In all of them, the mostly poor, struggling communities have produced street gangs, and some seem to be in the process of generating "mega-gangs." There are similarities in how these subcultural developments unfold across places and peoples, but there are also instances when historical and cultural factors make each community unique.

Ethnohistorical Considerations

To begin with, there are ethnohistorical nuances and contours to the ways in which gangs have unfolded within each ethnic population. Every ethnic group's history (as well as every nation's!) differs in such important areas as time, place, and people—that is, when and where the people settled, how their communities formed, and what distinguished them from other people in the city. Consideration of the time factor allows for an appreciation of the specific conditions in Los Angeles that affected members of the group when they arrived and how they settled.

Two of the communities in this assessment have been present in Los Angeles since its inception. Chicanos, as original inhabitants, were overwhelmed by Anglo newcomers, submerged by changes under Anglo influences, and later rediscovered as newcomers throughout different ebbs and flows of large-scale (and continuing) immigration since the 1920s (Vigil, 1998a, 1998b). Immigration augmented the original, native Mexican plaza settlement, and the focal area of the Mexican population moved eastward into *barrios* (neighborhoods). These barrios were often located in ecologically inferior spaces (low areas subject to periodic flooding or on hills that could only be reached by poor, winding roads; Vigil, 2000).

African Americans also have a long history in Los Angeles. Mestizos of African origin were an important part of the Mexican population from its beginnings, but American blacks migrated to Los Angeles in large numbers after both World War I and World War II, seeking to benefit from a somewhat booming economy and a tight labor market in each time period. Racism and discrimination in those decades segregated and isolated most blacks in a narrow belt along the Central Avenue district. The struggles to change those conditions grew during and after the 1960s with an acceleration of civil rights strivings and inroads (Alonso, 1999).

In these two ethnic groups the gangs have been around for at least a half century (Chicanos a decade or two longer), and because each group was relegated to certain places (East Los Angeles and South Central Los Angeles), territoriality and defense of space became an issue. In addition, both have experienced persistent and concentrated poverty and disruptions of social control. A rooted gang subculture of age-graded youths (more common among Chicanos) was spawned to dominate the streets of each neighborhood. Older gang veterans became role models to help guide and direct younger street youth in the ways of the street, especially in settling old scores with rival street gangs. This gang subculture, born of street socialization, eventually had rituals, routines, signs, and symbols to help in the perpetuation of this lifestyle for barrio and ghetto youth who had no other recourse.

In contrast to the above ethnic groups, the Salvadoran and Vietnamese populations share a more recent migratory background, in both cases from homelands wracked by civil war. Most of the Vietnamese immigrants and a large proportion of those from El Salvador arrived in the United States as political refugees. The unraveling of social control actually began, for both groups, in their home countries where the United States played a prominent role in volatile military situations sparked by the anti-Communism climate of the era. Thus, Cold War geopolitical considerations are paramount for both groups (Vigil, Yun, & Long, 1993).

The Salvadoran (and other Central American) populations in Los Angeles are relatively new, mostly since the early 1980s, and settled predominantly in the Pico-Union area just west of downtown Los Angeles. These groups had to find their way to America during a time of economic instability and an intense anti-immigrant social and political climate. The

Salvadorans carry the burden of having had to leave their homeland in the midst of a highly charged civil war, with death threats propelling hundreds of thousands out of the country.

Along similar lines, the Vietnamese are best examined within the context of a war-torn homeland and an equally strife-ridden journey to the United States, beginning after 1975. Most found their way to America as members of a second wave of refugees known as the "boat people," a process begun in the late 1970s and continuing into the early 1980s. Although dispersed throughout Southern California, these newcomers are heavily concentrated in and near Chinatown in north Los Angeles, and in the San Gabriel Valley and northern parts of Orange County.

In contrast to the two older gangs, these two new groups have had a decidedly different experience. Territoriality became a part of the gang identification process, but more so for the Salvadorans, who concentrated in a neighborhood near jobs (e.g., janitors, domestics) sought by their parents. For the Vietnamese, a fluid mobility prevailed because of the nature of their secondary migration and settlement and only recently has gang space (or where certain groups hang out) become important. Both groups had an accelerated street socialization to speed creation of street gangs and gang members because their neighborhoods and schools were rife with existing Chicano gangs. This was especially the case for the Salvadorans, who resided in the middle of one of the biggest gangs in Los Angeles, 18th Street. Although older gang veterans are just now becoming a factor, both of these groups are more likely to develop ties to established criminal elements and activities as gang members advance from street to illicit enterprises under the purview of older adults. Coming from civil war backgrounds, gang members sometimes get caught up in the political rivalries and controversies that persist from the home country; graffiti messages or tattoos often reflect these leanings.

A Cross-Cultural Approach

These four ethnic groups were examined cross-culturally to help generate trends and tendencies found in street youth populations (Vigil, in press). This comparative approach is beneficial because it facilitates interdisciplinary analysis and incorporates the multidimensional dynamics (discussed below) that must be considered in understanding the formation and evolution of street gangs. It adds breadth and depth to an appraisal because it helps account for historical, political, and ethnic group differences while examining those differences from a variety of perspectives. Moreover, it facilitates appreciation of each group's experiences, as that group understands them (Vigil & Long, 1990). Establishing a cross-cultural research framework will help illuminate most of the forces, events, and circumstances that push gangs to the forefront of contemporary Los Angeles issues and recent history.

Utilization of this framework, aside from noting obvious differences among ethnic groups, such as time of arrival, destination, and intragroup variation, can help us learn a great deal about gang dynamics and street life by controlling for ethnicity. Ethnicity becomes an important factor when cultural groups live in close contact and utilize their physical or cultural distinctions to create social boundaries. In Los Angeles, as elsewhere in the United States, ethnic minorities whose physical characteristics are readily distinguishable from those of the white majority have faced prejudice and discrimination to varying degrees. An examination of each ethnic group's integration and adjustment to Los Angeles permits us to observe similar and contrasting ways in which gangs have been formed within each ethnic community. The unique history and culture of each ethnic group and the families within them have interacted with overriding socioeconomic and social psychological forces in shaping the gang experience.

Multiple Marginality: A Conceptual Framework

The street gang is the result of complex processes that stem from multiple levels and forces over a long period of time. Macrohistorical and macrostructural forces lead to economic insecurity and lack of opportunity, fragmented social control institutions, poverty, and psychological and emotional barriers in broad segments of ethnic minority communities in Los Angeles. Race and class forces are heavily implicated in the marginalization of each of the four groups and the resultant social and cultural repercussions have led to street socialization.

Street socialization is the learning process that blurs the ethnic lines among all four groups because remarkably similar things are learned on the streets where fear and vulnerability generate the need for protection, friendship, loyalty, and other routines and rhythms provided by the gang. The street gang dominates the lives of untethered youth because other institutions have become undermined and fragmented and have been made fragile and largely ineffective. Nevertheless, each group has uniqueness about it, such as race being a focal issue for African Americans, and the dual nature relationship Chicanos have with the dominant society as both natives and immigrants. Salvadorans and Vietnamese both have global, cold war political ramifications to their entry into the United States. In large part, marginalization began for them before they entered the country.

In an earlier work dealing with Chicanos, I noted that the emergence of street gangs stems from the problems and strains associated with adaptation to American culture and city life (Vigil, 1988a). The series of breakdowns and readaptations is multiple (to reiterate, what I have referred to as "multiple marginality") and affects family structure and stability, schooling readiness in the context of language and cultural contrasts, and level of involvement with police and the criminal justice system. The phrase multiple marginality reflects the complexity and persistence of these forces (Vigil, 1988a, 1988b; Vigil & Yun, 1998). These communities face inadequate living conditions, stressful personal and family mutations, racism, and cultural repression in schools. It is a complex problem that necessitates multiple levels of analysis. Thus, as will be noted later, strategies for solutions must be a sophisticated mix of prevention, intervention, and law enforcement.

All these multiple strains take their toll and strip minority peoples of their coping skills. Being left out of the mainstream of society in so many ways and in so many places relegates urban youth to the margins of society in practically every conceivable area. This positioning leaves them with few traditional options or resources to better their lives. Thus, marginalization of all sorts leads to the emergence of street gangs and the generation of gang members.

A holistic, integrative assessment and interpretation of street gangs must recognize the many strands and sources of gang delinquency. A discussion of multiple marginality is a move in that direction. Its theory-building framework addresses ecological, economic, sociocultural, and psychological factors. Over the years, there have been many theories that incorporate these elements meaningfully (e.g., Covey et al., 1992; Vigil, 1988b). Most researchers are in accord that major macrohistorical and macrostructural forces form the backdrop to street gangs. The causation debate becomes contentious and heated when the focus is on the intermediate and micro levels of analysis. Barring a major overhaul of the social system, then, a systematic examination of the major socialization agents (i.e., families, schools, and law enforcement) would help our understanding of gangs and gang members and how a quasi-institutional gang subculture emerged. Set against a broad canvas, a cross-cultural analysis would add immensely to our insights on such street subcultures.

Time, place, and ethnicity are central to this dynamic (Vigil, 1998b). The context for looking at social control dynamics can be set in an examination of how each ethnic group has adapted to Los Angeles, detailing what their neighborhoods are like and how they became a part of the city. A macro-analysis sets the stage for other evidence showing how fractured and marginalized a people become, especially children and youth, undergoing major changes. From this broad backdrop, a look at the micro events in the life of a gang member will show how social control networks unfold, such as connections to family and significant others, engagements with a higher status, involvements with positive and constructive activities, and beliefs associated with the central value system of a society. Family organization, schooling experiences, and interactions with law enforcement institutions will surface as sources of problems in the lives of many youth, as illustrated in Figure 11.1. In assessing the different ethnic gangs along the four social control dimensions (i.e., connections, engagements, involvements, and beliefs), a common theme emerges—the weakening of these bonds "frees" the adolescent from the paths of conformity and, with street socialization and the acquisition of a street subculture, ensures that unconventional behavior is likely.

Aspects of Social Control

Anthropologists have long noted that social control is an important function of cultures and that the family universally plays a key role in this regard (Ember & Ember, 1990; Haviland, 1988). The structure and form of the family and other institutions of social control vary from society to society, and there are internalized (within the individual) and externalized (from outside) mechanisms, as well as various formal and informal sanctions. Social control "always . . . seeks to ensure that people behave in acceptable ways, and defines the proper action to take when they don't" (Haviland, 1988, p. 289). Families, schooling, and law enforcement are particularly important in examining how people learn to adjust and conform in a modern, urban society.

To apply social control theory to the street gangs of southern California, however, modifications are required, as certain elements of traditional social control theory fail to connect to other forces in the fuller equation of understanding gangs (Wiatrowski, Griswold, & Roberts, 1981). We believe, along with Covey et al. (1992), that social control theory, "as integrated into ecological and other perspectives [i.e., multiple marginality], appears to be fundamental to understanding the formation and illegal behavior of juvenile gangs" (p. 173; see also Cloward & Ohlin, 1960; Decker & Van Winkle, 1996; Hagedorn, 1988; Klein, 1995; Moore, 1978, 1991; Shaw & McKay, 1942; Spergel & Curry, 1995; Thrasher, 1927/1963; Vigil, 1988a, 1988b).

Families, schools, and law enforcement merit special scrutiny in this regard for two main reasons (Bursik & Grasmick, 1995a). First, they are the primary agents of social control in society. Second, they are uniquely adaptive and responsive to the concerns of society. Although each of these institutions has made its separate contributions to the gang problem, it is their joint actions (or inactions) that make the problem worse. It is in their collective failure that street socialization has taken over and rooted the quasi-institution of the street gang.

What Policymakers Need to Know

If family, schools, and law enforcement are the key elements of social control in any industrialized, urban society and are largely responsible for

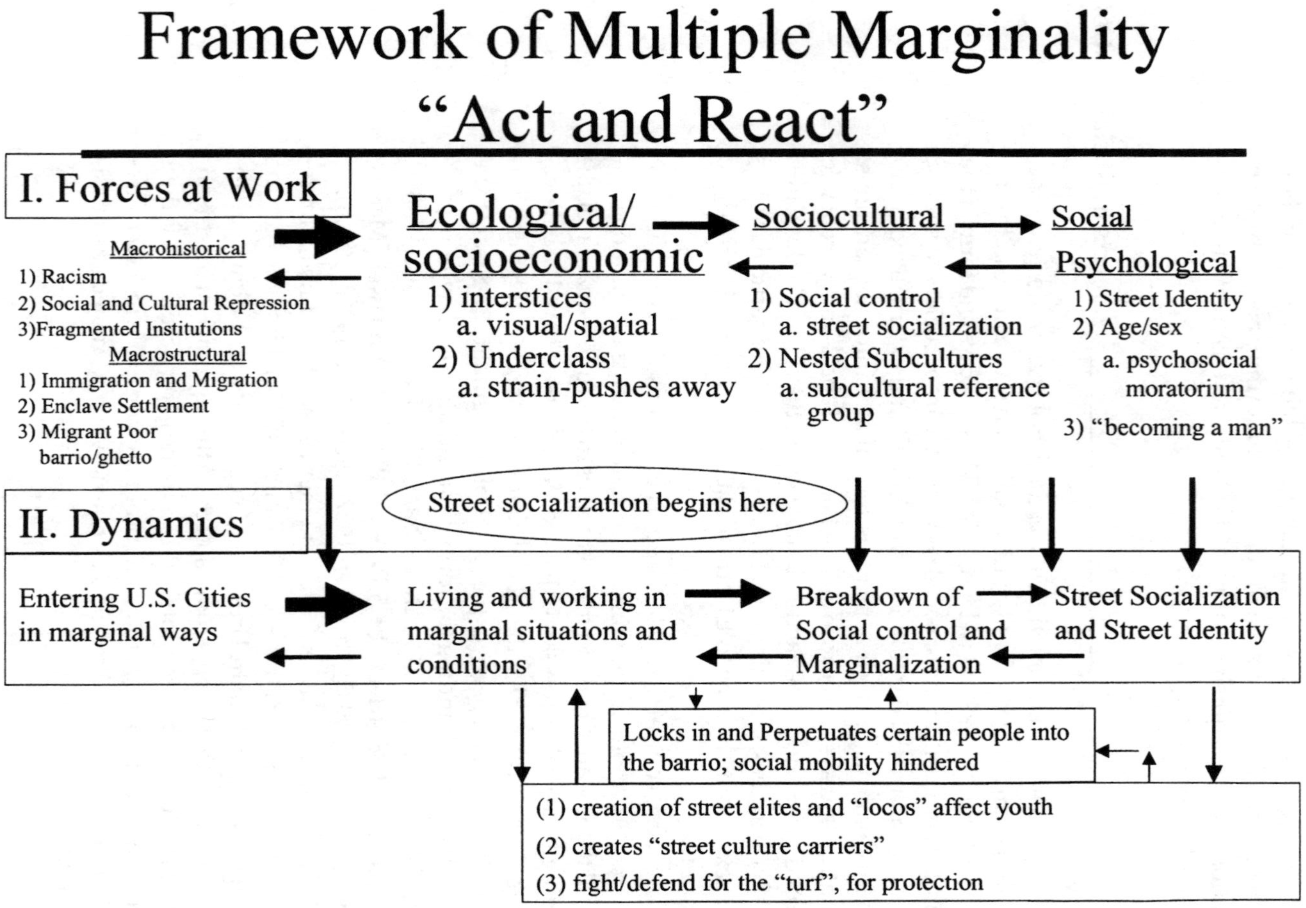

Framework of Multiple Marginality

"Act and React"

I. Forces at Work

Ecological/Socioeconomic → **Sociocultural** → **Social** → **Psychological**

Ecological/Socioeconomic

Macrohistorical
1) Racism
2) Social and Cultural Repression
3) Fragmented Institutions

Macrostructural
1) Immigration and Migration
2) Enclave Settlement
3) Migrant Poor barrio/ghetto

1) interstices
  a. visual/spatial
2) Underclass
  a. strain-pushes away

Sociocultural
1) Social control
  a. street socialization
2) Nested Subcultures
  a. subcultural reference group

Psychological
1) Street Identity
2) Age/sex
  a. psychosocial moratorium
3) "becoming a man"

II. Dynamics

Entering U.S. Cities in marginal ways

Living and working in marginal situations and conditions

Street socialization begins here

Breakdown of Social control and Marginalization

Street Socialization and Street Identity

Locks in and Perpetuates certain people into the barrio; social mobility hindered
(1) creation of street elites and "locos" affect youth
(2) creates "street culture carriers"
(3) fight/defend for the "turf", for protection

Figure 11.1. Framework of Multiple Marginality

street socialization developments, they are also accessible and open to human intervention and alteration. Adaptation and integration into the city for many racially distinct and culturally different newcomers usually entails starting on the bottom rung of the ladder, but barriers and hindrances keep them from climbing up. It is what researchers have referred to as a status that makes for strain (Merton, 1949) or differential opportunity structures (Cloward & Ohlin, 1960) thus having repercussions in other associated realms.

Structural causes must therefore be at the forefront of any serious discussion of what causes gangs and creates gang members. The multiple marginality framework begins with ecological and economic factors that are at the root of the breakdown of social control (Vigil, in press). Those who set policy have lapsed into facile answers, thus allowing ideological arguments (e.g., moral evaluations) to cloud the debate on how to guide our approach to this problem. To help guide our thinking about policy, it is imperative that we examine more closely the multiple factors that shaped the emergence of a street culture and subsociety from various ethnic backgrounds reflected in gangs.

The cross-cultural, comparative analysis suggested here will sharpen our policy formulations. When street socialization takes over, a remarkably similar street orientation and culture emerges for each group, irrespective of ethnic traditions, and with only slightly greater variation, regardless of gender. Moreover, a comparative examination will afford us a broad, historical approach to policy considerations in looking at how and why social control was disrupted, when and where groups and individuals became social outcasts, and what political forces overshadowed the process.

To combat the street gang subculture and subsociety, we must look at the ways separate social control influences are integrated and interact with each other. This reciprocal connection shows an action and reaction interplay that evolves over time. Larger dynamics strongly affected social control institutions that bear on the lives of gang members. Thus it is all the more laudable when success comes for families that survive, students who piece together an academic path, and more constructive relations with law enforcement are struck. Beginning with family life, what do we need to understand in order to make this more likely for more members of these and other afflicted communities (Jessor, 1998)?

Questions to Ask in Generating New Strategies

How can we address the absence of parenting and early voids in the development of connections, so necessary for leading the child to engagements, involvements, and beliefs? We must not forget that families and other household members are not situated in a vacuum. There is a long history of racism and poverty that has repercussive qualities and lingering effects on how, even whether, family life is structured and organized to participate in society effectively. Moreover, the state of schooling for minority youth and their relations with law enforcement in general have affected family life, in that poor people often receive short shrift from authorities.

As for law enforcement and the overall criminal justice system, the Rodney King affair (Oliver et al., 1993; *Los Angeles Times,* 1992), coupled with the dominant sentiment of distrust and fear of the police among blacks and Latinos in light of the Rampart Division (LAPD) scandal, tell it all. In sum, questions regarding the gaps and shortcomings found in the educational realm and the criminal justice system must also be considered, along with those addressed in the family.

We are not two Americas; we are one America. We are not two separate societies—an inner city and everything outside it. What is needed today to address gang problems (and other social problems as well) is a balance of prevention, intervention, and law enforcement (Goldstein & Huff, 1993), the carrots and sticks that enable parents to help their children conform. We must begin to think of the children of our society, particularly the less fortunate, as ours to care for at an early age, similar to the small-scale but sensitive efforts of reformers for white ethnic youth in the late 19th century. Detractors will claim that this strategy is unworkable, impractical, and if implemented, another "expensive" form of welfare. Failing to realize that the present criminal justice apparatus is also a form of welfare, criminal justice welfare, these naysayers forget that hundreds of billions of dollars are spent every year to warehouse hundreds of thousands of largely poor, ethnic minority peoples (Petersilia, 1992). Sadly, this continues to be the approach in spite of studies that show the cost and benefits of early inter-vention and prevention tactics, which far surpass in savings those of the current strategy (Greenwood, 1996; Rubin, 1999).

In California alone, the prison population has spiraled out of control. The costs for this narrow "punishment" strategy are exorbitant. For every new prison bed that is budgeted, there will be less money available for higher education. In 1995, the California state budget for 150,000 prisoners stood at $4 billion—the same amount as the budget for the Los Angeles Unified School District [LAUSD] to educate more than 700,000 children! With a rising state economy, the LAUSD budget since then has doubled to more than $8 billion, but prison costs have also increased sharply. More-over, a recent report underscored the same disparity for New York City, which now "spends $8,000 a year per child in its public schools but $93,000 a year per child in the new juvenile detention center in the South Bronx" (Huffington, 2000, p. M5).

In short, the unilateral suppression strategy is a failure, as the numbers of gangs, gang members, gang crimes and homicides, prisons, prisoners, and the overall street influences have risen dramatically (Klein, 1995). The nature of the public debate forces experts and observers to stake out an either "tough" or "soft" position on this problem, when in fact a balanced prevention, intervention, and law enforcement strategy is what is needed. Why not take this broader, reflective approach and be "smart" on crime?

_____ **A Balanced, Integrated Policy for Street Youth**

In this more holistic way, prevention, intervention, and suppression strategies can follow a logical, developmental route. Prevention must begin in the early childhood years up to age 8 or 9. Communities and agencies must take a proactive approach to addressing the primary problems of the general population in low-income areas as well as factor in secondary prevention for specific at-risk youth and/or related issues. Intervention actions must be aimed at the crucial preteen years, from about 9 to 12 or 13 years of age, and involve treatment and work with youths who are peripherally, but not yet deeply, connected to the streets. Dissuading and curtailing youth, at early ages, from the attitudes and behavior that clearly lead to delinquent and criminal paths opens the possibility for a return to more prosocial activities later. Finally, suppression is the strategy that we must rely on to stop the spread of delinquency and criminal behavior during the ages of 13 to 20 for those who, despite our best prevention and intervention efforts, have nevertheless joined in gang activities. Here, the criminal justice system applies a punitive and corrective approach to control destructive and violent behavior that often goes beyond members of the street populations. In tandem, and as needed, prevention, intervention, and law enforcement strategies can be utilized throughout the life course of an individual.

The Los Angeles County Sheriff's Department is moving in this even-handed direction. Community policing, the VIDA (Vital Intervention through Directional Alternatives) youth intervention program, and the formation of a police review board headed by experienced civil rights lawyers are examples of this new philosophy. In this vein, prevention, intervention, and law enforcement can often be interwoven. It requires, though, that various agencies and sectors agree to cooperate and coordinate efforts to address the gang problem in their communities. A few years ago, a Los Angeles City Council initiative took this integrated approach to the L.A. Bridges. The bridges metaphor emerged from the public hearings to underscore that a cooperative and coordinated structure was needed to combat gangs and violence. It was understood by most participants that a complex problem required a multilevel strategy, and early prevention and intervention efforts involving linkages and partnerships among educators, parents, and law enforcement. Recent research focusing on other programs from throughout the nation affirms that such initiatives can work (Catalano, Loeber, & McKinney, 1998).

A shift in public policy toward the family, similar to the changes underway in policing, should also be formulated and cultivated for low-income populations (Sampson & Laub, 1994). Numerous programs now exist—some only sketchily thought out and others quite successful innovations—to address the strains and problems of modern families (OJJDP, 1993). An investigation focusing on family life and dynamics, conducted between 1992 and 1995 in a housing project in East Los Angeles, found further that gang members tended to come from the poorest of the poor (Vigil, 1996), and the poorest reflected many more emotional and personal problems. Even in the same community, where welfare, housing assistance, food stamps, and so on, characterized almost all of the residents, there was internal variation. What this means for family support programs and assistance is that resources can be targeted for low-income areas, but with a special focus on the families and individuals most in need, who will warrant most of the time and attention.

Schooling and educational issues, in the context of social control dysfunctions, are of even higher import. Massive changes must be introduced in urban schools in general. We must hire thoroughly trained and prepared teachers; ensure that they are adequately paid; develop teacher training programs that explicitly address inner-city populations; reexamine the learning curriculum and formulate innovative strategies to revise and revamp it; initiate outreach efforts to forge stronger links to parents and communities; solicit and cultivate leadership and supervision styles and approaches that are change oriented; recruit leaders who take risks and are willing to experiment; and apply pressure on government bodies, local to national, to generate and contribute resources and research expertise to transform and improve urban inner-city schools and communities (Goldstein & Kodluboy, 1998).

Specifically, for the most marginalized, low-income children, many of whom are street socialized, we should begin to formulate a national strategy to guide and monitor them throughout their public school experience (Vigil, 1999). Key to this objective is ensuring that each child learns to read. For example, an experimental program in Los Angeles known as Ten Schools, with low-income, ethnic minority communities as a comparison group, has shown marked improvements in reading and math skills when additional staffing and resources were made available. Previously, I have argued for a continuation of the Headstart learning program by instituting a GetSmart phase in elementary school and a StaySmart component for the middle school (Vigil, 1993b), and a student of mine has suggested even more continuity by adding BeSmart for high school—a policy recommendation labeled Follow Through by other researchers. The basic goal in this sequence of developmental phases is to maintain a continuous hold on the child to help minimize the chances of anyone "falling through the cracks." In this way, the small percentage of children in any low-income neighborhood who might become gang members will receive extra attention and monitoring. Coordination with parents and the overall community, as envisioned in the L.A. Bridges program for example, is essential in this approach.

In short, there are many different strategies that can be utilized to regain control in the classroom and educate and better guide youth who might be street socialized and/or gang members (Heath & McLaughlin, 1993; Vigil, 1993b). In addition to those discussed above, there are others that directly deal with the gang subculture itself (Vigil, 1999). Students from a gang are bonded in ways that encourage hostile and negative behavior, teacher admonishments to the contrary. Ironically, many remedial learning programs in elementary or middle school that target gang children place them with similarly street-raised youth in the same learning groups; this practice often worsens in the later years in alternative and continuation high schools. Such placements actually further bond gang members and, in fact, bring many of them together for the first time. Thus, opportunities to learn on the streets are duplicated and reaffirmed in the classroom (Vigil, 1999).

Conclusion

Comprehending this process and the gang subcultures it has generated is augmented and strengthened by a cross-cultural investigation across groups along similar macro dimensions, and specifically within a social control framework. Although the results of this analysis are set in the same time (1990s) and place (Los Angeles), the background times and places of the communities made for different contrasting macrohistorical and macrostructural experiences (Vigil, in press). Within these peoples' histories and socioeconomic trajectories, multidimensional dynamics are important.

Multiple marginality, the framework within which our analysis was conducted, helps us pinpoint and highlight the ways ecological and economic marginalization affect and intersect with social, cultural, and psychological strains and stresses. These forces additively and cumulatively contribute to the breakdown of social control and the emergence of gangs and varieties of gang members (see Vigil, 1988a, for varieties of gang members). It is these broader forces that undermine and create social control dysfunctions, disrupting family life, undermining education, and leading law enforcement, inevitably, to play a stronger role as society's "conformity" safety net. To fill these gaps (Klein, 1971; Vigil, 1988a, 1993a), the gang replaces the parenting, schooling, and policing to regulate youth's lives to one of a street subculture where routines and regulations help guide gang members. The subculture that emerges varies somewhat between males and females, although as previously documented, there is a remarkable consistency in the major themes among them: multiple marginality, breakdown of social control, and even specific gang routines like initiation, tattoos and graffiti, and gang conflict.

To reiterate, the seeds of the solutions to gangs are found in the root causes. Even though larger-than-life historical and structural forces have undermined social control institutions, such as families, schooling, and law enforcement, there is an opportunity to salvage many of the children who have been marginalized and left to the streets. This cross-cultural assessment accounts for the differences in time, place, and peoples. However, there are striking similarities as well, enough to generate universal public policy ideas and plan concerted actions to make a difference. With such policies and programs we can assist and shape the future of families that until now have lost out; restructure and improve schools and schooling routines that have obviously fallen short; and develop partnerships to integrate peoples and communities into new criminal justice strategies that help encourage youth to respect society and its laws, because respect is tendered to them.

The Girls in the Gang[1]
What We've Learned From
Two Decades of Research

JODY MILLER

It is no longer accurate to say that female involvement in youth gangs is an understudied phenomenon. Since Anne Campbell's (1984) groundbreaking book *The Girls in the Gang,* a number of scholars have dedicated themselves to understanding the lives of young women in gangs. In the past 4 years, two monographs and an edited collection have specifically addressed girls' gang activities (Chesney-Lind & Hagedorn, 1999; Fleisher, 1998; J. Miller, 2001a). This is in addition to Joan Moore's (1991) landmark *Going Down to the Barrio,* the important ongoing research on female gang involvement in San Francisco (Hunt, Joe-Laidler, & Mackenzie, 2000; Hunt, Mackenzie, & Joe-Laidler, 2000; Joe-Laidler & Hunt, 1997; Lauderback, Hansen, & Waldorf, 1992), and other informative studies (see Joe & Chesney-Lind, 1995; Nurge, 1998; Portillos, 1999; Portillos, Jurik, & Zatz, 1996). In fact, though some gang researchers continue to ignore girls, a number of scholars have become attentive to the importance of examining gender in the context of gangs (see Bjerregaard & Smith, 1993; Curry, 1998; Curry & Decker, 1998; Deschenes & Esbensen, 1999a, 1999b; Esbensen & Deschenes, 1998; Esbensen, Deschenes, & Winfree, 1999; Esbensen & Winfree, 1998; Fagan, 1990; Hagedorn, 1998b; Klein, Maxson, & Miller, 1995).

It is safe to say that we now have more information about girls in gangs, and from a variety of methodological perspectives, than at any point in the long history of gang research. In fact, as David Curry (1999) points out in a recent essay, the foundations for contemporary research on girls in gangs were actually laid down earlier. As Curry reviews, Walter Miller (1973) first described two female gangs, the Molls and the Queens, active in the middle part of the 20th century. Waln Brown (1978) reported on his observations of African American female gang members in Philadelphia, and John Quicker (1983) studied Chicana gang members in Los Angeles around the same period. We also have historical evidence of the nature of female gang involvement from Laura Fishman's (1995) analysis of data collected on the Vice Queens for James Short and Fred Strodtbeck's (1965) Chicago-based research during the 1960s. Joan Moore's (1991) research was based on interviews with adults active in street gangs in the 1950s and 1970s; and Malcolm Klein's research during the same era documented the widespread involvement of young women in street gangs (see Klein, 2001; see also Bowker, Gross, & Klein, 1980; Bowker & Klein, 1983).

This early research is especially important to highlight, as it tempers popular claims of "new violent female offenders" routinely depicted as young women in gangs (see Chesney-Lind, 1993, and Chesney-Lind, Shelden, & Joe, 1996, for a discussion). From the available information, it appears that there has been both continuity and change in young women's participation in gangs. But overall the proportion of gang members who are girls, and the nature of girls' gang involvement, does not appear to have shifted substantially over the years. Klein documented that approximately a quarter of the gang members in his study were girls. Moore reports that females were nearly a third of the gang members she studied. As important, research from this earlier era shows that although there was variation in young women's gang involvement, girls were actively involved in violence, most often fighting. In addition, their place in gangs was never as mere "tomboys" or "sex objects." Instead, girls' roles and activities in gangs were negotiated, with varying results, in the context of male-dominated settings.

In the contemporary era, scholarly concern with young women's gang involvement has grown substantially. In part this is because of the growth in gangs since the 1980s and the tremendous growth in gang research during this same period. As other chapters in this volume illustrate, recent estimates suggest that there are now more than 1,000 cities and towns across the United States reporting gangs in their communities—more than five times the number that existed as recently as 1980 (Klein, 1995; Maxson, Woods, & Klein, 1995). This alone is not sufficient to account for the growth in research on girls in gangs, however. Instead, the move away from a primarily androcentric approach to the study of gangs is in large part because of the expansion of feminist criminology and its requisite attention to the experiences of women.

So then, what have we learned in the past two decades? For starters, we have come to recognize that young women's involvement in youth gangs is a varied phenomenon. Girls' experiences in gangs and the consequences of their gang involvement vary by—among other things—their ethnicity, the gender composition of their gangs, and the community contexts in which their gangs emerge. In this chapter, I provide an update of our current state of knowledge about girls in gangs. My focus is on four issues:

1. The level of female gang involvement
2. Risk factors for gang membership and girls' pathways into gangs
3. The level and character of gang girls' delinquency and its context in gang life for girls
4. The consequences of gang involvement for girls, including both victimization risks within gangs and evidence of long-term costs associated with gang involvement for girls

In discussing each of these issues, I draw from my own research (J. Miller, 2001a) and collaborations with others (Miller & Brunson, 2000; Miller & Decker, 2001; Peterson, Miller, & Esbensen, 2001), as well as from the wide range of studies documented at the start of this chapter. I take this approach to emphasize the comparisons that can be drawn across re- search methodologies, study sites, ethnicity, and gang structures. As Klein (2001) aptly notes, the examination of such differences is "instructive and re-mind[s] us properly that while we can generalize about gangs, we had best do so while recognizing that they reflect [a range of] different . . . contexts" (p. x).

Levels of Female Gang Involvement

Recent estimates suggest that female participation in gangs is more widespread than has typically been believed. Data from official sources continue to underestimate the extent of girls' gang membership. For instance, Curry, Ball, and Fox (1994) found that some law enforcement policies officially exclude female gang members from their counts. Controlling for data from these cities, they still found that females were only 5.7% of gang members known to law enforcement agencies. Part of law enforcement's underestimation of girls' gang involvement is attributable to male gang members' greater likelihood of being involved in serious crime, as well as average age differences between males and females in gangs (see Bjerregaard & Smith, 1993; Fagan, 1990). Whereas young men are more likely to remain gang involved into young adulthood, gang membership for girls is much more likely to remain a primarily adolescent undertaking (see J. Miller, 2001a; Moore & Hagedorn, 1996).

On the other hand, results from survey research with youths indicate that young women's gang involvement is relatively extensive and at levels only slightly below that of young men, particularly in early adolescence. For instance, findings from the Rochester Youth Development Study, based on a stratified sample of youths in high-risk, high-crime neighborhoods, actually found that a slightly larger percentage of females (22%) than males (18%) claimed gang membership when self-definition was used as a measure (Bjerregaard & Smith, 1993). Later evidence from this longitudinal study suggests that girls' gang involvement tends to be of a shorter duration than boys', with girls' peak gang involvement around eighth and ninth grades (Terence P. Thornberry, personal correspondence, April 2, 1999). Similarly, based on a sample of eighth graders in 11 cities, Esbensen and Deschenes (1998) report a prevalence rate for gang membership of 14% for males and 8% for females.

In addition to prevalence rates, two additional issues are important in considering the level of girls' participation in gangs. One is the proportion of gang members that are female versus male, and the other is the distribution of female gang involvement across various gang types. Estimates of the ratio of female to male members suggest that young women approximate between 20% and 46% of gang members (Esbensen & Huizinga, 1993; Esbensen & Winfree, 1998; Fagan, 1990; Moore, 1991; Winfree, Fuller, Vigil, & Mays, 1992). There is wide variation, however, across gangs. In my comparative study of female gang involvement in Columbus, Ohio, and St. Louis, Missouri, girls in mixed-gender gangs (i.e., gangs with both male and female membership) were as few as 7% or as many as 75% of the members of their gangs (J. Miller, 2001a). Overall, these girls were in predominantly male gangs: of the 42 girls in my sample who were in mixed-gender gangs, 74% were in groups that were majority-male, with just under a third (31%) in gangs in which 80% or more of the members were males. Male gang members in St. Louis provide even more extreme accounts. Although 39% of the boys we spoke to described their gangs as male-only, of the 61% of young men who described having both male and female membership in their gangs, two thirds reported that their membership was at least 80% male (Miller & Brunson, 2000).[2]

Though standard approaches for categorizing (presumably or implicitly) male gangs continue to focus on a broad range of issues exclusive of gender (see, e.g., Maxson & Klein, 1995; Spergel & Curry, 1993), studies of female gang types focus specifically on gender organization, most often drawing from Walter Miller's (1975) tripartite classification: (a) mixed-gender gangs with both female and male members; (b) female gangs that are affiliated with male gangs, which he refers to as "auxiliary" gangs; and (c) independent female gangs. Several scholars have noted that this tripartite division misses some of the complexity of gang formations, and also that it is androcentric to focus on gender organization when examining female but not male gang involvement (Hagedorn & Devitt, 1999; Nurge, 1998). Nonetheless, as I will discuss throughout this chapter, research on the gendered organization and gender ratio of girls' gangs has yielded important information.

There are several case studies of the various gang types Miller describes (see Fleisher, 1998; Lauderback, Hansen, & Waldorf, 1992; Quicker, 1983; Venkatesh, 1998), but less evidence of their prevalence. Curry's (1997) study of female gang members in three cities found that only 6.4% of girls described being in autonomous female gangs, whereas 57.3% described their gangs as mixed-gender, and another 36.4% said they were in female gangs affiliated with male gangs. It appears that there is some variation across ethnicity in the likelihood of each gang type. For example, Chicana/Latina gang members are those most likely to describe their gangs as female groups affiliated with male gangs, and African American young women are more likely to describe their gangs as mixed-gender. The handful of all-female gangs documented by scholars has largely been African American as well (Curry, 1997; Joe-Laidler & Hunt, 1997; Lauderback et al., 1992; J. Miller, 2001a; Venkatesh, 1998).

Nurge (1998) reports that the majority of girls in her study of girls in Boston gangs were in groups that were mixed-gender rather than auxiliary or female-only, but with varying gender compositions. She further differentiated mixed-gender gangs according to whether the groups were territorial and whether they referred to themselves as gangs or cliques. Likewise, in my comparative study of gangs in St. Louis and in Columbus, Ohio, the vast majority of girls interviewed were African American, and all of their gangs were predominantly African American. In all, 85% of girls described their gangs as mixed gender, with only three girls each describing their gangs as a female group affiliated with a local male gang, or as an independent female gang (J. Miller, 2001a). Because sampling was not representative, it is difficult to ascertain how generalizable such patterns are.

A recent analysis of the Gang Resistance Education and Training (G.R.E.A.T.) program data (Peterson et al., 2001) supports the finding that most youth gangs are composed of both male and female members. Of the 366 gang members reporting, 84% of male gang members described their gangs as having both female and male members and 16% said they were in all-male gangs. In terms of the ratio of males to females in their groups, approximately 45% of male gang members described their gangs as having a majority of male members; 38% said their gangs had fairly equal numbers of males and females; and just under 1% (2 cases) reported being in gangs that were majority female. Young women were more likely than young men to describe belonging to gender-balanced, rather than majority-male, mixed-gender gangs. Fully 64% of girls described their gangs as having equal numbers of males and females, followed by 30% in majority-male gangs, and 13% in majority female (8 cases) or all-female (10 cases) gangs. Thus, just 7% of girls described their gangs as having only female members.

Unfortunately, the measure of gender composition in the G.R.E.A.T. study did not allow an assessment of the prevalence of the gang types described above (i.e., affiliated vs. integrated groups). However, this and several additional studies suggest that the gender composition of gangs has a significant impact on the nature of gang members' activities, including their participation in delinquency (Joe-Laidler & Hunt, 1997; J. Miller, 2001a; Miller & Brunson, 2000; Peterson et al., 2001). I will highlight these findings further below.

Girls' Risk Factors for Gang Membership and Pathways Into Gangs

Gang membership doesn't happen overnight. Research shows that youths typically hang out with gang members for some time—often as much as a year—before making a commitment to join (Decker & Van Winkle, 1996). The young women in my study typically began hanging out with gang members when they were quite young—around age 12 on average—and they joined at an average age of 13. In fact, 69% of the girls in the sample described joining their gangs before they turned 14. This is quite similar to reports from other research, and appears to be relatively consistent across ethnic groups. Joe and Chesney-Lind's (1995) study of Samoan and Filipino gang youths in Hawaii reports an average age of entrée of 12 for girls and 14 for boys. Based on his study in Phoenix, Portillos (1999) reports that most of the Chicana girls in his study joined between ages 12 and 13. Recall also that the Rochester Youth Development Study found the highest prevalence rates of female gang participation in the early waves of their study, again suggesting that girls' gang membership starts quite young (see also Maxson & Whitlock, Chapter 2 of this volume).

Research on why girls join gangs has generally included two approaches. First are analyses of etiological risk factors for gang membership from survey research; second, qualitative analyses of girls' accounts of why they join gangs, what they gain from their gang participation, and their life contexts both prior to and at the time of joining. Though differing in approach, most studies focus on several or more of five sets of issues: structural and neighborhood conditions, the family, school factors, the influence of peers, and individual factors.

To account for the proliferation of gangs in recent decades, many scholars have focused on compelling evidence that much, though not all, of this growth has been spurred by the deterioration in living conditions for many Americans caused by structural changes brought about by deindustrialization (see Hagedorn, 1998b; Huff, 1989; Klein, 1995). The resulting lack of alternatives and sense of hopelessness are believed to have contributed to the growth of gangs in many cities, as scholars point to the gang as a means for inner-city youths to adapt to oppressive living conditions imposed by their environments. Though much of the focus of this research has been on gangs in general, or male gang members in particular, a few scholars have linked these conditions to female gang involvement as well. For example, findings from the Rochester Youth Development Study (RYDS) suggest that growing up in disorganized, violent neighborhoods is a risk factor for gang involvement for young women[3] (Thornberry, 1998).

Qualitative research highlights the importance of this link even further. Campbell (1990) notes that in addition to the limited opportunities and powerlessness of underclass membership shared with their male counterparts, young women in these communities also face the burden of child care responsibilities and subordination to men. The youths in Joe and Chesney-Lind's (1995) study were from impoverished communities, in what they note was a "bleak and distressing environment." They conclude from their research that "the gang assists [both] young women and men in coping with their lives in chaotic, violent and economically marginalized communities" (p. 411; see also Moore, 1991). Moreover, because these neighborhoods are often dangerous, gangs may assist young women in protecting themselves both by providing them the opportunity to learn street and fighting skills (Fishman, 1995), and by offering protection and retaliation against victimization in high-crime communities (J. Miller, 2001a).

The characteristics of the neighborhoods from which the young women in my study were drawn were very much in keeping with this image of urban poverty and racial segregation. In both cities, the vast majority of girls lived in neighborhoods that were economically worse off and more racially segregated than the cities as a whole (see J. Miller, 2001a). My project also included a comparative sample of nongang girls from the same communities. Although the neighborhood conditions were similar for both gang and nongang girls, there were important differences in girls' descriptions, particularly in relation to their exposure to gangs. In both Columbus and St. Louis, the vast majority of young women described some exposure to gangs in their neighborhoods. However, the extent and proximity of gang activity in girls' neighborhoods was a feature distinguishing gang and nongang girls' descriptions. More than four fifths of the gang members reported both "a lot" of gang activity in their neighborhoods and other gang members living on their streets, as compared to about half of the nongang girls. It appears that coupled with other risk factors, living in neighborhoods with gangs in *close* proximity increases the likelihood that girls will decide to join gangs.

Although impoverished and dangerous neighborhood conditions help answer the question of why girls come to join gangs, this remains only a partial explanation. Research shows that less than one quarter of youths living in high-risk neighborhoods claim gang membership (Bjerregaard & Smith, 1993; Winfree et al., 1992), and researchers have not found differences in perceived limited opportunities between gang and nongang youths in these communities (Esbensen, Huizinga, & Weiher, 1993). A factor that has received quite a bit of attention is the family, which has long been considered crucial for understanding delinquency and gang behavior among girls.

Findings from survey research have been somewhat inconsistent with regard to the family. Esbensen and Deschenes (1998), in a multisite study of risk factors for delinquency and gang behavior, found that weak supervision and low parental involvement were significant risk factors, though they suggest that lack of maternal attachment was more predictive of gang membership for males than females. Bjerregaard and Smith (1993) measured both parental supervision and parental attachment within the family, and found neither to be significantly related to gang membership for girls. However, Thornberry (1998) in his analysis including later waves of the RYDS project reports low parental involvement as a significant risk factor for girls.

Ethnographic and other qualitative studies are much more likely to suggest that serious family problems contribute significantly to girls' gang involvement. Joe and Chesney-Lind (1995) observe that the girls in their study had parents who worked long hours, or who were un- or underemployed—circumstances they suggest affected both girls' supervision and the quality of family relationships. Fleisher's (1998; see also Campbell, 1984) ethnographic study of gangs in Kansas City, Missouri, documents intergenerational patterns of abuse and neglect, exacerbated by poverty and abject neighborhood conditions, which he suggests are at the heart of the gang problem. Likewise, Moore (1991) documents a myriad of family problems that contribute to the likelihood of gang involvement for young women: childhood abuse and neglect, wife abuse, alcohol and drug addiction in the family, witnessing the arrest of family members, having a family member who is chronically ill, and experiencing a death in the family during childhood. Her conclusion, based on comparisons of male and female gang members, is that young women in particular are likely to come from families that are troubled. Portillos's (1999) study of Chicana gang members suggests that girls are also drawn to gang involvement as a means of escaping oppressive patriarchal conditions in the home.

In my study, gang members were significantly more likely than girls who were not in gangs to come from homes with numerous problems. Gang girls were significantly more likely to have witnessed physical violence between adults in their homes and to have been abused by adult family members. In addition, they were much more likely to report regular drug use in their homes. Most important, gang members were significantly more likely to describe experiencing *multiple* family problems—with 60% (vs. 24% of nongang girls) describing three or more of the following five problems: having been abused, violence among adults, alcohol abuse in the family, drug abuse in the family, and the incarceration of a family member. In fact, 44% reported that four or more of these problems existed in their families, compared to only 20% of the nongang girls (see J. Miller, 2001a).

In the in-depth interview portion of my study, the most common family-related themes described by young women as contributing to their gang involvement were drug addiction among primary caregivers and being physically and/or sexually abused by family members.[4] The ways in which family problems facilitated girls' gang involvement were varied, but they shared a common thread—young women began spending time away from home as a result of difficulties or dangers there, and consequently sought to get away and to meet their social and emotional needs elsewhere. A number of researchers have suggested that "the gang can serve as a surrogate extended family for adolescents who do not see their own families as meeting their needs for belonging, nurturance, and acceptance" (Huff, 1993, p. 6; see also Campbell, 1990; Joe & Chesney-Lind, 1995; but see Decker & Van Winkle, 1996; Hunt, Mackenzie, & Joe-Laidler, 2000). The gang can offer a network of friends for girls whose parents are unable to provide stable family relations; moreover, girls' friendships with other gang members may provide a support system for coping with family problems, abuse, and other life problems (Joe & Chesney-Lind, 1995). Regardless of whether gangs actually fulfill these roles in young women's lives,[5] it is clear that many girls believe they will when they become involved.

Some girls who lack close relationships with their primary caregivers can turn to siblings or extended family members to maintain a sense of belonging and attachment. However, if these family members are gang involved, it is likely that girls will choose to join gangs themselves. Moreover, even when relationships with parents or other adults are strong, having adolescent or young adult gang members in the family often heightens the appeal of gangs (see also Joe & Chesney-Lind, 1995; Moore, 1991). In fact, Hunt, Mackenzie, and Joe-Laidler (2000) have challenged the dichotomous treatment among gang researchers between "gang" and "family," noting that there are many cases in which both "real" and "fictive" kin are members of girls' gangs. Thus, when young women speak of the familial nature of their gang relationships, they sometimes are literally speaking about their family members.

In my own research, this was often the case. As compared with nongang girls, gang girls in my study were much more likely to have siblings in gangs and were more likely to have two or more gang-involved family members. Moreover, in the qualitative portion of the study, many young women described the significant influence that older siblings and relatives had on their decisions to join their gangs. More often than not, young women who joined gangs to be with or like their older siblings did so in the context of the types of family problems noted earlier (J. Miller, 2001a). In fact, in my study the themes just reviewed—neighborhood exposure to gangs, family problems, and gang-involved family members—were overlapping in most gang girls' accounts, further distinguishing them from nongang girls in the sample.[6] These were the primary issues I identified as contributing to girls' gang involvement.

Although qualitative studies are most likely to find family problems and community conditions at the heart of girls' gang involvement, a number of studies based on surveys of juvenile populations note school-based problems (see Thornberry, 1998, for an overview). Bjerregaard and Smith (1993) found that low expectations of completing school were a significant predictor of gang membership for young women. Likewise, Bowker and Klein (1983) report that female gang members are less likely than nonmembers to intend to finish high school or go to college. More recently, Esbensen and Deschenes (1998) report that school commitment and expectations are associated with gang involvement for girls, and Thornberry (1998) also describes negative attitudes toward school as a risk factor for girls.[7]

Survey research has also examined individual characteristics and behaviors as risk factors for gang membership, as well as relationships with delinquent peers. Based on their analysis of the G.R.E.A.T. project, Esbensen, Deschenes, and Winfree (1999) report that gang girls were more socially isolated and had lower self-esteem than their male gang peers. Comparing male and female nongang members, their findings were similar; however, the difference was more pronounced between gang girls and boys. G.R.E.A.T. findings also suggested that risk seeking was a predictor of female, but not male, gang membership (Esbensen & Deschenes, 1998). On the other hand, Bjerregaard and Smith (1993) did not find self-esteem predictive of gang membership for girls. With regard to values, activities, and exposure to antisocial peers and situations, Esbensen and Deschenes (1998) report that commitment to negative peers was associated with gang membership for girls; Thornberry (1998) reports that delinquency, drug use, and positive values about drugs are risk factors for girls; and Bjerregaard and Smith (1993) also report that both delinquent peers and early onset of sexual activity were associated with gang membership for girls. As Maxson and Whitlock (Chapter 2, this volume) suggest, these survey results suggest a "lack of stable, unique predictors" of gang membership for young women. Combined, however, survey and qualitative research highlight many of the salient issues researchers are continuing to examine.

_____ Gang Life, Delinquency, and Violence Among Girls

One reason gangs have received so much attention among criminologists is that we know from quite a bit of research that young people who are in gangs—male and female—are substantially more involved in delinquency than their nongang counterparts. Research comparing gang and nongang youths has consistently found that serious criminal involvement is a feature that distinguishes gangs from other groups of youths (see Battin, Hill, Abbott, Catalano, & Hawkins, 1998; Esbensen & Huizinga, 1993; Fagan, 1990; Klein, 1995; Thornberry, 1998; Thornberry, Krohn, Lizotte, & Chard-Wierschem, 1993). This pattern holds for female gang members as well as their male counterparts (Bjerregaard & Smith, 1993; Deschenes & Esbensen, 1999a, 1999b; Esbensen & Winfree, 1998; J. Miller, 2001a). The enhancement effect of gang membership is most noticeable for serious delinquency and marijuana use (Thornberry et al., 1993). Bjerregaard and Smith (1993) summarize:

> Our study suggests that for females [as well as males], gangs are consistently associated with a greater prevalence and with higher rates of delinquency and substance abuse. Furthermore, the results suggest that for both sexes, gang membership has an approximately equal impact on a variety of measures of delinquent behavior. (p. 346)

Perhaps what's most significant about this research is evidence that female gang members are more delinquent than their female nongang counterparts, but also more so than their *male* nongang counterparts. For instance, Fagan (1990) reports that "prevalence rates for female gang members exceeded the rates for non-gang males" for all the categories of delinquency he measured (see also Esbensen & Winfree, 1998). Fagan summarizes his findings in relation to girls as follows:

> More than 40 percent of the female gang members were classified in the least serious category, a substantial difference from their male counterparts. Among female gang members, there was a bimodal distribution, with nearly as many multiple index offenders as petty delinquents. Evidently, female gang members avoid more serious delinquent involvement than their male counterparts. *Yet their extensive involvement in serious delinquent behaviors well exceeds that of non-gang males or females.* (Fagan, 1990, p. 201, my emphasis).

As Fagan's findings suggest, there is also evidence of gender differences within gangs with regard to criminal involvement. Fagan (1990, pp. 196-197) reports greater gender differences in delinquency between gang members than between nongang youth. Male gang members were significantly more involved in the most serious forms of delinquency, while for alcohol use, drug sales, extortion, and property damage, gender differences were not significant. Specifically, as noted above, Fagan reports a bi-modal distribution among young women in gangs: Approximately 40% of the gang girls in his study were involved only in petty delinquency and a third were involved in multiple index offending, compared to 15% and 56%, respectively, for young men. Moreover, evidence from a number of studies suggests that gun use is much more prevalent among male than fe-male gang members (Decker, Pennell, & Caldwell, 1997; Fleisher, 1998; Hagedorn & Devitt, 1999; Miller & Brunson, 2000; Miller & Decker, 2001).

Several explanations have been offered for these differences. In keeping with a large body of literature showing that gender stratification is a key organizational element of delinquent and criminal street networks (see Maher, 1997; Miller, 1998b), there is evidence of the "structural exclusion of young women from male delinquent activities" within mixed-gender gangs (Bowker et al., 1980, p. 516; J. Miller, 2001a; Miller & Brunson, 2000). Bowker et al.'s (1980) male respondents suggested that not only were girls excluded from the planning of delinquent acts, but when girls inadver-tently showed up at the location of a planned incident, it was frequently postponed or terminated. Likewise, the majority of young women in my study did not participate routinely in the most serious forms of gang crime, such as gun use, drive-by shootings, and (to a lesser extent) drug sales. This was in part a result of exclusionary practices by male gang members, but in addition, many young women purposively chose not to be involved in what they considered dangerous and/or morally troubling activities (J. Miller, 2001a). Like Fagan (1990), I found that only about a quarter to a third of gang girls were routinely involved in serious delin-quency.

Other researchers suggest that gender differences in norms supportive of violence and delinquency accounts for differences in gang girls' and gang boys' delinquency. Joe and Chesney-Lind (1995; see also Campbell, 1993), for example, suggest that participation in violence is a stronger nor-mative feature of male gang involvement than it is for young women in gangs. They argue that for girls, "violence (gang and otherwise) is not cele-brated and normative; it is instead more directly a consequence of and a re-sponse to the abuse, both physical and sexual, that characterizes their lives at home" (Joe & Chesney-Lind, 1995, p. 428). As noted, some girls in my study suggested they avoided violence because they found it morally trou-bling, but I did not find this to be a consistent pattern. Instead, many young women in my study did describe violence as a normative activity for girls, though rarely at extreme levels such as gun use or homicide (J. Miller, 2001a; see also Hagedorn & Devitt, 1999).

There is growing evidence that part of the answer to these competing explanations for gender differences in gang delinquency and violence, as well as variations in young women's participation in gang crime, can be found by examining the gender organization and composition of girls' gangs (Joe-Laidler & Hunt, 1997; Miller & Brunson, 2000; Peterson et al.,

2001). It may also be the case—though more comparative research is needed—that ethnic differences may account for variations as well. Moore and Hagedorn (1996) suggest that Latina gang members are more bound by "traditional" community patriarchal norms than are African American gang girls (see also Portillos, 1999). Likewise, as noted, the young women in Joe and Chesney-Lind's (1995) study were from communities (Samoan and Filipino) with strong patriarchal norms for girls, particularly with regard to sexuality.

I did not find strong supportive relationships among most gang girls in my study; instead, many girls identified with masculine status norms in the gang and desired acceptance as "one of the guys." Given the extent to which this finding contradicted other research on girls in gangs (Campbell, 1984; Joe & Chesney-Lind, 1995; Lauderback et al., 1992), I sought explanation in gang structure. Kanter (1977) notes that often conclusions drawn about differences between males and females, and attributed to "gender roles" or cultural differences between women and men, are in fact more appropriately attributable to situational or structural factors such as the gender composition of groups. As I described above, the vast majority of girls in my study were in mixed-gender gangs that were numerically male dominated. Examining the data more closely, it did appear that the handful of girls in female-only gangs, or gangs with a substantial representation of female members, were more likely to emphasize the social and relational aspects of their gangs, particularly their friendships with other girls.

This also suggests that differences in girls' levels of participation in violence, and the normative salience of violence for girls, might also be influenced by the gender organization of their gangs. In an analysis of gang boys' perceptions of girls' activities in their gangs, we found that young men in gender-balanced groups highlighted the social aspects of their interactions with female gang members, but differentiated males' and females' participation in delinquent activities. Young men in gangs with a vast majority of male members embraced the few young women in their gangs as "one of the guys" and described these girls as essentially equal partners in many of their delinquent endeavors (Miller & Brunson, 2000).

Peterson et al.'s (2001) analysis of the G.R.E.A.T. project, described above, allowed for further examination of this question. We classified youths' gangs according to four types of gender composition: all male, majority-male but with female membership, gender-balanced, and majority- or all female. We compared youths' descriptions of their gangs' activities, as well as individual delinquency rates for males and females across these groups, and our findings offer support for the importance of gender composition in shaping both the nature of gang activities, and individual gang members' delinquency. Based on member characterizations of their *gangs*, majority-/all-female gangs were the least delinquent groups, followed by all-male gangs. Both gender-balanced and majority-male gangs were similar with regard to the gangs' involvement in delinquent activities. To the extent that these descriptions are a reflection of the goals and norms of respondents' gangs, these differences are noteworthy and suggest that delinquency, particularly of a serious nature, is a less normative feature of primarily female gangs than other gangs.

On the other hand, our findings are not fully supportive of the notion of "gender differences" between girls and boys with regard to the normative acceptance of violence and delinquency.[8] Instead, we found significant within-gender differences for both girls and boys with regard to their level of participation in delinquency across gang types (Peterson et al., 2001). Specifically, comparing youths by gender and across gang types, we found that girls in all-/majority-female gangs had the lowest rates of delinquency. They were followed by girls in gender-balanced gangs. Next lowest were *boys* in all-male gangs, followed by girls in majority-male gangs, boys in gender-balanced gangs, and finally, boys in majority-male gangs. For both boys and girls, but especially girls, membership in majority-male gangs was correlated with the highest rates of delinquency.[9] Thus, girls' (and boys') gang-related delinquency appears to be strongly associated with the gender organization of their groups.

Other research offers additional support for the importance of examining the types of gangs girls are involved in. For instance, Lauderback et al. (1992) provide one of the few thorough descriptions of an autonomous female gang (see also Venkatesh, 1998), the Potrero Hill Posse (PHP), a group that was heavily involved in drug sales in San Francisco. Lauderback and colleagues (1992) suggest that PHP actually came about because these young women were dissatisfied with a "less than equitable . . . distribution of the labor and wealth" (p. 62) that had been part and parcel of their previous involvement in selling drugs with males. Moreover, this was a gang characterized by close, familial-like relationships among its female members. Joe-Laidler and Hunt (1997) extended Lauderback et al.'s (1992) analysis of PHP, comparing the social contexts of violence for young women in PHP with the social contexts facilitating violence among female gang members in other gangs in San Francisco. Although members of PHP were African American, the vast majority of other young women were Latina (with a small number of Samoans), and were in female groups affiliated with male gangs.

Joe-Laidler and Hunt (1997) found important differences in young women's exposure to violence across gang types, and report that girls in auxiliary gangs were exposed to a greater variety of violence-prone situations, many of which were tied to their associations with young men. The young women in PHP described violence occurring in three types of situations: violence associated with the drug trade, fights with girls in other gangs (over both men and turf), and intimate partner violence at the hands of their male partners. In contrast, young women in auxiliary gangs were subject to more violence-prone situations: violence in the context of gang initiations, conflicts with rival gang members—both male and female[10]— and conflicts *among* homegirls in the same gang (over reputation, respect, jealousies over males, and fights instigated by males), as well as intimate partner violence at the hands of boyfriends.

Joe-Laidler and Hunt's (1997) findings offer further evidence that dynamics resulting from the gendered social organization of gangs shapes young women's exposure to and participation in violence. Though additional research is needed on the role of ethnicity in shaping girls' gang experiences, there appears to be a relationship between the ethnic composition of gangs and their gender organization, as well as young women's experiences in gangs (see also Moore & Hagedorn, 1996). Contemporary research on African American gang girls has not found evidence of a strongly sexualized component of their gang activities (J. Miller, 2001a). However, in his research on Chicana gang members in Phoenix, Portillos (1999) reports that gang girls' sexuality was often used as a means of setting up rival gang males. In contrast to my portrait of African American girls in majority-male gangs as "one of the guys," Portillos describes Chicana gang girls constructing an oppositional femininity that is clearly differentiated from (and subordinate to) male gang members' gang masculinity.

As this research suggests, gender plays a complicated role in girls' gang participation, including their involvement in delinquency and violence. It intersects with ethnicity and culture, and is a structural determinant of girls' experiences rather than simply a result of individual differences between young women and young men. For some girls, and in some contexts, delinquency is part of the allure of gang life. But evidence suggests that some girls (as well as boys) are fairly ambivalent about their criminal involvement, even though they report finding it fun or exciting at times. On one hand, it brings them status and recognition within the group, as well as economic remuneration; on the other, it can get them into trouble with the law or put them at greater risk for being victimized by rival gang members or others on the streets.

But for girls in particular, many aspects of gang involvement, including delinquency, go against dominant notions of appropriate femininity. This shapes girls' experience within and outside of their gangs, often locking them into what Swart (1991) describes as a series of double binds. This point brings me to the last topic I want to touch on—the consequences of gang involvement for girls. Here I will focus on two issues. First, what are the consequences of gang involvement for girls while they are active in gangs? Second, what evidence do we have about the long-term consequences of gang involvement for young women? Though young people often turn to gangs as a means of meeting a variety of needs within their lives, it is often the case that their gang affiliation does more harm than good by increasing their likelihood of victimization and decreasing their opportunities and life chances.

Consequences of Gang Involvement for Girls

Girls' gang participation can be viewed as transgressing social norms concerning appropriate feminine behavior; thus a number of scholars have discussed gang girls as constructing an "oppositional" or "bad girl" femininity (see Hagedorn & Devitt, 1999; Messerschmidt, 1995; Portillos, 1999). Research, however, has consistently shown that youth gangs—with the exception of autonomous female gangs—are by and large male dominated in structure, status hierarchies, and activities, even as young women are able to carve meaningful niches for themselves (see Campbell, 1984; Fleisher, 1998; Hagedorn, 1998b; Joe-Laidler & Hunt, 1997; J. Miller, 2001a; Moore, 1991). Even young women in all-female gangs must operate within male-dominated street networks (see Lauderback et al., 1992; Taylor, 1993). Thus, while some scholars would suggest that because they are challenging traditional gender roles, girls' gang participation can be viewed as liberating, most researchers highlight what Curry (1998) refers to as the "social injury" associated with gang involvement. During the course of their gang involvement, girls face a number of risks and disadvantages associated with gender inequality. Moreover, there is some evidence of long-term detrimental consequences for gang-involved young women (Moore, 1991; Moore & Hagedorn, 1996).

Research has shown that girls in gangs face social sanctions, both within and outside the gang, for not behaving in gender appropriate ways. For instance, Swart (1991) suggests that girls' experiences in gangs are complicated by the contradictions they face as they balance deviant and gender norm expectations. On the one hand, he argues, "the female gang member's behavior must be 'deviant' to those outside of the gang in order to ensure her place within the gang itself" (p. 45). On the other hand, if it is too deviant, it risks the danger of offending other gang members who maintain certain attitudes about appropriate female conduct when it comes to issues of sexual activity, drug use, violence, and motherhood. The likelihood of such social sanctions, however, is shaped by the gender composition of girls' gangs. As I described, young women accepted as "one of the guys" are better able to escape disapproval, particularly with regard to their participation in gang delinquency (see Miller & Brunson, 2000).

Thus, Swart's findings are complicated, as Curry (1998) notes, by evidence that also suggests that young women's gang involvement provides a means of resisting limitations placed on them by narrow social definitions of femininity, which they recognize as limiting their options in an environment in which they are already quite restricted. Campbell (1987), for instance, found that "gang girls see themselves as different from their [female] peers. Their association with the gang is a public proclamation of their rejection of the lifestyle which the community expects from them" (pp. 463-464; see also J. Miller, 2001a). Likewise, Taylor's (1993) study of female gang members in Detroit found young women highly critical of the entrenched misogyny on the streets and the difficulties females often face in interacting in these environments.

Regardless of girls' awareness of gender inequality, it remains an inescapable element of their experiences within gangs and brings with it particular sorts of consequences. For instance, there is a clear sexual double standard in operation within gangs, as in American society as a whole (Campbell, 1990; Fleisher, 1998; J. Miller, 2001a; Moore, 1991; Portillos, 1999; Swart, 1991). Moore (1991) suggests that some young men viewed young women as sexual objects, "a piece of ass," or "possessions" (pp. 52-53), while young women, though recognizing gender inequalities in their gangs, on the whole wanted to see themselves as respected by male members. Girls' dating options were narrowed as well. Being a gang member and having the look of a gang member was stigmatizing for girls, making them less attractive to boys outside the gang. On the other hand, male gang members frequently had girlfriends outside the gang who were "square," and these "respectable" girls were looked to by the boys as their future (Moore, 1991, pp. 74-76; see also Fishman, 1995).

Moreover, research suggests that rather than challenging this sexual double standard, young women often reinforce it in their interactions with one another. Several studies reveal that gang girls create hierarchies among themselves, sanctioning other girls both for being too "square" and for being too promiscuous. Typically, the sexual double standard is reinforced by girls as sanctions against those they perceive as too sexually active. Girls have not been found to gain status among their peers for sexual promiscuity (Campbell, 1990; J. Miller, 2001a; Swart, 1991); rather, they are expected to engage in serial monogamy. On the whole, the sexual double standard tends to disadvantage girls in their relationships with boys but also interferes with the strength of their own friendship groups (Campbell, 1987).

My research suggests additional problems exacerbated by gender inequality within gangs. Attention to the association between gang membership and delinquency has overlooked an equally important relationship: that between gang membership and victimization. Though few studies have been attentive to this question, there are reasons to consider it an important one. There is strong evidence that participation in delinquency increases youths' risk of victimization (Lauritsen, Sampson, & Laub, 1991). Given ample evidence linking youths' participation in gangs with increases in delinquency, it seems self-evident that gang membership likely increases youths' victimization risks. In my research, gang girls were significantly more likely than nongang girls to have been sexually assaulted,[11] threatened with a weapon, and stabbed, and to have witnessed stabbings, shootings, drive-bys, and homicides (J. Miller, 2001a).

Moreover, gender inequality in gangs and young men's greater participation in serious gang crime suggests that victimization risks within gangs will be shaped by gender. Because girls are less likely than their male counterparts to engage in serious forms of gang crime, they face less risk of victimization at the hands of rival gang males, because they are less likely to engage in those activities that would increase their exposure to violence. This lesser risk is bolstered to the extent that norms or rules exist against male gang members targeting rival females (Joe-Laidler & Hunt, 1997; J. Miller, 2001a). Thus girls' lesser risk is especially the case with regard to lethal and potentially lethal violence, particularly because young women themselves rarely engage in gun violence (Hagedorn & Devitt, 1999; J. Miller, 2001a).

For example, in an analysis of St. Louis homicide data (Miller & Decker, 2001), we found that women were more than twice as often (17% vs. 8%) nongang homicide victims as they were gang homicide victims. Moreover, the vast majority of female gang homicide victims were not the intended targets of these killings: the modal, and by far predominant, pattern for female gang homicides was for the victim to be killed when suspects opened fire into a group. In contrast, the majority of male gang homicide victims were the intended targets. Likewise, Hagedorn (1998b, p. 197) reports that female gang members in his sample reported having been shot at an average of 0.33 times, compared to 9.1 times for male gang members, a ratio of 27:1.

However, because leadership and status hierarchies in mixed-gender gangs are typically male dominated, and because girls are less likely to engage in those activities that confer status within the gang, they are often viewed as lesser members within their gangs. This devaluation of young women can lead to girls' mistreatment and victimization, especially by members of their own gang, because they aren't seen as deserving of the same respect (see Joe-Laidler & Hunt, 1997; J. Miller, 2001a). These problems are further exacerbated by the sexual double standard described above, as well as high rates of intimate partner violence among gang youth as documented by Joe-Laidler and Hunt (1997; see also Fleisher, 1998). One particularly troubling issue for some gang girls is the use of sexual initiations for entrée into the gang. Both my research and that of Portillos (1999) uncovered the use of this practice—having sexual relations with multiple male gang members—among gangs, though in neither instance did we find it to be the primary initiation pattern for girls.[12] When this occurs, girls are highly stigmatized and disrespected by other gang members, both male and female. They are viewed as promiscuous and sexually available, thus increasing their subsequent mistreatment. In addition, they are viewed as taking the "easy" way in and are not seen as valuable members of the gang (J. Miller, 2001a; Portillos, 1999).

Moreover, I found that the stigma could extend to female gang members in general, creating a sexual devaluation that all girls had to contend with. Nonetheless, there appears to be tremendous variation in girls' experiences within gangs. Among the girls in my study, some were able to carve a niche for themselves that put them, if not exactly in the same standing as young men, at least on a par in terms of much of their treatment. Other young women were severely mistreated, and there was a range of experiences in between. Ironically, those young women most respected within the gang were more likely to face gang-related victimization at the hands of rivals. Those young women defined as "weak" by their lack of participation in gang-related fighting and delinquency were more likely to face abuses at the hands of their gang peers (J. Miller, 2001a).

Thus far, I have specifically discussed the impact of gang involvement for girls while they are in their gangs. What about after they leave? Few studies offer evidence of the long-term consequences of gang involvement for girls (see Moore, 1991; Moore & Hagedorn, 1996). However, the available evidence suggests that young women in gangs are at greater risk than others for a number of problems into and within their adult lives. Whereas many opportunities for legitimate success are gravely limited for young women living in impoverished communities, the negative consequences associated with gang membership can prove crippling. Gang membership exacerbates already troubled lives (Fleisher, 1998). Moore and Hagedorn (1996) note that although many young women turn to gangs as a means of dealing with multiple life problems, "for most women, being in a gang does have a real impact on later life" (p. 215).

Moore's (1991) research on Chicano/a gang members in Los Angeles found that ex-gang members could be divided into three categories: *tecatos, cholos,* and *squares.* She reports that approximately a quarter of the males in her study, and "a much smaller proportion of the female sample" (p. 125) were *tecatos*—heroin addicts involved in street life; about a third of the men but more of the women were *cholos*—persisting in gang and criminal involvement into adulthood. Women and men in this category typically had not held down regular jobs and had unstable marriage patterns, often characterized by early marriage and childbearing, followed by early divorce (Moore, 1991, pp. 125-127). Finally, she reports that whereas around 40% of the males in her sample went on to lead conventional lives ("squares"), this was the case for fewer of the women[13] (p. 127).

While Moore's Los Angeles research concerned individuals who had been in gangs in the 1950s and 1970s, her more recent work with Hagedorn (Moore & Hagedorn, 1996) compared these with contemporary African American and Latina gang members in Milwaukee, Wisconsin. They report that substantially fewer of these women continued their gang involvement into adulthood, concluding that "for women—but not for men—the gang was almost completely an adolescent experience" (p. 209). Latinas were more likely to be involved in drug sales and use into adulthood, compared with African American women. Moore and Hagedorn (1996) conclude:

> For Latinas in both cities, gang membership tended to have a significant influence on their later lives, but for African American women in Milwaukee, the gang tended to be an episode. There is much less sense in Milwaukee that gang girls of any ethnicity were as heavily labeled in their communities as were Chicana gang girls in Los Angeles. (p. 210)

It seems reasonable to suggest that the earlier a girl exits the gang, the greater her chances for a better life. Some evidence suggests that childbearing and the child care responsibilities that result often facilitate young women's maturation out of gangs (J. Miller, 2001a; Moore & Hagedorn, 1996). However, though having children may expedite girls' leaving their gangs, doing so does not necessarily increase their chances for successful lives. Partly this is because stable marriages and jobs are less available in the current socioeconomic climate in urban communities in the United States than in the past. Communities where many gangs are located have dwindling numbers of males in the marriage pool; moreover, skyrocketing rates of incarceration and lethal violence have greatly contributed to this shortage (Moore & Hagedorn, 1996; Wilson, 1996). Considering the high unemployment rates in most gang neighborhoods, many young men have few conventional opportunities and are increasingly likely to continue their gang and criminal involvement into adulthood (Klein, 1995). The bleak futures that await the men in their communities often makes marriage no longer a desirable component of gang-involved women's lives (Moore & Hagedorn, 1996). The attacks on many social programs have also negatively affected women's lives after gang membership. Moore and Hagedorn (1996) observe,

> Ironically, the most important influence on gang women's future may be the dismantling of the nation's welfare system in the 1990s. This system has supported women with children who want to stay out of the drug marketing system and in addition has provided a significant amount of cash to their communities. Its disappearance will deepen poverty and make the fate of gang women ever more problematic. (p. 217)

These issues are of vital importance for gang-involved young women and represent an area strongly in need of further research.

Conclusion

This chapter has addressed a number of issues concerning young women's involvement in gangs—the extent of their gang involvement, why they become involved, and what their experiences in gangs are like, including their participation in delinquency and exposure to violence. As I have shown, young women join gangs in response to a myriad of problems in their lives. Gang involvement, though, tends to exacerbate rather than improve their situation. It increases the likelihood that young women will engage in delinquency and exposes them to risks of victimization, at the hands of both rival gangs and gang peers. Though young women are not as involved in the most serious forms of gang violence as young men, and gangs are less likely to be life threatening for their female than their male members, nonetheless, gang involvement often narrows young women's life options even further (see Moore, 1991).

A number of suggestions for policy and practice emerge from this overview. With regard to prevention, the research highlights several notable issues. Girls begin hanging out with gang members quite early and often join gangs in the first years of their teens. Thus prevention efforts must begin quite early. In addition, a series of risk factors appears to converge for girls, increasing the likelihood that gangs become an alluring option. These include living in neighborhoods where gangs are in close proximity; having multiple problems in the family, including violence and drug abuse; and having siblings or multiple family members in gangs. Most significant, it appears to be the convergence of such risk factors that particularly heighten girls' risks for gang involvement. Prevention efforts should be targeted especially to girls exposed to these problems. However, as Maxson and Whitlock (Chapter 2, this volume) suggest, etiological research on female gang involvement has not identified clear risk factors for girls, above and beyond those identified for girls' risks for delinquency. Their suggestions regarding gender-specific prevention approaches appear prudent, given the state of our knowledge about these issues.

Findings presented in this chapter also have implications for gang intervention with young women. Most notable is the need to recognize *variations* in young women's experiences and activities within and across gangs. My research suggests that although in some instances gender-specific interventions may be useful (particularly in dealing with sexual assault and abuse), it is also the case that some features of gang programming for young men are likely to be important for girls as well. For example, though girls are rarely as involved in serious violence as boys, it is nonetheless the case that group processes, conflicts, and rivalries provoke girls' participation in confrontations with rival gang members in ways similar to those of young men. Thus, interventions for girls need to take such issues into account (see Klein, 1995).

Intervention strategies should also be tailored to meet the diverse needs of female gang members, with sensitivity to ethnic and cultural differences. In addition, given variations across gangs, specific knowledge about girls' gangs can provide suggestions for effective approaches. Specifically, attention to the gender composition and organization of girls' groups is likely to provide important information about girls' victimization risks and their exposure to violence-prone situations (Joe-Laidler & Hunt, 1997). In particular, the level and nature of young women's participation in gang crime may be an indicator of the particular types of victimization risks these young women face: Girls who are heavily involved in street crime are at heightened risk for physical violence such as assaults and stabbings; other young women are at greater risk for ongoing physical and sexual mistreatment by male gang members (J. Miller, 2001a; Miller & Brunson, 2000). Most important is the need to recognize that young women in gangs are not a monolithic group and should be approached accordingly.

Unfortunately, responses to gangs and gang members are often primarily punitive in nature, disregarding the social, economic, and personal contexts that cause gang participation. This punitive orientation toward gang members means that gang-involved youths are not seen as in need of assistance and protection, and this—coupled with the problems they face in their daily lives—has further detrimental effects on these young people (see Fleisher, 1998; Moore & Hagedorn, 1996). Moreover, programming and policies targeted specifically to the needs of female gang members have been scant (see Curry, 1999). Given the findings I have detailed above, the best course of action with regard to young women's gang involvement should involve policies that consider the social, economic, and personal contexts that influence gang participation, gang crime, and young women's victimization within these groups. Initiatives that actually consider the best interest of youths are needed in order to rationally respond to gangs and young women's involvement in these groups.

Notes

1. This title is borrowed appreciatively from Anne Campbell's (1984) monograph of the same name—recognized by many as the force behind contemporary research on young women in gangs.

2. Part of this discrepancy is likely attributable to differences in youths' perceptions of what constitutes membership in their gangs. See Hagedorn and Devitt (1999) and Miller and Brunson (2000) with regard to the gendered social construction of gangs and gang membership.

3. However, family poverty was not a significant predictor of gang membership for young women in the RYDS study (Thornberry, 1998).

4. Although the RYDS study did not find family violence to be a significant risk factor for female gang involvement (Thornberry, 1998), there is a growing body of literature supporting the link between childhood maltreatment and youths' subsequent involvement in delinquency (see Smith & Thornberry, 1995; Widom, 1989). Maxson and Whitlock (Chapter 2, this volume) note that studies of risk factors for gang membership are better at distinguishing gang and nongang youth among males than females. They suggest that "male gang members may be more distinctive than their nongang counterparts than is true for females," and that prevention programming for girls, given our current state of knowledge, may be most suc-

cessful in targeting girls' risks for delinquency more generally rather than risks for gang involvement.

5. Recent evidence suggests that girls' supportive relationships in gangs may be stronger in all-female gangs and those with a substantial number of female members than in gangs that are numerically or ideologically male dominated. See my discussion later in this chapter of Joe-Laidler and Hunt (1997), J. Miller (2001a), Miller and Brunson (2000), and Peterson et al. (2001) regarding the impact of gendered gang structure on member activities and delinquency.

6. Taken individually, a majority of girls fit within each category: 96% described living in neighborhoods with gangs (vs. 59% of nongang girls). Of these, 69% explicitly described their neighborhood and peer networks as factors in their decisions to join. Likewise, 71% recognized family problems as contributing factors (26% of nongang girls reported similar problems); and 71% had siblings or multiple family members in gangs, or described the influence of gang-involved family members on their decisions to join (compared to a third of the nongang girls who had gang members in their immediate family or multiple gang members in their extended family). In all, 90% of the gang members in the study report two or more dimensions of these risk factors; and fully 44% fit within the overlap of all three categories. In contrast, only a third of the nongang girls experienced a multiple of these risk factors for gangs, and only four nongang girls (9% vs. 44% of gang girls) reported all three dimensions.

7. In my study, differences between gang and nongang girls did not emerge in school measures, nor did gang members describe school contexts as contributing to their decisions to join. This may be a result of differences across sites, or the result of sampling or methodological differences (see Esbensen & Winfree, 1998, for a discussion of sampling and methodology).

8. This is particularly the case since boys in all-male gangs also reported lower rates of gang delinquency than youths in gangs with both male and female membership.

9. And note that girls in majority-male gangs reported more individual delinquency than boys in all-male gangs.

10. In fact, Joe-Laidler and Hunt note that fights between rival girls were often instigated by males, who reportedly enjoyed watching females fight. Though they describe rules excluding girls from fighting males from rival gangs, young women sometimes got caught in these conflicts.

11. Sexual assault requires some clarification. In all, 25 gang girls (52%) in my study had been sexually assaulted a total of 35 times. Most of the sexual victimization young women reported occurred in the context of their families or by men they were exposed to through family members. On the whole, the gang context did not seem to increase girls' risk of sexual assault as it did for their risk of other violent crime. However, as I discuss, this is not to suggest that sexual assaults in gangs did not occur or that other forms of sexual exploitation were not present. In fact, as I will discuss, the less girls were involved in gang crime, the more vulnerable they appeared to be to sexual exploitation and other mistreatment within the gang.

12. In Portillos's (1999) research, girls from the neighborhood could be viewed as "born into" the gang by virtue of their close connections to the neighborhood, and girls could also be beaten in as a means of gaining status. It was also the case in his research that when girls were "trained into" gangs, this was not always consensual. In my research most girls were beaten or jumped into their gangs, though there was more fluidity in St. Louis because of gangs' strong neighborhood dimensions. It is notable that Joe and Chesney-Lind (1995) did not report initiation rituals among gang youth in their study in Hawaii, and Joe-Laidler and Hunt (1997) do not describe initiations for PHP members, but they do for members of other gangs.

13. Moore (1991) notes that this finding is partly an artifact of the underrepresentation of "square" women in her sample. She notes, "Some such women refused the interview because their husbands would not allow them to discuss their 'deviant' adolescence; others refused because they were afraid that they would be questioned about what they now define as 'deviance' —particularly about sexual activity" (p. 130). Moore concludes, "These views offer a poignant confirmation of the stigma attached to women's gang membership" (p. 130).

Doing Field Research on Diverse Gangs

Interpreting Youth Gangs as Social Networks

MARK S. FLEISHER

Fieldwork in gang neighborhoods allows for the firsthand collection of data about the social lives of gang members. Gang fieldwork gathers data, such as on-site interviews and observations, that may lead to insights otherwise overlooked or unattainable with off-site data-gathering practices, such as interviews in controlled settings (offices, correctional settings), and/or the use of official records, such as police arrest reports. Field-based data collection is significant in gang research. A dominant advantage of field research is that a researcher can investigate firsthand the multiple social contexts that influence, or are influenced by, gangs. These social contexts range in size and complexity from single families to public housing projects to neighborhoods and communities.

This chapter is based on two gang field studies. The term *gang* used here is equivalent to Klein's (1995) use of the term *street gang* (p. 132), which refers to younger members, weakly organized, who commit "cafeteria-

AUTHOR'S NOTE: I wish to express my appreciation to my research assistant Kelly Hird, and colleagues Jessie Krienert, Regina Day Langhout, and Stanley Wasserman for their assistance in the Champaign research. Of course, errors of fact and interpretation are mine alone. LaWanda Washington, Iresha Washington, and Burpee Thomas were my field assistants in Champaign. Their support and assistance was greatly appreciated.

style" crimes (see Short & Strodtbeck, 1965, pp. 81-93). The first gang study was conducted among the Fremont Hustlers in northeast Kansas City, Missouri. The second gang study was conducted in a highly impoverished gang neighborhood on the north end of Champaign, Illinois, some 120 miles southeast of Chicago.[1] These gang field studies combined three research approaches: anthropological ethnography (see Fleisher, 1998, chap. 15, for a full discussion of fieldwork techniques used in Kansas City; similar techniques were used in Champaign); sociological theory with data analysis; and social network theory with data analysis. The analysis in this chapter focuses specifically on gangs as social networks. A social network refers to the web of social relations within which individuals (gang members and others as well) are embedded.

This chapter first defines terms necessary to understand gangs, social networks, and social capital. Second, there is a discussion of the implications of the term *gang* used as an attribute of individuals or as a quality of a relationship between individuals. Third, the case of the Fremont Hustlers is presented to illustrate the concept of social capital from a cross-sectional and longitudinal perspective. Fourth, there is a discussion of Champaign's north-end gangs as social networks within an emerging community. Finally, the conclusion emphasizes the need for more sophisticated gang prevention and intervention initiatives that are based on social network concepts.

Gangs: A Social Network Perspective

The social network perspective focuses on describing and analyzing webs of social relations. This perspective, as it is applied to gang analysis, assumes that gangs are social networks composed of individual gang members, and that gang member behavior is determined in part by a gang member's location in the structure of the social network. That location in the social network structure determines opportunities and constraints that expand or limit a gang member's choices.

The Kansas City research was an ethnographic study of the social networks of the Fremont Hustlers but offered no formal social network data. Social network ethnography focuses on gang members, among others, and *describes* the type and quality of their interpersonal relations. The Champaign research used a fieldwork approach to gather systematically sociological and social network data (Fleisher & Langhout, 2001), as a supplement to ethnographic observations. These social network data describe the friendship networks of adolescent and adult women who are self-declared gang members. A social network analysis (vs. an ethnography of social networks) *measures* the nature (i.e., structure and dynamics) of the relations among fellow gang members and between friends who are members of different gangs. The term *relation* (or relationship) refers to the bond that links actors. An actor may be an individual (What are the specific relationships binding members of a gang?) or a gang (Are there specific relationships that bind or repel gangs from one another?). A relation is a type of attachment. Attachments have different degrees of strength (weak vs. strong; Granovetter, 1973). Attachments may be emotional (lovers), social (friends), hierarchical (boss-subordinate), or affiliational (belonging to the same club; Wasserman & Faust, 1994, p. 18).

Social network analysis uses terms that are consistent with a grounded, socially based, contextual analysis. This analysis of gangs as social networks rests on the following core assumption: Gangs do not exist sui generis. Analyzing the patterns of relations among gang members, the links between and among gangs, and the nature of the links binding gangs to their encompassing social contexts is critical to understanding gang structure and dynamics (Short & Strodtbeck, 1965, pp. 7-10). Network analysts would ask, among other questions, How does network size (the number of individuals who self-declare an affiliation to Gang X) influence violence? How does network density (how well, if at all, do network members know one another) influence violence? How do the type and quality of relations among female gang members and/or between female and male members influence violence? How does a member's position in a network influence violence, in general, or violence in specific relationship to particular victims?

Social network analysis measures, among many things, an actor's location in a social network. A significant network measurement is the number of social connections leading to and away from an actor and the value (positive, negative) of those links (ties). The number and quality of ties will determine the social and economic opportunities available to an actor (an individual, a group, a neighborhood). Research has shown, for example, that economically wealthy communities are also rich in social capital (i.e., social networks and expectations of reciprocity [Lin, 1999]); the reverse is true as well (Sampson, Raudenbush, & Earls, 1997; Simcha-Fagan & Schwartz, 1986; Wilson, 1987).

The Kansas City (Fleisher, 1998) and Champaign research shows that individuals increase social capital while affiliating with a gang (see also Macon & Hagedorn, 1998). Stated another way, individuals who share a gang affiliation become, to some degree, bonded to one another (i.e., they share some degree of *bonding* social capital; see Horowitz, 1983, p. 187). Bonding social capital increases gang members' solidarity to one another (a measurable, social network hypothesis), which simultaneously separates members of Gang X from other gangs (also a measurable network hypothesis). If, however, gangs had the ability to create *bridging* social capital, gangs would obtain for their members mainstream social and economic opportunities by eroding class and race boundaries as a concomitant to extending and strengthening relations between an impoverished neighborhood, like the north end, and a mainstream community. The assertion that gangs are positively linked to community institutions is a measurable hypothesis, but there have been no formal tests of such a hypothesis (see Macon & Hagedorn, 1998; Moore, 1978; Sanchez-Jankowski, 1991).

"Gang": An Attribute or a Relational Variable?

The Kansas City and Champaign research shows that a gang is a social network that increases a gang member's social capital. Gang research customarily uses respondents' self-declarations of a gang affiliation as *the* test of gang membership (Esbensen & Huizinga, 1993). Such a self-declaration can be either an attribute of an individual or used as an inference about an individual's relations to other individuals similarly self-nominated. Were a gang declaration used as an attribute (an attribute variable), it would assert that being a gang member is comparable to other personal attributes, such as race and gender, and in this sense infers no relational (or social network) qualities. Were a gang declaration used as a relation (a relational variable), it would necessarily infer reciprocal relations among others in the same gang. It could then be reasonably assumed that a cohort of gang members (the term gang being used as an attribute) would create a gang group (the term gang being used as a relational variable), which would have the property of exclusive, nonreciprocal relations with members of other gangs and/or strictly limit relations with individuals who are not gang members or members of their own gang. Sociological gang analysis sorts individuals by self-nomination (gang as attribute), infers relational conditions among those individuals and between members of one gang and another, and infers gang "group" effects on individual behavior, without the use of relational data. Further explanation of this critical point is necessary.

A sociological model of gangs is based on the correlation of gang members' behavior to the gang members' attributes (Short, 1998, p. 17). Research shows, for instance, that females act out less violently than male gang counterparts (Miller & Decker, 2001). The correlation of gender and violence recurs in gang research (Fleisher, 1998), but the correlation itself cannot explain why females are less violent. Miller and Decker (2001) write, "Women's lower levels of involvement in gang homicide, as both victims and offenders, may reflect their lower rates of participation in gang life. Apparently, however, it is the *nature* of young women's gang involvement that is at issue" (p. 138; italics in original). The authors identify two key relational concepts: "participation in gang life" and the "nature of involvement [in gang life]," but astutely did not draw inferences about these relational concepts using correlational data.

The social network approach in Champaign used the variable "gang" as an attribute and then carefully defined its relational qualities, to explore in detail *the nature of relations as relations affect participation* in gang life. The term gang used as an attribute variable simply arranged respondents by self-declared gang affiliation; its use as a relational variable surprisingly discovered complex relational ties among members of the same gang and *between members of different gangs*. This finding clearly suggests that gangs are not closed or near-groups (see Yablonsky, 1959), but complex, interwoven networks of relations.

In summary, the sociological approach to gangs interprets gangs as collectives of individuals bound by a common variable: a gang label. Individual gang members are seen as bundles of attributes (age, class, education, gang affiliation) that cause behavior (see Abbott, 1997, p. 1152). Research measures individual attributes and correlates them. A social network approach identifies attribute variables as well, but focuses on the nature and quality of attachments among actors. This approach argues that the structure of a social network and the relations among its actors directly influence individual behavior. The use of the term gang as a relational variable must include the analysis of relational data; however, sociological gang studies have often inferred network attachments without appropriate supporting data. This data-collection omission has led to a number of problematic interpretations of concepts linked to gang life. These concepts include the meaning of "membership," "recruiting," "gang crime," "gang-related crime," and "gang-motivated crime." More discussion on this follows below.

The Ego-Gang Network

Klein (1995) strikes at a critical issue in the social nature of gangs as a structured arrangement of networks when he argues that a street gang is not a highly cohesive group: "What we see is a rather amorphous collection of subgroups, cliques, pairs, and loners. . . . It's loose and somewhat fragmented" (p. 61). The objective of a social network analysis of gangs would be to describe these subgroups, cliques, and dyads (pairs) and show how these units are structurally arranged and then discuss how such an arrangement influences the behavior of individuals and/or subgroups, cliques, and dyads.

A preliminary analysis of Champaign social network data (Fleisher & Langhout, 2001) has isolated an operational social unit called an ego-gang network. The ego-gang network is the total set of social relations of a gang member. The Champaign data show that ego-gang networks of female gang members include (male and female) gang members and (male and female) non-gang members. Ego-gang networks also have a spatial dimension: Ego-gang network actors reside in different locations. Thus, an ego-gang network may be widely scattered in locations, such as apartments, houses, parks, jails, and street corners.

The analysis of 51 ego-gang networks shows that included in each ego-gang network were males and/or females of a gang or gangs different from ego's (respondent). This means that ego-gang networks are socially flexible, and as the analysis below shows, enable a young woman to meet her complex set of material, social, and emotional needs. Ethnographic observations and interview data show, as well, the absence of formal intra- and intergang relations, in such activities as planning crime conspiracies. This suggests that these (to reemphasize, youth) gangs do not exist as formal organizational entities, as Klein (1995, p. 61) believed. This conceptualization of a gang views it as a complex, interwoven system of ego-gang networks. A more complete discussion of ego-gang networks and related implications follows below.

The next sections show the utility of the ego-gang network in two ecological settings. The Fremont Hustlers case shows that the ego-gang network offered alienated youth an opportunity to establish bonding social capital. The limitation of the Fremont Hustlers' research is that formal network data were not gathered; however, cognitive, social domain data were elicited (Fleisher, 1998, pp. 39-43; also, Fleisher, 2000). The Champaign case suggests that ego-gang networks are the social expression of the emergence of structural and relational ties within a newly established black community, and within that context, ego-gang networks have obtained social and economic value.

Fremont Hustlers

The Fremont Hustlers were a gang with some 72 members. They had a community reputation, according to local police, for violence and drug distribution. Gender and ethnicity made Fremont an interesting study case: Males and females were black, white, and Hispanic. Ethnographic observations did not show that gender and race restricted access to drug markets nor that race interfered in interpersonal relations (i.e., black members did not remain away from white and Hispanic members because of color). Many of them had been abused by parents or stepparents and had run away from home; others were continuously embroiled in emotional battles with parents and/or stepparents and stayed away from home as much as possible. Ardent members were school failures and had long records of suspension and expulsion. Most had been confined in juvenile institutions, and some had been arrested as youth and transferred to adult courts and, by their late teenage years, had served sentences in adult prisons. Nearly all of the ardent members had known one another long before the self-conscious formation of the Fremont Hustlers in the summer of 1992. Even without a gang label, these youth needed one another: In fact, they had nowhere else to go, no one else to count on but one another.

A few of the ardent members had been reared in or near the Fremont area and still had parents residing there. Nearby parents did not mitigate these youth's survival issues, especially if these youth were alienated from their parents and/or if parents had personal problems similar to their children's. How can a drug-addicted mother help her son or daughter deal with addiction? How can an ill-educated mother convince her daughter to remain in school after being expelled? How can a woman whose son was born when she was 16 convince her son (or daughter) that teenage pregnancy was the first step toward life-long economic problems? There was a clear link between the dilemmas of the parents and those of their children.

The Fremont data show that the notion of gang "membership" can be misleading, especially in light of the operational definition of ego-gang networks. The term *membership* may be misleading because it easily conjures familiar images: member of a family (denoting life-long affiliation); member of a country club (denoting status and achievement); member of a fraternal organization (denoting a formal and informal screening process, initiation, rules). Fremont research did not reveal a systematic process of "recruiting" potential members nor did research find a formal mechanism of group affiliation. Fremont ethnography shows that so-called membership was identical with friendship and that youth who were friends with a "member" were considered to be members once they became familiar to other youth.

Fremont's ego-gang network, reported ethnographically but not formally, united its members by satisfying their personal needs. Despite various degrees of reciprocity, Fremont was not a peaceful brotherhood and sisterhood. There were animosities among females and males over lovers and insults, and many members did not know one another well enough to hang out. In fact, only about one third of Fremont's 72 named members hung out on Fremont and 13th Street. The concept of the gang as a group far exceeded the social nature of the group.

Fremont was a neighborhood gang that was not located in a gang neighborhood. The gang's location in the Fremont neighborhood was fortuitous and based on the fact that a female member's mother owned a house at the corner of Fremont and 13th Street. That house soon became the physical location of Fremont, because the house owner's drug and alcohol addiction meshed with the crimes of Fremont members. Figure 13.1 summarizes key points in the life histories of Fremont youth and their parents, as well as observational data collected through participant observation gathered during the study period from 1995 to 1997. It also identifies individual and family risk factors that have been linked to gangs (Howell, 1998). Risk factors have effects on individual and family levels of intergenerational human and social capital. *Human capital* refers to the capacity (education, training) of an individual to be economically productive. Fremont and Champaign research indicates that low levels of family-based human capi-

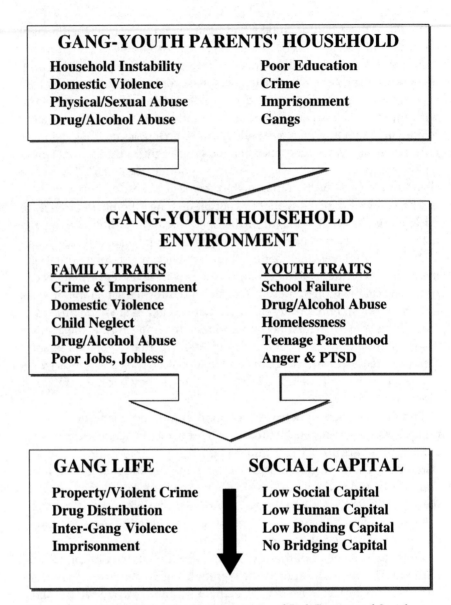

Figure 13.1. Fremont Hustlers' Intergenerational Risk Factors and Social Capital Assessment

tal contribute directly to the low human and social capital of a family's descendants.

A review of the three-generation model begins with the Gang-Youth Household Environment. The left side of this box shows Family Traits and on the right side, Youth Traits (PTSD refers to post-traumatic stress disorder, which is an outcome of harsh early-life socialization; see Fleisher, 2000). The Youth Traits are linked to Family Traits and are an outcome of inadequate and harsh childhood socialization (McCord, 1991; Moffitt, 1993). The traits in this box are linked in a left-to-right, or family-to-individual pattern, and in an intergenerational progression, as well. Children born into households defined by such harsh Family Traits will realistically have few chances to overcome them and will realistically end up with, to some degree, the personal deficits identified in Youth Traits.

The upper-most box, Gang-Youth Parents' Household, summarizes the traits of the households, which were identified in life history interviews with the parents of Fremont members. Domestic violence, drug abuse, poor education, and imprisonment (among other destructive family traits) necessarily reduce a family's collective level of human and social capital. Poorly educated, alcohol- and/or drug-addicted individuals with poor employment records cannot reasonably establish the basis for a strong social and economic position within a community. Such social and human capital deficits are the context within which the next generation is born. Such household deficits are worsened when households are located in racially marginal, economically isolated communities. Were we to know little more about a Fremont member's family life than the traits of his or her grandparent's family, we would have the basis for the prediction that the grandchild (a Fremont member) would likely be a marginal child.

The lowest-level box shows the link between the traits of Gang Life and their effects on Social Capital. Crime, drugs, violence, and imprisonment tell only part of the tragic story. The long-term persistent deficits faced by a Fremont member are: low social capital; low human capital; low bonding capital; and low bridging capital. Each Fremont member is an adolescent with a poor education and low-value employment skills. Even if these adolescents were not gang members with rap sheets, their social and economic fate would be dismal. A criminal record seals their fate. Unlike the bonding effect of a gang label in the context of an emerging, racially isolated community (as in Champaign's north end), the Fremont Hustlers, in general, tolerated one another but never acted as a unit. The social unit often fragmented into small networks of adolescents who "hated" other members. This was especially common among females who "fought" over boyfriends. Such "child-like" feuds weakened one of the primary, positive outcomes of being a Fremont Hustler: bonding social capital, which could unite and, for a while, offer protection.

The Fremont Hustlers were known for violence and drug distribution. Whether the reputation was "deserved" is immaterial; an affiliation with Fremont did not open doors in the mainstream community, except perhaps prison doors. Being a Fremont member destroyed an attempt to bridge the gap between the street and reasonably good employment. Fremont had no political prowess; its leaders could not meet with the mayor and the police chief to broker education and employment opportunities for members. The gang was simply what it appeared to be: poor, marginal youth who hung out together, sold and used drugs, and occasionally acted out in violent ways. Fremont members in the mid-1990s did not have the social and human capital to overcome social and human capital deficits set in motion two generations before their birth.

Champaign's North End

Fieldwork interviews show that the adolescent and young-adult gang members of the north end are the grandchildren and great-grandchildren of the north end's founding generation of immigrants, who moved to Champaign directly from southern states (Mississippi, Arkansas, Alabama) or moved to Champaign from Chicago (see Grossman, 1991, for a thorough discussion of black migration to Chicago). Census data in 1990 show 2,152 residents residing in the north-end study site; 94.2% of those residents were black. The earliest immigrants to the north end appeared in the 1940s and 1950s. Census data show that the north-end study site has been the poorest neighborhood in Champaign since 1970, when economic data on Census tracts first appeared (before 1970, data cannot be segmented by Census tract). In Champaign, the mean white household income in 1990 (in 1998 dollars) was $55,532, and the mean black household income was $22,263; however, the mean household income on the north end decreased (in 1998 dollars) from $25,798 in 1970 to $15,594 in 1990.

Interviews with north-end residents who are over 50 years old reveal that, for as long as they remember, the north end had (what they call) gangs, with familiar names: Vice Lords, Gangster Disciples, Black P-Stones, and Black Disciples. In the 1960s and 1970s, Mad Black Souls and Black Panthers were common, too. Intra-state migration from Chicago to Champaign and back again may account for the migration of gang members (or simply the diffusion of gang names), but this notion must remain speculation until more interview data are collected (movement between Champaign and Chicago is common today). North-end residents also say that their community was socially and economically isolated from white Champaign until recent decades. Desegregation and busing are still vivid in the memories of community elders. Also remembered is violence. Middle-aged and older residents can point to the physical boundaries around the north end. Elders say that the Champaign police did not go beyond those boundaries on daily patrols unless they had to. A long-term employee of the Champaign Police Department remembers when police cruisers were targets of gunfire as they entered the community. A career employee of the Champaign School District remembers occasions when he "had to be escorted" into the north end by local black residents to visit students' families. Whites were not welcome in the north end, he said. Blacks were not welcome in the white community, they said.

Fieldwork shows that there are no institutional forms of bridging social capital between the north end and the mainstream community. Even though the north end is no longer highly segregated (i.e., whites enter freely and without danger), black freedom and social and economic progress have been slow, as the above Census data show. In a real sense, the north-end black community has had to acquire social and economic mechanisms to meet the conditions of poverty within its boundaries. Fieldwork shows that today's residents rarely leave the north end for social occasions during which they interact with people who do not reside in the north end. There are few north-end jobs and no job recruiting within the north end by community employers. Residents who are employed elsewhere, work and return home. The black north end has no institutional means to enter the white community. The white community has no reason to enter the black north end. These communities live apart; however, it would be easier for north-end residents to live separately if they earned middle-class incomes.

A variable-based, sociological concept of gangs as it applies to the north end does not explain how or why crime-oriented gang groups emerged in the 1950s and 1960s or how these groups function in the community (see Short & Strodtbeck, 1965, p. 270). Were gang groups to function primarily with a crime orientation, the north end would soon be depleted of adolescent and adult males and females as they were arrested and imprisoned. The north-end gangs do not attract attention to themselves. Territory has been reduced to someone's apartment or a corner of a park. There is no graffiti; such markings are targets for police suppression. Age grades are, of course, a natural occurrence in a multigenerational community where friends and kinsmen who share a gang affiliation will naturally be stratified by age. Were gangs conceptualized as closed or near-closed groups in a community typified by long-term poverty, such groups would be socially and economically maladaptive and likely lead to intra-community strife (as an effect of bonding social capital) rather than the inter-household cooperation that is necessary to cope with poverty.

The fundamental issue of north-end life is this: Needs of the north-end's residents must be satisfied given the resources available on the north end and to north-end residents. Government assistance contributes financial wealth to households (nearly 100% of adolescent and adult residents receive or have received some form of public aid). Public housing, Section 8, and food stamps prevent homelessness and starvation. Legitimate employment provides income to an undefined percentage of adult men and women. Income-producing crime, such as low levels of drug selling, provides household assistance to women with children and too little money. To be sure, years of fieldwork have shown that drug sellers who flaunt their behavior (by selling on street corners and lawns) and profits (newer cars, motorcycles) are soon arrested and imprisoned as part of the police department's drug-selling suppression strategy.

Ego-gang network data were gathered from 51 gang members, ranging in age from the mid-teens to the early thirties. Gangs in the sample are the Vice Lords, Black Disciples, Black P-Stones, and Gangster Disciples. Ego (respondent) was asked to provide a list of friends, close friends, and best friends, using field-tested operational definitions (Fleisher & Langhout, 2001). Respondents were asked if they were actively involved in gangs or were no longer actively involved; operational definitions were provided. The ego-gang networks were stratified by activity level. Ego was asked to list each friend's gang affiliation, when ego met each friend, how many hours each week ego hung out with each friend, how well ego liked each friend, and a series of questions designed to measure reciprocal relations between ego and alters.

Fifty-one respondents named 360 alters (or friends): 100 were Gangster Disciples; 72 were Black P-Stones; 96 were Vice Lords; 26 were Black Disciples; 13 included members of smaller gangs (4, Mickey Cobras; 7, Four Corner Hustlers; 1, 26 Playboy; and 1 Black Gangster), and 53 were unaffiliated with any gang (see Tables 13.1 and 13.2). Table 13.1 is a descriptive analysis of the ego-gang networks of women who are still active in gangs. These women said they still hang out with gang friends most to all the time; are involved in street activities, including fights, drug selling, and other offenses; and obtain most of their personal income in gang activities (hanging out, street activities, and street-related sources of income are the operational criteria for active gang life).

The ego-network size varied widely, from 5 to more than 32, with a mean ego-network size of 12.9. No ego knew all members of her gang. In fact, the central-most Vice Lords (i.e., the Vice Lords who knew the highest number of Vice Lords and were known to the highest number) knew fewer than 10% of all Vice Lords listed as alters in the sample. This finding is highly significant: Social networks, by definition, involve mutual obligations and specific and/or generalized reciprocity (specific reciprocity means, "I'll scratch your back if you scratch mine"; generalized reciprocity means, "I'll scratch your back but you don't have to scratch mine"). If gang members do not know one another, there can be no mutual obligations and reciprocity, and thus the notion of the gang as a "group" (a type of network) is extremely suspicious.

This fact argues against gang members' facile claims of being a unified group, or that "our gang" has hundreds or even thousands of members, as some Gangster Disciples have asserted in Champaign field research. This fact also challenges police estimates of gang membership when such estimates use a gang label as the only criterion for asserting that a city has, for instance, 1,500 Vice Lords, without demonstrating the relations among these 1,500 gang members. To assert that there is a Vice Lord gang "group" with more than 100 members in Champaign is, based on ego-gang data, a

Table 13.1 Ego-Gang Network Descriptive Characteristics:
Active Female Gang Respondents (*N* = 25)

Gang Name	Sample Size	Age Range	Range in Ego-Gang Network Size	Range in the Number of Males in Ego-Gang Networks	Range in the Number of Opposite-Gang Female Alters in Ego-Gang Networks
Black Disciples	1	17	6	0	2
Gangster Disciples	8	16-21	5-32	0-10	2-17
Black P-Stones	10	16-20	6-23	0-9	2-16
Vice Lords	6	16-25	7-25	0-10	0-8
Mean		18.2	12.9	3.9	6.8

Table 13.2 Ego-Gang Network Descriptive Characteristics:
Inactive Female Gang Respondents (*N* = 26)

Gang Name	Sample Size	Age Range	Range in Ego-Gang Network Size	Range in the Number of Males in Ego-Gang Networks	Range in the Number of Opposite-Gang Female Alters in Ego-Gang Networks
Black Disciples	1	18	4	0	2
Gangster Disciples	9	20-27	3-21	0-5	1-17
Black P-Stones	3	14-18	8-12	1-3	2-5
Vice Lords	13	18-33	4-29	0-7	1-15
Mean		21.6	9.4	1.5	4.5

factual error. In the absence of relational data, an assertion about "gang group size" means only that more than 100 youth refer to themselves with the same attribute variable, Vice Lord. The inference that these 100 individuals are a gang "group" (if a group is a type of social network) may lead to faulty inferences about gang-group crime. Were "gang crimes" aggregated solely on the basis of a gang attribute variable (Vice Lord, Black Disciple), to the exclusion of relational data, then to refer to "Vice-Lord crime" would be both a conceptual error and a factual error, given the nature of ego-gang networks.

Yet another extension of the inference of relations among gang members without the benefit of relational data appears in classifying offenses as "gang-motivated" and "gang-related" (Maxson & Klein, 1990, 1996; Spergel, 1995, p. 24). More accurate characterizations would be "ego-gang network-motivated" and "ego-gang network-related" crime, because the operational unit of street crime is not a gang group but rather the ego-gang network or some segment of it. Although the ego-gang network has social reality, the *gang group* may be only a metaphor of expression used by youth being queried about gang crime, gang initiation, gang exit, and the like.

Ego-gang network data show that the range in the number of males in female egos' ego-gang networks ranged from zero to 10, with a mean of 3.9. This means that some females had no male gang or nongang friends (see Campbell, 1990) and some had many. Who are these males? Interview data show that males are often kinsmen (brothers, cousins, boyfriends, former boyfriends) or childhood friends who grew up near ego, on the same street or in the same housing project. Do these males have a function beyond friendship? Indeed they do. When asked which of their friends would be called upon for assistance in the event of a physical threat made by a male in another gang, female egos almost unanimously selected male friends, especially kinsmen. Their selection, however, was not predicated on a male's gang affiliation being the same as ego's; rather, friendship super-ceded a gang affiliation. Ego's best male friends, no matter what gang they claimed, would be sought for protection and thus, at least temporarily, in-crease ego-gang network cohesion but not gang group cohesion (cf. Klein, 1995, pp. 61-62; Klein & Crawford, 1967).

The gender composition of female-ego's ego-gang networks is mostly female. If the opposite were true, that male gang members, when asked to cite friends, cited few or no female friends in their ego-gang networks, gangs would appear to be all or mostly male. Answering the questions—What is the role of females in gangs? What is the role of males in gangs? Are there female gangs?—seems to depend, it is suggested here, almost en-tirely on the gender of the ego who is providing ego-gang network data.

The fact that females have few male ego-gang friends could help to ex-plain the social dynamics of why females report committing less crime than males. Gang research repeatedly reports that male gang members commit the most crime. Ego-gang data suggest that less-crime-involved females have few or no high-crime males in their ego-gang networks. High-crime-involved females seem to have a higher percentage of high-crime males as ego-gang friends; such associations may pull these females into street crime (Fleisher & Langhout, 2001; see J. Miller, 2001a, chap. 6; Miller & Decker, 2001, pp. 126-128). Access to and participation in high-crime ego-gang networks (i.e., those ego-gang networks whose members commit more crime; Short & Strodtbeck, 1965, referred to *"cliques* of *conflict gangs"* [p. 98; italics in original]) may be the social network counterpart of gang researchers' finding that delinquent acts increase with gang affilia-tion and gangs that facilitate crime (Thornberry, 1998).

Female egos' inclusion of few males in ego-gang networks has another interpretation. Black culture has been stabilized by female-headed house-holds (Stack, 1974). What's more, with aggressive antigang and antidrug policing in Champaign, survival-oriented females would be ill advised to rely on males for financial and social support. Ego-gang network data show that females do not rely on males for financial needs and child care. With this in mind, it is consistent with black culture for females to exclude males as friends in ego-gang networks, especially in critical relationships, such as a need for protection.

Inclusion in an ego-gang network might be conceptualized as *joining a gang*. Joining simply means spending more time weekly with more gang-active, ego-gang network alters; however, according to youth, one can be considered an active gang member without committing crime (see Klein, 1995, p. 20; Short, 1997, p. 81; and more generally, Short & Strodt-beck, 1965, for a discussion of gangs and delinquency). Interview data strongly suggest that spending more time with ego-gang network com-panions is frequently coterminous with becoming socially and economi-cally independent from parents', grandparents', or extended relatives' households.

Nine out of 54 respondents said they had to commit an act of *initiation*. In one case, an adolescent said she had to beat up someone who was known to be tougher than she. In another case, a young woman had to at-tack and beat up any stranger. All nine cases share a similarity: A young woman was coerced into violence by a male, most often a relative (brother, cousin), who was much older (often 10 years older). Had the young woman not followed orders, she would have been beaten by the older male or by someone he ordered to beat her. These cases suggest that these young women were moving into an aggressive male's ego-gang network. Once included in his ego-gang network, these women negotiated their own so-cial life and gradually formed a nonviolent (or less violent) ego-gang net-work. The details of such social negotiation have yet to be completely un-derstood.

The most interesting and significant finding is that ego-gang networks in this sample were *never* gang homophilous; that is, ego-gang networks always included members of gangs other than ego's. A Vice Lord's ego-gang network, for instance, included non-Vice Lords and often included friends without a gang affiliation; the same is true for other gangs, as Table 13.1 shows. In one case, a respondent reported that her ego-gang network had no members of her gang. In no case did the number of opposite-gang alters exceed 50% of an ego-gang network. The average number of alters in respondents' gangs was 6.8.

What does this finding mean? First, it shows the difference between the use of "gang" as an attribute and as a relational variable. In neighborhoods where youth have no friends other than those in their own gang (Decker & Van Winkle, 1996), such a finding may not occur. Middle-aged residents say that social life on the north end has always included multiple gangs. The bonding social capital effect of gang affiliation has been mitigated by the need for a social structure that allows for social flexibility. In this sense, an ego-gang network structures potential relations; however, there is no rule of single-gang interaction that requires members of Gang A to interact only with other members of Gang A or interact more with members of Gang A than with outsiders. Ego-gang networks show that individuals in any gang may interact with members of other gangs as well as gang-unaffiliated friends. The nature of ego-gang networks also shows that sentimental ties, expressed by limiting interaction only to individuals in the same gang, do not necessarily emerge in ego-gang networks.

In the social reality of the north end, a gang affiliation (attribute) is one thing, a friendship (relation) is another. For instance, it is common for a young woman to "rollover" or "jump" (change gang affiliation) when she gets a new boyfriend. A Vice Lord woman today may be a Black Gangster tomorrow, because her new boyfriend is a Black Gangster. Rolling over *never* has violent repercussions. Women who jump are called "renegades." Young women who are "true" say that renegades have an inability to "settle," cannot make a decision, and make bad girlfriends and wives.

Table 13.2 provides ego-gang network data on inactive females. Note the decrease in the number of mean network size from 12.9 (active) to 9.4. Although the relative percentage of opposite-gang, female alters remained fairly constant (52.7% for active, 47.8% for inactive), the relative percentage of males in ego-gang networks decreased dramatically from 30.2% (active) to 15.9% (inactive).[2] This decrease has several causes. Males' residences shift frequently, making them unavailable to females who withdraw from active gang life; males are also more likely to be arrested and imprisoned. More important, males lose interest in pregnant females and in the mothers of their children once these women withdraw from street life, especially if these women cannot offer males a place to hang out, sleep, and sell illegal drugs.

All of the inactive females interviewed, without exception, said that having a child was the benchmark event that slowed and eventually ended active gang life. Pregnancy and childbirth required a recomposition of ego-gang networks: Strong ties to high-crime and/or aggressive males and females were replaced with strong ties to residentially stable, low-crime or "no-crime" females. Such a recomposition of the ego-gang network is the social network counterpart of *exiting a gang*. New mothers' ego-gang network relations were vital, especially in the absence of natal and extended family ties, to assist in pregnancy and creating a household. In this process of settling down in the community and establishing a household, as their mothers did before them, gang women said that their ego-gang network friends helped the most in pregnancy and aided in creating a household. These gang friends were these young mothers' oldest and most durable relations.

Network structures broader than the ego-gang network influence continued gang participation for new mothers. Fieldwork observations and interviews with inactive women suggest that if gang activity continues post-childbirth, that activity depends to a large extent on whether a new mother has female kin who are willing to care for infants. A 19-year-old mother of a 2-year old son said she continued active gang involvement for almost a year after her son's birth, because her mother, aunts, and/or grandmother cared for her son. A shift from a gang to a nongang lifestyle is compelled, to some degree, by family structure and the economics of parenthood.

Many friendships in ego-gangs have a long duration. Inactive females in their late twenties report lifelong friendships with men and women in their ego-gang networks. Here is a summary of key points about ego-gang networks on the north end: Friends are often lifelong; cohesion among friends within and between gangs is high, as measured by reliance on one another for social support and during events of potential violence; intimacy is high as well, as measured by their reliance on one another to care for children, provide emergency residence, and share property. Stack's (1974) findings parallel these for the north end.

North-end ego-gangs allow the richness of social life to be flexible, supportive, and ever present. Gang relations are, respondents agree, the best way to offer protection in the event of outsider threats, especially to females. If a young woman is threatened, all she needs to do is call her brother or male cousin, or in some cases, three or four of her most aggressive female friends—all accessible in the ego-gang network—and she will be protected.

Conclusion

This chapter discusses ego-gang networks. The Fremont Hustlers is an example of ego-gangs used in a specific situation of youth alienation. The ego-gang networks supported these youth and provided them with a survival setting. Fremont's ego-gang networks did not extend widely into the Fremont neighborhood, and in this sense, Fremont was a gang in a neighborhood. The Champaign example is quite different: This complicated setting shows how ego-gangs are a flexible social mechanism that allows for integrating households by linking youth, even though many are not members of the same gang. Such data suggest that inter-gang hostility is not a necessary element in gang affiliation, and that it may be influenced more by individuals' propensity toward violence than by the inherent nature of a gang group (as conceptualized sociologically) or an ego-gang network.

Ego-gang networks have specific functions. A gang affiliation is the first step in creating bonding social capital, but that affiliation alone is insufficient to actually bond individuals. Bonding requires mutual relations, trust, cooperation, and attention to the quality of relations. Friendships reported in ego-gang networks are the high-value relations in respondents' lives: These are the people who, experience shows, can be trusted in particular situations. Even though there are more than 100 Vice Lords, a Vice Lord can trust only 8, 9, or 10 of them. This social network is small but valuable, in its social and economic relations, in the absence of other social capital.

Champaign data show that ego-gang networks emerge prior to self-reported gang affiliations; most friendships in ego-gang networks have preceded "joining a gang." Joining meant only that a woman began to spend more time with a particular set of friends, to the exclusion of other friends. These are the friends, or some of the friends, with whom an adolescent female will spend her life. Women in their forties and fifties still hang out with friends they had as adolescents on the north end.

Fremont Hustlers and Champaign's Vice Lords, Gangster Disciples, Black P-Stones, and Black Disciples focused and facilitated the creation of bonding social capital, but ego-gang networks did not create the bridging social capital necessary to help gang youth leave the streets. Overcoming intergenerational human and social capital deficits is the most challenging issue in gang intervention and prevention. Gang prevention in at-risk families may be able to provide crime resiliency through after-school programs, athletics, and drug education, but unless such intervention and prevention increases an actor's level or potential for increasing bridging social capital, prevention and intervention initiatives will likely fall short.

These social network research findings suggest that gang interventionists must be mindful of the nature of intra- and inter-gang social life, especially with youth gangs that are customary in the social-scape of impoverished communities. Such gangs have deep community roots. Simple forms of intervention, prevention, and/or suppression will likely fail. Poverty will keep generating the need for ego-gang networks; police suppression will fill the prisons but will always fail to solve the problem of poverty. Prevention is difficult if people are continuously hungry. Intervention has a chance of success, if it is well planned. If today's intervention enables a gang member to earn a General Education Diploma, and if his son earns an associate's degree and his grandson earns a bachelor's degree, only then would such intervention have a real human capital benefit in modern society. That human capital benefit would be unrealized, however, if the educated grandson still resides in the same socially and economically isolated, impoverished community as his grandfather.

Gang prevention and intervention initiatives must go hand in hand with community-based economic and social development. Helping a person at risk is good; aiding a community at risk is better. Ensuring that poor communities, like Champaign's north end, are linked in long-term relationships to the mainstream community is best.

Notes

1. The Kansas City research was conducted with a grant from the Harry Frank Guggenheim Foundation, between 1995 and 1997. The initial research in Champaign (1995-1999) was conducted when I was a local evaluator in a national youth gang suppression, intervention, and prevention demonstration project, under the direction of Professor Irving A. Spergel, funded by the U.S. Department of Justice, Office of Juvenile Justice and Delinquency Prevention. Then, with a grant from the Office of Juvenile Justice and Delinquency Prevention (2000-2002), research in Champaign continued and focused on women's involvement in gangs.

2. These percentages were derived by dividing the mean for opposite-gang alters and male alters by the mean network size of active and inactive, ego-gang networks.

Chinese Gangs
Familial and Cultural Dynamics

SHELDON X. ZHANG

**Delinquency in the Chinese Community—
Beyond the Model Minority Myth**

The perceptions of Chinese American youth in the mainstream American culture have been dominated by the image of a model minority for decades. This view of Chinese American youths as hard-working, high achieving, and well disciplined first came into vogue in the 1950s when the mainstream media, as well as politicians, began to praise their academic success, good behavior, and success in entering white-collar professions (Chun, 2000, p. 89; Tong, 2000, p. 174). As a corollary, popular magazines of the 1950s publicized the absence of juvenile delinquency among Chinese American youths (Chun, 2000, p. 89).[1]

Such celebrations of Asian Americans' achievements have, however, exaggerated their success and created a damaging image that glossed over the structural barriers and cultural adversities for many who have struggled to overcome socioeconomic hardships and racial discrimination (Tong, 2000, p. 174). In short, the idealized portrait of Chinese American youth had not been drawn from reality.

AUTHOR'S NOTE: The author would like to acknowledge the helpful comments received from Therese Baker-Degler and Zhiwei Xiao. This study was partially supported by a grant from the National Science Foundation (SBR-9300919). The author is solely responsible for the points of view expressed here.

Because of the restrictive immigration policies against Chinese nationals between 1882 and 1964, the size of the Chinese youth population in the United States was small (Chin, 1996; Tong, 2000). During this period of time, which included two world wars, the few Chinese youths in America were reported to be law-abiding and hard-working students (Chin, 1996). This myth of the Chinese American youth as a "model minority" has largely continued until today, obscuring the many recent young Asian immigrants whose opportunities in life rarely extend beyond the edges of their urban neighborhoods and whose often poor academic performance pushes them to seek recognition among gangs and delinquent peers (Chun, 1993; Kitano, 1997; McGrath, 1983). In Chinese neighborhoods, behind the bustling restaurants and glitzy gift shops, it is not hard to find business owners and small vendors struggling to fend off Chinese youth gangs whose harassing tactics include extortion, scams, and outright violence (Chin, 1996).

The repeal of the Exclusion Act in 1943 and passage of the War Brides Act in 1946 resumed Chinese immigration to the United States. More recently two historical events have further boosted the number of Chinese youths entering the United States. First, after the fall of Saigon in 1975, tens of thousands of refugees were allowed entry into the United States, many of whom were of Chinese descent (Vigil & Yun, 1990). Second, in 1978, the U.S. government established diplomatic relations with Mainland China, opening up formal immigration channels to a vast population.

The increase of the Chinese youth population in the United States has also brought about various social problems, particularly youth gangs in many major urban Chinese communities. In fact, at the same time that the mainstream media were touting the Chinese success stories, Chinatowns in San Francisco and New York were already experiencing the effects of increasing numbers of youth gangs that were disrupting the otherwise seemingly "peaceful" Chinese community. In the late 1960s and early 1970s, the violent activities of Chinatown gangs began to appear in newspapers in San Francisco and New York City (Chernow, 1973; Howe, 1972; Pak, 1972).

"Hardly a week-end passes," reported a San Francisco local Chinese paper, "without some disruptive incident and rarely is there a dance without these small gangs spoiling the whole evening"("The Open Forum," 1950, p. 8). Far from being model sons and daughters, these troubled youths badgered their community with their violent acts and extortion (Tong, 2000, p. 91). Gang members were usually drawn from recent immigrants with few marketable skills and weak educational backgrounds. Yet these gangs succeeded in terrorizing merchants and residents with street fights and extortion schemes (Chin, 1996; Kelly, Chin, & Fagan, 1993).

The problems of youth gangs in Chinatowns took a drastic turn when calculated murders and senseless massacres erupted in several major urban Chinese communities in the late 1970s and early 1980s. The first incident of this magnitude occurred in 1977 in San Francisco when three heavily armed Chinese gang members walked into the Golden Dragon Restaurant and opened fire on customers, killing 5 and wounding 11; none of the victims were members of a rival gang (Ludlow, 1987). In New York, on Christmas Eve in 1982, three masked gunmen randomly shot customers inside a Chinatown bar (Blumenthal, 1982). Similar gang-related violent incidents broke out in Los Angeles, Houston, Boston, Chicago, Vancouver, and Toronto (Daly, 1983; Dubro, 1992). Chinatown gangs by now have gained nationwide notoriety through these media reports, aided by such Hollywood portrayals as *The Year of the Dragon* and *China Girl*. As a result, police agencies in major metropolitan areas moved to establish special task forces to combat Chinese youth gangs (Chin, 1996, p. 10).

Although many American criminologists had marveled at the absence of juvenile delinquency in Chinese neighborhoods (Sollenberger, 1968), the growing evidence of delinquency gathered attention only slowly. Until very recently, Asian Americans were underrepresented among social scientists so that few "insiders" with the needed linguistic and cultural skills were available to conduct community-oriented research among Asian youths. For instance, in the past 15 years (1986-2000), there have been fewer than 10 entries in *Sociological Abstracts* on subjects that had anything to do with crime and delinquency in the Chinese American community, many fewer than those about Chinese delinquents living in Hong Kong, Canada, Australia, or China. Of the few studies found, only three dealt directly with Chinese youth gangs. Chin and his colleagues (Chin, 1996; Kelly, Chin, & Fagan, 1993) are among the very few who have ever conducted systematic empirical inquiry into Chinatown youth gangs.

Much of the existing literature to date has argued that the success of Chinese American youth in educational and economic advancement stemmed from deeply held cultural values and traditions, including strong familial ties, parental control, and the priority of collective solidarity over individual gain. Not surprisingly, these same cultural attributes have also been used to explain the low rate of delinquency in the Chinese community as early as 1937 (see Haynor & Reynolds, 1937, and, more recently, Tsai, 1986). However, to examine youth gangs or delinquency effectively, it is necessary to consider family values and how parents may contribute to the development of delinquency because of their own problems or their inability to handle their children (Zhang, 1995). Considering the central role of parents in the Chinese family, it is fair to say that any systematic study of youth gangs or juvenile delinquency in general in the Chinese community requires an understanding of how parents deal with their delinquent children. This study attempts to examine the little-known family dynamics of how Chinese parents apply their cultural values and traditions from the Old World to manage and control their delinquent children in the New World.

Defining the Chinese Culture

Chinese are often treated as a homogeneous group and lumped together for analytical purposes. Although it may seem like splitting hairs to differentiate the subgroups among Chinese, it should be acknowledged that much diversity exists in terms of language and customs. These differences have arisen from such elements as history, geographical origin, area of settlement, time and circumstances of entry into the United States, and levels of acculturation.

The most obvious source of cultural identity is the place in which one has spent one's childhood. This geo-cultural imprint at an early age sets a cultural orientation that prompts one to identify oneself not only as a Chinese, but a Chinese from a specific region: They are Cantonese, Fujianese, Shanghainese, or Chinese from Hong Kong, Malaysia, the Philippines, or Vietnam. They speak different languages, eat different foods, and worship different gods. These patterned differences in customs, languages, and lifestyles obviously bear consequences that are worth exploring, and oversimplification will occur if these groups of Chinese are treated as a homogeneous cultural entity.

On the other hand, the task of doing research on youth gangs in the Chinese community does not easily lend itself to the luxury of appreciating the many fine cultural nuances because of the overall small Chinese population in the United States and the even smaller number of youths who get in trouble with the law. Political and cultural sensitivity, therefore, may have to give way to empirical pragmatism. This study deals with this issue by identifying what may be considered common cultural norms and beliefs that mark the accepted boundaries of the ethnic group called "Chinese." The purpose here is not to engage in a detailed discussion of what constitutes Chinese culture, but rather to capture commonly shared cultural expectations that help to define social control in the Chinese culture and therefore make it possible to systematically examine how delinquency is handled in a Chinese family.

Confucianism, Family Hierarchy, and the Face-Saving Mentality

Chinese culture (as well as many East Asian cultures) is heavily influenced by Confucianism, which advocates social order through the maintenance of a hierarchically arranged social structure, where roles are clearly ascribed to each individual and adhered to within the family and community. Most of Confucian thought that has come to dominate Chinese cultural practices for 2,500 years centers on the cultivation of one's proper conduct in relationship to others in different social positions (de Barry & Bloom, 1999, p. 42). The development of an awareness of and concern with human interrelatedness and reciprocity is considered fundamental to achieving moral nobility. A "virtuous" person, or *junzi*, in Confucius's teachings, should possess three essential qualities—filial devotion *(xiao)*; humaneness *(ren)*; and ritual decorum *(li)*; all of which are crucial in the maintenance of proper social order.

Rituals and protocols guiding social interactions are well defined and reinforced through a myriad of highly developed feelings of obligation, most of which are hierarchical in nature (such as those of a son to his parents and of a common man to his emperor). The family and community supersede the individual (Chun, 2000, p. 89). The importance of the family and the high level of respect and reverence for authority figures are values learned from an early age through the rituals and customs of the Chinese patriarchal culture (Chao, 1994, 1995).

Rules of conduct are formalized and prescribed for specific roles to a greater extent than in most other cultures (Shon & Ja, 1982). Because of the cultural emphasis on interconnections, one's behavior not only reflects one's adherence to these rules, but also the family and kinship network to which one belongs. Unlike Western culture, which emphasizes self-sufficiency and mastery of one's own destiny, Chinese culture views individuals as the product of their relationships to their family, especially their parents (Wong, 1988).

Social control is accomplished through the teaching of "face" at a young age. Social and legal transgressions are considered a disgrace to one's parents and to the family and detrimental to one's social standing within the community (Hu, 1975). Shame (or losing "face") is most often used to reinforce the adherence to shared social expectations and norms of acceptable behavior, because the consequence of a transgression will lead to the withdrawal of the family's confidence and support. In a culture where interdependence is important, the actual or threatened renouncement by others, especially one's own parents, raises the existential anxiety of being left alone to face the world. Because individualism is less highly valued than it is in the Western culture, being left alone is a more punishing threat.

Family and Kinship Patterns

Many Chinese scholars have argued that there are no "typical Chinese families," just as there are no typical American families. They argue that the variations within a culture are as wide as between cultures (Kitano, 1997). The structure and style of family and kinship patterns largely reflect the level of acculturation, exposure to the mainstream culture, and life circumstances in the host society. Wong (1995) argued that the Chinese American family is best viewed as a product of the interaction between structural factors (i.e., restrictive immigration policies and racism) and cultural factors (i.e., Confucian ethics). Because these factors are constantly changing, the Chinese American family is also undergoing constant change and adaptation to the changing social environment.

However, in contrast to other ethnic groups in the United States, such as whites or African Americans, there are a few identifiable patterns of Chinese family relations, at least among first-generation immigrant families (where most juvenile delinquents are concentrated). Multiple generations living under one roof is a common phenomenon. Members of a family network tend to be blood/marriage related and remain stable over time with clear hierarchical arrangements. Divorces and remarriages are less common than in other ethnic groups; thus, frequent exit from and entry by relatives is rare.[2] These family and kinship patterns in Chinese culture bear direct consequence on how delinquent youths are perceived and handled. Family stability has often been cited as a pillar in the control of Chinese youths.

Method

Data for this study were collected from in-depth interviews with 15 Chinese parents whose sons were adjudicated offenders and placed under the supervision of the Asian Gang Unit at the Los Angeles County Probation Department.[3] The interview questions revolved around three main themes—(a) their reactions to the instant arrests, (b) their interpretations of the delinquency events, and (c) and their responses to the subsequent events as a result of the justice procedures (i.e., dealing with the child's probation activities). The offenses that these gang members committed ranged from receiving stolen goods and burglary to robbery and aggravated assault with deadly weapons.

Because of the study's goal of exploring the familial and cultural dynamics in dealing with and responding to Chinese youth gang members, a set of predetermined criteria was used to select parents with similar exposures to the justice system. Although these gang members varied in the type and severity of their offenses, the parents were similar in many ways.

First, only parents of male gang members were considered for this study. Because of the rare occurrence of female Asian gang members, and the complex sociocultural constructs surrounding the differential treatment of female delinquents in Chinese culture, this study chose not to include parents of female gang members. It is common in Chinese culture that parenting practices vary along gender lines (Gorman, 1998; Ho, 1989). Second, only parents whose children were on formal probation for the first time were eligible. This was because chronic or repeat offenders might be dealt with differently at home than would first-time offenders. Third, only parents whose children were placed at home on probation (HOP), the most common sanction for juvenile offenders, were eligible because of the study's intention to explore parent-child interaction while under official sanction. In addition, youngsters placed on HOP are exposed to the same level of supervision treatment, more similar than those placed on other probation programs—such as juvenile camps or out-of-home placement (e.g., group homes or treatment centers). By limiting subject selection to the same supervision program, the impact of differential official treatment on parental response would thus be avoided. By holding these variables constant, this study chose a group of parents who were confronted with an event of similar or comparable magnitude, as opposed to chronic youth offenders with longer criminal histories and more serious offenses.

These 15 parents consisted of eight mothers and seven fathers.[4] Except for two mothers, who were born and raised in the United States, all respondents were first-generation immigrants with limited English-language skills. All interviews were conducted in the parents' language of choice (which included Mandarin, Cantonese, and English) and at locations convenient to them, which included their homes and probation area offices.[5] Subjects were paid a nominal fee for their participation.

Data analysis was driven by the thematic content of the interviews, and two strategies were applied—(a) the explicit wording of these parents' responses and (b) conceptual similarity. A theme was established if at least half of the parents (or 8) used the same or similar wording for a concept or an elaboration of a concept (Chao, 1995; Gorman, 1998). In a few cases, themes generated by a small number of parents were also developed because of their conceptual significance.

_____ **Findings**

The Sky Is Falling

The instant arrest and subsequent sanction were overwhelmingly perceived as an emotionally upsetting event, so much so that most respondents reported that their entire families went into a state of crisis. The responses were clearly one sided, with respondents emphasizing how the arrests ruined their otherwise peaceful lives and how the court-ordered probation activities came to dominate their daily routines and became the focal concern of the families. It was apparent during the interviews that few of these parents had any prior experience with or knowledge of the justice system. Most parents had never thought that any member of their family would be arrested. To most of these respondents, the worst encounter with police they had ever imagined would be getting a traffic ticket. After learning her son was arrested for possessing a weapon, a 34-year-old mother, whose income came from her part-time job in a restaurant and welfare subsidy, felt her world was caving in:

> The police called me. I was so scared. I dropped my work immediately and went to the police station at once. I was shaking so hard that I didn't even think I could drive. It was the first time in my whole life that I was in contact with the police. I was crying that day. I got out a vacuum cleaner pole and threatened to hit [minor's name] if he would ever get in trouble again.

These parents were unprepared for events of this nature, and their centuries-old traditions only exacerbated their emotional upheavals. Getting in trouble with an authority figure was perceived as a violation of a fundamental cultural tradition. For these immigrant parents, who were struggling to survive in their new country, having to divert time and attention to deal with the justice system (of which few had any prior knowledge) was overwhelming. For many parents, it was more than a stressful event; it was a crisis. A mother, who was recently divorced, said,

> I have developed a lot of physical illnesses because of my worries about [minor's name]. I have an ulcer now and have gone into hospital three times and the doctors told me to reduce my worries and stress. How can I? I was very hurt to find out that [son's name] was arrested. I felt I had failed on everything in my life, my family and my marriage. After the arrest, I just wanted to forget everything. I took up alcohol and drank until I passed out so I didn't have to deal with all the pain. My older daughter was very mad at me and I was mad at my son and myself. I asked myself why I even bothered to bring children into this world.

As for the interpretation of the arrest event, the majority of the parents were quick to accept the offense as charged by the police. Despite the justice process, which presumes that those charged are innocent until proved guilty, all the respondents immediately assumed that their children must have done something wrong, even though some parents thought the police blew the incident out of proportion, as a 51-year-old mother said:

> I knew he liked to play with the *nunchaku* [martial arts instrument] at home, but I never thought he would bring them to school. Nor did I think that doing so would get him arrested. I guess the police considered them weapons.

It was rare for Chinese parents to deny any wrongdoing on behalf of their children, to blame someone else, or to accuse the police of arresting the wrong person. When probed about possible causes of their children's transgression, Chinese parents, in general, went through long periods of soul searching and sought explanations from within. Most cited reasons included poor parenting, inadequate supervision, and overindulgence. Their cultural background did not allow them to adopt many of the standard answers that were often used in the mainstream culture—blaming the government, the society, the justice system, racial discrimination, or poverty. In fact, when prompted with questions on these external sociolegal factors, many parents found it odd that the interviewer would suggest that government or the police might have caused their children to get in trouble. As one Chinese mother put it,

> I don't know why you keep asking whether the government or police have anything to do with my son's bad behavior. They care enough to help me. They order me to come and I have to come [to court]. [Minor's name] deserves the punishment. He should do his time. I don't know much about this country and its law. Whatever they tell me to do, I will do it.

The most these parents could find outside their immediate family as causes were the bad friends their children were keeping. Even the association with the bad friends was often brought forth in the context of their lack of supervision, which gave rise to the opportunities for their children to go out and play in the neighborhood. A mother wept as she described how she had not paid attention to whom her son was socializing with and now it was hard for her to stop him:

> I was busy working and did not spend enough time with [minor's name]. He came home every day from school and had a lot of time by himself. When I found out he was going out with bad friends, I tried to stop him. I would block the hallway with my arms and refused to let him pass. He would go into his room and climbed out of the window. I couldn't stop him. I even fought to restrain him from leaving the house.

To most respondents, it was neither customary nor culturally acceptable in their home countries to blame the government or the authorities for a child's misconduct. This was in contrast to the mainstream American culture in which delinquency is often explained and studied in the context of such factors as poverty, lack of job opportunities, racism/white oppression, and decaying neighborhoods where street crime of various sorts is common.

Feelings of Embarrassment and Self-Blame

Feelings of embarrassment and disgrace were the most common emotional reactions among the parents, many of whom openly called themselves incompetent parents. They took responsibility for their child's behavior, asking repeatedly what could have gone wrong with their parenting that led their child astray. Accepting responsibility for their child's behavior and blaming themselves for having failed to steer their child in the right course exemplifies the Chinese cultural tradition of filial devotion. Most mothers broke into tears during interviews and described how embarrassed they felt after receiving the phone call from the police. To many, the memory of the event (i.e., having to face the police and probation officer) was nightmarish enough to sustain feelings of shame and disgrace for the rest of their lives. A mother who was a waitress in a seafood restaurant said,

> I feel I have lost all my face. In all my life, I have been honest and trustworthy. How embarrassing it was for me, a Chinese mother, to go to the police to pick up my son. I could tell he was embarrassed too. I was scared to death when I went to the court. I had not even dreamed of a day when I might have to go to court. It must have been my fault. I must have put too much pressure on him to do well at school. I used to hit him a lot, a couple of years ago, and blame him for not working hard at school.

One could not fail to notice the intensive feelings of embarrassment of these parents. This transference of shame onto the parents because of their child's bad behavior represents a cultural response to traditional Chinese belief that "bad" children are the product of "bad" parents. Moreover, the displays of parental disapproval and embarrassment seemed to be a culturally conditioned practice that aimed at inducing the reciprocity of similar emotions in their delinquent child. When probed as to whether they shared these embarrassing feelings with their delinquent child, all parents reported that they wanted their child to be fully aware of their disapproval so that the child would feel bad for what he had brought upon the family. Another waitress mother, who was raising her son by herself for about 10 years while waiting for her husband to join her from mainland China, said,

> I keep telling my son that even though we are very poor, I still have managed to find money to hire a private tutor for him. On the day of the arrest, it just happened that the tutor did not show up on time. He should have waited at home. Instead, he ran out with his friends and got arrested. I almost fainted when I got a call from the police. Now look what I have to do for [minor's name]. I lose my face every time the stern-looking judge wants to see me and do whatever the court tells me to do. I am scared to death each time when I go to the court, all because of my son.

Acculturation and Education—
From Enmeshment to Differentiation

This study found that in a small number of cases, the native-born and college-educated (in the U.S.) parents were somewhat less inclined to feel personally responsible for their children's troubles with the law. Even though all expressed disapproval and disappointment in their delinquent boys, the intensity of their reactions was noticeably reduced. These parents were the only ones in the sample who were able to see causes in the larger society as contributing to their children's downfall, such as the lack of job opportunities and structured activities for their children, the bad influence of street gangs, the corrupting effects of poor neighborhoods, and the exploitation by the media. Such was the case for an engineer father, trained in the United States, who placed much of the blame on the gang members with whom his son was socializing. His son was on probation for receiving stolen goods and possessing weapons. The 56-year-old father said,

> His problem started when he was transferred from Downey to Alhambra High. At the new school, he became really out of control. The government should control gangs at school. Right now there is no control at all. I don't think parents are responsible for their children's wrongdoings. He chose his way. As parents, we can't choose his friends.

Though shocked to hear about her son's arrest for vandalism, a U.S.-born mother seemed able to differentiate herself from the incident and found an external contributing factor to her son's arrest:

> After we moved to Torrance and he went to a public school at 10th grade, he has been exposed to all types of kids. [Minor's name] is a bold child and likes to take risks. And also there is the bad influence of violent movies. Now I keep telling [minor's name] "you have to be responsible for yourself." His psychologist said he was looking for excitement.

To the less educated and new immigrant parents, placing the blame on external and larger social factors was a foreign idea. To think otherwise, like a native-born American, would require successful acculturation, which may happen in time. For example, most of the respondents in the sample were ordered by the court to attend parenting classes, which was a common probation condition for most juvenile offenders who were placed at home on probation. These court-ordered parenting classes appeared to enable some parents to mimic the vocabulary of the mainstream culture and lessen their self-blaming and emotional enmeshment with their children. After taking these parenting classes, a Chinese father said,

> We were devastated at first. It [delinquency] was not acceptable in this family. We became very upset and sad at not being able to control [minor's name]. Now we know we can only provide him with as many tools as possible. We can only point him to the right direction, but we can't make choices for him. We don't know whether he will get arrested again. There is no way to choose friends for him. Now we know better from the court-ordered parenting classes. We have a support group to call on each other for help.

Although he acknowledged the different concepts he acquired from the parenting classes, he also complained that parents were powerless in the United States and remembered his days in Hong Kong where parents routinely used corporal punishment to rein in their wayward children. These parenting classes appeared to point to an effect of acculturation on parental perception of and response to their delinquent children. The more acculturated Chinese parents became, the more likely they would be inclined to externalize family and personal problems and find external causes for their child's delinquent behavior that were acceptable in the host culture and that released them from the burdens of their original culture. The new immigrant parents, however, had not had the time to acquire these cultural responses.

Role Reversal and Breakdown
of Traditional Family Hierarchy

Many parents noted that they felt powerless in front of their children, because they were busy making ends meet and had little time or knowledge of how their children were doing at school or with whom they were socializing. Their children were often forced into playing the adult roles, such as doing the family banking, filling out paperwork from public authorities (such as the DMV), and interacting with social service agencies. Parental control was thus significantly weakened. The hierarchy that traditionally maintains the stability of many immigrant Chinese families was no longer viable. These youngsters made their own decisions and socialized with whomever they chose. In short, they were no longer looking up to their parents for guidance, protection, or even financial assistance.

After her son was arrested for burglary, a 45-year-old mother said that she had seen it coming because her son was running around with "bad friends." At the time of the interview, a bench warrant had been issued to arrest this delinquent offender for probation violations. He was in hiding with the help of his gang friends and stopped contacting his parents. The mother said,

> I want the police to arrest him and put him away because I have no control over him anymore. He is driving me and his two sisters crazy. We used to drive around every night to look for him and make many phone calls to find out where he was. Now I don't know where to look for him. I am a bad parent and can't live up to my duties. I have tried everything. I can't control him. I am frustrated, angry, and sad. He is out there every day. I don't know where he sleeps and whether he has enough to eat. Who is preparing the three meals for him these days? I am so worried. All parents love their children. But I often wonder why I even gave birth to him.

Because of their limited knowledge of the host society, schools, and the justice system, these parents were unable to exercise their traditional roles. Their attempts at providing guidance and protection, or imposing discipline were easily dismissed by their children as useless or simply "stupid." Many delinquent children simply took advantage of their parents' ignorance about the host society. One mother with limited English found out from a court-appointed interpreter only after her son's arrest and probation hearing that her son had previously been suspended from school several times. All along, she had been led to believe that because her son was doing so well at school he had been given extra "vacations" from school. Another mother concurred with this observation:

> I can't read English and don't know how to supervise his homework. I really wish I could help him with his homework, but I can't and don't know how.

Managing the Aftermath

When discussing what might have contributed to their children's involvement in youth gangs and delinquent activities, the most often cited reasons were (a) the lack of supervision and (b) the influence of bad friends. Correspondingly, two themes ran through most of the conversations with these parents about what to do with their children on probation: (a) increase supervision and (b) control the selection of friends.

Although these two strategies were not new to these parents, what made the difference this time was the restored parental authority, backed by the explicit coercion from the court and the probation officer. To them, probation officers seemed to enhance their parental authority, enabling them to give orders that would be obeyed. Most Chinese parents reported that they appreciated the structure and rules imposed by the court. They were even grateful that probation officers spent time with their children and worked with the parents to impose the court order. Parents who previously felt powerless in front of their wayward child now were able to call on the probation officer to intervene. In fact, many parents often threatened to call their probation officers if they believed their child was behaving badly.

The mother who became an alcoholic welcomed the intervention from the court and probation office wholeheartedly. She reported that her son was listening to her again, and that she felt her relationship with him had never been better, thanks to probation:

> Probation is good. It puts more discipline and structure in his life. I welcome all court orders. They are positive. He is really afraid of his probation officer. Mr. Lewis [minor's probation officer] did a lot of good for [minor's name]. Probation has changed [minor's name]'s attitude and behavior. He doesn't wear baggy pants anymore. Now we do everything together. I take [minor's name] with me everywhere. When he comes home from school and I am at work, the first thing he does is to call and let me know he is home. We are to-

gether more often. I stay home more. I don't drink anymore. Now I am happy. I see [minor's name] every day at home.

Because of the culturally prescribed fear of authority, many parents became consumed in court-ordered activities. The respondents reported that they would spend most of their nonworking time in making sure their sons followed the rules set by the court or probation (e.g., attending counseling classes, paying restitution, and doing community service). Even during working hours, these parents continued to worry about their delinquent child and feared possible relapses. All parents seemed to have established their own ways to check on their children. A mother and her husband, a banquet coordinator, used a pager to accomplish this task:

There is a lot more stress in our life and more time is spent on watching him. We have to tell him not to stay out late and make sure he comes home on time. We have given him a pager and page him often. He has to report to us all the time. Whenever he goes out he has to get permission from us. We have gotten tougher with him and become more involved with him.

Despite their culturally conditioned reverence for authority, parents complained about the rising stress as a result of their need to comply with court orders and to supervise their child. There were many activities that these parents must do to assist their child on probation. They would need to assist their child in paying restitution, to drive him to his community service or to see his probation officer, to accompany him at tutoring and counseling classes, and to attend parenting classes themselves. These activities did not seem to ease the parents' worries. A mother, whose son was arrested for auto theft, said,

I am very worried he might be in trouble again. There are too many distractions in his life now. This is a very confusing age for him. Psychological counseling is not helping me; it only gives me headaches. I have to go everywhere [minor's name] goes. I feel so tired most of the times. Each month we have to see his probation officer once. For the whole month my heart feels heavy.

Although these parents complained about the stress and worries they experienced in supervising their children, all respondents reported significantly improved family relationships because of the increased interactions and time spent between parents and the delinquent child. These parents hoped the improved parent-child relationship would prevent their boy from getting in trouble again. As a Chinese father put it,

We grew closer. We talk to him a lot about his day or his activities at school. Actually we channel all of our energy into his life. We have nothing else in our mind but his well-being. I am taking him to school every morning, making sure he is there. His mother calls him at school every day to check up on him. Right now I don't want him to socialize with anyone, especially his gang friends.

As a part of parental involvement and watchfulness, the control over the selection of friends came naturally to these respondents, who were eager to exercise their regained authority. Given that all court orders for identified gang members on probation include provisions against socializing with certain individuals in the neighborhood, this effectively increases parents' control over who their children can go out with. Moreover, the probation officer has the authority to add names to the list, thus increasing the range of undesirable associates to be avoided. All parents appeared to agree on what kind of people their children should not socialize with, and they shared surprisingly similar definitions of "bad friends." These were youths who did not do well in school, who were disrespectful and seemingly out of their parents' control, and who wore gang-like clothing. Doing well in school consistently appeared to be the number one criterion in the definition of a "good" child. Frequent questioning about where and with whom the child was playing became an essential part of parental supervision, as most of the parents were very worried that their children would succumb to bad influences. As a mother said,

My son complained that I don't let him do anything. I am just afraid he might go back to his friends. I don't let him play with his friends anymore. He can't play at the video arcade. I bought him video games to play at home. I only allow one friend to come to our house, and he is in college. Maybe he'll be a good influence.

In sum, increased parent-child activities were reported among most respondents. Respondents in general relied on themselves to supervise their delinquent children. Most participate actively in their children's probation-related activities, including driving them to community services and helping pay fines and restitutions. Besides probation and the court-ordered parenting classes, Chinese parents sought little external assistance from established social agencies or social workers, from community-based counseling agencies, support groups, or school counselors. Several factors could contribute to their lack of utilization of formal social services. The Chinese families may be less familiar with such community agencies. Their limited language ability and restricted social networks further hamper their efforts to take advantage of many social services. There is also a lack of cultural support and tradition for turning to social support systems for personal problems and the even stronger cultural stigma attached to using services associated with mental health (Fong, 1998). Probation services therefore became the social agency on which these parents relied the most in their efforts to control their child.

Discussion

Parents in this study seemed most distraught by their inability to maintain their traditional family hierarchy and to exercise effective control over their wayward child. The situation was exacerbated by the long hours they had to spend at work due to financial pressure as well as limited employment opportunities.

The parents needed to maintain their precarious economic situation. Because most of the parents had few marketable skills for joining the mainstream economy, their livelihood was confined within the ethnic Chinese enclave economy. A majority of the mothers worked in restaurants where 10- to 12-hour working days were the norm. Several fathers held more than one job to bring in extra income. Working long hours in low-paying jobs reduced their time with their families. Overwhelmed with fatigue, the exhausted parents often gave up interaction with their children to attend to the bare essentials of family matters, such as buying groceries, cooking, and resting.

Tong (2000) pointed out that most working-class immigrant parents have to forsake parental supervision as a result of their labor-intensive jobs in the secondary labor market or enclave economy. In these dual-worker families, husbands and wives experience a complete segregation of work and family life. Sung in her 1987 study, conducted among Chinese immigrants in New York City, found that although 82% of the children lived with both mother and father, 32% did not see their fathers from one day to the next, and 21% never even caught a glimpse of their mothers.

Therefore, prolonged parental absence or inadequate supervision due to chronic financial pressure and physical exhaustion undermined parental supervision over the youngsters. It was only natural that these youngsters would gravitate toward friends from the neighborhood and seek comfort and companionship in the pseudo-family of similar peers. These youngsters were marginalized at the outskirts of both cultures—rejecting their parental values and refusing to follow their steps into the "slavish" labor market, and yet unable to assimilate into the mainstream culture of the host country. All concerned youngsters in this study were either first-generation immigrants or children of at least one new immigrant parent. Cultural maladjustment was likely a main cause of their delinquency involvement.

At a more fundamental level, a repeated theme throughout the interviews was the apparent breakdown of the traditional family hierarchy, which could be attributed to a host of cultural factors besides parental fatigue from working long hours. The concept of role reversal is likely to become an important issue in explaining the causes of delinquency in the Chinese immigrant community. A well-functioning Chinese family rests on an effective parental hierarchy. Unfortunately, when such a hierarchical structure is not present, children are left to their own proclivities, leading to delinquency. Linguistic and cultural barriers rendered these parents impotent in dealing with their children. Because of the rapid increases in immigrant families in the United States, it is important to understand these families and the unique experiences that characterize the process of striving for a better life in a new society. With few exceptions, there are two themes that dominate the life experiences of most racial and ethnic minority immigrants—their cherished American dream and their inability to speak the language (Balcazar & Qian, 2000).

Regardless of country of origin and socioeconomic status, most immigrants come to the United States to seek opportunities to improve their material life, and all face various challenges and pressures, among which English fluency is probably the most critical determinant of adjustment in the United States. Those who cannot speak English well often find themselves unprepared for fulfilling their dreams, especially those with little formal education and few employable skills, who often end up in low-paying and low-status jobs (Balcazar & Qian, 2000, p. 360).

Although small in its sample size, this study nevertheless revealed surprisingly consistent responses from the parents. I hope these findings can serve to increase the understanding of how delinquency arises in immigrant Chinese neighborhoods in the United States. With the rapid increase of the Chinese population in this country, juvenile delinquency among Chinese communities has become a recognized social problem that requires systematic examination. In a culture heavy on tradition and hierarchy, the recognition of how Chinese parents perceive and respond to delinquent children is crucial to establishing effective policies for the prevention and control of wayward youngsters.

It is hoped that this study will bring about more systematic inquiry into the causes of delinquency among Chinese immigrant youth, to examine the interplay of Chinese cultural traditions and norms with those of the larger society as they are related to the rise of delinquency, and to seek empirical data that may provide helpful guidance in prescribing effective social control policies. With further research on Chinese delinquents, evidence will accumulate to better understand the causes of delinquency. That understanding can, in turn, be helpful in formulating justice policies.

Notes

1. A few examples include: "No Chinese American Juvenile Delinquency," *America* (July 6, 1955), *93*, p. 402; "Our Amazing Chinese Kids," *Coronet* (December 1955), *39*, pp. 31-36; "Why No Chinese American Delinquents? Maybe It's Traditional Respect for Parents," *Saturday Evening Post* (April 30, 1955), *227*, p. 12; "Americans Without a Delinquency Problem," *Look* (April 29, 1958), *22*, pp. 75-81; "Chinatown Offers Us a Lesson," *New York Times Magazine* (October 6, 1957), pp. 49ff.

2. For instance, the percentage of divorced Asians and Pacific Islanders was about one half the percentage of whites (U.S. Bureau of the Census, 1999).

3. These subjects represent a subset of a larger sample of Asian parents in a study funded in part by the National Science Foundation (SBR-9300919). Additional interviews were conducted at a later time with other Chinese parents and probation officers at the Asian Gang Unit.

4. One respondent served as a guardian for his delinquent brother, who was 15 years younger, and appeared in front of the judge and probation officer because their parents could not speak a word of English.

5. Through this exploratory study, methodological problems were uncovered during interviews with Chinese respondents. Most of them had little or no prior experience with this type of interview. Many parents had little formal education and were unfamiliar with many concepts common in Western culture. Thus extra explanations were needed, hence significantly lengthening the interview and increasing the possibility for "noise" in data collection. Readers should, therefore, be cautious in the interpretation of the findings.

15

Street Gangs

A Cross-National Perspective

MALCOLM W. KLEIN

In the fall of the year 2000, an international group of European scholars submitted a proposal for funding to the European Union (Weitekamp, 2000). The purpose was to establish, over a 3-year period, an interactive network of researchers interested in studying street gangs and developing principles for the prevention and control of gang activities. Because it was generally thought up to that time that street gangs were principally an American problem, this chapter will review the history of this new development—known as the Eurogang Program—and place it in the context of this volume of *Gangs in America*. Why should one include a chapter on street gangs outside the United States in such a volume? At least four reasons offer themselves.

1. We have "exported" our American street gang culture abroad. For example, there are Crips in the Netherlands (van Gemert, 2001). As we come to understand foreign variations of our own gang structures, we will learn more about what the sine qua non of street gangs is, and what is peripheral to their necessary nature.

2. The particular forms of European gangs seem similar to those to be found in the United States, although with differences in prevalence and in ethnic makeup. These structural similarities and variations inform us about both European and American youth cultures.

3. The Eurogang Program was initiated by a few Americans on the basis of American gang experiences. We are naturally curious to study our own impact (or lack thereof) in this new setting.

4. The very considerable generic knowledge we have accumulated over the past 70 years in the United States may be quite culture bound. Comparative research elsewhere can illuminate our own knowledge limitations with respect to such well-studied issues as gang location, diffusion, structure, ethnicity, age, gender, cohesiveness, and behavior patterns (including crime).

Gangs Elsewhere

Although this chapter deals principally with the cities of Western Europe, it is clear from a scattered literature that street gangs have been noted in many other locations. Most of this literature, unfortunately, notes but does not describe these gangs: Our empirical knowledge of street gangs in foreign lands is skimpy at best. Here are a number of examples:

- Japan, South Africa, Zambia, Kimshasa, Dakar, the Cameroons, Ceylon (now Sri Lanka), Thailand, Malaysia, Chile, Argentina, India, and Egypt (Clinard & Abbott, 1973)

- Kenya, Tanzania, South Africa, Australia, Mexico, Brazil, Peru, Taiwan, South Korea, Hong Kong, China, and Japan (Spergel, 1995)

- Ghana, Montreal, Australia, Puerto Rico, Jamaica, India, Indonesia, and Thailand (Covey, Menard, & Franzese, 1997). The Ghanaian case is described in sufficient detail to show resemblance to some American street gangs.

- Canada, Mexico, Japan, South Africa, the Philippines, Hong Kong, China, New Zealand, Australia, and Papua-New Guinea (Klein, 1995). The descriptions cited for the Philippines and Papua-New Guinea (Port Moresby in particular) provide some structural and criminal details that both contrast with and exemplify American counterparts.[1]

- A number of Canadian scholars are now reporting on street gangs in Vancouver, Toronto, Winnipeg, and Montreal. They include Caucasian, Aborigine, Vietnamese, Chinese, and Haitian gangs. What structural information exists to date suggests general similarities to U.S. street gangs, although descriptions range from "youth movements" to "criminal business organizations."

- In New Zealand, a more detailed report by Eggleston (1996) depicts primarily Maori gangs that are clearly crime oriented, male dominated, and involved in intergang rivalries. We are told little about their structures, however.

- In El Salvador, both news reports and visits by American gang experts yield a clear picture of gang culture exported to San Salvador, the capital city, by Salvadoran immigrants to the United States who return or are deported back to that country. *Placas* (graffiti) on the walls advertise "homies unidos" (homeboys united).

- In Argentina, DeFleur (1967) many years ago sought counterparts to some highly structured, large, big-city U.S. gangs depicted in American gang treatises of the time. Instead, she found small, leaderless but internally cohesive gangs, quite different in form from what she had anticipated.

In sum, street gangs, or groups subsumed under similar terminology, have been reported in Asia, Africa, Southeast Asia, Latin America, and Canada. Few of the reports, however, have been based on first-hand research. The "gangs" are mostly of unknown size, structure, and behavior patterns. The exceptions, such as those in Canada, Argentina, Papua-New Guinea, and the Philippines, whet the appetite for further study but provide few clues for new directions. Comparative research is badly needed, and the Eurogang Program at last holds promise for an organized approach to the issues at hand.

The Eurogang Program: Definitions and Issues

Although a few American researchers initiated the Eurogang Program, it soon became, by design, a decidedly European venture with Americans as principal consultants. The first step was an informal survey I made of European cities, establishing locations in which street gang activity had emerged during 1980s and 1990s. There followed several meetings of a small steering committee (members from the United States, Canada, Belgium, Holland, Germany, and Sweden) and a series of four workshops between 1997 and 2000 in Germany, Norway, Belgium, and Holland. Other countries represented in one or more of these were Finland, Denmark, England, France, Spain, Italy, Slovenia, Croatia, Greece, and Russia. Street gangs, or "gang-like youth groups" as a few preferred to call them, were found to exist, in some cases in small numbers, in almost all of the European nations. A commonality of interests soon developed among more than 100 participants, most of whom were researchers but some of whom were policymakers in public agencies such as ministries of justice and the police.

Throughout the developmental process, four key issues emerged and drew the most attention, issues whose resolution was required before the agreed-upon goals of cross-national and multimethod research could comfortably be undertaken. The first of these was to achieve a common definition of "street gangs" capable of applying to a variety of such groups as well as distinguishing them from other groups. The latter include motorcycle gangs, prison gangs, terrorist groups, and the very large number of other, less troublesome youth groups that exist in all countries (often school and youth culture based) that are not much of a danger to others.

The second issue, shared less among active gang researchers but more among others becoming interested in the Program's research goals, was the possible creation of a "moral panic" (Cohen, 1972). The concern here was that undertaking research on groups specifically labeled "gangs" could reify the concept, create greater public concern about it, and indeed help to create the phenomenon to a degree greater than originally existed. Some felt it might indeed be a wiser policy to deny or ignore gangs, or at least to develop alternative terminology than the gang terms so common in the United States.

Third, and inextricably tied to the first two, was the issue of setting street gangs into the broader context of youth groups generally. If street gangs are in any sense a unique form of group, we can only know and appreciate their unique qualities through contrast with other youth groups not labeled as gangs. Although this issue has not been a central issue in most American gang research, it has greater meaning in many European countries where there has been a tradition of studying youth groups and youth movements over many decades.

The fourth issue was the most engaging, at least to the American gang scholars. It came to be known as the "Eurogang Paradox."[2] Simply stated, the paradox consists of two elements, the first being the denial by numerous European researchers and policymakers that their jurisdictions have street gangs, because they don't have gangs that are large, highly structured, with strong cultural codes of loyalty and territoriality, and a commitment to violence as seen in American gangs. That is, they don't have "American style" street gangs. The second element of the paradox, of course, is that most American gangs also don't fit this publicly held stereotype of street gangs. Thus the paradox: The denial of gangs in Europe is based on a "typical" American gang that is not at all typical in America.

Very briefly, before moving on to characterizing European gangs as they have been described recently, I will comment on those four issues as they have been addressed in the Eurogang Program. Again, the issues are gang definitions, the concern about moral panic, the context of other youth groups, and the Eurogang Paradox.

Definitions. In a major set of annual surveys of U.S. police agencies designed to assess the prevalence of street gangs, the National Youth Gang Center (NYGC) offered the following approach to defining gangs for its police respondents: "A group of youths or young adults in your jurisdiction that you or other responsible persons in your agency or community are willing to identify or classify as a 'gang.' " The Eurogang participants determined that such a broad definition would be *too* inclusive—almost a "non-definition" as noted by some. But choosing an acceptable alternative proved—as it has for decades in the United States—to be a thorny problem.

The first solution was to accept, for working purposes, a minimal nominal definition that includes the elements of stability over time, street orientation, and a self-identity based on criminal involvement. The definition drafted for these purposes was this: "A street gang (or a problematic youth group corresponding to a street gang elsewhere) is any stable, street-oriented youth group whose own identity includes involvement in antisocial activity" (Weitekamp, 2000).

Note the phrase in parentheses above. For those wishing to avoid gang terminology, the definition can be applied to "problematic youth groups" without explicitly saying, "this is a gang." The second solution was also adopted to meet the concerns of those wishing or needing to avoid gang terminology. This approach, itself having two alternative forms, was to define the issue of whether a group under study is a "gang" or not *operationally*, rather than nominally as above.

The first operational procedure, common to many interview and questionnaire surveys of youth, is to use a set of "funneling" questions. These start with broad questions about one's friends and groups of friends, then narrow slowly to descriptions of groups such as size, activities, reasons for joining, and tendencies to get into trouble. Only at the end is the respondent asked if he or she considers this particular group of friends to be a gang. If the answer is yes, this is generally taken at face value. If the answer is no, the researcher can determine if this is also to be taken at face value or as a denial of "true" gang membership based on the previous answers to the funneling questions. Some of those questions reveal typical gang characteristics.

The second operational procedure is based on the Maxson-Klein typology of gang structures described later in this chapter. The typology describes five gang structures that encompass most gangs found in the United States.[3] It asks youth respondents in two ways to describe their "special group of friends" in line with the five gang types. The first, indirect way is to ask them to describe the group with respect to its size, age range, duration, presence of subgroups, territoriality, and antisocial behavior patterns. These are the dimensions that determine placement of the group in one of the five gang types, or into none of them. The second, more direct way is to present the respondent with very brief scenarios of the five gang types, asking the respondent which of these best describes his special group of friends, or if none of them do.

In sum, the operational definition of a youth's description of his or her group as a street gang can be determined by the funneling questions, or by the indirect or direct approach to the use of the five types of gang structures. The designation of a youth group as nongang or gang is thus achieved by the operations described—that is, by the youth's responses to questions shown in research to distinguish street gangs from other youth groups. These survey approaches can also be applied, with minor modifications, for use in gang observations and ethnographies and for use in surveys of adult experts such as police, school personnel, and community youth agencies. All those procedures are being planned for the developing Eurogang research projects.

Moral Panic. Interestingly, the European colleagues most concerned with creating a moral panic about street gangs tended to be those not yet directly engaged in gang research. Those already so engaged had not found the concern to be very tangible. Nonetheless, the operational definition approach outlined above was designed to make gang research more palatable to those genuinely concerned with the issue. For example, the funneling technique allows one to go all the way through the determination of gang membership by a youth respondent without that youth ever having to admit to gang membership. The phrase adopted—"your special group of friends"—allows avoidance of gang terminology yet permits determination by the researcher of the youth's gang or nongang status.

By the same token, the gang structures approach, both in the questions about size, duration, antisocial activities, and so on, and in the presentation of the five scenarios, uses the word *group,* not gang, in their language. Again, this allows the researcher to determine gang status without directly asking about it. Further, it allows for those youths responding in gang-like fashion to be fitted into one of the five types so that comparisons across sites and with U.S. data can readily be made. Any moral panic resulting from these procedures will not result from the research process, but only from the manner in which the results are presented to the public (if indeed they are made public).

The Youth Group Context. Here, too, the operational approach outlined above serves a secondary purpose, namely the application of gang-relevant survey instruments to a broader array of youth groups. By comparing youth responses from gang and nongang respondents, the distinction between the two types of groups can readily be illuminated. Youth group researchers will undoubtedly wish to ask a far more extensive set of questions in addition, depending on their particular interests. Having the gang comparisons available to them will simply amplify one issue of concern. A fine example can be found in the comparative study in Bremen, Germany, and Denver, Colorado (Huizinga & Schumann, 2001), using common survey instruments applied to large samples of school students in the two cities. A funneling technique for gang determination was employed amid a far broader set of questions about individuals, families, schools, and communities. Excellent contrasts were thus drawn between gang and nongang youth and between both of these cross-nationally.

The Eurogang Paradox. This fourth issue raised during the development of the Eurogang Program has not yet been fully resolved for two reasons. First, the stereotype of American gangs is fairly fixed in many minds and constantly reinforced by naïve, poorly informed representatives of the media and some law enforcement agencies. Second, as the program has expanded its membership, new colleagues continually appear who have not yet been alerted to the nature of the paradox. In my view, following the initiation of the program discussions there have been two principal contributions by the American participants. One is the collaborative process of gang definition statement and measurement. The second, designed to reduce the paradox, is to bring to the European colleagues (admittedly with some repetition and insistence) the most recent data from the 1980s and 1990s on the true nature of U.S. gangs (see, e.g., chaps. 1-7 in Klein, Kerner, Maxson & Weitekamp, 2001). By showing, with both case studies and national surveys, that the stereotypical gang is the exception rather than the rule, and by illustrating the five structural types of the gang typology, the Americans have attempted to demonstrate the variety of gangs in the United States. By doing this, they have allowed European observers to understand that some of their groups, while not fitting the old stereotype, do indeed resemble some of the other, more common U.S. gangs. The resemblance between U.S. and European gangs has been documented (Klein, 1997) and now allows far more useful comparisons of both similarities and differences. It has been a "hard sell," but progress along these lines has been steady.

Characteristics of American Gangs

Though we have established that street gangs probably exist or have existed on every continent, it seems clear that they are most evident in the United States. In attempting to understand street gangs elsewhere, it makes sense to establish their basic elements first in the United States, where seven decades of gang research has taken place. In particular, because American gangs have changed over time and have proliferated in just the past 20 years in particular, it seems sensible to establish the base of knowledge principally on more recent research. The most significant changes have probably taken place with respect to prevalence (there are now thousands of gang-involved jurisdictions), crime patterns (more lethal violence now, due to the availability of modern firearms), and structures (the emergence of several types of nonstereotypical gang forms). In addition to these three characteristics, it seems useful to review several others briefly: location; ethnicity; gender; cultural diffusion; cohesiveness; and two additional crime patterns, versatility and amplification.

Location. In the days of the most "classic" American gang research, from the 1920s to the mid-1970s, gangs known to exist were located principally in large urban centers or their immediate surroundings. These included most notably New York, Philadelphia, Boston, Chicago, Los Angeles, San

Francisco, San Antonio, and El Paso. Prior to 1960, there were about 50 communities in these areas with gang problems; street gangs were an urban problem. The number of gang jurisdictions grew slowly but steadily through the mid-1980s, and then exploded to the point that the National Youth Gang Center has reported several *thousand* gang-involved communities, encompassing more than 26,000 gangs and almost 850,000 gang members (NYGC, 2000a).

Almost every urban center is now involved, but there are not 3,000 urban centers in the United States; this means that gangs now exist in many large and even many small towns. Recent data from the NYGC (2000a) show the following (according to police reports and NYGC's very broad definition):

Large cities:	12,538 gangs	482,380 members
Small cities:	8,413 gangs	94,875 members
Suburban counties:	6,040 gangs	176,610 members
Rural counties:	1,716 gangs	26,368 members

The data are a bit misleading, because NYGC defines as large cities those above 25,000 in population. Nonetheless, it is clear from the above figures that gangs *cannot* be considered just a "big city" problem. For those who think of gangs as an East Coast phenomenon, the NYGC data are equally surprising. Seventy-two percent of reporting jurisdictions in the West indicate active gangs, as opposed to 48% in the Midwest and South and only 29% in the Northeast. The *West Side Story* now has a new meaning.

Clearly, as we look at the street gang situation in Europe or elsewhere, we will need to assess their location in urban *and* nonurban areas. The character of gangs is affected by their location on the landscape.

Ethnicity. In the earlier, classic period, American gangs of many backgrounds were reported: German, Scandinavian, Italian, Polish, Irish, Jewish, and other European immigrant populations fueled the inner-city gangs along with black and Hispanic groups. But with the absorption of most immigrant populations into the multiethnic fabric of our nation, it came to be more and more the still-marginalized minorities—blacks, Hispanics, and to a lesser extent various Asian groups—that have composed most of our modern street gangs. This history makes it clear that it is not a particular nationality, ethnicity, or race that makes up the street gang problem, but rather the disadvantaged, marginalized, and alienated status of youth segments that gravitate to the gang world. Even in the case of Caucasian groups such as the Skinheads, a review of their membership reveals that they are drawn from those who perceive themselves to be socially marginalized.

When we look at the composition of street gangs reported in connection with the Eurogang Program, obviously we should not expect to find a pre-ponderance of blacks or Hispanics, but we should be on the lookout for other marginalized populations there.

Gender. Until recently, the prevalence and behavior of girls in street gangs had received moderate attention at best. A very few autonomous female gangs had been described. More commonly, girls were described either as occasional participants in male gangs or as members of auxiliary groups, as small adjuncts to larger male gangs. It was generally acknowledged that female gang members were fewer in number (ratios of from 1 to 10 to 3 to 10 female to male were noted), younger on average by several years, and less criminally involved than males (although manifesting similarly versatile crime patterns). Female gang members were largely ignored by the police and courts, and stereotypes abounded that the females were sex objects for the males ("toys for boys"), carried concealed weapons for the males, spread rumors to incite rivalries between male gangs, and were generally subservient in a male-dominated street world.

More recently, especially with the advent of feminist criminology, a number of more careful and considered works on female gang members have appeared (see, e.g., Chesney-Lind, Shelden, & Joe, 1996; Fleisher, 1998; Hagedorn, 1999; J. Miller, 2001a; Moore, 1991). Less importance is now given to female subservience and more to female gang participation in serving specific needs, much as male participation serves such needs. Also, it now appears that the prevalence of female gang members is higher than was estimated earlier (percentages in the 20% to 40% range are more common) and fewer auxiliary groups are reported, with more of the girls to some extent integrated with the boys' groups. Male domination, nonetheless, continues to be the typical pattern. Finally, it is still the case that female gang participation is largely unknown to or downplayed by the police and courts.

The Eurogang Program, unlike the earlier days of American gang research, has been alerted to the issues of female gang members (see J. Miller, 2001b). Perhaps attention to females early in the development of European gangs will yield more accurate data, although some European scholars, more than Americans, place heavy weight on the issue of "masculinities" (see, e.g., Kersten, 2001).

Cultural Diffusion. In earlier decades, street gangs seemed to appear in major cities as independent phenomena, arising in each case as responses to local patterns of immigration, central city structure, culture clash, and economic disadvantage. None of the earlier gang literature suggested effective ties between gangs in New York and Chicago and Los Angeles and the other known gang locations. Indeed, one noted scholar almost scoffed at the notion of inter-city gang recognition (Campbell, Munce, & Galea, 1982).[4]

Since the mid-1980s, it has become rather commonplace to assign the responsibility for the proliferation of street gangs across the country to one of three processes. The first is a shadow of the earlier thinking: Gangs have emerged in many localities because of similar conditions that are gang-spawning in their nature. These include racism, relative poverty or deprivation, poor local resources, inadequate employment opportunities for youth (and minority youth in particular), and the general marginalization of black, Hispanic, and other minority groups. Many scholars, myself among them, are inclined to this view, noting that the social and political conservatism of the country over the past 20 years has exacerbated these processes.

A second commonly offered explanation is the advent of crack cocaine and its franchising across the country. Promulgated principally by law enforcement agencies who saw crack cocaine as a new epidemic being fueled by drug kingpins and distributed through the auspices of organized street gang networks, this explanation did receive support from incidents in widely scattered parts of the country. More careful research, however, has downplayed the importance of gang member migration and street gang capacities to market drugs extensively (Decker & Van Winkle, 1996; Hagedorn, 1988; Howell & Gleason, 1999; Klein, 1995; Maxson, 1998).

The third explanation, propounded by myself (Klein, 1995) and a number of police gang experts in the late 1980s, has gained general acceptance over the past decade. It notes the general diffusion of street gang culture—the dress and ornamentation styles, the postures, the argot of gang members—to the general youth population of the country. The press, gang-oriented movies, television news and documentaries, entertainment venues such as MTV, and "gangsta rap" music forms have all served to inculcate original street gang culture into a far broader youth culture. Most young people in America recognize the look, the walk, and the talk of gang members. Many mimic it in part or in whole. Many try it out as a personal style, some to discard it and some to retain it. Play groups, break-dancing groups, taggers, and school peer groups experiment with gang life. For some, it becomes all too real (Hagedorn, 1988; Klein, 1995).

In Europe, a number of new street gangs seem to have taken on the trappings of this gang culture. Needed now is a more careful assessment of the degree to which the exportation of the American style is a cause, or merely the external trappings, of European gang forms.

Cohesiveness. Two characteristics of street gangs, important in themselves, lead to a third. The first of these is group cohesiveness, although we must be careful not to overstate the extent to which gang members are tied to each other. Surprisingly few American scholars have paid much attention to group dynamics within gangs. Notable exceptions have been Yablonsky (1963), Short and Strodtbeck (1965), Jansyn (1966), and Klein (1971, 1995). What has been learned is that group cohesion in gangs is highly variable, both over time and across gangs. Generally, street gangs have only moderate levels of cohesiveness, with the result that this can be reduced sometimes to the point of gang dissolution but also that it can be increased to yield gangs that are more resistant to intervention and more involved in gang-related delinquency and crime. The more cohesive gang usually is the more criminally involved. Paradoxically, data from several projects suggest that the inadvertent effect of direct intervention with street gangs is to *increase* gang cohesiveness and thus gang crime. European policymakers must take very careful note of this process before launching naively into either social welfare *or* suppression programs to deal with their gangs.

Crime Patterns. One finding about street gangs has been consistently reported in research over the past seven decades. For the most part, gangs and gang members do not specialize in particular forms of offending but, rather, display considerable versatility in offending.[5]

Thus it is usually inappropriate to speak of violent gangs or theft gangs or graffiti gangs. They do a little of everything, but alcohol use, minor drug use, petty theft, and vandalism are probably the most common forms of crime. Violent offenses are the exception rather than the rule, a fact consistently overlooked in the media and among political figures. The stereotype of the violent American gang is one important factor underlying the Eurogang Paradox noted earlier.

Crime Amplification. There is, not surprisingly, a selection factor by which more delinquently inclined youth in a neighborhood are more likely to join street gangs than are their less delinquently inclined peers. Perhaps more important, recent longitudinal studies of gangs (Battin, Hill, Abbott, Catalano, & Hawkins, 1998; Huizinga, 1996; Thornberry, Krohn, Lizotte, Smith, & Tobin, in press) have already confirmed a pattern more informally noted in earlier observational and ethnographic research. Joining a street gang greatly increases one's involvement in criminal activity, and especially in violent activity. Conversely, leaving the gang results in a significant reduction in criminal involvement. It is the combination of group cohesiveness and the crime patterns of gang members that together account for much of this amplification of criminal activity.

It is not just that "birds of a feather flock together." Being with other delinquents is only part of the process; the rest is the triggering of group processes as gang members intermingle and join forces against common enemies (Battin et al., 1998). One sees an amplification of group identity, group pride and status, need for protection, diffusion of responsibility, mutual reinforcement of antisocial moral codes, and similar social psychological processes that both allow and encourage engagement in the very behaviors—criminal behaviors—that give the gang its unique identity. Because normal moderate levels of cohesiveness allow for their own increase, these processes can and do result in serious crime amplification. Because most descriptions of European gangs suggest only moderate levels of cohesiveness and versatile patterns of criminal offending (except among skinhead groups), there is good reason to be worried about crime amplification, much as it has been demonstrated in the United States.

Application to European Gangs

The seven descriptors noted above certainly are not exhaustive. One might add leadership, clique structures, family background, neighborhood characteristics, and so on. Yet the seven listed here provide a sound base from which we might ask about European gangs. There is, however, one additional factor that will help considerably. This is the description of street gang structures.

For this purpose, I turn to the Maxson/Klein (1995) typology of five street gang structures, developed from descriptive data gathered from hundreds of police departments and applied in a preliminary way to European gangs in two publications (Klein, 1997; Klein et al., 2001). As outlined in the pending proposal to the European Union, these five structural types contain descriptors related to subgrouping, size, age range, duration, territoriality, and crime patterns (all are versatile except for the Specialty Gangs). Brief scenarios describing the five as seen in the United States are as follows.

Five Street Gang Scenarios

The Traditional Gang. Traditional gangs have generally been in existence for 20 or more years—they keep regenerating themselves. They contain fairly clear subgroups, usually separated by age. O.G.s or Veteranos, Seniors, Juniors, Midgets, and various other names are applied to these different age-based cliques. Sometimes neighborhoods rather than age separate the cliques. More than other gangs, Traditional gangs tend to have a wide age range, sometimes as wide as from 9 or 10 years of age into the 30s. These are usually very large gangs, numbering one hundred or even several hundred members. Almost always, they are territorial in the sense that they identify strongly with their turf, 'hood, or barrio, and claim it as theirs alone.

In sum, this is a large, enduring, territorial gang with a wide range and several internal cliques based on age or area.

The Neotraditional Gang. The Neotraditional gang resembles the Traditional form, but has not been in existence as long—probably no more than 10 years, and often less. It may be medium size—say 50 to 100 members—or also into the hundreds. It probably has developed subgroups or cliques based on age or area, but sometimes may not. The age range is usually smaller than in the classical Traditional gangs. The Neotraditional gang is also very territorial, claiming turf and defending it.

In sum, the Neotraditional gang is a newer territorial gang that looks on its way to becoming Traditional in time. Thus at this point it is subgrouping, but may or may not have achieved territoriality, and size suggests that it is evolving into the Traditional form.

The Compressed Gang. The Compressed gang is small—usually in the size range of up to 50 members—and has not formed subgroups. The age range is probably narrow—10 or fewer years between the younger and older members. The small size, absence of subgroups, and narrow age range may reflect the newness of the group, in existence less than 10 years and maybe for only a few years. Some of these Compressed gangs have become territorial, but many have not.

In sum, Compressed gangs have a relatively short history, short enough that by size, duration, subgrouping, and territoriality it is unclear whether they will grow and solidify into the more traditional forms, or simply remain as less complex groups.

The Collective Gang. The Collective gang looks like the Compressed form, but bigger and with a wider age range—maybe 10 or more years between younger and older members. Size can be under one hundred, but is probably larger. Surprisingly, given these numbers, it has not developed subgroups, and may or may not be a territorial gang. It probably has a 10- to 15-year existence.

In sum, the Collective gang resembles a kind of shapeless mass of adolescent and young adult members that has not developed the distinguishing characteristics of other gangs.

The Specialty Gang. Unlike these other gangs that engage in a wide variety of criminal offenses, crime in this type of group is narrowly focused on a few offenses; the group comes to be characterized by the specialty. The Specialty gang tends to be small—usually 50 or fewer members—without any subgroups in most cases (there are exceptions). It probably has a history of less than 10 years, but has developed a well-defined territory. Its territory may be either residential or based on the opportunities for the particular form of crime in which it specializes. The age range of most Specialty gangs is narrow, but in others is broad.

Table 15.1 Characteristics of Five Gang Types

Type	Subgroups	Size	Age Range	Duration	Territorial	Crime Versatility
Traditional	Yes	Large (> 100)	Wide (20-30 years)	Long (> 20 years)	Yes	Yes
Neotraditional	Yes	Medium-Large (> 50)	(no pattern)	Short (< 10 years)	Yes	Yes
Compressed	No	Small (< 50)	Narrow (< 10 years)	Short (< 10 years)	(no pattern)	Yes
Collective	No	Medium-Large (> 50)	Medium-Wide (> 10 years)	Medium (10-15 years)	(no pattern)	Yes
Specialty	No	Small (< 50)	Narrow (< 10 years)	Short (< 10 years)	Yes	No

In sum, the Specialty gang is crime-focused in a narrow way. Its principal purpose is more criminal than social, and its smaller size and form of territoriality may be a reflection of this focused crime pattern. Typical examples are drug sales gangs and skinhead groups.

Reference to Table 15.1 suggests that modifications may benefit the application of the typology to the European situation. For instance, these relatively new gangs in Europe *at the present time* will seldom reach the size or age-range or duration of the Traditional gangs in the United States. Yet Traditional gangs have been noted in at least three cities—Glasgow, Berlin, and Kazan. The availability of the typology allows a preliminary assessment of the degree to which one can find gangs that are structurally similar in the United States and Europe, thus overcoming the Eurogang Paradox.

Weitekamp's (2001) review of European gang descriptions collected in the book *The Eurogang Paradox* (Klein et al., 2001) reports Traditional gangs in Kazan, Neotraditional and Compressed gangs in Manchester, Specialty Gangs in The Hague and Rotterdam, as well as Compressed gangs in Copenhagen, Frankfurt, and Oslo. Klein (1997) found similar typology counterparts in Paris, Stockholm, Stuttgart, and Brussels. In sum, European nations have street gangs very similar in structure to the street gangs in America. Only future research can reveal variations or prevalence of the types, existence of other types, and the salience of other descriptors.

And what of the seven other gang characteristics listed above; how do they compare in Europe? Here we are severely limited by the few clear depictions currently available in the European gang literature, much of which was written without explicit attention to U.S./European comparisons. I will rely for this analysis on the eight chapters in *The Eurogang Paradox* that describe street gangs in Europe.

Location. The cities involved in these chapters are Rotterdam, den Haag, Manchester, Oslo, Copenhagen, Frankfurt, Kazan, Paris, and Bremen. Within these cities gang locations are described as inner city in Manchester, Oslo, and Kazan. Suburban locations are suggested in Manchester, Oslo, and Paris. In a number of these European cities, the location in suburban areas is explained by the placement there of housing projects designed for or occupied by immigrant and refugee populations.

Ethnicity. Many European countries, especially following the second World War, have welcomed substantial numbers of immigrants—often as "guest workers" to fill low-paying jobs not acceptable to sufficient numbers of the indigenous population. The second-generation offspring of the guest workers have in some locations gravitated toward street gang structures. In addition, some of these same countries have been receptive to large numbers of refugees from countries experiencing various kinds of nationalism and persecution of minority populations. Younger refugees and second-generation offspring have also fueled some of the gang problems. A review of *The Eurogang Paradox* reports reveals the following national and ethnic gang compositions:

Holland:	Moroccan, Antillian, and Surinamese
Manchester:	Afro-Caribbean, indigenous white
Oslo:	Vietnamese, Filipino, Pakistani, Somali, Iranian, Moroccan, Turkish, and indigenous white
Copenhagen:	Muslim, indigenous white
Frankfurt:	Turkish, Croatian, Italian, and Russian
Kazan:	Indigenous white, Tatars
Paris:	Algerian
Bremen:	Turkish, indigenous white

Other reports from Stockholm, London, Berlin, Stuttgart, Spain, and Switzerland confirm this highly varied pattern of both indigenous and, especially, nonindigenous gang composition. The contrast to the United States is obviously fairly striking. It should be added that much of the indigenous white gang activity in these European locations, more so than in the United States, is comprised of skinheads and similar racist groups, most of which fit fairly well into the Specialty gang structure.

Gender. With the exception of a mention in the report from Paris, none of the reports in this collection speaks of female gang participation. Whether this reflects a one-sex gang situation or the absence of researchers' attention to the issue cannot be determined. If the former, this is an important departure from the American experience. If the latter, it may be a reflection of a mostly male research enterprise not unlike that found in earlier American studies. The enrollment of female researchers in the Eurogang Program can certainly be encouraged to help open the window on the gender issue there.

Diffusion. There are no American gangs in Europe, nor have I heard of any American gang members migrating to Europe and influencing gang genesis there. But the reports from Holland, Manchester, and Oslo do suggest that the diffusion of American *gang culture* has had an effect. American gang movies and books (including translations from the English) are specifically cited. And of course much European television fare is imported from the United States, as is gang-oriented popular or rap music. How much we have spread our gang influence is not clear, but it is certain that some level of gang culture diffusion has taken place.

Cohesiveness. The picture on concern for and measurement of gang cohesiveness in Europe is mixed. The reports from Holland, Paris, and Frankfurt make no explicit reference to the topic. The Manchester report suggests low levels, and the Copenhagen and Bremen reports are of medium levels. Some of the Oslo material suggests high gang cohesiveness, and the Kazan report describes a transformation over time from medium to high cohesiveness as those gangs have become more organized and explicitly criminal in focus. None of these reports uses empirical measures of group cohesiveness, to say nothing of common measures. This, then, is a most promising area for future gang research in European settings.

Crime Patterns. The Dutch gangs observed in The Hague and Rotterdam were small Specialty gangs. In Oslo and Paris, both specialized and versatile crime patterns were reported. In all the other sites, versatility was the reported pattern. The parallel to the American experience is quite striking. The patterns of most concern to American officials—drug sales and violence—are in most cases lower in the European cities, and firearm violence there is practically nonexistent. One can only hope this is a difference that will persist.

Crime Amplification. The major effect on levels of criminal activity occasioned by joining street gangs in the United States is mentioned in only three of the European reports, those from Oslo, Kazan, and Bremen. One suspects that this pattern has simply not been a paramount concern for European gang observers, but only future, focused research can clarify this.

Summary

Although European gang research is quite new, and the gangs themselves have had little opportunity to evolve in form, some comparisons to the U.S. situation are already becoming clear. U.S. gangs are far, far more prevalent, and far more involved in serious and lethal violence. Our ethnic gang composition has over time become narrow, whereas that in Europe is highly varied. Still, on both continents street gangs are composed primarily of youth from marginalized segments of their societies. Gender and cohesiveness patterns may be different, but may also only seem so due to a lack of research attention.

But in contrast to these differences, one is struck by the similarities to be found between American and European gang situations (in the absence of, it should be noted, almost any deliberately comparative research). Two sets of attributes, when compared across the two continents, suggest we are viewing one older and one newer variation on a similar theme attributable to common group processes and similar combinations of societal variables that produce marginalization of some youth populations.

First, there are those attributes of gang structure that produce a typology of five gang types roughly applicable in both the United States and Europe. Group placements on subgrouping, size, age range, duration, territoriality, and crime versatility serve to reduce the "Eurogang Paradox" and reveal that current European street gangs can largely be subsumed under the Maxson/Klein typology developed in the United States. To deny street gang existence in Europe, in these circumstances, would be more foolish than useful.

Second, analyses of European gang reports in eight general locations show that, to the extent they are covered, seven gang-relevant descriptions from U.S. research are applicable to European research. One can obtain clarification of European gangs by reference to such variables as location, ethnicity, gender, cultural diffusion, cohesiveness, crime patterns, and crime amplification. These are variables additional to the structural attributes of the typology (except for crime pattern).

There is much room in all this for future research to elucidate the unique natures of European gangs, and the developing Eurogang Program will likely provide such clarification. But the uniqueness will be bounded by the discovered similarities to American street gangs. This means that the American gang knowledge accumulated over the past 70 years provides a major resource for research in Europe, the kind of research not available to the Americans until only very recently. As suggested above, I would urge special attention to group processes and youth marginalization as pivotal concerns for understanding and controlling street gang developments in Europe.

Notes

1. The Port Moresby "Rascals" have been described in Biles (1976), and by Sundeen (1981).

2. A book by that name includes many of the papers produced for the first Eurogang workshop: see Klein et al. (2001).

3. Klein (1997) and Klein et al. (2001) have expanded on the five gang types revealed in the original research by Maxson and Klein (1995). These types have been confirmed in a statewide study in Illinois by Scott (2000) and by the National Youth Gang Center (2000b) in a comprehensive national survey of law enforcement agencies.

4. Campbell and her coauthors noted, "youth in one part of the country are relatively ignorant of others' activities until it reaches the point of mass movement or violence. The net effect is that New York teenagers, already factioned within the city into their own areas, have virtually no knowledge of the situation of gang members in Chicago, Los Angeles, or Philadelphia."

5. This has also been labeled "cafeteria-style" offending ("Smorgasbord offending" has been suggested by a Swedish scholar). The major exception to this versatile pattern is to be found in Specialty gangs described later in this chapter.

PART

4

Gang Research
and Public Policy

16

Ganging Up on Gangs
Anti-Loitering and Public Nuisance Laws

GILBERT GEIS

The current legislative and law enforcement drive to control juvenile gangs by passing laws specifically targeting them reflects the temper of our times, both figuratively and literally. As one writer notes, life in the United States today is characterized by what he calls "social demoralization"—"the fear, the crime, the class warfare, the murderous difficulties of the poor, and the consolidation of political will against them" (Denby, 1996, p. 197). We are living in a period in American history in which people insist that they themselves, though not necessarily others, have every right to the Good Life. There are heady expectations and a strong belief in personal rights as contrasted to social responsibility. Litigation is ardently pursued to see that we get what we presume we deserve. Deferring gratification or otherwise reigning in whims is considered old-fashioned. The desire is for "self-fulfillment" and "growth," matters that involve a dedication to leisure activities, the quest for adventure, the embracing of the "joy of living," and the accumulation of a store of material objects (Patterson, 1996, p. 712).

A strong element of this ethos emphasizes health and self-protection. Americans jog, frequent gyms, and hire personal trainers. Well-being is essential for better enjoyment of the goodies of contemporary existence. The spirit of the times proclaims that seeming threats to such well-being and to the pursuit of bliss must be drastically reduced, if not eliminated. Cigarette smoking should be prohibited if the fumes might waft in our direction. Some day soon, perhaps, it will be illegal to be overweight, with a mandatory visit to a law enforcement scale every 3 months to detect those who exceed the stipulated heft limit (Geis, 1968).

We particularly demand protection from criminal harm. Such harm unequally is the lot of the have-nots, who also yearn for a reasonable share of the good life that they see so intensely promoted by television and other media (Campbell, 1991). They too can be enrolled, though much less readily, in tough-minded crusades against law-breakers. Their lesser enthusiasm for draconian penalties for criminals and delinquents is rooted in their awareness that it is from within their ranks that most of the malefactors will be seized, and not from the suites or the legislative halls. Besides, as one writer notes, "police interventions directed at crime and disorder have generated concern, anxiety, and outright anger about police intrusiveness, particularly as directed at minority populations" (Livingston, 1999, p. 142).

Tensions arise because traditional methods for defining and dealing with outlawry do not produce notable results. Few burglaries and auto thefts will be solved, because offenders are very infrequently observed at the crime scene. Murder rates fluctuate for obscure reasons that have little if anything to do with either capital punishment or enforcement tactics. This situation induces a mind-set that seeks to locate novel methods to deal with crime, methods that, even if they are at best marginally successful, appear to demonstrate concern for possible victims—the Good People, the voters. Increasing punishment for offenses such as homicide, robbery, rape, and burglary can accomplish only so much—or so little. Therefore we look for innovative approaches, such as "three strikes" laws that reduce the on-the-street population of repeat offenders (not to mention persons who pose little or no real criminal threat) and Megan's Law notifications that offer, besides scenarios of meanness, a largely false sense of security against persons released from prison who had been convicted of child molestation.

To protect us better, further attempts have proliferated to identify and distinguish subsets of criminal offenses and to impose additional punitive consequences for their commission. Among the better known of such efforts is the denomination of "hate crimes." Statutes add additional punishment onto an act that can be claimed to have been committed for motives rooted in bias toward members of groups other than one's own. Such a newly minted offense turns its back on the common-law principle that people ought to be dealt with in regard to what they do, not in regard to what they might have been thinking when they did it (Jacobs & Potter, 1998; Jenness, 1997).

Organized crime represents a particularly tough law enforcement target. For one thing, many of its activities—such as the drug trade—involve victimless crimes, in the sense that the parties are consensually involved in illicit transactions (Meier & Geis, 1997); and second, it is notoriously hazardous for victims to cooperate with the police to try to bring organized criminals to justice. To overcome such barriers prosecutors lobbied for the enactment of the RICO (Racketeer Influenced and Corrupt Organizations) statute to target organized criminals who can be prosecuted not for a specific common-law statutory offense but for engaging in a "pattern" of illegal behavior. As the title of a law review commentary suggests, RICO has created "the crime of being a criminal" (Lynch, 1987).

Increasingly, there are clarion calls to extend RICO prosecutions to juvenile gangs, thereby lowering standards of proof and making alleged gang members vulnerable to penalties that are tied to the group to which they are said to belong and its pattern of behavior rather than to what the individuals themselves specifically have done (Bonney, 1993; see also Gartenstein & Warganz, 1990; Parker, 1996; Truman, 1995).

Juvenile gangs, like organized crime syndicates, are part of the world of Others. Their members are ethnically, economically, and socially different from those who wield power and make laws. It is no longer acceptable in American society to demonstrate prejudice overtly. But the same end can be achieved by pinpointing activities that are very largely those of the socially disenfranchised and inventing special kinds of laws that will bring persons who violate them to grief.

Juvenile gangs are seen as particularly threatening because they are formed by persons in an age range that is notorious for a predilection for violence. Gangs also receive considerable publicity when they engage in drive-by shootings and random acts of terror. Gangs can be fearsome for people who view themselves as likely (however improbably in statistical terms) to be killed or seriously injured because they are in the wrong place at the wrong time, and not because of anything "improper" that they might have done. There is no true protection against random acts of violence, especially those committed with high-tech weaponry.

To respond to citizen concerns, legislative bodies have sought to formulate laws and ordinances that provide new weapons to make it easier to harass and punish presumed members of juvenile gangs. Underlying such enactments is the belief that alleged gang members by their very interaction with each other are or will be engaged in illegal behavior. These laws, it might be noted, do not have parallels that decree that it is illegal for two or more corporate executives who represent supposedly competing businesses with a history of antitrust violations to congregate in posh hotel meeting rooms and to fail to check out when so ordered by a regulatory enforcement agent.

The anti-gang laws, which can be loosely classified as anti-loitering or public nuisance provisions, gain a certain legitimacy by their focus on juveniles, since, beginning in 1899 with the establishment in Illinois of the nation's first juvenile court, it has been permissible to hold underage persons responsible for acts such as truancy, sexual promiscuity, and "being out of control" that are perfectly permissible for adults. The rationale is that intervention in the lives of youngsters who engage in such behavior is for their own good—a highly questionable assumption. The District of Columbia city council, which enacted a curfew law to keep juveniles off the streets after 11 p.m. on weekdays and midnight on weekends, used just such a defense of the tactic: it was "to protect the welfare of minors by reducing the likelihood that minors will perpetrate or become victims of crime and by promoting parental responsibility" (*Hutchins v. District of Columbia,* 1996, pp. 681-682; see also Sasse, 2000). The latter part of the justification reflects another prong of the attempt to contain delinquency by holding parents and guardians criminally responsible for the misdeeds of their offspring (Geis & Binder, 1991). Almost invariably, the parents charged are inner-city single mothers exhausted by demanding, low-paying jobs and overwhelmed by an inability to shield their children from the ubiquitous opportunities and inducements for law-breaking in the slums where they live.

There is a sizeable body of law review analyses of appellate court decisions dealing with statutes and ordinances directed against gang members. Virtually all of it takes as given the high-blown rhetoric that accompanies the enactment of such laws, rhetoric that melodramatically spells out the presumed horrors of uncontrolled gang activity and employs such statements to justify what often are infringements of the constitutional rights of all citizens, including gang members. Typical of such rhetoric is the observation that life in southern California is lived "in the midst of an unprecedented gang holocaust" (Burrell, 1990, p. 741). Similarly, an anti-gang ordinance was justified because "California is in a state of crisis which has been caused by violent street gangs whose members threaten, terrorize, and commit a multitude of crimes against peaceful citizens of their neighborhood" (Yeager, 1998, p. 595).

At times statistics are presented, courtesy of district attorneys, that are said to demonstrate the striking impact of such laws and ordinances on the reduction of crime and delinquency. None of the law review writers question the authenticity of such statistics or note that they may merely duplicate the downswing in all crime that has occurred in recent years throughout the nation. Juvenile crime, for instance, was reported at the end of 2000 to have dropped precipitously in the past half decade. Murders by juveniles were down 68% since 1993 to the lowest level in three decades. These declines occurred in sites both with anti-gang laws and those without them (Lichtblau, 1999). It is also possible that lowered rates in one area may indicate no more than that gang activity has migrated to other parts of the city where enforcement is more lax.

The law review writers also spend a great deal of intellectual energy dissecting the contents of the enactments to determine if they do or do not violate such standards as First Amendment guarantees of free association and free speech, or infringe on the right to travel, or whether they should be voided because of vagueness. But they rarely pause to ask if the enactments are sensibly justified in a democratic society, regardless of how they square with judicial precedent and legislative intent. The assumption is that if they are found to be "constitutional," then they must be morally correct.

Lanzetta v. New Jersey (1939)

Though it dealt with adult offenders, the *Lanzetta* decision by the U.S. Supreme Court is the grandfather of subsequent judgments about the constitutionality of laws directed against juvenile gang members. New Jersey's legislature in 1934 enacted a law that read as follows:

> Any person, not engaged in any lawful occupation, known to be a member of any gang consisting of two or more persons, who has been convicted at least three times of being a disorderly person, or who has been convicted of any crime, in this or in any other state, is declared to be a gangster. (Chapter 155, Laws 1934)

The penalty for those convicted of violating the law was a fine not to exceed $10,000, or imprisonment not to exceed 20 years, or both. Frank Pius (also known as Ignatius Lanzetta), Michael Falone, and Louie del Rossi were found guilty of breach of the law and sentenced to not more than 10 years and not less than 5 years imprisonment. Their appeal to the Supreme Court of New Jersey (*New Jersey v. Pius,* 1937) and ultimately to the state's highest tribunal, the Court of Errors and Appeals (*New Jersey v. Pius,* 1938), fell on deaf ears. The first court declared that "the statute is not aimed at punishing convicted criminals because they are convicted criminals, but because, being such, they become members of a gang organized to commit further crimes, and neglect or refuse to engage in any lawful occupation" (*New Jersey v. Pius,* 1937, p. 214). It took only a few lines for the state's highest court to note that it was "in full accord" with this conclusion (*New Jersey v. Pius,* 1938, p. 1189).

The U.S. Supreme Court, however, would have none of this, and so indicated in a sharply worded opinion, written by Justice Pierce Butler (Brown, 1945), an arch-conservative and one of the "nine old men" whose wings Franklin D. Roosevelt had tried to clip in 1937 by pushing an ill-fated bill calling for an additional appointment to the court whenever one of the incumbents refused to quit on reaching the age of 70. Butler tied the court's opinion on New Jersey's anti-gang law to the juridical axiom that "[n]o one may be required at peril of life, liberty or property to speculate as to the meaning of penal statutes. All are entitled to be informed as to what the State commands or forbids" (*Lanzetta v. New Jersey,* 1939, p. 453).

Butler noted that the phrase "consisting of two or more people" was the only definition provided of "gang." He then took a tour through the history of English and American law and found no definition of gang there. Nor did a search of the leading dictionaries shed any useful light on precisely what "gang" meant (see generally Thumma & Kirchmeier, 1999). Finally, he examined the definitions offered by Frederic M. Thrasher (1927, 1931) and Herbert Asbury (1928), the only two scholars who at that time had dealt in a reasonably comprehensive manner with gangs. Neither provided any satisfactory clue to precisely what "gang" meant. Indeed, later writers would note that Thrasher, in his pioneering study of juvenile gangs, had failed to come close to indicating exactly what he was studying (Bookin-Weiner & Horowitz, 1983). One set of writers has maintained that under the amorphous definition Thrasher offered, the Harvard and Notre Dame football teams could be regarded as gangs, as could Mardi Gras revelers (Covey, Menard, & Franzese, 1992; Esbensen, Winfree, He, & Taylor, 2001; see also Geis & Dodge, 2000).

Butler's conclusion was that the statute was unconstitutional:

> The challenged provision condemns no act or omission, the terms it employs to indicate what it purports to denounce are so vague, indefinite and uncertain that it must be condemned as repugnant to the due process clause of the Fourteenth Amendment [to the Constitution]. (*Lanzetta v. New Jersey*, 1939, p. 459)

The California Putsch

Perhaps because Justice Butler had made it clear that broad-ranging legislative sweeps seeking to corral vaguely specified gangs were constitutionally unacceptable, no further such attempts occurred until recent decades. The current effort got under way when gang behavior became an item of great social concern and derivatively, therefore, of great political concern. By the mid-1990s seven states had passed laws that forbade participation in gangs and five had declared that gang members would receive enhanced sentences if convicted of specified offenses (Yoo, 1994). Many municipalities joined in the fray, formulating ordinances, many of which, as one commentator noted, "operate on the fringes of the Constitution" (Steel, 2000, p. 255). Such enactments have been derisively labeled "street-cleaning statutes" by their critics (Jeffries, 1985, p. 216).

California, which is believed to have the most extensive gang problem in the nation, led the law-making crusade against street gangs. Its anti-gang legislation took two forms: (a) the enactment of a state law and (b) parallel to this, the passage by cities of ordinances that declared street gangs to be public nuisances and their members subject to civil injunctions under specified conditions (Astvasadoorian, 1898; Boga, 1994). The civil injunction tactic was favored by the police and prosecutors not only because it expanded the arsenal of weapons available to reach presumed law-breakers, but also because injunctions are not subject to the more rigorous constitutional privileges associated with criminal trials (Cheh, 1991; Maxson, Hennigan, & Sloane, 2001).

The injunctive approach also often proves more effective than criminal charges because the ordinances allow the police to net the entire group or large portions of it. Injunctions may be sought for such matters as associating with gang members, demanding entry to a residence not one's own, and wearing gang-identified clothing and insignias. As one writer observes, the ordinances often can "induce cooperation [that is, "ratting"] by providing negotiable sentence enhancements" (Hard, 1998, p. 631; see also Werdegar, 1998).

The 1988 Street Terrorism and Prevention Act (STEP)

California's STEP law defines a gang member in the following terms:

[A]ny person who actively participates in any criminal street gang with knowledge that its members engage in or have engaged in a pattern of criminal gang activity, and who willfully promotes, furthers, or assists in any felonious criminal conduct by members of that gang. (California Penal Code §§ 186.20-27)

The law permits courts to escalate the penalties for gang-related behavior and for gang offenses committed within 1,000 feet of a school. There are, in addition, sanctions against gang members using buildings as their headquarters and for recruiting new members (Bjerregaard, 1998; Martinez, 1997). The statute was declared to be within constitutional limits after being challenged in California appellate courts—in one because it was said to be unacceptably vague (*People v. Green*, 1991), and in the other on the allegation of overreach (or overbreadth in legal terminology; *People v. Gamez*, 1991: see generally Isserles, 1998).

The Injunctive Approach

A number of municipalities throughout California supplemented state law by enacting ordinances that sought to disable gang activity through the use of injunctions. The first injunction was issued in Los Angeles in December 1987 against a group known as the Playboy Gangster Crips. Three hundred members were declared to constitute a public nuisance and enjoined from gathering within a 26-block area. Oddly, the Los Angeles ordinance was not renewed after its stipulated run of a year; authorities said that it had been so effective that there was no need to keep it on the books.

Six years later, the Los Angeles city attorney opted for a civil injunction approach tied to the statutory definition of public nuisance. The authorities can file a complaint (a) if a gang meets the STEP definition; (b) if it is deemed a public nuisance in a specific geographic area; and (c) if there is evidence that specified individuals are members of the criminal gang responsible for the nuisance. Each gang member is sought out and given a copy of the complaint. The injunction specifies now-forbidden acts; in Los Angeles the emphasis tends to be a ban on association among gang members. If the injunction is violated, the city pursues a criminal remedy for failure to obey the order. The possible penalty is a one-year jail term and/or a $1,000 fine (Vranicar, telephone interview, December 14, 2000). Inevitably the broad-ranging prohibitions in most of the California municipal ordinances have come under court challenge. The leading case, *People ex rel. Gallo v. Acuna* (1997), concerned a Santa Clara ordinance that forbade "standing, sitting, walking, driving or appearing anywhere in public view with . . . any other known gang members." The case involved a Latino group in San Jose, the Varrio Surrea Locos, whose members were alleged to be creating an urban war zone in the Rocksprings area of the city. The California Supreme Court in a split decision ruled that the ordinance met constitutional standards, though in a partial dissent one of the judges noted that the gang was only a loosely organized association of individuals with no express purpose and no central leadership. He pointed out that the people responsible for the alleged gang unruliness could have been only a small minority of its membership and that it was sweeping with a very broad brush to enjoin 38 individuals. The dissenting justice singled out the situation of Blanca Gonzalez. She admitted gang membership and she wore the gang outfit of a black top and black jeans, but the justice noted pointedly that this did not prove that she itended to further the gang's aims. A law review critic echoes this point, observing that "*Acuna* is bad law because the court ignored the fundamental legal principle that guilt is personal and that liability should only be imposed upon a showing of individual wrongdoing" (Allen, 1998).

The City of Chicago v. Morales (1999)

Half a century after the *Lanzetta* decision, the U.S. Supreme Court was faced with a juvenile gang clone of that case in the *City of Chicago v. Morales*. Jesus Morales and others had been convicted under an ordinance promulgated by the Chicago City Council after it heard testimony on the dire threat posed by gang behavior. Among other things, the Council offered as a basis for the ordinance the rather strange observation that "members of criminal street gangs avoid arrest by committing no offense punishable under existing law when they know police are present" (*City of Chicago v.*

Morales, 1997, p. 58). Council members apparently believed that more responsible people would not hesitate to commit crimes when the police are in sight.

The Chicago ordinance had four prongs: First, a police officer must reasonably believe that one of two or more persons present in a place open to the public is a "criminal street gang member." A criminal street gang was defined as

> any ongoing organization . . . or group of three or more persons, whether formal or informal, having as one of its substantial activities the commission of one or more [enumerated] criminal acts, and whose members individually or collectively engage in or have engaged in a pattern of criminal gang activity.

Second, the persons must be "loitering," a behavior defined as "remaining in one place with no apparent purpose." Third, the officer must order all of the persons to disperse and remove themselves from the area. Fourth, a person must disobey the officer's order. If any individual, whether a gang member or not, disobeys the order, that person is guilty of violating the ordinance. Such guilt was punishable by a fine of not less than $100 and up to $500, imprisonment for not more than 6 months, and a requirement to perform up to 120 hours of community service (Municipal Code 8-4-015, 1993; see also Poulos, 1995).

The Chicago police department had urged the council to keep the wording of the ordinance loose because it intended to promulgate specific enforcement guidelines. These guidelines permitted only members of the force's Anti-Gang unit to use the ordinance. Ironically, members of that Unit would face charges in 2000 of buying and selling drugs and ripping off drugs and cash from other dealers (Slater, 2000). The guidelines also listed enforcement areas where gangs were said to have a detrimental effect, though the location of the specified areas was not made public. As the U.S. Supreme Court would point out, the guidelines did not have the force of law and the ordinance could be applied in any part of the city. Justice Stevens underlined that point by noting that a gang member and his father might loiter near Wrigley Field to rob an unsuspecting baseball fan or merely to get a glimpse of Sammy Sosa leaving the ballpark: "In either event, if their purpose is not apparent to a nearby police officer, she may, indeed, she 'shall'—order them to disperse" (*City of Chicago v. Morales*, 1999, p. 60).

During the 3 years in which the anti-gang provision was in force, the Chicago police issued more than 89,000 dispersal orders and arrested some 42,000 persons for its violation. Two Chicago trial judges held the ordinance to be constitutionally valid; 11 thought otherwise. In one of these latter cases, the judge declared that the ordinance improperly authorized arrest on the basis of a person's status instead of that person's conduct, and that the failure to allow freedom of association resembled what goes on in a "police state" (*City of Chicago v. Youkhana*, 1995, p. 39). When the Illinois Supreme Court agreed with that conclusion, Chicago ceased to enforce the ordinance pending the outcome of an appeal to federal courts.

The U.S. Supreme Court in *City of Chicago v. Morales* struck down the ordinance, ruling that it was void because it was unsatisfactorily vague (see generally Clark, 1999). The verdict overturned the jail sentences of 1 to 27 days that had been imposed on Morales and his codefendants (Mann, 2000). The court employed two precedent standards to characterize "vagueness"—itself a vague term unless clearly pinned down. A law would be unacceptable if (a) it is so vague and lacking in standards that it fails to "define the criminal offense with sufficient definiteness so that ordinary people can understand what conduct is prohibited" and/or (b) it fails to establish guidelines to prevent "arbitrary and discriminatory enforcement" (*Kolender v. Lawson*, 1983, p. 357).

Writing for the majority, Justice Stevens wondered how it could satisfactorily be established whether a loiterer has "an apparent purpose." The court also looked askance at the prohibition of "loitering," declaring that the right of individuals to remain in a public place of their choice is a fundamental part of their liberty. The decision repeated a hypothetical that had been used by one of the Illinois trial courts:

> Suppose a group of gang members were playing basketball in the park, while waiting for a drug delivery. Their apparent purpose is that they are in the park to play. The actual purpose is that they are waiting for the drugs. Under [the ordinance's] definition of loitering, a group of people innocently sitting in the park discussing their futures would be arrested, while the "basketball players" . . . would be left alone. (*City of Chicago v. Morales*, 1999, p. 50)

Nor, the court declared, could the warning to disperse overcome the inadequacy of the anti-loitering rule, because "if the loitering is in fact harmless and innocent, the dispersal order itself is an unjustified impairment of liberty" (*City of Chicago v. Morales*, 1999, p. 16).

At the same time, the court offered strong support for a possible ordinance that would in more precise terms produce the intended outcome. Thus, Justice Stevens observed,

> The basic factual predicate for the city's ordinance is not in dispute. As the city argues in its brief, "the very presence of a large collection of obviously brazen, insistent, and lawless gang members and hangers-on . . . intimidates residents, who become afraid even to leave their homes and go about their business. This in turn imperils community residents' sense of safety and security, detracts from property values, and can ultimately destabilize entire neighborhoods. (*City of Chicago v. Morales*, 1999, p. 51)

A law "that directly prohibited such intimidating conduct," Justice Stevens declared, undoubtedly would be constitutional, presumably meaning by this that "brazenness" and "insistency" could be outlawed if such conduct were defined with adequate specificity. But perhaps the Justice meant that *acts* of intimidation that included such characteristics might be reached by ordinance. Similarly, in a potpourri of exegetic exercises, various combinations of Justices looked at different elements of the Chicago ordinance and offered both objections and suggestions about how the enactment might be more satisfactorily drafted.

There were two dissents from the majority opinion—one by Justice Scalia and the second by Justice Thomas. Scalia's commentary, considerably longer than the majority opinion, must have been an irritant to his colleagues. It is condescending, adopting the tone of a law school professor, which Scalia had been, trying to point out to a bunch of rather dim-witted students their inability to understand the true nature of the law and their substitution of personal preferences for constitutional standards. Scalia scored a number of debating points, scolding Justice Stevens for a sentence that, in his opinion, Scalia (correctly) found incomprehensible, and ridiculing Justice O'Connor's suggestion that if it was things such as brazenness that the Chicago City Council desired to proscribe then it ought to say just that. Scalia scoffed: "If the majority considers the present ordinance too vague, it would be fun to see what it makes [of that formula]" (*City of Chicago v. Morales*, 1999, p. 96).

Polemics aside, the essence of Scalia's position was not impressive. He argued that the ordinance was "a perfectly reasonable measure" and represented only "a minor limitation upon the free state of nature" and seemed "a small price to pay for liberation of [the] streets" (*City of Chicago v. Morales*, 1999, p. 74). The majority specifically disagreed, labeling the ordinance a "major" limitation, a viewpoint that undoubtedly reflected the thoughts of the 42,000 persons who had been arrested during the 3 years the provision was in force. Scalia also noted that the majority had favored "gang members and associated loiterers over the beleaguered law-abiding residents of the inner city" (*City of Chicago v. Morales*, 1999, p. 81). But the majority pointed out that it was not only the right of gang members to loiter with no apparent purpose that it was defending, but the right of "associated loiterers," including law-abiding citizens, to be free from harassment and arrest. Scalia tried to shore up his viewpoint by granting that much harmless behavior might become the object of police attention, but that, after all, freedom to loiter was not a constitutionally protected right, like free speech and religious freedom. Nor did he find the phrase "with no apparent purpose" unacceptable. "No one in his right mind," Scalia retorted to the majority's position, "would read the phrase . . . to mean anything other than 'without any apparent lawful purpose' " (*City of Chicago v. Morales*, 1999, p. 94). Scalia's conclusion was predictably bombastic:

The citizens of Chicago have decided that depriving themselves of the freedom to "hang out" with a gang member is necessary to eliminate pervasive gang crime and intimidation—and that the elimination of one is worth the deprivation of the other. The Court has no business second-guessing either the degree of necessity or the fairness of the trade. (*City of Chicago v. Morales,* 1999, p. 98)

Justice Thomas, for his part, revisited the history of vagrancy laws, both in pre-colonial England and in early and later American history (see generally Adler, 1989; Chambliss, 1964). He sought to buttress his dissent by arguing that because such laws had a long history they must therefore be reasonable impositions on the freedom of contemporary citizens. "[I]t is anomalous to characterize loitering as 'innocent' conduct,' " Thomas wrote, "when it has been disfavored throughout American history. When a category of conduct has been consistently criminalized, it can hardly be considered 'innocent' " (*City of Chicago v. Morales,* 1999, p. 113). This conclusion is reminiscent of Sir Matthew Hale's benighted justification in 1662 when he sentenced to death two women convicted of witchcraft. Witchcraft is a real crime, Hale said in his instructions to the jury, because there had from ancient times been laws against it in all nations (Geis & Bunn, 1997). Hale was wildly wrong: There were no actual witches cavorting with the devil, and the women he sentenced to death were totally innocent of the crime with which they were charged. Justice Thomas portrayed the consequences of the court's decision in melodramatic terms: "I fear the court has unnecessarily sentenced law-abiding citizens to lives of terror and misery" (*City of Chicago v. Morales,* 1999, p. 98). He called the penalties for violation "modest" and believed that the police could be trusted to exercise their discretion wisely.

Predictably, the Chicago city council quickly framed a new ordinance in light of the Supreme Court opinion. There were tighter requirements for documentation of arrests and dispersal orders. Designated "hot spots" still were not made public but now the list would be updated every 3 months, making it tougher for gangs to relocate to a site where they would be immune from the loitering restrictions, though such movement was restricted by the boundaries of rival gangs and the need for prearranged meeting sites for drug transactions. The new ordinance presumably will in time face court challenges to determine whether it has overcome the unconstitutional elements of its predecessor (Bellock, 2000).

Conclusion

Americans are justifiably proud of the freedom and opportunity that their country offers to citizens and to immigrants seeking a better life. There are endless heart-warming stories of men and women who by the dint of hard work and, perhaps, unusual intelligence and some good luck have moved from poverty to affluence, from noxious overcrowded slums to secluded, upscale suburbs. But there is a significant element of hypocrisy—or, at least, denial—when Americans look only at the wonderful things that their nation offers.

The disciplined workers for Amnesty International paint a much different picture of the United States than our typical one-sided self-portrait. Jonathan Powers (2001, pp. 235-236) in his history of Amnesty International notes that the United States

> was founded in the name of democracy, political and legal equality, and individual freedom. However, despite its claim to leadership in the field of human rights, . . . it is failing to deliver the fundamental promise of rights for all. . . . The picture painted of the United States by Amnesty International is a grim, even sadistic one.

Much of that portrait focuses on the way we treat street offenders, persons overwhelmingly from the lower and dispossessed class of our society. Amnesty International notes that we have 5% of the world's people but that our prison population is 25% of the world's total and that half of these prisoners are blacks. Besides, we rank fifth in the world for the number of executions of prisoners—behind China, Congo, Saudi Arabia, and Iran— hardly company that we would prefer to keep. State-imposed criminal penalties fall distressingly often on people who start out far behind in the social race and are not afforded reasonable opportunities to catch up.

Gangs have become the new focus of a cold war that presumes that the infliction of punishment is the best method to coerce conformity. As social commentator Mike Davis (1990) observes, "Like the Tramp scares in the nineteenth century, or the Red scares in the twentieth, the contemporary Gang scare has become a . . . terrain of pseudo-knowledge and fantasy" (p. 270).

Loitering, vagrancy, and public nuisance laws are notorious for their inherent racial bias (Jeffries, 1985). A leading case in which one such law was ruled unconstitutional, *Papachristou v. City of Jacksonville* (1972), involved two black men driving in a car with two white women. All four had clean records but nonetheless were arrested for vagrancy in a case that reeked of racial discrimination. The charge was "prowling by auto," supported by the allegation that the group had stopped near a used car lot that recently had been robbed. The city ordinance was declared unconstitutional by the U.S. Supreme Court on the ground of vagueness.

A law review writer has pointed out the boomerang effect the current incarnation of enforcement approaches directed against gangs may well produce:

Incarceration of so many young black males contributes to the very problems that are often pointed to as the source of higher crime rates in the black community. By removing so many black men from the community and stigmatizing them forever with a criminal conviction, criminal law enforcement is likely to mean more single-parent families, less adult supervision of children, more unemployed and unemployable members of the community, more poverty, and, in turn, more drugs, more crime and more violence. (Stewart, 1998, p. 2256)

"This is to suggest," Stewart (1998) observes, "that incarceration—especially on so large a scale in a well-defined community—is far from an adequate solution and may exacerbate the problems associated with crack and crime" (p. 2257).

There is no question that juvenile gangs can be unruly and can make life wretched and sometimes dangerous for people who live in their midst. But there is a good deal of question concerning the validity of the idea that laws that target gang members and that at best are only arguably acceptable in a free society are the most effective way to deal with problems that gangs may present.

It is an irrefutable fact that youngsters who own cars do not often steal other cars. People who enjoy a decent standard of living, a good education in a well-supplied school with first-rate teachers, and similar things that give them a stake in conformity, by and large will behave in the same manner as do others who enjoy such opportunities. The observation of a scholar who has worked for more than 30 years on gang issues pinpoints the superficial sense of safety offered by today's spate of anti-gang laws:

Were these new and expanded forms of suppression based on the expanded knowledge base about gangs, it would have been fine. But instead most of them ignored knowledge in favor of ideology. Indeed, many of them were directly opposite what was being learned about gangs and how they respond to efforts at control. Street gangs . . . develop an "oppositional culture": the more attention paid to them, the more society intervenes in their world, the stronger become the bonds between gang members. . . . Young people join gangs first and foremost out of needs for identity, status, and protection. The effect of most interventions . . . is to increase the identity and status and to glorify the gang to potential recruits. We have the data to demonstrate this, but law enforcement, the courts, and political leaders do not attend to such data in formulating their practices and pronouncements. (Klein, in press)

17

New Approaches to the Strategic Prevention of Gang and Group-Involved Violence

ANTHONY A. BRAGA
DAVID M. KENNEDY
GEORGE E. TITA

A number of jurisdictions have been experimenting with new problem-solving frameworks to prevent gang and group-involved violence. These new strategic approaches have shown promising results in the reduction of violence. Pioneered in Boston, these new initiatives have followed a core set of activities to reduce violence. These activities have included the "pulling levers" focused deterrence strategy, designed to prevent violence by and among chronic offenders and groups of chronic offenders; the convening of an interagency working group representing a wide range of criminal justice and social service capabilities; and jurisdiction-specific assessments of violence dynamics, perpetrator and victim characteristics, and related issues such as drug market characteristics and patterns of weapons use and acquisition. All of these initiatives have been facilitated by a close, more or less real-time, partnership between researchers and practitioners. In many jurisdictions, an initial interest in "juvenile violence" or "gun violence" has shifted, as the problem assessments have proceeded, to a focus on understanding and controlling violence, regardless of age or weapon type, associated with chronic offenders and groups of chronic offenders. This chapter traces the development of these new problem-solving frameworks, discusses the commonalities and divergences across jurisdictions that have experimented with these approaches, and synthesizes the key elements of the new strategic prevention frameworks.

The Development of the New Strategic
Prevention Frameworks: The Boston Gun Project _____

The Boston Gun Project was a problem-solving enterprise expressly aimed at taking on a serious, large-scale crime problem—homicide victimization among young people in Boston. Like many large cities in the United States, Boston experienced a large, sudden increase in youth homicide between the late 1980s and early 1990s. Boston youth homicide (ages 24 and under) increased 230%—from 22 victims in 1987 to 73 victims in 1990 (Braga, Kennedy, Waring, & Piehl, 2001). Youth homicide remained high well after the 1990 peak; Boston averaged 44 youth homicides per year between 1991 and 1995 (Braga et al., 2001). The Boston Gun Project proceeded by (a) assembling an interagency working group of largely line-level criminal justice and other practitioners; (b) applying quantitative and qualitative research techniques to create an assessment of the nature of, and dynamics driving, youth violence in Boston; (c) developing an intervention designed to have a substantial, near-term impact on youth homicide; (d) implementing and adapting the intervention; and (e) evaluating the intervention's impact (Kennedy, Piehl, & Braga, 1996). The Project began in early 1995 and implemented what is now known as the Operation Ceasefire intervention, which began in the late spring of 1996.

The trajectory of the Project and of Ceasefire is by now well known and extensively documented (Kennedy et al., 1996; Kennedy, Braga, & Piehl, 1997; Kennedy, 1997; Kennedy, 1998; Kennedy, 2001; Braga et al., 2001). Briefly, the working group of law enforcement personnel, youth workers, and researchers diagnosed the youth violence problem in Boston as one of patterned, largely vendetta-like ("beef") hostility among a small population of chronically criminal offenders, and particularly among those involved in some 60 loose, informal, mostly neighborhood-based groups (these groups were called "gangs" in Boston, but were not Chicago- or LA-style gangs). As this diagnosis developed, the focus of the Project shifted from its initial framework of "juvenile violence" and "gun violence" to "gang violence." The Operation Ceasefire "pulling-levers" strategy was designed to deter violence by reaching out directly to gangs, saying explicitly that violence would no longer be tolerated, and backing up that message by "pulling every lever" legally available when violence occurred (Kennedy, 1997, 1998). Simultaneously, youth workers, probation and parole officers, and later churches and other community groups offered gang members services and other kinds of help. The Ceasefire Working Group delivered this message in formal meetings with gang members; through individual police and probation contacts with gang members; through meetings with inmates of secure juvenile facilities in the city; and through gang outreach workers. The deterrence message was not a deal with gang members to stop violence. Rather, it was a promise to gang members that violent behavior would evoke an immediate and intense response. If gangs committed other crimes but refrained from violence, the normal workings of police, prosecutors, and the rest of the criminal justice system would deal with these matters. But if gang members hurt people, the Working Group focused its enorcement actions on them.

A central hypothesis within the Working Group was the idea that a meaningful period of substantially reduced youth violence might serve as a "firebreak" and result in a relatively long-lasting reduction in future youth violence (Kennedy et al., 1996). The idea was that youth violence in Boston had become a self-sustaining cycle among a relatively small number of youth, with objectively high levels of risk leading to nominally self-protective behavior such as gun acquisition and use, gang formation, tough "street" behavior, and the like: behavior that then became an additional input into the cycle of violence (Kennedy et al., 1996). If this cycle could be interrupted, a new equilibrium at a lower level of risk and violence might be established, perhaps without the need for continued high levels of either deterrent or facilitative intervention. The larger hope was that a successful intervention to reduce gang violence in the short term would have a disproportionate, sustainable impact in the long term.

A large reduction in the yearly number of Boston youth homicides followed immediately after Operation Ceasefire was implemented in mid-1996. As discussed earlier, Boston averaged 44 youth homicides per year between 1991 and 1995. In 1996, with Ceasefire in place for roughly half the year, the number of Boston youth homicides decreased to 26 and then further decreased to 15 youth homicides in 1997, a level below that characteristic of Boston in the pre-epidemic period. The low level of youth homicides has continued through 1998 (18) and 1999 (15; Braga & Kennedy, 2001). A formal evaluation of Operation Ceasefire revealed that the intervention was associated with a 63% decrease in the monthly number of Boston youth homicides, a 32% decrease in the monthly number of shots-fired calls, a 25% decrease in the monthly number of gun assaults, and, in one high-risk police district given special attention in the evaluation, a 44% decrease in the monthly number of youth gun assault incidents (Braga et al., 2001). The evaluation also suggested that Boston's significant youth homicide reduction associated with Operation Ceasefire was distinct when compared with youth homicide trends in most major U.S. and New England cities (Braga et al., 2001).

Experiences in Other Jurisdictions

At first blush, the effectiveness of the Operation Ceasefire intervention in preventing violence may seem unique to Boston. Operation Ceasefire was constructed largely from the assets and capacities available in Boston at the time and deliberately tailored to the city's particular violence problem. Operational capacities of criminal justice agencies in other cities will be different, and youth violence problems in other cities will have important distinguishing characteristics. However, the basic working group problem-solving process and the pulling-levers approach to deterring chronic offenders are transferable to violence problems in other jurisdictions. A number of cities have begun to experiment with these analytic frameworks and have experienced some encouraging preliminary results. Consistent with the problem-solving approach, these cities have tailored the approach to fit their violence problems and operating environments.

Minneapolis, Minnesota

Homicide in Minneapolis, traditionally a city with a very low homicide rate, increased dramatically from 59 victims in 1994 to 97 victims in 1995. In 1996, the number of homicides remained unusually high at 83 victims. In response to these unprecedented increases, a group of community members, law enforcement officers, government officials, and corporate representatives retained Police Executive Research Forum (PERF) and Harvard University researchers to help analyze their homicide problem and develop appropriate preventive strategies (Kennedy & Braga, 1998). The Minneapolis problem-solving enterprise was organized as an integrated academic-practitioner partnership and involved a working group composed of Minneapolis Police Department officers, Hennepin County probation officers, local and federal prosecutors, ATF field agents, and other local, state, and federal criminal justice agency representatives.

Using a blend of quantitative and qualitative exercises, the research team closely examined all homicide incidents between January 1994 and May 1997. The problem analysis revealed that homicide victims and offenders tended to have criminal histories, often substantial ones, and committed a wide variety of crimes including drug offenses, property crimes, disorder offenses, weapons offenses, and violent crimes (Kennedy & Braga, 1998). Many homicide victims and offenders were under probation supervision, sometimes at the time of the homicide incident. Gang-related violence played an important role in Minneapolis homicides. Reviews with Minneapolis practitioners suggested that Minneapolis did indeed have both "native" and Chicago-style gangs, plus groups linked to other cities and to Native Americans. Nearly 45% of the homicide incidents were considered to be gang related (Kennedy & Braga, 1998). Of all homicide incidents during the period examined, 26% of the victims and slightly more than 45% of the offenders were gang members (Kennedy & Braga, 1998). Some 32 active gangs with about 2,650 members were identified as being central to gang violence in Minneapolis; these individuals represented less than 3.5% of Minneapolis residents between the ages of 14 and 24 (Kennedy & Braga, 1998). These gangs tended not to be territorial, but operated fluidly geographically across Minneapolis and other local jurisdictions.

The working group decided that the results of the problem analysis supported the use of a pulling-levers ceasefire-style intervention. The working group responded to outbreaks of gang violence with a wide variety of criminal justice activities focused on the gang or gangs in question, communicated this new policy directly to gangs and gang members as the implementation unfolded, and matched the criminal justice intervention with social service and community-based interventions wherever possible (Kennedy & Braga, 1998). A key element in the enforcement portfolio was the creation, in the Hennepin County Probation Department, of a small number of field probation officers dedicated to the project and detailed to conducting home visits, street enforcement, and the like, in the company of Minneapolis Police Department officers.

The enforcement phase of the operation was kicked off by selecting a particularly violent gang, the Bogus Boyz, that was ultimately largely dismantled through the use of federal weapons prosecutions. The Minneapolis working group pursued a wide variety of means to deliver the deterrence message to the target audience. The Mayor and the enforcement team held a press conference to announce the Bogus Boyz arrests and their antiviolence rationale; teams of police and probation officers made home visits to troublesome gang members and paid special visits to gang-involved victims of gang violence (often in the company of their friends) in the hospital where they would warn against retaliation; and posters detailing the city's new gang violence policy were displayed prominently in the Hennepin County jail for viewing by the arrestees.

Although a formal evaluation of this effort has not been conducted, preliminary findings suggest that the intervention had an impact on homicide. After the intervention was implemented in June 1997, monthly homicide counts during the summer of 1997 showed a sharp reduction compared to monthly counts of homicide over the previous two summers (1995, 28 victims; 1996, 41 victims; 1997, 8 victims; Kennedy & Braga, 1998). After the initial success of the operation, adherence to the core strategy by the agencies involved slackened, and homicide in the city increased, though not to the levels observed immediately prior to the initial intervention.

Baltimore, Maryland

Baltimore has long suffered from high yearly counts of homicides. During the 1990s, however, Baltimore experienced more than 300 homicides per year between 1990 and 1997, with a 30-year peak of 353 homicides in 1993 (Kennedy, Braga, & Thomson, 2000). In 1996 and 1997, Baltimore had the fourth highest homicide rate in the United States among cities with more than 250,000 residents (Pastore & Maguire, 1999). Beginning in 1998, with the support of the Baltimore Safe and Sound Campaign, a working group composed of Baltimore Police Department officers, Baltimore State's Attorney's Office and U.S. Attorney's Office prosecutors, probation and parole officers, juvenile corrections officers, federal law enforcement agencies (ATF, FBI, and DEA), and Harvard University researchers engaged in a problem-solving enterprise to unravel the dynamics underlying the homicide problem, develop a comprehensive violence reduction strategy, and implement the strategy (Kennedy et al., 2000).

The research team began the homicide problem analysis by obtaining official data on 303 homicide victims and 211 homicide suspects from 1997. A close examination of the criminal history data revealed that 74% of the victims and 87% of the suspects had adult and/or juvenile charges filed against them in court (Kennedy et al., 2000). Some 53% of the victims and 68% of the offenders had been under either adult or juvenile court-ordered supervision. Among those with criminal records, victims averaged about 8 prior charges and offenders nearly 10 prior charges; these prior offenses include a wide range of violent, drug, and property offenses (Kennedy et al., 2000). Using semi-structured qualitative data collection techniques, the research team closely examined the circumstances of the homicide victimizations. About 20% of the homicide incidents involved an ongoing dispute that was not about drug business between individuals or groups. Disputes involving drug business were involved in 18% of the homicides, and street drug robberies characterized 10% of the homicides. The remaining incidents were characterized as the result of robberies (nonstreet drug, 10%), spontaneous arguments (9%), domestic violence (6%), other circumstances (4%), or unknown circumstances (22%). Some 59% of the incidents occurred in or near a street-level drug market, and about 46% of the suspects and 37% of the victims were members of a drug organization or some recognized neighborhood criminal network (Kennedy et al., 2000). The project research identified some 325 drug groups in Baltimore that ranged in nature from rather sophisticated drug organizations, to structured neighborhood groups or "gangs" that sold drugs, to loose neighborhood groups that sold drugs (Kennedy et al., 2000).

The overall picture that emerged from this research suggested that violent groups of chronic offenders immersed in Baltimore's drug markets were responsible for the bulk of the city's homicides. As such, the working group felt that a pulling-levers-focused deterrence strategy was a promising way to reduce the city's homicide problem. Unlike Boston and Minneapolis, the sheer number of groups, the high homicide rate—averaging nearly one a day—and the clear role of street drug activity as a driver of the violence made the idea of an operation focused solely on groups implausible. Instead, the Baltimore strategy took *violent street drug market areas* as the basic unit of work. The basic operational idea was to take these areas in turn, reaching out to the groups in a particular area, "calming" the violence, establishing a maintenance strategy for the area, and then expanding the operation to new areas.

The first application of Operation Safe Neighborhoods, as the operation was called, focused on a very violent drug market area in the Park Heights neighborhood (Kennedy et al., 2000). The strategy proceeded by delivering a benchmark intervention that focused a varied menu of criminal justice operations on the violent groups in the target area. Selected members of the violent groups, usually those members on probation or under some form of criminal justice supervision, were then required to attend a forum where the new strategy was explained to the offenders. The forum was supplemented by a variety of other communication strategies, including the posting of fliers in the area and direct one-on-one communications with offenders on the street. Beyond the communication of cause and effect between violent behavior and law enforcement actions, the offenders were also offered access to social intervention and opportunity provision programs organized by the Safe and Sound Campaign. The violence prevention strategy was designed to ensure compliance in the targeted area, and new violent areas were addressed until the strategy was implemented citywide. Although a formal evaluation of the strategy has not been completed, preliminary analyses suggest that the intervention was associated with a 74% reduction in shootings and a 22% reduction in homicides in Park Heights during the 5 months following the intervention relative to shootings and homicides in the target area during the same time period one year earlier (Kennedy et al., 2000).

Boyle Heights, City of Los Angeles, California

In March 1998, the National Institute of Justice (NIJ) funded RAND to develop and test strategies for reducing gun violence among youth in Los Angeles. In part, the goal was to determine which parts of the Boston Gun Project might be replicable in Los Angeles. In designing the replication, RAND drew a clear distinction between the process governing the design and implementation of the strategy (data-driven policy development, problem solving, working groups) and the elements and design (pulling levers, collective accountability, retailing the message) of the Boston model. Processes, in theory, can be sustained and adaptive, and as such can be utilized to address dynamic problems. By singling out process as an important component, the RAND team hoped to make clear that process can affect program effectiveness independently of the program elements or the merits of the actual design (see Tita, Riley, & Greenwood, 2001, for a detailed analysis of the project).

The Los Angeles replication is unique in several important ways. First, the implementation was not citywide, but only within a single neighborhood (Boyle Heights) within a single Los Angeles Police Department Division (Hollenbeck). The project site, Boyle Heights, also differs from other sites in that the population is relatively homogenous. Well over 80% of the residents are Latinos of Mexican origin. The same is true for the gangs, many of which were formed prior to the Second World War. These gangs are clearly "traditional" gangs, with memberships exceeding a hundred members. The gangs are strongly territorial, contain age-graded substructures, and are intergenerational in nature (Maxson & Klein, 1996).

Unlike the other cities where gang and group-involved violence is a rather recent phenomenon, Los Angles represents an attempt to reduce gun violence in a "chronic gang city" with a long history of gang violence and an equally long history of gang reduction strategies. The research team first had to convince members of the local criminal justice and at-large community that the approach we were espousing differed in important ways from these previous efforts to combat gangs. In fact, it does—the RAND project was not about "doing something about gangs," but rather "doing something about gun violence" in a community where gang members committed an overwhelming proportion of the gun violence. The independent analysis of homicide files confirmed the perception held by police and community alike that gangs were highly overrepresented in homicidal acts. From 1995 to 1998, 57% of all homicides had a clear gang motivation. Another 25% of the homicides could be coded as "gang related" because they involved a gang member as a victim or offender but were motivated for reasons other than gang rivalries.

The analysis found very little evidence that drug dealing motivated much of the violence. Among the 90 gang-motivated homicides, less than 10% (8) also included a drug component. Law enforcement officials from the working group were skeptical and insisted, "These kids are . . . being killed because of [dope]." The group revisited the homicide files with the gang detective personally responsible for assembling the cases. In the end, 4 homicides out of the 90 were recoded: Three homicides that were originally coded "gang-motivated only" were changed to "gang-/drug-motivated" and 1 case was recoded from "gang-/drug-motivated" to "gang-motivated only" (Tita et al., 2001).

Given the social organization of violence in Boyle Heights, the multidisciplinary working group fully embraced the pulling-levers-focused deterrence strategy developed in Boston. The processes of communicating the message have also been formally adopted, though to date this has been accomplished through personal contact rather than in a group setting. Police, probation, community advocates, street gang workers, a local hospital, and local clergy are all passing along the message of collective accountability for gangs continuing to commit gang violence.

It is too early to comment on any successes that the actual implementation of the strategy has had on reducing gun violence. However, participants are encouraged that in 2000, a year in which the citywide homicide rate in Los Angeles increased by 30% (and is being attributed to a rise in gang violence), homicide within the Hollenbeck area decreased by 15%. This at least suggests that the working group process and the collection and sharing of information among agencies may be responsible for some level of proactive responses to potential incidents of violence, as opposed to purely reactive responses.

Strategic Approaches to Community Safety Initiative in Five Cities

The Strategic Approaches to Community Safety Initiative (SACSI) is a U.S. Department of Justice pilot project that follows the Boston Gun Project's strong emphasis on partnerships, knowledge-driven decision making, and ongoing strategic assessment (Coleman, Holton, Olson, Robinson, & Stewart, 1999). The project is spearheaded by U.S. Attorneys and has been implemented in five cities—Indianapolis, Indiana; Memphis, Tennessee; New Haven, Connecticut; Portland, Oregon; and Winston-Salem, North Carolina. The crime problems addressed vary across the cities and range from gun violence (Indianapolis, Portland, and Winston-Salem), to community fear (New Haven), to sexual assault (Memphis). Several of the sites have adopted pulling-levers strategies that are well enough along to discuss here. In addition, although not formally part of SACSI, U.S. Attorneys have spearheaded pulling-levers operations in High Point, North Carolina, and in Omaha, Nebraska. We will discuss these operations as a group.

The Indianapolis project's working group is composed of Indiana University researchers and federal, state, and local law enforcement agencies (McGarrell & Chermak, 2001). During the problem analysis phase, the researchers examined 258 homicides from 1997 and the first 8 months of 1998 and found that a majority of homicide victims (63%) and offenders (75%) had criminal and/or juvenile records. Those with a prior record often had a substantial number of arrests. The working group members followed the structured qualitative data gathering exercises used in Boston to gain insight into the nature of homicide incidents. The qualitative exercise revealed that 59% of the incidents involved "groups of known chronic offenders" and 53% involved drug-related motives such as settling business and turf disputes (McGarrell & Chermak, 2001). It is worth noting that the terminology "groups of known chronic offenders" was used because there was not a consensual definition of *gang*, and the reality of much gang activity in Indianapolis is of a relatively loose structure (McGarrell & Chermak, 2001).

The working group developed two sets of overlapping strategies. First, the most violent chronic offenders in Indianapolis were identified and targeted for heightened arrest, prosecution, and incarceration (McGarrell & Chermak, 2001). Second, the working group engaged the pulling-levers approach to reduce violent behavior by groups of known chronic offenders (McGarrell & Chermak, 2001). The strategy implemented by the Indianapolis working group closely resembled the Boston version of pulling levers. The communications strategy, however, differed in an important way. The deterrence and social services message was delivered in meetings with high-risk probationers and parolees organized by neighborhoods. Similarly, home visits to probationers and parolees were generally organized by neighborhood. As the project progressed, when a homicide or series of homicides involved certain groups or gangs, the working group attempted to target meetings, enforcement activities, and home visits on the involved groups or gangs (McGarrell & Chermak, 2001). The research team has not yet completed a formal evaluation of the intervention. However, homicides citywide in Indianapolis fell from roughly 150 a year in the 2 years preceding the intervention to 100 in the year following implementation (Edmund F. McGarrell, personal communication, March 25, 2001). In addition, a preliminary analysis following an application of the pulling-levers approach in the Brightwood neighborhood suggests that the approach significantly reduced gun assaults and robbery incidents in the targeted area (McGarrell & Chermak, 2001).

High Point, North Carolina, is a city that began experiencing a quite severe street homicide problem in the mid-1990s. Working with Kennedy, U.S. Attorney Walter Holton, members of his staff, and members of the High Point police department determined that the problem fit the groups-of-chronic-offenders mold and instituted a pulling-levers strategy in late 1998. The High Point working group was quite robust and, in addition to the usual state and local actors, included very active participation by ATF, FBI, and DEA. As in Indianapolis, High Point followed a mixed strategy that focused both on repeat drug, gun, and violent offenders and on violent groups. The working group identified several hundred violent offenders and held a series of meetings with them; these meetings were formatted such that community representatives and service providers met privately with the offenders first, then enforcement representatives met with them subsequently. The operation was launched in the wake of the federal prosecution of a repeat gun offender, a prosecution that was then heavily "marketed" to offenders through the meeting process. In addition, as violence occurred in the community, the groups involved were identified and targeted for enforcement.

Homicides in High Point had numbered 14 (5 firearm) in 1994; 11 (9 firearm) in 1995; 11 (8 firearm) 1996; 16 (11 firearm) in 1997; and 14 (14 firearm) in 1998. After the operation began in late 1998, homicides fell to 5 (2 firearm) in 1999 and 9 (8 firearm) in 2000. According to High Point officials and the U.S. Attorney's office, none of the 1999 or 2000 homicides was the drug/gang type targeted by the strategy (Caren Johnson, personal communication, March 26, 2001).

The Winston-Salem operation is similar to High Point's, with an interesting elaboration. The Winston-Salem SACSI team was quite deeply focused on preventing juvenile offending. As the problem assessment proceeded, it became clear to the Winston-Salem team that juvenile offending, especially violent offending, was often the result of juveniles being incorporated into the criminal activity of older offenders, for instance as drug couriers and enforcers. Therefore, while maintaining its focus on juveniles and holding meetings with juvenile offenders, the Winston-Salem working group also sought to break this cycle by holding meetings with older offenders in which they were warned quite explicitly that incorporating juveniles into their illegal activity would result in focused state and federal enforcement attention (Coleman et al., 1999). In Winston-Salem, SACSI has focused on the four areas of the city that account for the vast majority of juvenile violent offenses. In these four areas, since the implementation of the SACSI strategy in September 1999, the city has seen a 36% reduction in juvenile violent offenses and a 60% reduction in the use of firearms by juveniles (Caren Johnson, personal communication, March 26, 2001).

Stockton, California

Beginning in mid-1997, criminal justice agencies in Stockton began experimenting with the pulling-levers approach to address a sudden increase in youth homicide. The Stockton Police Department and other local, state, and federal law enforcement agencies believed that most of the youth violence problem was driven by gang conflicts and that the pulling-levers approach used in Boston might be effective in reducing Stockton's gang violence problem. The strategy was implemented by the Stockton Police Department's Gang Street Enforcement Team and grew into what is now known as Operation Peacekeeper as more agencies joined the partnership. The Peacekeeper intervention is managed by a working group of line-level criminal justice practitioners; social service providers also participate in the working group process as appropriate. As street gang violence erupts or when it comes to the attention of a working group member that gang violence is imminent, the working group follows the

Boston model by sending a direct message that gang violence will not be tolerated and pulling all available enforcement levers to prevent violence while continuing communications and providing social services and opportunities to gang members who want them.

To better document the nature of youth homicide in Stockton, the working group retained Harvard University researchers to conduct an analysis of youth (age 24 and under) homicide incidents between 1997 and 1999 (see Braga, Thomson, & Wakeling, 2000). The research revealed that many offenders and victims involved in youth homicide incidents had noteworthy criminal histories and criminal justice system involvement. Following the same qualitative research methods used in Boston and elsewhere, gang-related conflicts were identified as the motive in 48% of the youth homicides. The research analysis also revealed that there were 44 active gangs with a total known membership of 2,100 individuals. Most conflicts among Stockton gangs fall into three broad categories: Asian gang beefs, Hispanic gang beefs, and African American gang beefs. Within each broad set of ethnic antagonisms, particular gangs form alliances with other gangs. Conflicts among Asian gangs were among clusters of different gangs composed mostly of Laotian and Cambodian youth. Conflicts among Hispanic gangs mainly involved a very violent rivalry between Norteño gangs from Northern California and Sureño gangs from Southern California. African American gangs tended to form fewer alliances and divided along well-known Blood and Crip lines. The research also suggested that Operation Peacekeeper was a promising approach to preventing gang violence as youth homicides in Stockton dropped by 54% between 1997 (24) and 1998 (11) and remained low in 1999 (14).

Key Elements of the New Approaches

The available research evidence suggests that these new approaches to the strategic prevention of gang and group-involved violence have generated promising results. It is important to recognize that, with the exception of the Boston experience, rigorous evaluations of the interventions implemented in the various cities have not been completed. As such, these promising results should be interpreted with caution. Nevertheless, there are some core elements of this approach that seem to be the key ingredients in their apparent success. These key elements are worth delineating here.

Recognizing that violence problems are concentrated among groups of chronic offenders who are often, but not always, gang involved. Research has demonstrated that the character of criminal and disorderly youth gangs and groups varies widely both within cities and across cities (see, e.g., Curry, Ball, & Fox, 1994; Maxson & Klein, 1995). The diverse findings on the nature of criminally active groups and gangs in the jurisdictions described in this chapter certainly support this assertion. The research also suggests that the terminology used to describe the types of groups involved in urban violence matters less than their behavior. Gangs, their nature, and their behavior remain central questions for communities, police, and scholars. At the same time, where violence prevention and public safety are concerned, the gang question is not the central one (Kennedy, 2001). The more important observation is that urban violence problems are in large measure concentrated among groups of chronic offenders and the dynamics between and within these groups (Kennedy, 2001). This is an old observation in criminology, and is essentially well known among line law enforcement personnel, prosecutors, probation and parole officers, and the like. These new strategies offer a way of responding to this reality without setting the usually unattainable goals of eliminating chronic offending and/or eliminating criminal gangs and groups.

At the core of much group and gang violence is a dynamic or self-reinforcing positive feedback mechanisms. The research findings indicate that groups of chronic offenders are locked in a self-sustaining dynamic of violence often driven by fear, "respect" issues, and vendettas. The promising reductions observed in the cities engaging these strategic crime prevention frameworks suggest that the "firebreak hypothesis" may be right. If this cycle of violence among these groups can be interrupted, perhaps a new equilibrium at a lower level of risk and violence can be established. This may be one explanation for the rather dramatic impacts apparently associated with what are in fact relatively modest interventions.

The utility of the pulling-levers approach. The pulling-levers deterrence strategy at the heart of these new approaches was designed to influence the behavior, and the environment, of the groups of chronic-offenders that were identified as the core of the cities' violence problems. The pulling-levers approach attempted to prevent gang and group-involved violence by making these groups believe that consequences would follow violence and gun use and that they would, therefore, choose to change their behavior. A key element of the strategy was the delivery of a direct and explicit "retail deterrence" message to a relatively small target audience regarding what kind of behavior would provoke a special response and what that response would be.

Several of these sites have modified Boston's basic approach in interesting ways. Indianapolis and the North Carolina sites have incorporated a focus on individual dangerous offenders as well as on groups, and Indianapolis has a focus on neighborhoods as well. Indianapolis has also extended the strategy to felons returning from prison, warning them as part of the release process about the new enforcement regime to which they will be exposed. Winston-Salem has incorporated an intriguing attempt to prevent juveniles from being drawn into criminal activity. Those sites using Boston-style offender call-ins have developed their own variations on that theme, whereas Minneapolis and the Boyle Heights project in Los Angeles have relied on one-on-one outreach to their target populations. In addition, none of the sites have working groups or sets of partners that look exactly like Boston's or like each other's. This all fits with the original idea behind the Boston project and the pulling-levers idea, which was that the intervention and the logic behind the intervention were both flexible, open to adaptation according to local conditions, local preferences, and the strengths and weaknesses of variable sets of partners (Kennedy, 1997, 2001).

Drawing on practitioner knowledge to understand violence problems. The experiences, observations, local knowledge, and historical perspectives of police officers, street workers, and others with routine contact with offenders, communities, and criminal networks represent an underutilized resource for describing, understanding, and crafting interventions aimed at crime problems (Kennedy et al., 1997). The semi-structured qualitative research performed by the academics in these initiatives essentially refined and specified existing practitioner knowledge. Combining official data sources with street-level qualitative information helped to paint a dynamic, real-life picture of the violence problem.

Convening an interagency working group with a locus of responsibility. Criminal justice agencies work largely independent of each other, often at cross-purposes, often without coordination, and often in an atmosphere of distrust and dislike (Kennedy, 2001). This is also often true of different elements operating within agencies. The ability of the cities to deliver a meaningful violence prevention intervention was created by convening an interagency working group of line-level personnel with decision-making power that could assemble a wide range of incentives and disincentives. It was also important to place on the group a locus of responsibility for reducing violence. Prior to the creation of the working groups, no one in these cities was responsible for developing and implementing an overall strategy for reducing violence.

Researcher involvement in an action-oriented enterprise. The activities of the research partners in these initiatives depart from the traditional research and evaluation roles usually played by academics (see, e.g., Sherman, 1991). The integrated researcher/practitioner partnerships in the working group setting more closely resembled policy analysis exercises that blend research, policy design, action, and evaluation (Kennedy & Moore, 1995). Researchers have been important assets in all of the projects described above, providing what is essentially "real-time" social science aimed at refining the working group's understanding of the problem; creating information products for both strategic and tactical use; testing—often in a very elementary, but important, fashion—prospective intervention ideas; and maintaining a focus on clear outcomes and the evaluation of performance. They have begun to produce accounts both of basic findings and of intervention designs and implementation processes that will be helpful to other jurisdictions. In addition, in several sites, researchers played important roles in organizing the projects.

_____ **Conclusion**

We have provided here an account of a number of related violence prevention efforts. We underscore, again, that none of these have been fully evaluated, nor have they used desirable controlled experimental designs. However, we interpret the cumulative experience described above as supportive, at this preliminary stage, of the proposition that the basic Boston approach has now been replicated, with promising results, in a number of disparate sites.

If this is true, it suggests that there was nothing particularly unique about either the implementation or the impact of Operation Ceasefire in Boston. It suggests further that the fundamental pulling-levers framework behind Ceasefire can be successfully applied in other jurisdictions; with other sets of partners; with different particular activities; and in the context of different basic types of gangs and groups. Further operational experience and more refined evaluation techniques will tell us more about these questions, as experience and analysis continue to accumulate. At the moment, however, there appears to be reason for continued optimism that serious violence by gangs and other groups is open to direct and powerful prevention strategies.

18

Gangs and Public Policy
Prevention, Intervention, and Suppression

C. RONALD HUFF

This volume includes contributions from some of the nation's leading scholars and practitioners on the subject of gangs. The foregoing chapters not only contribute to the growing body of knowledge concerning gangs but also have many implications for public policy formulation, implementation, and evaluation. All too often we forget to ask the question, "So what?" What are the implications for the ways in which society chooses to address the gang problem?

This closing chapter will attempt to pull together some of the implications of the collective research presented in this book for public policy—specifically for prevention, intervention, and suppression.[1] Those three elements are essential ingredients in any community's approach to the gang problem, and if the community can combine these components in a balanced manner, it is more likely that it can develop a comprehensive, rather than fragmented, strategy that will address not only the immediate short-term challenge of *controlling* gang-related crime but also the longer-term challenge of *preventing* it. As Kent Shafer and I noted in Chapter 9, the most typical response of a community, when initially confronted with an emerging gang problem, is to rely solely or heavily on law enforcement and its expertise in suppression. We tried to summarize some of the dangers inherent in overreliance on that approach. In this chapter, drawing on the collective contributions in the preceding chapters, I outline an alternative to that approach that will serve communities much better in the longer term.

Prevention

All of us grew up hearing that "an ounce of prevention is worth a pound of cure." Never has that axiom been more accurate than with respect to the problem of gang-related crime and, in fact, crime in general. Our society has recently been pursuing an extraordinarily expensive policy agenda that tends to rely heavily on suppression and the extensive use of incarceration. In human history, it is rare for a society to incarcerate such a large proportion of its citizens, often removing them from the productive labor force (and, in the U.S., often from the rolls of taxpayers as well) and imprisoning them at great cost to the public, while also disrupting their families and causing many of their families to receive public assistance, thus driving up the costs even farther. In fact, the recent rates of incarceration in the United States put us in such illustrious company as the gulags of the former Soviet Union.

Let us compare this policy preference with our perspective on health care in the United States. By analogy, if we pursued similar policy preferences in health care, we would concentrate our public expenditures solely on those at the end of the medical care continuum—those who are dying. We would not focus on preventive health measures, even though they are much less expensive in the long run. Instead, we'd concentrate on end-of-life care, such as hospices and units for terminal cancer patients. Likewise, the massive investment we've been making in prisons represents a public policy choice—a choice to concentrate our resource expenditures and our hopes on a policy of punishment and incapacitation for criminal behavior after it has occurred. But by then, the offender has already been transformed into a criminal, thus damaging his or her life chances. And by then, there are victims whose victimization might have been prevented.

Among the strategies available to us for attempting to prevent gang-related crime, *primary prevention* is the foundation on which we should build. In this approach, it is not necessary for us to identify specific individuals who are *likely* to become gang members or to engage in gang-related criminal behavior. The rationale for this approach is as follows: By providing effective programs to *entire groups* we will be able to involve a number of individuals who, without such programming, would become involved in gang-related crime. Programs of this genre include both community-wide approaches (e.g., the Communities That Care model and the Spergel/OJJDP comprehensive community strategy) and those that target specific groups (e.g., DARE and G.R.E.A.T., which concentrate on entire classes of school children). Careful evaluation of such programs is essential, and we know that our programmatic efforts must continue to be refined as we understand their effects and are able to improve their content.

But what do we know about the optimal target groups for such prevention efforts? Those that focus on entire communities and seek to engage the citizens and their local agencies and organizations in the effort to build human capital are addressing many of the points raised in the preceding chapters. But what about those that target specific groups for the purpose of primary prevention? Some of the research reported in this volume and elsewhere suggests that an optimal age to focus on the prevention of such high risk behaviors as using drugs and joining gangs might be between 10 and 12; in other words, children in the fifth to seventh grades in school. For example, interviews with 140 gang members in Ohio, Florida, and Colorado indicate that their first association with a gang occurred at ages ranging from about 12½ to 13, and they then joined a gang about 6 months to 1 year after their first association. Those data also demonstrated that their first arrest occurred after they began their involvement with the gang. At the aggregate level, this relationship was invariant across all samples in all three states (Huff, 1998b).[2]

Further evidence for this recommended target age range is provided in this volume by Esbensen, Peterson, Freng, and Taylor (Chapter 3) and by Miller (Chapter 12). Esbensen et al.'s data, based on part of a national evaluation of the G.R.E.A.T. program, showed that delinquent activity most commonly began in the year in which the youth joined a gang, and they found that a sizeable proportion of their sample was using drugs by the eighth grade. Miller, focusing on female involvement in gangs, recommended that prevention efforts begin prior to age 12, although she also recommended targeting such prevention efforts to girls with specific risk factors (an example of *secondary* prevention, rather than primary prevention).

Also, it is important to ask whether some current efforts at prevention may be targeting students *too early*. Should such programs be targeting classes of third graders, for example? Do the lives of third graders generally provide the kind of context in which such prevention programming is likely to be perceived as relevant and therefore more likely to be efficacious? It seems more likely that the kinds of behavioral rehearsal and other social learning techniques employed in such programming will be perceived as relevant only in the context of the day-to-day, lived experience of the children being targeted. Arguably, third graders would rarely be at a point where anticipatory socialization techniques would be salient to their lived experience. So, the challenge is to introduce such prevention programming at an optimal time—a time that fits into a range between the loss of "childhood innocence" and the beginning of significant adolescent peer pressures toward conformity—including conformity to deviant and delinquent behavioral expectations of some individuals and groups.

What kinds of programming might be useful at this age range? Interestingly, both Maxson and Whitlock (Chapter 2) and Miller (Chapter 12) commented on the importance of conflict resolution skills. Although their chapters focused on female involvement in gangs, the literature on male gang behavior suggests that conflict resolution skills would be no less important for boys, as well. Both boys and girls need to develop their social competence and their problem-solving and conflict resolution skills, not only to resist such high-risk behaviors as joining a gang or using or selling drugs, but also to prepare them for the everyday challenges they will face as citizens living and working in increasingly diverse communities and organizations in which conflict is an expected and normal part of daily life. Many of these skills can be taught in the schools, whose leaders can also improve their working partnerships with the community and their development of comprehensive safety and security plans, as recommended by Trump (Chapter 8), to prevent gang-related violence, as well as the kinds of tragedies that have been reported in recent years, though still quite rare statistically.

Prevention can, and should, also occur at the macrolevel, of course. Cureton (Chapter 6), Hagedorn (Chapter 7), Vigil and Yun (Chapter 11), and Fleisher (Chapter 13) all make this point—each in his own way. Taken collectively, those chapters provide powerful evidence for and advocacy of a stronger commitment to enhance economic opportunity for all our citizens, rather than to allow the illegal opportunity structure to compete for "job creation" in our cities (drug dealers are often more "equal opportunity employers" than are legitimate businesses); to celebrate, rather than to marginalize, diversity; and to focus our longer-term efforts on the development of human capital for our citizens and "social glue" for our communities, rather than to pursue policies that result in disinvestment, despair, multigenerational unemployment, and gangs in many of our communities. Zhang (Chapter 14) focuses on sociocultural and macrolevel factors and how they affect those who have immigrated to the United States from China. His documentation of, and insights into, the breakdown of social control in the families of Chinese immigrants whose children have broken the law provides additional evidence of the need for more effective efforts to support families and children in a society with a demanding and highly segmented economy that often contributes to disruptions in social control.

Finally, with respect to prevention, we lack a comprehensive youth policy perspective at the federal, state, and local levels of our society. By that, I mean a coordinated effort to assign a very high priority to the welfare of children and to ask ourselves when formulating public policies how they are likely to affect the welfare of our children. Although our children are our nation's most important resource for the future, we often pay more attention, in the public policy arena, to our physical infrastructure than to our human infrastructure. For example, it is unclear why, in a nation with such enormous economic resources, children should have to live in poverty and other conditions that greatly constrain their life chances and often contribute to their involvement in the alternative illegal economic opportunities made available to them. A coordinated effort at the national, state, and local levels to strengthen neighborhoods and families could help address the issues raised in Bursik's insightful discussion (Chapter 5) and could enhance the chances that the kind of "social capital" described by Bursik can be transferred to children by their parents and other adults in the community, thus increasing the chances that they will become law-abiding citizens, rather than being forced to adapt to the "code of the street" (Anderson, 1999), which may often mean gang-related crime and violence in response to the daily, lived experience of marginalization.

_____ **Intervention**

Discussing prevention, I referred to an early "window of opportunity" for prevention that I believe occurs around ages 10 to 12. My own research has also indicated a second window of opportunity—this one for *intervention* with those who have already committed a criminal or delinquent act. This second opportunity occurs between the time gang members are arrested for property crimes (which typify first arrests for most gang members) and their subsequent involvement in more serious offenses. This period, according to my data (see Huff, 1998b), lasts about 1½ or 2 years. Intervention during that period affords us a chance to divert young offenders from the gang subculture before they further endanger their own lives and victimize other citizens. Successful intervention at this stage, through such programs as prosecutorial diversion targeting first-time, gang-involved property offenders, can save lives (of both the offenders and the victims) and can save society the enormous costs associated with arresting, convicting, and incarcerating serious offenders.

Although the best thing we can do is to prevent someone from ever becoming an offender, the second best thing we can do is to remove an offender from the pool of offenders. In the case of gang members, Decker and Lauritsen's research (Chapter 4) provides evidence that we have another window of opportunity for intervention when a gang member is confronted with the reality of a violent event and may be more motivated at that point to leave the gang. They advocate more detailed studies of the factors and processes associated with leaving the gang, as well as crime desistance in general. Why, for example, do some gang members decide to leave the gang in response to a violent event, but others stay? As Decker and Lauritsen note, there may be important developmental and maturational variables at work that we simply do not understand well. Gang members' decisions may be driven by the cumulative nature of their experiences, by differential support networks, and by other key factors that we have not identified at this point.

The research reported by Braga, Kennedy, and Tita (Chapter 17) also has important implications for intervention strategy. The "pulling-levers" approach (a form of suppression), when combined with intervention at optimal times (as discussed by Decker & Lauritsen) and appropriate social services, can yield effective results, as has been shown in Boston, for example, in addressing problems associated with gangs and guns. Their work has stimulated other communities to examine the factors associated with the local supply of guns and how youth obtain those weapons. Some of the renewed efforts I have witnessed include a more aggressive stance toward obtaining information when juveniles with guns are taken into custody. For example, a youth might be asked to provide information concerning how he or she obtained the gun, with a clear statement that the cooperativeness of the youth will be taken into account in determining the prosecution's recommendation concerning a proper disposition of the case. On the other hand, failure to provide information about how the weapon was obtained will also be taken into account by the prosecutor's office. If the youth states that the gun was obtained from an adult, then law enforcement is immediately instructed to investigate and, if appropriate, arrest the adult involved, who is then prosecuted aggressively. Finally, if the adult is convicted, the prosecutor's office works cooperatively with the news media to ensure heavy news coverage, with the rationale of promoting general deterrence by "getting the word out" that adults who furnish weapons to youth will be aggressively targeted for prosecution and conviction. This blend of intervention and suppression strategies provides a useful transition to the final focus of this closing chapter: suppression.

Suppression

Finally, several chapters in this volume have focused on issues that are important in any discussion of suppression. Clearly, suppression is a necessary but not sufficient strategy for dealing with gang-related crime. I always ask my students, when discussing gangs, "Who invented the DARE Program?" They seldom know that it originated in the Los Angeles Police Department (LAPD) in recognition of the fact that law enforcement simply cannot successfully deal with the gang problem via arrests only. The LAPD recognized that it was essential that prevention efforts begin with young children, before they became involved with gangs.

The LAPD is, of course, a police organization that has evolved from a nationally respected model to one that has witnessed a series of challenges that have called into question the department's relationship with minority citizens and the overzealous and lawless behavior of some of its elite gang unit officers in the Rampart Division. In Chapter 9, Kent Shafer and I focus on the advantages to be gained by changing the culture of law enforcement organizations from a paramilitary, suppression-focused approach to one that views law enforcement as partners with the community, rather than engaging in a war against the community. The fact is that most citizens are on the side of law enforcement, and even in the highest crime areas, most citizens do not want crime and violence, and want to find ways of dealing

with them. The community-oriented, problem-solving approach to policing has much to recommend it, and it also seems to offer greater potential
for addressing the gang problem, because community policing officers are
likely to obtain more information that is relevant than are officers assigned
to a centralized unit.

One useful tool for law enforcement, in improving its understanding of
gang incidents and how they are distributed spatially, is the Orange
County Gang Incident Tracking System described by Meeker and Vila
(Chapter 10). The changing nature of gang turf and gang-related crimes is
such that they cut across jurisdictions. This requires cooperation among
law enforcement agencies, including a shared database whenever possible. Meeker and Vila also found that communication among these entities
is essential to the success of such collaborative efforts. Their discussion of
the issues associated with such shared databases is important for those
who are now confronting emerging and/or growing gang problems.
Properly utilized, such shared databases have great potential.

Finally, Geis's discussion of civil injunctions (Chapter 16) has enormous
implications for scholars, policymakers, and practitioners as we consider
where, or if, civil injunctions should be employed as weapons in dealing
with the gang problem. As Geis points out, such injunctions are often
drafted in impermissibly broad language and have great potential for mis-
use and abuse, given the broad discretion afforded law enforcement officers in the United States. Such injunctions clearly have the potential to be
utilized for the "profiling" of certain groups (generally minorities), who
may then be harassed and/or arrested, even though no criminal behavior
was evident on their part. Geis eloquently argues that in this case, "the cure
is worse than the disease," so to speak, because the freedoms that we all
cherish so much are endangered whenever any of us is deprived of them
without due process of law and without proof beyond a reasonable doubt
that we have committed a crime. We must, then, ask ourselves whether,
were we to apply a balancing test (our interest in preserving our freedom
to associate with each other as we please vs. our desire to control gang-related crime), it is worth the tradeoff involved in allowing law enforcement
the discretion to enforce such civil injunctions.

It is fitting that we conclude a volume on the subject of gangs with such
a cautionary note, because gangs are not *the* problem; they are instead a *dependent* variable—a *symptom* of more fundamental, causally prior independent variables that have numerous dysfunctional consequences for
our society, one of which is gang-related crime. The underlying factors that
contribute to the formation of gangs and to gang-related crime have been
well documented in this book and its two preceding editions. It is my hope
that we will continue to make progress in our understanding of gangs and
that we will improve our ability to translate that research into sound public
policy and programmatic initiatives because in the end, our research dem-

onstrates that gangs generally have two kinds of victims—those who join the gang and those who are victimized by the gang. As a society, we have a responsibility to try to prevent both kinds of victimization.

Notes

1. For an overview and assessment of appropriate prevention and intervention strategies, see Goldstein and Huff (1993), Klein (1995), and Tonry and Farrington (1995).

2. Longitudinal cohort studies have provided extensive data that demonstrate the relationship between gang membership and criminal behavior. See Esbensen and Huizinga (1993, pp. 565-589); Thornberry, Krohn, Lizotte, and Chard-Wierschem (1993, pp. 55-87); and Battin, Hill, Abbott, Catalano, and Hawkins (1998, pp. 93-115).

References

Abbott, A. (1997). Of time and space: The contemporary relevance of the Chicago School. *Social Forces, 75*, pp. 1149-1182.

Abbott, E. (1931). *Report on crime and criminal justice in relation to the foreign born for National Commission on Law Observance and Enforcement.* Washington, DC: Government Printing Office.

Adler, J. S. (1989). A historical analysis of the law of vagrancy. *Criminology, 27*, 209-229.

Allen, R. (1998). (Ab)using California's nuisance law to control gangs. *Western State University Law Review, 25*, 257-311.

Allison, A. (1840). *The principles of population and the connection with human happiness.* Edinburgh: Wm. Blackwood and Son.

Alonso, A. (1999). *Territoriality among African-American street gangs in Los Angeles.* Unpublished master's thesis, Department of Geography, University of Southern California.

Anderson, E. (1999). *Code of the street: Decency, violence, and the moral life of the inner city.* New York: Norton.

Anderson, E., & Short, J. F., Jr. (in press). Delinquent and criminal subcultures. In *Encyclopedia of crime and justice* (2nd ed.). New York: Macmillan.

Asbury, H. (1928). *The gangs of New York: An informal history of the underworld.* New York: Knopf.

Astvasadoorian, R. (1998). California's two-prong attack against gang crime and violence: The Street Terrorism Enforcement and Prevention Act and anti-gang injunctions. *Journal of Juvenile Justice, 19*, 272-300.

Balcazar, H., & Qian, Z. (2000). Immigrant families and sources of stress. In P. C. McKenry & S. J. Price (Eds.), *Families and change: Coping with stressful events and transitions* (2nd ed., pp. 359-377). Thousand Oaks, CA: Sage.

Ball, R., & Curry, G. D. (1995). The logic of definition in criminology: Purposes and methods for defining "gangs". *Criminology, 33*(2), 225-245.

Bankston, C. L., III. (1998). Youth gangs and the new second generation: A review essay. *Aggression and Violent Behavior, 3*, 35-45.

Battin, S. R., Hill, K. G., Abbott, R. D., Catalano, R. F., & Hawkins, J. D. (1998). The contribution of gang membership to delinquency beyond delinquent friends. *Criminology, 36*(1), 93-115.

Battin-Pearson, S. R., Guo, J., Hill, K. G., Abbott, R. D., & Hawkins, J. D. (1999). Early predictors of sustained adolescent gang membership. Seattle: School of Social Work, Social Development Research Group.

Battin-Pearson, S. R., Thornberry, T. P., Hawkins, J. D., & Krohn, M. D. (1998). *Gang membership, delinquent peers, and delinquent behavior* (Juvenile Justice Bulletin, NCJ No. 171119). Washington, DC: U.S. Department of Justice, Office of Juvenile Justice and Delinquency Prevention.

Bellair, P. E. (1995). *The consequence of crime for social disorganization theory: An examination of reciprocal effects between crime and social interaction.* Unpublished doctoral dissertation, State University of New York at Albany, Department of Sociology.

Bellair, P. E. (1997). Social interaction and community crime: Examining the impact of neighbor networks. *Criminology, 35,* 677-704.

Bellair, P. E. (2000). Informal surveillance and street crime: A complex relationship. *Criminology, 38,* 137-165.

Bellock, P. (2000, August 31). Chicago makes another effort to disrupt gangs. *New York Times,* p. A14.

Bernard, J. (1970). *The sociology of community.* Glenview, IL: Scott, Foresman.

Best, J., & Hutchinson, M. M. (1996). The gang initiation rite as a motif in contemporary crime discourse. *Justice Quarterly, 13,* 383-404.

Biernacki, P., & Waldorf, D. (1981). Snowball sampling: Problems and techniques of chain referral sampling. *Sociological Methods and Research, 10,* 141-163.

Biles, D. (Ed.). (1976). Introduction. In *Crime in Papua New Guinea.* Canberra: Australian Institute of Criminology.

Bjerregaard, B. (1998). The constitutionality of anti-gang legislation. *Campbell Law Review, 21,* 31-47.

Bjerregaard, B., & Smith, C. (1993). Gender differences in gang participation, delinquency, and substance use. *Journal of Quantitative Criminology, 9*(4), 329-355.

Black, D. (1989). Social control as a dependent variable. In D. Black (Ed.), *Toward a general theory of social control* (Vol. 1, pp. 1-36). Orlando, FL: Academic Press.

Block, C. R., Christakos, A., Jacob, A., & Przybylski, R. (1996). *Street gangs and crime: Patterns and trends in Chicago.* Chicago: Illinois Criminal Justice Information Authority.

Blumenthal, R. (1982, December 24). Gunmen firing wildly kill 3 in Chinatown bar. *New York Times,* sec. A1.

Boga, T. R. (1994). Turf wars, street gangs, local governments and the battle for public space. *Harvard Civil Rights-Civil Liberties Law Review, 29,* 477-503.

Bonney, L. S. (1993). The prosecution of sophisticated urban street gangs: A proper application of RICO. *Catholic University Law Review, 42,* 579-613.

Bookin-Weiner, H., & Horowitz, R. (1983). The end of the youth gang: Fad or fact? *Criminology, 21,* 585-602.

Bowker, L. H., Gross, H. S., & Klein, M. W. (1980). Female participation in delinquent gang activities. *Adolescence, 15,* 509-519.

Bowker, L. H., & Klein, M. W. (1983). The etiology of female juvenile delinquency and gang membership: A test of psychological and social structural explanations. *Adolescence, 18,* 739-751.

Braga, A. A., & Kennedy, D. M. (2001). Reducing gang violence in Boston. In *Responding to gangs: Research and evaluation.* Washington, DC: U.S. Department of Justice, National Institute of Justice.

Braga, A. A., Kennedy, D. M., Waring, E. J., & Piehl, A. M. (2001). Problem-oriented policing, deterrence, and youth violence: An evaluation of Boston's Operation Ceasefire. *Journal of Research in Crime and Delinquency, 38,* 195-225.

Braga, A. A., Thomson, G., & Wakeling, S. (2000). *The nature of youth homicide in Stockton, California.* Unpublished report. Cambridge, MA: Harvard University, John F. Kennedy School of Government.

Braga, A., Weisburd, D., Waring, E., Mazerolle, L. G., Spelman, W., & Gajewski, F. (1999). Problem-oriented policing in violent crime places: A randomized controlled experiment. *Criminology, 37,* 541-580.

Brown, F. J. (1945). *The social and economic philosophy of Pierce Butler.* Washington, DC: Catholic University of America Press.

Brown, W. K. (1978). Black female gangs in Philadelphia. *International Journal of Offender Therapy and Comparative Criminology, 21,* 221-228.

Burch, J., & Kane, C. (1999). *Implementing the OJJDP comprehensive gang model* (Fact Sheet #112). Washington, DC: U.S. Department of Justice, Office of Justice Programs, Office of Juvenile Justice and Delinquency Prevention.

Bureau of Justice Statistics. (2001, February). *Community policing in local police departments, 1997 and 1999.* Washington, DC: U.S. Department of Justice, Bureau of Justice Statistics.

Burgess, E. W. (1925). The growth of the city. In R. E. Park, E. W. Burgess, & R. D. McKenzie (Eds.), *The city.* Chicago: University of Chicago Press.

Burrell, S. L. (1990). Gang evidence issues for a criminal defense. *Santa Clara Law Review, 30,* 739-783.

Bursik, R. J., Jr. (1988). Social disorganization and theories of crime and delinquency: Problems and prospects. *Criminology, 26,* 519-551.

Bursik, R. J., Jr. (1999). The informal control of crime through neighborhood networks. *Sociological Focus, 32,* 85-97.

Bursik, R. J., Jr. (2000). The systemic theory of neighborhood crime rates. In S. S. Simpson (Ed.), *Of crime and criminality: The use of theory in everyday life.* Thousand Oaks, CA: Pine Forge Press.

Bursik, R. J., Jr., & Grasmick, H. G. (1993). *Neighborhoods and crime: The dimensions of effective community control.* New York: Lexington Books.

Bursik, R. J., Jr., & Grasmick, H. G. (1995a). Defining gangs and gang behavior. In M. W. Klein, C. L. Maxson, & J. Miller (Eds.), *The modern gang reader* (pp. 8-13). Los Angeles: Roxbury.

Bursik, R. J., Jr., & Grasmick, H. G. (1995b). Neighborhood-based networks and the control of crime and delinquency. In H. D. Barlow (Ed.), *Crime and public policy: Putting theory to work.* Boulder, CO: Westview.

Campbell, A. (1984). *The girls in the gang.* New York: Basil Blackwell.

Campbell, A. (1987). Self definition by rejection: The case of gang girls. *Social Problems, 34*(5), 451-466.

Campbell, A. (1990). Female participation in gangs. In C. R. Huff (Ed.), *Gangs in America: Diffusion, diversity, and public policy* (pp. 163-182). Newbury Park, CA: Sage.

Campbell, A. (1991). *The girls in the gang* (2nd ed.). Cambridge, MA: Basil Blackwell.

Campbell, A. (1993). *Men, women and aggression.* New York: Basic Books.

Campbell, A., Munce, S., & Galea, J. (1982). American gangs and British subcultures. A comparison. *International Journal of Offender Therapy and Comparative Criminology, 26,* 76-89.

Cannold, M., Kane, M., Nozik, N., & Reuther, S. (Producers), & Ferrara, A. (Director). (1987). *China girl* [Film]. (Available from Great American Films Limited; Street Lite; and Vestron Pictures)

Caruso, F. C., & De Laurentis, D. (Producers), & Cimino, M. (Director). (1985). *Year of the dragon* [Film]. (Available from Metro-Goldwyn-Mayer)

Castells, M. (1996). *The information age: Economy, society and culture: Vol. 1. The rise of the network society.* Malden, MA: Blackwell.

Castells, M. (2000). *The rise of the network society* (2nd ed.). Oxford, UK: Blackwell.

Catalano, R. F., Loeber, R., & McKinney, K. C. (1998). *School and community interventions to prevent serious and violent offending.* Washington, DC: U.S. Department of Justice, Office of Juvenile Justice and Delinquency Prevention.

Chambliss, W. (1964). A sociological analysis of the law of vagrancy. *Social Problems, 12,* 67-77.

Chandler, K. A., Chapman, C. D., Rand, M. R., & Taylor, B. M. (1998). *Students' reports of school crime: 1989 and 1995.* Washington, DC: U.S. Department of Education and U.S. Department of Justice.

Chao, R. K. (1994). Beyond parental control and authoritarian parenting style: Understanding Chinese parenting through the cultural notion of training. *Child Development, 65,* 1111-1119.

Chao, R. K. (1995). Chinese and European American cultural models of the self-reflected in mothers' childrearing beliefs. *Ethos, 23*(3), 328-354.

Cheh, M. M. (1991). Constitutional limits on using civil remedies to achieve criminal law objectives: Understanding and transcending the criminal-civil law distinction. *Hastings Law Journal, 42,* 1325-1413.

Chernow, R. (1973, June 11). Chinatown, their Chinatown: The truth behind the faade. *New York Magazine,* pp. 39-45.

Chesney-Lind, M. (1993). Girls, gangs and violence: Anatomy of a backlash. *Humanity & Society, 17,* 321-344.

Chesney-Lind, M., & Hagedorn, J. M. (1999). *Female gangs in America: Essays on girls, gangs and gender.* Chicago: Lake View.

Chesney-Lind, M., Shelden, R. G., & Joe, K. A. (1996). Girls, delinquency, and gang membership. In C. R. Huff (Ed.), *Gangs in America* (2nd ed., pp. 185-204). Thousand Oaks, CA: Sage.

Chin, K. (1996). *Chinatown gangs—Extortion, enterprise, and ethnicity.* New York: Oxford University Press.

Chun, G. H. (2000). *Of orphans and warriors—Inventing Chinese American culture and identity.* New Brunswick, NJ: Rutgers University Press.

Chun, K. T. (1993). The myth of Chinese American success and its educational ramifications. In Y. I. Song & E. C. Kim (Eds.), *American mosaic: Selected readings on America's multicultural heritage*. Englewood Cliffs, NJ: Prentice Hall.

City of Chicago v. Morales, 527 U.S. 41 (1999).

City of Chicago v. Morales, 687 N.E.2d 53 (Ill. 1997).

City of Chicago v. Youkhana, 660 N.E.2d 34 (Ill. 1995).

Clark, A. L. (1999). *City of Chicago v. Morales:* Sacrificing individual liberty interests for community safety. *Loyola University of Chicago Law Review, 38*, 113-149.

Clark, K. B. (1965). *Dark ghetto: Dilemmas of social power.* New York: Harper & Row.

Clayton, R. R. (1992). Transition in drug use: Risk and protective factors. In M. Glantz & R. Pickens (Eds.), *Vulnerability to drug abuse.* Washington, DC: American Psychological Association.

Clinard, M. B., & Abbott, D. J. (1973). *Crime in developing countries: A comparative perspective.* New York: John Wiley.

Cloward, R., & Ohlin, L. (1960). *Delinquency and opportunity.* Glencoe, IL: Free Press.

Cohen, S. (1972). *Folk devils and moral panics.* London, UK: MacGibbon and Kee.

Coleman, J. S. (1988). Social capital in the creation of human capital. *American Journal of Sociology, 4*(Suppl.), S95-S120.

Coleman, J. S. (1990). *Foundations of social theory.* Cambridge, MA: Harvard University Press.

Coleman, J. S., & Hoffer, T. (1987). *Public and private high schools: The impact of communities.* New York: Basic Books.

Coleman, V., Holton, W. C., Olson, K., Robinson, S., & Stewart, J. (1999, October). Using knowledge and teamwork to reduce crime. *National Institute of Justice Journal*, pp. 16-23.

Covey H. C., Menard, S., & Franzese, R. J. (1992). *Juvenile gangs.* Springfield, IL: Charles C Thomas.

Covey, H. C., Menard, S., & Franzese, R. J. (1997). *Juvenile gangs* (2nd ed.). Springfield, IL: Charles C Thomas.

Criminal justice innovations earn a place in the limelight for three agencies. (2000, September 30). *Law Enforcement News.*

Curry, G. D. (1997). *Selected statistics on female gang involvement.* Paper presented at the Fifth Joint National Conference on Gangs, Schools, and Communities, Orlando.

Curry, G. D. (1998). Female gang involvement. *Journal of Research in Crime and Delinquency, 35*(1), 100-118.

Curry, G. D. (1999). Responding to female gang involvement. In M. Chesney-Lind & J. Hagedorn (Eds.), *Female gangs in America* (pp. 133-153). Chicago: Lake View.

Curry, G. D. (2000). Self-reported gang involvement and officially recorded delinquency. *Criminology, 38*(4), 1253-1274.

Curry, G. D., Ball, R. A., & Decker, S. H. (1996). Estimating the national scope of gang crime from law enforcement data. In C. R. Huff (Ed.), *Gangs in America* (2nd ed.). Thousand Oaks, CA: Sage.

Curry, G. D., Ball, R. A., & Fox, R. J. (1994). *Gang crime and law enforcement recordkeeping* (NIJ Research in Brief No. NCJ 148345). Washington, DC: U.S. Department of Justice.

Curry, G. D., & Decker, S. H. (1997). Understanding and responding to gangs in an emerging gang problem context. *Valparaiso University Law Review, 31*(2), 523-533.

Curry, G. D., & Decker, S. H. (1998). *Confronting gangs: Crime and community.* Los Angeles: Roxbury.

Curry, G. D., Fox, R. J., Ball, R. A., & Stone, D. (1992). *National assessment of law enforcement anti-gang information resources. Final Report.* Washington, DC: U.S. Department of Justice, National Institute of Justice.

Curtis, R. A. (1999). The ethnographic approach to studying drug crime. *Looking at crime from the street level: Plenary papers of the 1999 Conference on Criminal Justice Research and Evaluation—Enhancing Policy and Practice Through Research (Vol. 1).* Washington, DC: U.S. Department of Justice, National Institute of Justice.

Daly, M. (1983, February 14). The war for Chinatown. *New York Magazine*, pp. 31-38.

Davis, M. (1990). *City of quartz: Evaluating the future of Los Angeles.* New York: Verso.

Dawley, D. (1992). *A nation of lords: The autobiography of the vice lords (2nd ed.).* Prospect Heights, IL: Waveland Press.

De Barry, T. W., & Bloom, I. (1999). *Sources of Chinese tradition.* New York: Columbia University Press.

de Soto, H. (1990). *The other path: The invisible revolution in the Third World*. New York: Harper & Row.

Decker, S. H., Bynum, T., & Weisel, D. (1998). A tale of two cities: Gang as organized crime groups. *Justice Quarterly, 15*(3), 395-425.

Decker, S. H., & Curry, G. D. (2000). Addressing key features of gang membership: Measuring the involvement of young members. *Journal of Criminal Justice, 28*, 473-482.

Decker, S., & Kempf, K. (1991). Constructing gangs: The social definition of youth activities. *Criminal Justice Policy Review, 5*, 271-291.

Decker, S. H., & Lauritsen, J. L. (1996). Breaking the bonds of membership: Leaving the gang. In C. R. Huff (Ed.) *Gangs in America* (pp. 103-122). Thousand Oaks, CA: Sage.

Decker, S. H., Pennell, S., & Caldwell, A. (1997). *Arrestees and guns: Monitoring the illegal firearms market* (Final report submitted to the National Institute of Justice). Washington, D.C.

Decker, S. H., & Van Winkle, B. (1996). *Life in the gang: Family, friends, and violence*. Cambridge, UK, & New York: Cambridge University Press.

DeFleur, L. (1967). Delinquent gangs in cross-cultural perspective: The case of Cordoba. *Journal of Research in Crime and Delinquency, 4*, 132-141.

Denby, D. (1996). *Great books*. New York: Simon & Schuster.

Deschenes, E. P., & Esbensen, F.-A. (1999a). Violence among girls: Does gang membership make a difference? In M. Chesney-Lind & J. Hagedorn (Eds.), *Female gangs in America* (pp. 277-294). Chicago: Lake View.

Deschenes, E. P., & Esbensen, F.-A. (1999b). Violence and gangs: Gender differences in perceptions and behavior. *Journal of Quantitative Criminology, 15*, 63-96.

Drake, St. C., & Cayton, H. R. (1962). *Black metropolis: A study of Negro life in a northern city*. New York: Harper.

Drucker, P. F. (1985). *Innovation and entrepreneurship: Practice and principles*. New York: Harper & Row.

Dubro, J. (1992). *Dragons of crime: Inside the Asian underworld*. Markham, ON: Octopus.

Duneier, M. (1999). *Sidewalk*. New York: Farrar, Strauss & Giroux.

Eggleston, E. J. (1996). *Youth perspectives on gangs and crime: An ethnography from New Zealand*. Unpublished manuscript, Massey University, New Zealand.

Egley, A., Jr. (2000). *Highlights of the 1999 National Youth Gang Survey* (Fact Sheet #2000-20). Washington, DC: U.S. Department of Justice, Office of Juvenile Justice and Delinquency Prevention.

Elliott, D. S., Huizinga, D., & Menard, S. (1989). *Multiple problem youth*. New York: Springer.

Ember, C. R., & Ember, M. (1990). *Cultural anthropology*. Englewood Cliffs, NJ: Prentice Hall.

Esbensen, F.-A., & Deschenes, E. P. (1998). A multi-site examination of gang membership: Does gender matter? *Criminology, 36*(4), 799-827.

Esbensen, F.-A., Deschenes, E. P., & Winfree, L. T. (1999). Differences between gang girls and gang boys: Results from a multi-site survey. *Youth and Society, 31*(1), 27-53.

Esbensen, F.-A., & Huizinga D. (1993). Gangs, drugs, and delinquency in a survey of urban youth. *Criminology, 31*(4), 565-589.

Esbensen, F.-A., Huizinga, D., & Weiher, A. W. (1993). Gang and non-gang youth: Differences in explanatory factors. *Journal of Contemporary Criminal Justice, 9*, 94-116.

Esbensen, F.-A., Miller, M. H., Taylor, T. J., He, N., & Freng, A. (1999). Differential attrition rates and active parental consent. *Evaluation Review, 23*(3), 316-335.

Esbensen, F.-A., & Osgood, D. W. (1997). *National evaluation of G.R.E.A.T.* (Research in Brief). Washington, DC: U.S. Department of Justice, National Institute of Justice.

Esbensen, F.-A., & Winfree, L. T., Jr. (1998). Race and gender differences between gang and non-gang youth: Results from a multi-site survey. *Justice Quarterly, 15*(4), 505-526.

Esbensen, F.-A., Winfree, L. T., Jr., He, N., & Taylor, T. J. (2001). Youth gangs and definitional issues: When is a gang a gang, and why does it matter? *Crime and Delinquency, 47*(1), 105-130.

Etten, T. J., & Petrone, R. F. (1994). Sharing data and information in juvenile justice: Legal, ethical, and practical considerations. *Juvenile and Family Court Journal, 45*(3), 65-90.

Fagan, J. E. (1989). The social organization of drug use and drug dealing among urban gangs. *Criminology, 27*(4), 633-669.

Fagan, J. E. (1990). Social processes of delinquency and drug use among urban gangs. In C. R. Huff (Ed.), *Gangs in America: Diffusion, diversity, and public policy* (pp. 183-219). Newbury Park, CA: Sage.

Fagan, J. E. (1996). Gangs, drugs, and neighborhood change. In C. R. Huff (Ed.) *Gangs in America* (2nd ed., pp. 39-74). Thousand Oaks, CA: Sage.

Fagan, J. E., Weis, J. G., & Cheng, Y.-T. (1990). Delinquency and substance use among inner-city students. *The Journal of Drug Issues, 20*(3), 351-402.

Fearn, N. E., Decker, S. H., & Curry, G. D. (2000). Public policy responses to gangs: Evaluating the outcomes. In J. Miller, C. L. Maxson, & M. W. Klein (Eds.) *The modern gang reader* (2nd ed., pp. 330-344). Los Angeles, CA: Roxbury.

Fernandez, M. E. (1998). An urban myth sees the light again. *Washington Post*, p. B2.

Finestone, H. (1976). *Victims of change: Juvenile delinquents in American society.* Westport, CT: Greenwood.

Fishman, L. T. (1995). The Vice Queens: An ethnographic study of black female gang behavior. In M. W. Klein, C. L. Maxson, & J. Miller (Eds.), *The modern gang reader* (pp. 83-92). Los Angeles: Roxbury.

Fleisher, M. S. (1995). *Beggars and thieves: Lives of urban street criminals.* Madison: University of Wisconsin Press.

Fleisher, M. S. (1998). *Dead end kids: Gang girls and the boys they know.* Madison: University of Wisconsin Press.

Fleisher, M. S. (2000). (Counter-)transference and compassion fatigue in gang ethnography. *Focal, 36*, 77-94.

Fleisher, M. S., & Decker, S. H. (2001). "Going home, staying home": Approaches to integrating prison gang members into the community. *Correctional Management Quarterly, 5*(1), 66-78.

Fleisher, M. S., Decker, S., & Curry, G. D. (2001a). An overview of the challenge of prison gangs. *Corrections Management Quarterly, 5*(1), 1-9.

Fleisher, M. S., Decker, S., & Curry, G. D. (Eds.). (2001b). Responding to the threat of gangs: Leadership and management strategies. *Corrections Management Quarterly, 5*(1).

Fleisher, M. S., & Langhout, R. D. (2001, April). *Gang networks as a subset of friendship network: A preliminary analysis.* Paper presented at the 21st International Sunbelt Social Network Conference, Budapest, Hungary.

Fong, R., Vogel, R., & Buentello, S. (1995). Blood-in, blood-out: The rationale behind defecting from prison gangs. *Gang Journal, 2*, 45-51.

Fong, T. P. (1998). *The contemporary Asian-American experience: Beyond the model minority.* Upper Saddle River, NJ: Prentice Hall.

Fritsch, E. J., Caeti, T. J., & Taylor, R. W. (1999). Gang suppression through saturation patrol, aggressive curfew, and truancy enforcement: A quasi-experimental test of the Dallas anti-gang initiative. *Crime and Delinquency, 45*(1), 122-139.

Fyfe, J. (1997). Good policing. In G. Alpert & R. Dunham (Eds.), *Critical issues in policing: Contemporary readings* (3rd ed., pp. 194-213). Prospect Heights, IL: Waveland.

Gartenstein, D. W., & Warganz, J. E. (1990). RICOs "pattern" requirement: Void for vagueness? *Columbia Law Review, 90*, 489-527.

Geis, G. (1968). The fable of a fatty. *Issues in Criminology, 3*, 211-213.

Geis, G., & Binder, A. (1991). Sins of their children: Parental responsibility for juvenile delinquency. *Notre Dame Journal of Law, Ethics & Public Policy, 5*, 302-322.

Geis, G., & Bunn, I. (1997). *A trial of witches: A seventeenth century witchcraft prosecution.* London: Routledge.

Geis, G., & Dodge, M. (2000). Frederic M. Thrasher (1892-1962) and *The gang* (1927). *Journal of Gang Research, 8*, 41-49.

Goldstein, A. P., & Huff, C. R. (Eds.). (1993). *The gang intervention handbook.* Champaign, IL: Research Press.

Goldstein, A. P., & Kodluboy, D. W. (1998). *Gangs in schools: Signs, symbols, and solutions.* Champaign, IL: Research Press.

Gorman, J. C. (1998). Parenting attitudes and practices of immigrant Chinese mothers of adolescents. *Family Relations, 47*(1), 73-80.

Granovetter, M. (1973). The strength of weak ties. *American Journal of Sociology, 78*, 1360-1380.

Greenwood, P. W. (1996). *Diverting children from a life of crime: Measuring costs and benefits.* Santa Monica, CA: RAND.

Grossman, J. R. (1991). *Land of hope.* Chicago: University of Chicago Press.

Hagedorn, J. M. (1988). *People and folks: Gangs, crime and the underclass in a rustbelt city.* Chicago: Lake View.

Hagedorn, J. M. (1990). Back in the field again: Gang research in the 1990s. In C. R. Huff (Ed.), *Gangs in America: Diffusion, diversity, and public policy* (pp. 240-259). Newbury Park, CA: Sage.

Hagedorn, J. M. (1994a). Homeboys, dope fiends, legits, and new jacks: Adult gang members, drugs, and work. *Criminology, 32,* 197-219.

Hagedorn, J. M. (1994b). Neighborhoods, markets, and gang drug organization. *Journal of Research in Crime & Delinquency, 32,* 197-219.

Hagedorn, J. M. (1998a). *The business of dealing drugs in Milwaukee.* Milwaukee: Wisconsin Policy Research Institute.

Hagedorn, J. M. (1998b). *People and folks: Gangs, crime, and the underclass in a rustbelt city* (2nd ed.). Chicago: Lake View.

Hagedorn, J. M. (1998c). Post-industrial gang violence. In M. Tonry & M. H. Moore (Eds.), *Crime and justice: Vol. 24. Youth violence* (pp. 457-511). Chicago: University of Chicago Press.

Hagedorn, J. M., & Devitt, M. L. (1999). Fighting female: The social construction of female gangs. In M. Chesney-Lind & J. Hagedorn (Eds.), *Female gangs in America: Essays on girls, gangs and gender* (pp. 256-276). Chicago: Lake View.

Hagedorn, J. M., & Goldstein, P. J. (1999). *Murder and drugs in the information age: An urban political economy approach to variation in homicide rates* (Unpublished report for Great Cities Institute by University of Illinois, Chicago).

Hagedorn, J. M., Torres, J., & Giglio, G. (1998). Cocaine, kicks, and strain: Patterns of substance use in Milwaukee gangs. *Contemporary Drug Problems, 15.*

Hard, B. (1998). Injunctions as a tool to fight gang-related problems in California after *People ex rel. Gallo v. Acuna:* A suitable solution. *Golden Gate Law Review, 28,* 629-680.

Harris, F. R., & Curtis, L. A. (Eds.). (1998). *Locked in the poorhouse: Cities, race, and poverty in the United States.* A Milton S. Eisenhower Foundation update of the Kerner Commission Report. Boulder, CO: Rowman & Littlefield.

Harris, M. C. (1988). *Cholas: Latino girls and gangs.* New York: AMS Press.

Haviland, W. A. (1988). *Cultural anthropology.* New York: Holt, Rinehart & Winston.

Haynor, N. S., & Reynolds, C. N. (1937). Chinese American family life in America. *American Sociological Review, 2,* 630-637.

Hazlehurst, K., & Hazlehurst, C. (Eds.). (1998). *Gangs and youth subcultures: International explorations.* New Brunswick, NJ: Transaction Publishing.

Heath, B., & McLaughlin, M. (Eds.). (1993). *Identity and inner-city youth: Beyond ethnicity and gender.* New York: Teachers College Press.

Higgins, D., & Coldren, J. D. (2000). *Evaluating gang and drug house abatement in Chicago.* Chicago: Illinois Criminal Justice Information Authority.

Hill, K. G., Howell, J. C., Hawkins, J. D., & Battin, S. R. (1999). Childhood risk factors for adolescent gang membership: Results from the Seattle Social Development Project. *Journal of Research in Crime and Delinquency, 36*(3), 300-322.

Hirschi, T. (1969). *Causes of delinquency.* Berkeley: University of California Press.

Ho, D. Y. F. (1989). Continuity and variation in Chinese patterns of socialization. *Journal of Marriage and the Family, 51,* 149-163.

Hoover, J. E. (1937, October 4). *Present-day police problems.* Address before the Convention of the International Association of Chiefs of Police, Baltimore, MD. (Washington, DC: U.S. Department of Justice, Federal Bureau of Investigation, 1937).

Horowitz, R. (1983). *Honor and the American dream: Culture and identity in a Chicano community.* New Brunswick, NJ: Rutgers University Press.

Horowitz, R. (1990). Sociological perspectives on gangs: Conflicting definitions and concepts. In C. R. Huff (Ed.) *Gangs in America: Diffusion, diversity, and public policy* (pp. 37-54). Newbury Park, CA: Sage.

Howe, C. (1972, July 7). The growth of gangs in Chinatown. *San Francisco Chronicle,* sec. 1.

Howell, J. C. (1998). *Youth gangs: An overview* (Juvenile Justice Bulletin, Youth Gang Series, NCJ No. 167249). Washington, DC: U.S. Department of Justice, Office of Juvenile Justice and Delinquency Prevention.

Howell, J. C. (2000). *Youth gang programs and strategies.* Washington, DC: U.S. Department of Justice, Office of Juvenile Justice and Delinquency Prevention.

Howell, J. C., & Decker, S. H. (1999). *The youth gangs, drugs, and violence connection* (Juvenile Justice Bulletin, Youth Gang Series, NCJ No. 171152). Washington, DC: U.S. Department of Justice, Office of Juvenile Justice and Delinquency Prevention.

Howell, J. C., Egley, A., Jr., & Gleason, D. K. (2000, November). *Youth gangs: Definitions and the age-old issue.* Paper presented at the annual meeting of the American Society of Criminology, San Francisco.

Howell, J. C., Egley, A., Jr., & Gleason, D. K. (in press). *Modern day youth gangs* (Juvenile Justice Bulletin, Youth Gang Series). Washington, DC: U.S. Department of Justice, Office of Juvenile Justice and Delinquency Prevention.

Howell, J. C., & Gleason, D. K. (1999). *Youth gang drug trafficking* (Juvenile Justice Bulletin, NCJ No. 178282, pp. 1-11). Washington, DC: U.S. Office of Juvenile Justice and Delinquency Prevention.

Howell, J. C., & Lynch, J. (2000). *Youth gangs in schools* (Juvenile Justice Bulletin, Youth Gang Series, NCJ No. 183015). Washington, DC: U.S. Department of Justice, Office of Justice Programs, Office of Juvenile Justice and Delinquency Prevention.

Hu, H. C. (1975). The Chinese concepts of face. In D. G. Haring (Ed.), *Personal character and cultural milieu.* Syracuse, NY: Syracuse University Press.

Huff, C. R. (1988, May). *Youth gangs and public policy in Ohio: Findings and recommendations.* Paper presented at the Ohio Conference on Youth Gangs and the Urban Underclass, Ohio State University, Columbus.

Huff, C. R. (1989). Youth gangs and public policy. *Crime and Delinquency, 35,* 524-537.

Huff, C. R. (1990). Denial, overreaction, and misidentification: A postscript on public policy. In C. R. Huff (Ed.), *Gangs in America* (pp. 310-317). Newbury Park, CA: Sage.

Huff, C. R. (1993). Gangs in the United States. In A. P. Goldstein & C. R. Huff (Eds.), *The gang intervention handbook* (pp. 3-20). Champaign, IL: Research Press.

Huff, C. R. (1996). The criminal behavior of gang members and nongang at-risk youth. In C. R. Huff (Ed.), *Gangs in America* (2nd ed., pp. 75-102). Thousand Oaks, CA: Sage.

Huff, C. R. (1998a). *Comparing the criminal behavior of youth gangs and at-risk youths* (Research in Brief, NIJ 172852). Washington, DC: U.S. Department of Justice.

Huff, C. R. (1998b). Criminal behavior of gang members and at-risk youths. *National Institute of Justice, Research Preview.* Washington, DC: U.S. Department of Justice, National Institute of Justice, March.

Huff, C. R., & McBride, W. D. (1993). Gangs and the police. In A. P. Goldstein & C. R. Huff (Eds.), *The gang intervention handbook* (pp. 401-415). Champaign, IL: Research Press.

Huff, C. R., & Trump, K. S. (1996). Youth violence and gangs: School safety initiatives in urban and suburban school districts. *Education and Urban Society, 28,* 492-503.

Huffington, A. (2000, May 14). Building prisons, not schools. *Los Angeles Times,* p. M5.

Huizinga, D. H. (1996). *The influence of delinquent peers, gangs, and co-offending and violence* (Fact Sheet). Washington, DC: U.S. Office of Juvenile Justice and Delinquency Prevention.

Huizinga, D. (1997). *Gangs and the volume of crime.* Paper presented at the Annual Meeting of the Western Society of Criminology, Honolulu.

Huizinga, D., Loeber, R., Thornberry, T. P., & Cothern, L. (2000). *Co-occurrence of delinquency and other problem behaviors* (Juvenile Justice Bulletin, NCJ No. 182211). Washington, DC: U.S. Department of Justice, Office of Juvenile Justice and Delinquency Prevention.

Huizinga, D. H., & Schumann, K. F. (2001). Gang membership in Bremen and Denver: Comparative longitudinal data. In M. W. Klein, H.-J. Kerner, C. L. Maxson, & E. G. M. Weitekamp (Eds.), *The Eurogang paradox: Street gangs and youth groups in the U.S. and Europe.* Dordrecht, The Netherlands: Kluwer Academic.

Hunt, G., Joe-Laidler, K., & Mackenzie, K. (2000). "Chillin,' being dogged and getting buzzed": Alcohol in the lives of female gang members. *Drug Education and Prevention Policy, 7,* 331-353.

Hunt, G., Mackenzie, K., & Joe-Laidler, K. (2000). "I'm calling my mom": The meaning of family and kinship among homegirls. *Justice Quarterly, 17,* 1-31.

Hunter, A. J. (1985). Private, parochial and public social orders: The problem of crime and incivility in urban communities. In G. D. Suttles & M. N. Zald (Eds.), *The challenge of social control: Citizenship and institution building in modern society.* Norwood, NJ: Ablex.

Hutchins v. District of Columbia. 942 F. Supp. 665 (D.D.C. 1996).

Hutson, H. R., Anglin, D., Kyriacou, D. N., Hart, J., & Spears, K. (1995). The epidemic of gang-related homicides in Los Angeles County from 1979 through 1994. *The Journal of the American Medical Association, 274,* 1031-1036.

Isserles, M. E. (1998). Overbreadth: Facial challenges and the valid rule requirement. *American University Law Review, 48,* 359-462.

Jacobs, J. (1977). *Stateville.* Chicago: University of Chicago Press.

Jacobs, J. B. (2001). Focusing on prison gangs. *Corrections Management Quarterly, 5*(1), vi-vii.

Jacobs, J. B., & Potter, K. (1998). *Hate crimes: Criminal law and identity policies.* New York: Oxford University Press.

Jansyn, L. (1966). Solidarity and delinquency in a street corner group. *American Sociological Review, 31,* 600-614.

Jargowsky, P. A. (1998). Urban poverty, race, and the inner city: The bitter fruit of thirty years of neglect. In F. R. Harris & L. A. Curtis (Eds.), *Locked in the poorhouse: Cities, race, and poverty in the United States.* A Milton S. Eisenhower Foundation update of the Kerner Commission Report. Boulder, CO: Rowman & Littlefield.

Jeffries, J. C., Jr. (1985). Legality, vagueness, and the construction of penal statutes. *Virginia Law Review, 71,* 189-245.

Jenness, V. (1997). *Hate crimes: New social movements and the politics of violence.* New York: Aldine de Gruyter.

Jessor, R. (Ed.). (1998). *New perspectives on adolescent risk behavior.* New York: Cambridge University Press.

Jimenez, J. B. (1989). Cocaine, informality, and the urban economy in La Paz, Bolivia. In A. Portes, M. Castells, & L. A. Benton (Eds.), *The informal economy: Studies in advanced and less developed countries* (pp. 135-149). Baltimore: Johns Hopkins University Press.

Joe, K. A., & Chesney-Lind, M. (1995). "Just every mother's angel": An analysis of gender and ethnic variations in youth gang membership. *Gender & Society, 9,* 408-430.

Joe-Laidler, K. A., & Hunt, G. (1997). Violence and social organization in female gangs. *Social Justice, 24,* 148-169.

Johnson, E. A., & Monkkonen, E. H. (Eds.). (1996). *The civilization of crime: Violence in town and country since the Middle Ages.* Urbana: University of Illinois Press.

Johnson, J. H., Farrell, W. C., Jr., & Stoloff, J. A. (2000). An empirical assessment of four perspectives on the declining fortunes of the African-American male. *Urban Affairs Review, 35,* 695-716.

Kanter, R. M. (1977). Some effects of proportions of group life: Skewed sex ratios and responses to token women. *American Journal of Sociology, 82,* 965-990.

Katz, J. (1988). *Seductions of crime: Moral and sensual attractions in doing evil.* New York: Basic Books.

Kelling, G. L., & Coles, C. M. (1996). *Fixing broken windows: Restoring order and reducing crime in our communities.* New York: Free Press.

Kelly, R. J., Chin, K., & Fagan, J. A. (1993). The dragon breathes fire: Chinese organized crime in New York City. *Crime, Law and Social Change, 19*(3), 245-269.

Kennedy, D. M. (1997). Pulling levers: Chronic offenders, high-crime settings, and a theory of prevention. *Valparaiso University Law Review, 31,* 449-484.

Kennedy, D. M. (1998, July). Pulling levers: Getting deterrence right. *National Institute of Justice Journal,* pp. 2-8.

Kennedy, D. M. (2001). A tale of one city: Reflections on the Boston gun project. In G. Katzmann (Ed.), *Managing youth violence.* Washington, DC: Brookings Institution.

Kennedy, D. M., & Braga, A. A. (1998). Homicide in Minneapolis: Research for problem solving. *Homicide Studies, 2*(3), 263-290.

Kennedy, D. M., Braga, A. A., & Piehl, A. M. (1997). The (un)known universe: Mapping gangs and gang violence in Boston. In D. L. Weisburd & J. T. McEwen (Eds.), *Crime mapping and crime prevention.* New York: Criminal Justice Press.

Kennedy, D. M., Braga, A. A., & Thomson, G. (2000, November). *Problem solving for homicide prevention in Baltimore.* Paper presented at the annual meeting of the American Society of Criminology, San Francisco.

Kennedy, D. M., & Moore, M. H. (1995). Underwriting the risky investment in community policing: What social science should be doing to evaluate community policing. *The Justice System Journal, 17,* 271-290.

Kennedy, D. M., Piehl, A. M., & Braga, A. A. (1996). Youth violence in Boston: Gun markets, serious youth offenders, and a use-reduction strategy. *Law and Contemporary Problems, 59*(1), 147-196.

Kennedy School of Government & National Research Council. (1994). *Violence in urban America: Mobilizing a response.* Washington, DC: National Academy Press.

Kersten, J. (2001). Groups of violent young males in Germany. In M. W. Klein, H.-J. Kerner, C. L. Maxson, & E. G. M. Weitekamp (Eds.), *The Eurogang paradox: Street gangs and youth groups in the U.S. and Europe.* Dordrecht, The Netherlands: Kluwer Academic.

Kitano, H. H. L. (1997). *Race relations* (5th ed.). Upper Saddle River, NJ: Prentice Hall.

Klein, M. (1971). *Street gangs and street workers.* Englewood Cliffs, NJ: Prentice Hall.

Klein, M. W. (1995). *The American street gang: Its nature, prevalence, and control.* New York: Oxford University Press.

Klein, M. W. (1997). Gangs in the United States and Europe. *European Journal on Criminal Policy and Research, 4,* 63-80.

Klein, M. W. (2001). Foreword. In J. Miller, *One of the guys: Girls, gangs and gender.* New York: Oxford University Press.

Klein, M. W. (in press). Surrounded by crime: Lessons from one academic career. In G. Geis & M. Dodge (Eds.), *Lessons of crime.* Cincinnati, OH: Anderson.

Klein, M. W., & Crawford, L. Y. (1967). Groups, gangs and cohesiveness. *Journal of Research in Crime and Delinquency, 4,* 63-75.

Klein, M. W., Kerner, H.-J., Maxson, C. L., & Weitekamp, E. G. M. (Eds.). (2001). *The Eurogang paradox: Street gangs and youth groups in the U.S. and Europe.* Dordrecht, The Netherlands: Kluwer.

Klein, M. W., Maxson, C. L., & Miller, J. (1995). *The modern gang reader.* Los Angeles: Roxbury.

Kodluboy, D. W., & Evenrud, L. A. (1993). School-based interventions: Best practices and critical issues. In A. P. Goldstein & C. R. Huff (Eds.), *The gang intervention handbook* (pp. 257-294). Champaign, IL: Research Press.

Kolender v. Lawson, 461 U.S. 352 (1983).

Kornblum, W. (1974). *Blue collar community.* Chicago: University of Chicago Press.

Lal, S. R., Lal, D., & Achilles, C. M. (1993). *Handbook on gangs in schools: Strategies to reduce gang-related activities* (pp. 7-8). Thousand Oaks, CA: Corwin Press.

Lane, R. (1997). *Murder in America: A history.* Columbus: Ohio State University Press.

Lanzetta v. New Jersey, 306 U.S. 451 (1939).

Lauderback, D., Hansen, J., & Waldorf, D. (1992). "Sisters are doin' it for themselves": A black female gang in San Francisco. *The Gang Journal, 1,* 57-72.

Lauritsen, J. L., Sampson, R. J., & Laub, J. H. (1991). The link between offending and victimization among adolescents. *Criminology, 29,* 265-292.

Lichtblau, E. (1999, December 15). Youth crime rate plunges, Justice Dept. study says. *Los Angeles Times,* p. A51.

Lin, N. (1999). Sunbelt keynote address: Building a network theory of social capital. *Connections, 22*(1), 28-51.

Liska, A. (1987). *Perspectives on deviance* (2nd ed.). Englewood Cliffs, NJ: Prentice Hall.

Livingston, D. (1999). Gang loitering, the court, and some related realism about police patrol. *The Supreme Court Review, 1999,* 141-202.

Los Angeles Times. (1992, November 16). Understanding the riots: Six months later. Los Angeles before and after the Rodney King case (Special 4-part supplement).

Ludlow, L. (1987, May 10). Golden Dragon massacre: Pain still felt a decade later. *San Francisco Examiner,* sec. B1.

Lynch, G. E. (1987). RICO: The crime of being a criminal: Parts I and II. *Columbia Law Review, 87,* 551-764.

Macon, P., & Hagedorn, J. M. (1998). *People and folks: Gangs, crime and the underclass in a rustbelt city* (2nd ed.). Chicago: Lake View.

Maher, L. (1997). *Sexed work: Gender, race and resistance in a Brooklyn drug market.* Oxford, UK: Clarendon.

Mann, A. J. (2000). A plurality of the Supreme Court asserts a due process right to do absolutely nothing in *City of Chicago v. Morales. Creighton Law Review, 33,* 579-641.

Martinez, C. J. (1997). The Street Terrorism Enforcement and Prevention Act: Gang members and guilt by association. *Pacific Law Journal, 28,* 711-714.

Martinez, R., Jr., & Lee, M. T. (2000). On immigration and crime. In G. LaFree, J. F. Short, Jr., R. J. Bursik, Jr., & R. B. Taylor (Eds.), *Criminal justice 2000: Vol. 1. The nature of crime: Continuity and change.* Washington, DC: National Institute of Justice.

Maruna, S. (2001). *Making good: How ex-convicts reform and rebuild their lives.* Washington DC: American Psychological Association.

Maxson, C. L. (1998). *Gang members on the move* (Juvenile Justice Bulletin, Youth Gang Series, NCJ No. 171153). Washington, DC: U.S. Department of Justice, Office of Juvenile
Justice and Delinquency Prevention.

Maxson, C. L., Hennigan, K., & Sloane, D. (2001). For the sake of the neighborhood? Civil gang
injunctions as a gang intervention tool in Southern California. In S. Decker & E. Connors
(Eds.), *Youth violence and community policing*. Belmont, CA: Wadsworth.

Maxson, C. L., & Klein, M. W. (1990). Street gang violence: Twice as great, or half as great? In
C. R. Huff (Ed.), *Gangs in America: Diffusion, diversity, and public policy* (pp. 71-100). Newbury
Park, CA: Sage.

Maxson, C. L., & Klein, M. W. (1995). Investigating gang structures. *Journal of Gang Research, 3*,
33-40.

Maxson, C. L., & Klein, M. W. (1996). Defining gang homicide: An updated look at member
and motive approaches. In C. R. Huff (Ed.), *Gangs in America* (2nd ed., pp. 3-20). Newbury
Park, CA: Sage.

Maxson, C. L., & Klein, M. W. (2000). Defining gang homicide: An updated look at the member
and motive approaches. In J. Miller, C. L. Maxson, & M. W. Klein (Eds.), *The modern gang
reader* (2nd ed.). Los Angeles: Roxbury.

Maxson, C. L., Whitlock, M. L., & Klein, M. (1997). *Developing resistance to street gangs and violence: Research-based guidelines for more effective programs and policies* (Report to the California
Wellness Foundation). Los Angeles: University of Southern California, Social Science Research Institute.

Maxson, C. L., Whitlock, M. L., & Klein, M. (1998). Vulnerability to street gang membership:
Implications for practice. *Social Service Review, 72*(1), 70-91.

Maxson, C. L., Woods, K., & Klein, M. W. (1995). *Street gang migration in the United States* (Final
report to the National Institute of Justice). Washington, DC: U.S. Department of Justice, National Institute of Justice.

Maxson, C. L., Woods, K., & Klein, M. W. (1996). Street gang migration: How big a threat? *National Institute of Justice Journal, 230*(February), 26-31.

McCord, J. (1991). Family relationships, juvenile delinquency, and adult criminality. *Criminology, 29*, 297-417.

McCorkle, R. C., & Miethe, T. D. (1998). The political and organizational response to gangs: An
examination of a "moral panic" in Nevada. *Justice Quarterly, 15*(1), 41-64.

McDermott, T. (2000, December 31). Perez's bitter saga of lies, regrets, and harm. *Los Angeles
Times*, pp. A1, A22-A24.

McGarrell, E., Giacomazzi, A., & Thurman, Q. (1997). Neighborhood disorder, integration,
and the fear of crime. *Justice Quarterly, 14*, 479-497.

McGarrell, E. F., & Chermak, S. (2001). Problem solving to reduce gang and drug-related violence in Indianapolis. In S. H. Decker & E. Connors (Eds.), *Gangs, youth violence, and community policing*. Belmont, CA: Wadsworth.

McGrath, E. (1983, March 28). Confucian work ethic. *Time*, p. 52.

Medaris, M. L., Campbell, E., & James, B. (1997). *Sharing information: A guide to the Family Edu-
cational Rights and Privacy Act and participation in Juvenile Justice programs*. Washington, DC:
U.S. Department of Education and U.S. Department of Justice, Office of Justice Programs,
Office of Juvenile Justice and Delinquency Prevention.

Meeker, J. W. (1999). Accountability for inappropriate use of crime maps and the sharing of inaccurate data. *Crime Mapping and Data Confidentiality Roundtable*, July 8-9, National Institute
of Justice, Crime Mapping Research Center.

Meeker, J. W., Vila, B., & Parsons, K. J. B. (in press). Developing a GIS-based regional gang incident tracking system. In W. Reed (Ed.), *Responding to gangs: Evaluation and research*. Washington, DC: National Institute of Justice.

Meier, R. F., & Geis, G. (1997). *Victimless crime? Prostitution, narcotics, homosexuality, and abor-
tion*. Los Angeles: Roxbury.

Merry, S. E. (1981). *Urban danger: Life in a neighborhood of strangers*. Philadelphia: Temple University Press.

Merton, R. K. (1949). *Social theory and social structure*. Glencoe, IL: Free Press.

Messerschmidt, J. W. (1995). From patriarchy to gender: Feminist theory, criminology and the
challenge of diversity. In N. H. Rafter & F. Heidensohn (Eds.), *International feminist perspectives in criminology: Engendering a discipline* (pp. 167-188). Philadelphia: Open University
Press.

Messner, S. F., & Rosenfeld, R. (1994). *Crime and the American dream.* Belmont, CA: Wadsworth.

Miethe, T. D., & McCorkle, R. C. (1997). *Evaluating Nevada's anti-gang legislation and gang prosecution units.* Washington, DC: U.S. Department of Justice, National Institute of Justice.

Miller, J. (1998a). Gender and victimization risk among young women in gangs. *Journal of Research in Crime and Delinquency, 35*(4), 429-453.

Miller, J. (1998b). Up it up: Gender and the accomplishment of street robbery. *Criminology, 36,* 37-66.

Miller, J. (2001a). *One of the guys: Girls, gangs and gender.* New York: Oxford University Press.

Miller, J. (2001b). Young women's involvement in gangs in the United States: An overview. In M. W. Klein, H.-J. Kerner, C. L. Maxson, & E. G. M. Weitekamp (Eds.), *The Eurogang paradox: Street gangs and youth groups in the U.S. and Europe.* Boston & Dordrecht, The Netherlands: Kluwer Academic.

Miller, J., & Brunson, R. K. (2000). Gender dynamics in youth gangs: A comparison of male and female accounts. *Justice Quarterly, 17*(3), 801-830.

Miller, J., & Decker, S. H. (2001). Young women and gang violence: Gender, street offending, and violent victimization in gangs. *Justice Quarterly, 18*(1), 115-140.

Miller, J., Maxson, C. L., & Klein, M. W. (Eds.). (2001). *The modern gang reader* (2nd ed.). Los Angeles: Roxbury.

Miller, W. (1973). The molls. *Society, 2,* 11, 32-35.

Miller, W. B. (1958). Lower class culture as a generating milieu of gang delinquency. *Journal of Social Issues, 14,* 5-19.

Miller, W. B. (1975). *Violence by youth gangs and youth groups as a crime problem in major American cities.* Washington, DC: Government Printing Office.

Miller, W. B. (1990). Why the United States has failed to solve its youth gang problem. In C. R. Huff (Ed.), *Gangs in America* (pp. 263-286). Newbury Park, CA: Sage.

Miller, W. B. (1992). *Crime by youth gangs and groups in the United States* (Rev. ed.). Washington, DC: U.S. Department of Justice, Office of Juvenile Justice and Delinquency Prevention.

Miller, W. B. (2001). *The growth of youth gang problems in the United States: 1970-1998.* Washington, DC: U.S. Department of Justice, Office of Juvenile Justice and Delinquency Prevention.

Moffitt, T. E. (1993). Adolescence-limited and life-course-persistent antisocial behavior: A developmental taxonomy. *Psychological Review, 100,* 674-701.

Moore, J. W. (1978). *Homeboys: Gangs, drugs, and prison in the barrios of Los Angeles.* Philadelphia: Temple University Press.

Moore, J. W. (1990). Gangs, drugs, and violence. In M. De La Rosa, E. Y. Lambert, & B. Gropper (Eds.), *Drugs and violence: Causes, correlates, and consequences.* Rockville, MD: National Institute on Drug Abuse.

Moore, J. W. (1991). *Going down to the barrio: Homeboys and homegirls in change.* Philadelphia: Temple University Press.

Moore, J. W. (1993). Gangs, drugs, and violence. In S. Cummins & D. J. Monti (Eds.), *Gangs* (pp. 27-46). Albany: State University of New York Press.

Moore, J. W., & Hagedorn, J. M. (1996). What happens to girls in the gang? In C. R. Huff (Ed.), *Gangs in America* (2nd ed., pp. 205-218). Thousand Oaks, CA: Sage.

Moore, J. W., & Hagedorn, J. M. (2001). *Female gangs: A focus on research* (Juvenile Justice Bulletin, Youth Gang Series, NCJ No. 186159). Washington, DC: U.S. Department of Justice, Office of Juvenile Justice and Delinquency Prevention.

National Crime Prevention Council. (1994, August). Partnerships to prevent youth violence. *BJA Community Partnerships Bulletin.* Washington, DC: U.S. Department of Justice, Office of Justice Programs.

National Drug Intelligence Center. (1995). *NDIC Street Gang Symposium.* Johnstown, PA: U.S. Department of Justice, National Drug Intelligence Center.

National Youth Gang Center. (1999a). *1996 National Youth Gang Survey.* Washington, DC: U.S. Department of Justice, Office of Juvenile Justice and Delinquency Prevention.

National Youth Gang Center. (1999b). *1997 National Youth Gang Survey.* Washington, DC: U.S. Department of Justice, Office of Juvenile Justice and Delinquency Prevention.

National Youth Gang Center. (2000a). *1998 National Youth Gang Survey.* Washington, DC: U.S. Department of Justice, Office of Juvenile Justice and Delinquency Prevention.

National Youth Gang Center. (2000b). 1998 National Youth Gang Survey: Program summary. Washington DC: U.S. Department of Justice, Office of Juvenile Justice and Delinquency Prevention.

National Youth Gang Center. (2001a). *A guide to assessing a community's youth gang problems.* Washington, DC: U.S. Department of Justice, Office of Juvenile Justice and Delinquency Prevention.

National Youth Gang Center. (2001b). *Planning for implementation of the OJJDP comprehensive gang model.* Washington, DC: U.S. Department of Justice, Office of Juvenile Justice and Delinquency Prevention.

Needle, J., & Stapleton, W. V. (1983). *Police handling of youth gangs.* Washington, DC: U.S. Department of Justice, Office of Juvenile Justice and Delinquency Prevention.

New Jersey v. Pius, 192 Atl. 89 (1937).

New Jersey v. Pius, 198 Atl. 837 (1938).

Nurge, D. (1998, November). *Female gangs and cliques in Boston: What's the difference?* Paper presented at the annual meeting of the American Society of Criminology, Washington, D.C.

Office of Juvenile Justice and Delinquency Prevention (OJJDP). (1993). *Strengthening America's families: Promising parenting strategies for delinquency prevention* (September, pp. 4-12). Washington, DC: U.S. Department of Justice.

Office of Juvenile Justice and Delinquency Prevention. (2000). *1998 National youth gang survey.* Washington, DC: U.S. Department of Justice, Office of Juvenile Justice and Delinquency Prevention.

Oliver, M. L., Johnson, J. H., & Farrell, W. C. (1993). Anatomy of a rebellion: A political-economic analysis. In R. G. Williams (Ed.), *Reading Rodney King/Reading urban uprising* (pp. 117-141). New York: Routledge.

Orange County Chiefs' and Sheriff's Association. (1999). *The final report of the Orange County Consortium COPS Project.* Westminster, CA: County Chiefs' and Sheriff's Association County-Wide Gang Strategy Steering Committee.

Pak, R. (1972, July 6). Chinatown gangs—Ex-member talks. *San Francisco Chronicle,* p. 1.

Papachristou v. City of Jacksonville, 405 U.S. 156 (1972).

Park, R. (1969). The city: Suggestions for the investigation of human behavior in the urban environment. In R. Sennett (Ed.), *Classic essays on the culture of cities* (pp. 91-130). Englewood Cliffs, NJ: Prentice Hall. (Original work published 1916)

Park, R. E., & Burgess, E. W. (1924). *Introduction to the science of sociology.* Chicago: University of Chicago Press.

Parker, A. M. (1996). Stretching RICO to the limit and beyond. *Duke Law Journal, 45,* 819-848.

Pastore, A. L., & Maguire, K. (Eds.). (1999). *Sourcebook of criminal justice statistics, 1998.* Washington, DC: U.S. Department of Justice, Bureau of Justice Statistics.

Patterson, J. T. (1996). *Great expectations: The United States, 1945-1974.* New York: Oxford University Press.

Pattillo, M. E. (1998). Sweet mothers and gangbangers: Managing crime in a black middle-class neighborhood. *Social Forces, 76,* 747-774.

Pattillo-McCoy, M. E. (1999). *Black picket fences: Privilege and peril among the black middle class.* Chicago: University of Chicago Press.

People ex rel. Gallo v. Acuna, 929 P.2d 596 (1997).

People v. Gamez, 286 Cal Rptr. 894 (1991).

People v. Green, 278 Cal. Rptr. 140 (1991).

Perkins, U. E. (1987). *Explosion of Chicago's black street gangs: 1900 to the present.* Chicago: Third World Press.

Pertersilia, J. (1992). Crime and punishment in California: Full cells, empty pockets, and questionable benefits. In J. B. Steiner, D. W. Lyon, & M. E. Vaiana (Eds.), *Urban America: Policy choices for Los Angeles and the nation* (pp. 175-206). Santa Monica, CA: RAND.

Peterson, D., Miller, J., & Esbensen, F.-A. (2001). The impact of sex composition on gangs and gang member delinquency. *Criminology, 39*(2), 411-439.

Platt, A. M. (1969). *The child savers: The invention of delinquency.* Chicago: University of Chicago Press.

Police Executive Research Forum. (1999). *Northeast Gang Information System: Description of the system and lessons learned.* Washington, DC: Police Executive Research Form. (Web site: www. nlectc.org/)

Porter, M. E. (1995). The competitive advantage of the inner city. *Harvard Business Review, 73,* 55-71.

Portes, A. (1998). Social capital: Its origins and applications in modern sociology. *Annual Review of Sociology, 24,* 1-24.

Portes, A., Castells, M., & Benton, L. A. (1989a). Conclusion: The policy implications of informality. In A. Portes, M. Castells, & L. A. Benton (Eds.), *The informal economy: Studies in advanced and less advanced countries* (pp. 298-311). Baltimore, MD: Johns Hopkins University Press.

Portes, A., Castells, M., & Benton, L. A. (Eds.). (1989b). *The informal economy: Studies in advanced and less advanced countries.* Baltimore, MD: Johns Hopkins University Press.

Portillos, E. (1999). Women, men and gangs: The social construction of gender in the barrio. In M. Chesney-Lind & J. Hagedorn (Eds.), *Female gangs in America: Essays on girls, gangs and gender* (pp. 232-244). Chicago: Lake View.

Portillos, E., Jurik, N., & Zatz, M. (1996). Machismo and Chicano/a gangs: Symbolic resistance or oppression? *Free Inquiry in Creative Sociology, 24,* 175-184.

Poulos, P. W. (1995). Chicago's ban on gang loitering: Making sense of vagueness and overbreadth in loitering laws. *California Law Review, 83,* 379-417.

Powers, J. (2001). *Like water on a stone: The story of Amnesty International.* London: Penguin.

Quicker, J. C. (1983). *Homegirls: Characterizing Chicana gangs.* San Pedro, CA: International University Press.

Rand, A. (1987). Transitional life events and desistance from delinquency and crime. In M. Wolfgang, T. Thornberry, & R. Figlio (Eds.), *From boy to man, from delinquency to crime* (pp. 134-162). Chicago: University of Chicago Press.

Reisig, M. D., & Parks, R. B. (2000). Experience, quality of life, and context: A hierarchical analysis of satisfaction with police. *Justice Quarterly, 17,* 607-630.

Reynolds, P., & White, S. (1993). *Wisconsin's entrepreneurial climate study.* Milwaukee: Wisconsin Innovation Network.

Rivera, R. J., & Short, J. F., Jr. (1967). Significant adults, caretakers, and structures of opportunity: An exploratory study. *Journal of Research in Crime and Delinquency, 4,* 76-97.

Romenesko, J. (1990, November). The last days of the struggle. *Milwaukee Magazine,* pp. 88-96.

Rose, D. R., & Clear, T. R. (1998). Incarceration, social capital, and crime: Implications for social control theory. *Criminology, 36,* 441-480.

Rose, D. R., Clear, T. R., & Ryder, J. A. (2000). *Drugs, incarceration, and neighborhood life: The impact of reintegrating offenders into the community* (Final report). Washington, DC: National Institute of Justice.

Rosenbaum, D. P., & Grant, J. A. (1983). *Gangs and youth problems in Evanston: Research findings and policy options.* Evanston, IL: Northwestern University, Center for Urban Affairs and Policy Research.

Rothman, D. (1971). *The discovery of the asylum.* Boston: Little, Brown.

Rountree, P. W., & Warner, B. D. (1999). Social ties and crime: Is the relationship general? *Criminology, 37,* 789-813.

Rubin, E. L. (Ed.). (1999). *Minimizing harm: A new crime policy for America.* Boulder, CO: Westview.

Russell Sage Foundation. (2001). *Examining the future of America's low-skilled workers.* New York: Author.

Sampson, R. J., & Bartusch, D. J. (1998). Legal cynicism and (subcultural?) tolerance of deviance: The neighborhood context of racial differences. *Law and Society Review, 32,* 777-804.

Sampson, R. J., & Groves, W. B. (1989). Community structure and crime: Testing social disorganization theory. *American Journal of Sociology, 94,* 774-802.

Sampson, R. J., & Laub, J. H. (1993). *Crime in the making: Pathways and turning points through life.* Cambridge, MA: Harvard University Press.

Sampson, R. J., & Laub, J. H. (1994). Urban poverty and the family context of delinquency: A new look at structure and process in a classic study. *Child Development, 65,* 523-540.

Sampson, R. J., & Lauritsen, J. L. (1997). Racial and ethnic disparities in crime and criminal justice in the United States. In M. Tonry (Ed.), *Crime and justice: A review of research: Vol. 21. Ethnicity, crime, and immigration.* Chicago: University of Chicago Press.

Sampson, R. J., Morenoff, J. D., & Earls, F. (1999). Beyond social capital: Spatial dynamics of collective efficacy for children. *American Sociological Review, 64,* 633-660.

Sampson, R. J., & Raudenbush, S. W. (1999). Systematic social observation of public spaces: A new look at disorder in urban neighborhoods. *American Journal of Sociology, 105,* 603-651.

Sampson, R. J., Raudenbush, S. W., & Earls, F. (1997, August 15). Neighborhoods and violent crime: A multilevel study of collective efficacy. *Science, 277,* 918-924.

Sampson, R. J., & Wilson, W. J. (1995). Toward a theory of race, crime, and urban inequality. In J. Hagan & R. D. Peterson (Eds.), *Crime and inequality.* Stanford, CA: Stanford University Press.

Sanchez-Jankowski, M. (1991). *Islands in the street: Gangs and American urban society.* Berkeley: University of California Press.

Sanders, W. B. (1994) *Gangbangs and drive-bys: Grounded culture and juvenile gang violence.* New York: Aldine de Gruyter.

Sante, L. (1991). *Low life: Lures and snares of old New York.* New York: Vintage.

Sasse, B. C. (2000). Curfew laws, freedom of movement, and the rights of juveniles. *Case Western Law Review, 50,* 681-728.

Sassen-Koob, S. (1998). *Globalization and its discontents.* New York: New Press.

Scott, G. (2000). *Illinois law enforcement responses to street gangs.* Chicago: Office of the Illinois Attorney General, Gang Crime Prevention Center.

Shafer, K. (1999). *Mission aligned policing philosophy.* Columbus, OH: Columbus Division of Police.

Shaw, C. R., & McKay, H. D. (1931). *Social factors in juvenile delinquency* (National Commission on Law Observation and Enforcement, No. 13, Report on the Causes of Crime, Vol. 2). Washington, DC: Government Printing Office.

Shaw, C. R., & McKay, H. D. (1942). *Juvenile delinquency and urban areas.* Chicago: University of Chicago Press.

Shaw, C. R., Zorbaugh, F. M., McKay, H. D., & Cottrell, L. S. (1929). *Delinquency areas.* Chicago: University of Chicago Press.

Sherman, L. (1991). Herman Goldstein: Problem-oriented policing. *Journal of Criminal Law and Criminology, 82,* 693-702.

Shon, S. P., & Ja, D. D. (1982). Chinese families. In M. McGoldrick, J. K. Pearce, & J. Giordano (Eds.), *Ethnicity and family therapy.* New York: Guilford.

Short, J. F., Jr. (1963). Introduction to the abridged edition. In F. M. Thrasher, *The gang,* (Abridged ed., pp. xv-liii). Chicago: University of Chicago Press.

Short, J. F., Jr. (1968a). Comment on Lerman's "Gangs, networks and subcultural delinquency." *American Journal of Sociology, 73,* 513-515.

Short, J. F., Jr. (1968b). *Gang delinquency and delinquent subcultures.* New York: Harper & Row.

Short, J. F., Jr. (1974). Youth, gangs and society: Micro and macrosociological processes. *Sociological Quarterly, 15,* 20-31.

Short, J. F., Jr. (1990). Gangs, neighborhoods, and youth crime. *Criminal Justice Research Bulletin, 5*(4), 1-11.

Short, J. F., Jr. (1997). *Poverty, ethnicity, and violent crime.* Boulder, CO: Westview.

Short, J. F., Jr. (1998). The level of explanation problem revisited—The American Society of Criminology 1997 Presidential Address. *Criminology 36*(1), 3-36.

Short, J. F., Jr., Rivera, R., & Marshall, H. (1964). Adult-adolescent relations and gang delinquency. *Pacific Sociolgoical Review, 7*(Fall), 59-65.

Short, J. F., Jr., & Strodtbeck, F. L. (1965). *Group process and gang delinquency.* Chicago: University of Chicago Press.

Short, J. F., Jr., & Strodtbeck, F. (1974). *Group process and gang delinquency.* Chicago: University of Chicago Press. (Original work published 1965)

Simcha-Fagan, O., & Schwartz, J. E. (1986). Neighborhood and delinquency: An assessment of contextual effects. *Criminology, 24*(4), 667-703.

Simon, R. J. (1985). *Public opinion and the immigrant: Print media coverage, 1880-1980.* Lexington, MA: Lexington Books.

Skogan, W. G. (1990). *Disorder and decline: Crime and the spiral of decay in American neighborhoods.* New York: Free Press.

Skolnick, J. (1988). *The social structure of street drug dealing* (BCS Forum). Sacramento: State of California.

Skolnick, J. H. (1989). *Gang organization and migration.* Sacramento: Office of the Attorney General of the State of California.

Skolnick, J. H. (1990). The social structure of street drug dealing. *American Journal of Police, 9,* 1-41.

Skolnick, J. H., Correl, T., Navarro, E., & Rabb, R. (1988). *The social structure of street drug dealing. Report to the Office of the Attorney General of the State of California.* Berkeley: University of California Press.

Slater, E. (2000, March 30). Scandal forces Chicago police to overhaul anti-gang unit. *Los Angeles Times*, p. A5.

Slayton, J. (2000). Establishing and maintaining interagency information sharing. *Juvenile Accountability Incentive Block Grants Program Bulletin*. Washington, DC: U.S. Department of Justice, Office of Justice Programs, Office of Juvenile Justice and Delinquency Prevention.

Smith, C., & Thornberry, T. P. (1995). The relationship between childhood maltreatment and adolescent involvement in delinquency. *Criminology, 33,* 451-479.

Snyder, H. N., & Sickmund, M. (1999). *Juvenile offenders and victims: 1999 national report*. Washington, DC: U.S. Department of Justice, Office of Juvenile Justice and Delinquency Prevention.

Sollenberger, R. (1968). Chinese-American child-rearing practices and juvenile delinquency. *Journal of Social Psychology, 74,* 13-23.

Spergel, I. A. (1990). Youth gangs: Continuity and change. In M. Tonry & N. Morris (Eds.), *Crime and justice: A review of research* (Vol. 12). Chicago: University of Chicago Press.

Spergel, I. A. (1995). *The youth gang problem: A community approach*. New York: Oxford University Press.

Spergel, I. A., & Bobrowski, L. (1989). Minutes from the "Law Enforcement Youth Gang Definitional Conference: September 25, 1989". Rockville, MD: Juvenile Justice Clearinghouse.

Spergel, I. A., Chance, R., Ehrensaft, C., Regulus, T., Kane, C., Laseter, R., Alexander, A., & Oh, S. (1994). *Gang suppression and intervention: Community models*. Washington, DC: U.S. Department of Justice, Office of Juvenile Justice and Delinquency Prevention.

Spergel, I. A., & Curry, G. D. (1990). Strategies and perceived agency effectiveness in dealing with the youth gang problem. In C. R. Huff (Ed.) *Gangs in America* (pp. 288-309). Newbury Park, CA: Sage.

Spergel, I. A., & Curry, G. D. (1993). The National Youth Gang Survey: A research and developmental process. In A. P. Goldstein & C. R. Huff (Eds.), *The gang intervention handbook* (pp. 359-400). Champaign, IL: Research Press.

Spergel, I. A., & Curry, G. D. (1995). The National Youth Gang Survey: A research and development process. In M. W. Klein, C. L. Maxson, & J. Miller (Eds.), *The modern gang reader* (pp. 254-265). Los Angeles: Roxbury.

Spergel, I. A., Curry, G. D., Chance, R., Kane, C., Ross, R., Alexander, A., Simmons, E., & Oh, S. (1994). *Gang suppression and intervention: Problem and response*. Washington, DC: U.S. Department of Justice, Office of Juvenile Justice and Delinquency Prevention.

Spergel, I. A., Turner, C., Pleas, J., & Brown, P. (1969). *Youth manpower: What happened in Woodlawn*. Chicago: University of Chicago, School of Social Service Administration.

Stack, C. B. (1974). *All our kin: Strategies for survival in a black community*. New York: Harper & Row.

Starbuck, D., Howell, J. C., & Lindquist, D. J. (2001). *Hybrids and other modern gangs* (Juvenile Justice Bulletin, Youth Gang Series, NCJ No. 18916). Washington, DC: U.S. Department of Justice, Office of Juvenile Justice and Delinquency Prevention.

Steel, M. C. (2000). Constitutional law—The vagueness doctrine: Two-part test of two conflicting tests? *City of Chicago v. Morales*, 119 S. Ct. 1949 (1999). *Land and Water Law Review, 35,* 255-274.

Stepick, A. (1989). Miami's two informal sectors. In A. Portes, M. Castells, & L. A. Benton (Eds.), *The informal economy: Studies in advanced and less advanced countries* (pp. 111-134). Baltimore, MD: Johns Hopkins University Press.

Stewart, G. (1998). Black codes and broken windows: The legacy of racial hegemony in anti-gang civil injunctions. *Yale Law Journal, 107,* 2249-2279.

Sullivan, M. (1989). *"Getting paid": Youth crime and work in the inner city*. Ithaca, NY: Cornell University Press.

Sundeen, R. A. (1981). Juvenile arrests in Papua New Guinea. In G. F. Jensen (Ed.), *Sociology of delinquency: Current issues*. Beverley Hills, CA: Sage.

Sung, B. L. (1987). *The adjustment experience of Chinese immigrant children in New York City*. New York: Center for Migration Studies.

Suttles, G. D. (1968). *The social order of the slum: Ethnicity and territory in the inner city*. Chicago: University of Chicago Press.

Swart, W. J. (1991). Female gang delinquency: A search for "acceptably deviant behavior." *Mid-American Review of Sociology, 15,* 43-52.

Taylor, C. S. (1988). Youth gangs organize quest for power, money. In *School Safety: National School Safety Center News Journal* (pp. 26-27).

Taylor, C. (1989). *Dangerous society*. East Lansing: Michigan State University Press.

Taylor, C. S. (1990). *Dangerous society*. East Lansing: Michigan State University Press.

Taylor, C. S. (1993). *Girls, gangs, women and drugs*. East Lansing: Michigan State University Press.

Taylor, R. B. (1997). Social order and disorder of street blocks and neighborhoods: Ecology, microecology, and the systemic model of social disorganization. *Journal of Research in Crime and Delinquency, 34*, 113-155.

The open forum: 'Punk' fights harm community. (1950, May 5). *Chinese Press*, p. 8.

Thomas, W. I., & Znaniecki, F. (1920). *The Polish peasant in Europe and America: Vol. 4*. Boston: Gorham Press.

Thompkins, D. (2000). [Untitled manuscript on inmate social organization.] (Available from D. Thompkins, Criminal Justice Department, University of Illinois-Chicago)

Thornberry, T. P. (1998). Membership in youth gangs and involvement in serious and violent offending. In R. Loeber & D. P. Farrington (Eds.), *Serious and violent juvenile offenders: Risk factors and successful interventions* (pp. 147-166). Thousand Oaks, CA: Sage.

Thornberry, T. P., & Burch, J. H., II. (1997). *Gang members and delinquent behavior* (Juvenile Justice Bulletin, NCJ No. 165154). Washington, DC: U.S. Department of Justice.

Thornberry, T. P., Krohn, M. D., Lizotte, A. J., & Chard-Wierschem, D. (1993). The role of juvenile gangs in facilitating delinquent behavior. *Journal of Research in Crime and Delinquency, 30*(1), 55-87.

Thornberry, T. P., Krohn, M. D., Lizotte, A. J., Smith, C. A., & Tobin, K. (in press). *Gangs: The origins and consequences of gang membership in developmental perspective*. New York: Cambridge University Press.

Thornberry, T. P., Lizotte, A. J., & Krohn, M. D. (1994). Delinquent peers, beliefs, and delinquent behaviors: A longitudinal test of interactional theory. *Criminology, 32*, 47-83.

Thornberry, T. P., Lizotte, A. J., Krohn, M. D., Farnworth, M., & Jang, S. J. (1994). Delinquent peers, beliefs, and delinquent behavior: A longitudinal test of interactional theory. *Criminology, 32*, 47-84.

Thoumi, F. E. (1995). *Political economy & illegal drugs in Colombia*. Boulder, CO: Lynne Rienner.

Thrasher, F. M. (1931). The gang. *Encyclopedia of the Social Sciences, 6*, 564.

Thrasher, F. M. (1963). *The gang: A study of 1,313 gangs in Chicago*. Chicago: University of Chicago Press. (Original work published 1927)

Thumma, S. L., & Kirchmeier, J. L. (1999). The lexicon has become a fortress: The United States Supreme Court's use of dictionaries. *Buffalo Law Review, 47,D 227-296*.

Tita, G. E., Riley, K. J., & Greenwood, P. (2001). From Boston to Boyle Heights: The process and prospects of a "pulling levers" strategy in a Los Angeles barrio. In S. H. Decker & E. Connors (Eds.), *Gangs, youth violence, and community policing*. Belmont, CA: Wadsworth.

Tong, B. (2000). *The Chinese Americans*. Westport, CT: Greenwood.

Tonry, M. (Ed.). (1997). *Crime and justice: A review of research: Vol. 21. Ethnicity, crime, and immigration: Comparative and cross-national perspectives*. Chicago: University of Chicago Press.

Tonry, M., & Farrington, D. (Eds.). (1995). *Building a safer society: Strategic approaches to crime*. Chicago: University of Chicago Press.

Tonry, M., & Moore, M. H. (Eds.). (1998). *Crime and justice: A review of research: Vol. 24. Youth violence*. Chicago: University of Chicago Press.

Torok, W. C., & Trump, K. S. (1994). Gang intervention: Police and school collaboration. *FBI Law Enforcement Bulletin, 63*(5), 3-17.

Touraine, A. (1995). *Critique of modernity*. Oxford, UK: Blackwell.

Truman, D. R. (1995). The Jets and the Sharks are dead: State statutory responses to criminal street crimes. *Washington University Law Quarterly, 73*, 683-735.

Trump, K. S. (1993a, Winter). Knowing no boundaries. *School Safety: National School Safety Center News Service*, pp. 8-11.

Trump, K. S. (1993b). Tell teen gangs: School's out. *The American School Board Journal, 180*(7), 39-42.

Trump, K. S. (1996). Gang development and strategies in schools and suburban communities. In C. R. Huff (Ed.), *Gangs In America* (2nd ed., pp. 270-280). Thousand Oaks, CA: Sage.

Trump, K. S. (1998). *Practical school security: Basic guidelines for safe and secure schools* (pp. 11-15). Thousand Oaks, CA: Corwin.

Trump, K. S. (2000). *Classroom killers? Hallway hostages? How schools can prevent and manage school crises.* Thousand Oaks, CA: Corwin.

Tsai, S. H. (1986). *The Chinese experience in America.* Bloomington: Indiana University Press.

U.S. Bureau of the Census. (1999). *The Asian and Pacific Islander population in the United States.* Washington, DC: U.S. Department of Commerce.

Valdez, A. (2000). *Gangs: A guide to understanding street gangs* (3rd ed.). San Clemente, CA: LawTech Publishing.

Valdez, A., Alvarado, J., & Arcos, R. (2000, November). *The effects and consequences of selling and using heroin among Mexican American street gang members.* Paper presented at the annual meeting of the American Society of Criminology, San Francisco.

Valentine, B. (1978). *Hustling and other hard work: Life styles in the ghetto.* New York: Free Press.

Van Gemert, F. (2001). Crips in orange: Gangs and groups in the Netherlands. In M. W. Klein, H.-J. Kerner, C. L. Maxson, & E. G. M. Weitekamp (Eds.), *The Eurogang paradox: Street gangs and youth groups in the U.S. and Europe.* Dordrecht, The Netherlands: Kluwer Academic.

van Kammen, W., & Loeber, R. (1994). Are fluctuations in delinquency activities related to the onset and offset in juvenile illegal drug use and drug dealing? *Journal of Drug Issues, 24*(1), 9-24.

van Kammen, W., Maguin, E., & Loeber, R. (1994). Initiation of drug selling and its relationship with illicit drug use and serious delinquency in adolescent boys. In E. G. W. Weitekamp & H.-J. Kerner (Eds.), *Cross-national longitudinal research on human development and criminal behavior.* Dordrecht, The Netherlands: Kluwer Academic.

Venkatesh, S. A. (1996). The gang in the community. In C. R. Huff (Ed.), *Gangs in America* (2nd ed., pp. 241-256). Thousand Oaks, CA: Sage.

Venkatesh, S. A. (1997). The social organization of street gang activity in an urban ghetto. *American Journal of Sociology, 103,* 82-111.

Venkatesh, S. A. (1998). Gender and outlaw capitalism: A historical account of the Black Sisters United "girl gang." *Signs, 23,* 683-709.

Venkatesh, S. A. (2000). *American project: The rise and fall of a modern ghetto.* Cambridge, MA: Harvard University Press.

Vigil, J. D. (1987, April). *Youth gangs and delinquency: A cross-cultural look at the children of immigrants.* Paper presented at the 47th annual meeting of the Society for Applied Anthropology, Oaxaca, Mexico.

Vigil, J. D. (1988a). *Barrio gangs: Street life and identity in Southern California.* Austin: University of Texas Press.

Vigil, J. D. (1988b). Group processes and street identity: Adolescent Chicano gang members. *Ethnos, 16*(4), 421-445.

Vigil, J. D. (1993a). The established gang. In S. Cummings & D. Monti (Eds.), *Gangs: The origins and the impact of contemporary youth gangs in the United States* (pp. 95-112). New York: State University of New York Press.

Vigil, J. D. (1993b). Gangs, social control, and ethnicity: ways to redirect street youth. In S. B. Heath & M. W. McLaughlin (Eds.), *Identity and inner-city youth: Beyond ethnicity and gender* (pp.94-119). New York: Columbia University Press.

Vigil, J. D. (1996). *Understanding life in an East Los Angeles public housing project: A focus on gang and non-gang families.* Working paper, Center for the Study of Urban Poverty, University of California, Los Angeles.

Vigil, J. D. (1998a). *From Indians to Chicanos: The dynamics of Mexican American culture.* Prospect Heights, IL: Waveland.

Vigil, J. D. (1998b). Time, place, and story in the formation of Chicano identity. In G. Campbell (Ed.), *Many Americas: Critical perspectives on race, racism, ethnicity* (pp. 111-118). Dubuque, IA: Kendall/Hunt.

Vigil, J. D. (1999). Streets and schools: How educators can help Chicano marginalized gang youth. *Harvard Educational Review, 69*(3), 270-288.

Vigil, J. D. (2000). Community dynamics and the rise of street gangs. Conference, *Latinos and the 21st century: Mapping a research strategy.* The David Rockefeller Center for Latin American Studies, Harvard University.

Vigil, J. D. (in press). *A rainbow of gangs: A cross-cultural look at street youth in Los Angeles.* Austin: University of Texas Press.

Vigil, J. D., & Long, J. M. (1990). Etic and emic perspectives on gang culture: The Chicano case. In C. R. Huff (Ed.), *Gangs in America: Diffusion, Diversity, and Public Policy*. Newbury Park, CA: Sage.

Vigil, J. D., & Yun, S. D. (1990). The Vietnamese youth gangs in Southern California. In R. Huff (Ed.), *Gangs in America: Diffusion, diversity, and public policy* (pp. 146-162). Newbury Park, CA: Sage.

Vigil, J. D., & Yun, S. D. (1998). Vietnamese youth gangs in the context of multiple marginality and the Los Angeles youth gang phenomenon. In K. Hazlehurst & C. Hazlehurst (Eds.), *Gangs and youth subcultures: International explorations* (pp. 117-139). New Brunswick, NJ: Transaction Publications.

Vigil, J. D., Yun, S. C., & Long, J. M. (1993). Youth gangs, crime, and the Vietnamese in Orange County. In J. Fagan (Ed.), The ecology of crimes and drugs in the inner city (pp. 1-56). New York: Social Science Research Council.

Vila, B., Meeker, J. W. (1997). A regional gang incident tracking system. *Journal of Gang Research, 4*(3), 23-36.

Vila, B., & Meeker, J. W. (1999). *Gang activity in Orange County, California: Final report to the National Institute of Justice* (Award Number 96-IJ-CX-0030). Washington, DC: U.S. Department of Justice.

Vila, B., & Morris, C. (Eds.). (1999). *The role of police in American society: A documentary history*. Westport, CT: Greenwood.

Vogel, R. E., & Torres, S. (1998). An evaluation of Operation Roundup: An experiment in the control of gangs to reduce crime, fear of crime and improve police community relations. *Policing, 21*(1), 38-53.

Vollmer, A. (1969). *The police and modern society*. College Park, MD: McGrath. (Original work published 1936 by the Regents of the University of California)

Wacquant, L. (2000). The new "peculiar institution": On the prison as surrogate ghetto. *Theoretical Criminology, 4*, 377-389.

Waldorf, D. (1993). When the Crips invaded San Francisco—Gang migration. *Journal of Gang Research, 1*, 11-16.

Warner, B. D., & Rountree, P. W. (1997). Local social ties in a community and crime model: Questioning the systemic nature of informal social control. *Social Problems, 44*, 520-536.

Wasserman, S., & Faust, K. (1994). *Social network analysis: Methods and applications* (Structural Analysis in the Social Sciences, Vol. 8). Cambridge, UK: Cambridge University Press.

Weisel, D. L., & Painter, E. (1997). *The police response to gangs: Case studies of five cities*. Washington, DC: Police Executive Research Forum.

Weitekamp, E. G. M. (2000). *Eurogang: A thematic network for comparative, multi-method research on violent youth groups* (The E.U. Eurogang proposal). Tübingen, Germany: Institute of Criminology.

Weitekamp, E. G. M. (2001). Gangs in Europe: Assessments at the millennium. In M. W. Klein, H.-J. Kerner, C. L. Maxson, & E. G. M. Weitekamp (Eds.), *The Eurogang paradox: Street gangs and youth groups in the U.S. and Europe*. Dordrecht, The Netherlands: Kluwer Academic.

Werdegar, M. M. (1998). Enjoining the Constitution: The use of public nuisance abatement injunctions against urban street gangs. *Stanford Law Review, 51*, 409-445.

Whyte, W. F. (1943). *Street corner society*. Chicago: University of Chicago Press.

Wiatrowski, M. D., Griswold, D. B., & Roberts, M. K. (1981). Social control theory and delinquency. *American Sociological Review, 46*, 525-541.

Widom, C. S. (1989). Child abuse, neglect, and violent criminal behavior. *Criminology, 27*, 251-271.

Wiebe, D. (1998, November). *Targeting and gang crime: Assessing the impacts of a multi-agency suppression strategy in Orange County, California*. Paper presented at the annual meeting of the American Society of Criminology, Washington, D.C.

Wilson, J., & Herrnstein, R. J. (1985). *Crime and human nature: The definitive study of the causes of crime*. New York: Simon & Schuster.

Wilson, W. J. (1987). *The truly disadvantaged: The inner city, the underclass, and public policy*. Chicago: University of Chicago Press.

Wilson, W. J. (1996). *When work disappears: The world of the new urban poor*. New York: Knopf.

Wilson, W. J., Quane, J. M., & Rankin, B. H. (1998). The new urban poverty: Consequences of the economic and social decline of inner-city neighborhoods. In F. R. Harris & L. A. Curtis

(Eds.), *Locked in the poorhouse: Cities, race and poverty in the United States.* Lanham, MD: Rowman and Littlefield.

Winfree, L. T., Jr., Fuller, K., Vigil, T. B., & Mays, G. L. (1992). The definition and measurement of "gang status": Policy implications for juvenile justice. *Juvenile and Family Court Journal, 43*(1), 20-37.

Wong, M. G. (1988). The Chinese American family. In C. H. Mindel, R. W. Habenstein, & R. Wright, Jr. (Eds.), *Ethnic families in America: Patterns and variations.* New York: Elsevier.

Wong, M. G. (1995). Chinese Americans. In P. G. Min (Ed.), *Asian Americans: Contemporary trends and issues.* Thousand Oaks, CA: Sage.

Yablonsky, L. (1959). The delinquent gang as near-group. *Social Problems, 7,* 108-117.

Yablonsky, L. (1963). *The violent gang.* New York: Macmillan.

Yablonsky, L. (1973). *The violent gang.* New York: Penguin.

Yamaguchi, K., & Kandel, D. B. (1984). Patterns of drug use from adolescence to young adulthood: Sequences of progression. *American Journal of Public Health, 74,* 668-672.

Yeager, M. (1998). *People ex rel. Gallo v. Acuna:* Cities allowed a new weapon in their arsenal for the crackdown on gangs. *Whittier Law Review, 19,* 595-654.

Yoo, C. S. (1994). The constitutionality of enjoining street gangs as a public nuisance. *Northwestern University Law Review, 89,* 212-267.

Zatz, M. S., & Portillos, E. L. (2000). Voices from the barrio: Chicano/a gangs, families, and communities. *Criminology, 38,* 369-401.

Zevitz, R. G., & Takata, S. R. (1992). Metropolitan gang influence and the emergence of group delinquency in a regional community. *Journal of Criminal Justice, 20*(2), 93-106.

Zhang, S. X. (1995). Measuring shaming in an ethnic context. *British Journal of Criminology, 35* (2), 248-262.

Index

About the Editor

C. Ronald Huff is Professor of Criminology, Law and Society and Dean of the School of Social Ecology at the University of California, Irvine. He previously taught at Ohio State University (1979-1999), Purdue University (1976-1979), and UC Irvine (1974-1976) and served as a visiting professor at the University of Hawaii (1995). The most recent of his other books include *Youth Violence: Prevention, Intervention, and Social Policy* (1999) and *Convicted but Innocent: Wrongful Conviction and Public Policy* (Sage, 1996), which received an Academic Book of the Year award from the nation's academic and research libraries. He has also published more than 60 journal articles and book chapters. In addition to his academic research and teaching, he has served as a consultant on gangs, youth violence, and public policy to the U.S. Senate Judiciary Committee, the F.B.I. National Academy, the U.S. Department of Justice, numerous other federal agencies, five states, and a number of police departments throughout the nation and has served as an expert witness in a number of court cases. He is currently (2000-2001) President of the American Society of Criminology. His other honors include the Donald Cressey Award from the National Council on Crime and Delinquency (1992), the Paul Tappan Award from the Western Society of Criminology (1993), and the Herbert Bloch Award from the American Society of Criminology (1994).

About the Contributors

Anthony A. Braga is a Senior Research Associate in the Program in Criminal Justice Policy and Management of the Malcolm Wiener Center for Social Policy at Harvard University's John F. Kennedy School of Government and a Visiting Fellow at the National Institute of Justice. His research focuses on developing problem-oriented policing strategies to control violent crime hot spots, disrupt drug markets, and reduce firearms violence. He has served as a consultant on these issues to the RAND Corporation; National Academy of Sciences; U.S. Department of Justice; U.S. Department of the Treasury; Bureau of Alcohol, Tobacco, and Firearms; Boston Police Department; New York Police Department; and other state and local criminal justice agencies. He received his Ph.D. in Criminal Justice from Rutgers University.

Robert J. Bursik, Jr., is Curators' Professor of Criminology and Criminal Justice at the University of Missouri-St. Louis. He is a Fellow of the American Society of Criminology and former vice-president of that organization, as well as the current editor of *Criminology.*

Steven R. Cureton is an Assistant Professor at the University of North Carolina, Greensboro. He received his Ph.D. in Sociology from Washington State University. His research interests include race and crime, gangs, and race relations. His publications have appeared in *The Journal of Black Studies, African-American Research Perspectives, The Journal of Gang Research, Journal of Criminal Justice,* and *The System in Black and White.* He is currently completing a book titled *Hoover: A Gangster's Perspective.*

Scott H. Decker is Curator's Professor of Criminology and Criminal Justice at the University of Missouri-St. Louis. He received a B.A. in Social Justice from DePauw University and an M.A. and Ph.D. in Criminology from Florida State University. His primary research focus has been on criminal justice policy, gangs, violence, and the offender's perspective. He is co-author of *Burglars on the Job* (1994); *Life in the Gang: Family, Friends and Violence* (1996), a field-based study of gang members; *Armed Robbers in Action* (1997); and *Confronting Gangs* (1998). He is currently conducting an evaluation of the SafeFutures program in St. Louis and directing the evaluation of the Strategic Approaches for Community Safety Initiative (SACSI) in St. Louis.

Arlen Egley, Jr., is Research Associate with the National Youth Gang Center, Institute for Intergovernmental Research, Tallahassee, Florida, and a doctoral candidate in the Department of Criminology and Criminal Justice at the University of Missouri-St. Louis. He is completing his dissertation, titled *Levels of Involvement: Differences Between Gang, Gang-Marginal, and Non-Gang Youth,* which examines the relationship between social factors and differing levels of gang membership in a sample of middle school youth. His research interests include juvenile delinquency, youth gangs, and public policy responses.

Finn-Aage Esbensen is the E. Desmond Lee Professor of Youth Crime and Violence in the Department of Criminology and Criminal Justice at the University of Missouri-St. Louis. His publications include a textbook, *Criminology: Explaining Crime and Its Context* (4th ed., with Stephen E. Brown and Gilbert Geis), and recent journal articles that have appeared in *Criminology, Justice Quarterly, Crime and Delinquency, Evaluation Review, Youth and Society, The Journal of Research in Crime and Delinquency,* and *Quantitative Criminology.*

Mark S. Fleisher is Professor of Criminal Justice Sciences at Illinois State University. He has published journal articles and book chapters on corrections and on street gangs, and three books: *Warehousing Violence* (Sage, 1989); *Beggars and Thieves* (1995); and *Dead End Kids* (1998).

Adrienne Freng is Assistant Professor in the Department of Criminal Justice at the University of Wyoming. Her current research interests include race and crime issues (specifically dealing with Native Americans), gangs, and juvenile delinquency. Currently, she is completing research examining the role of race in gang membership.

Gilbert Geis is Professor Emeritus, Department of Criminology, Law and Society at the University of California, Irvine. He is a former president of the American Society of Criminology and recipient of its Edwin H. Sutherland award for outstanding research. His most recent books are *A Trial of Witches,* with Ivan Bunn (1997), and *Crimes of the Century,* with Leigh Bienen (1998).

John M. Hagedorn is Associate Professor of Criminal Justice at the University of Illinois-Chicago. He has authored a number of books and articles on the subject of gangs, and he is currently engaged in research on the history of gangs in Chicago.

James C. Howell, Ph.D., is a criminologist and Adjunct Researcher with the National Youth Gang Center (NYGC), Institute for Intergovernmental Research, in Tallahassee, Florida. Formerly Director of Research and Program Development at the federal Office of Juvenile Justice and Delinquency Prevention, he conducts research on youth gangs at the NYGC and with other youth gang research teams. His gang research has addressed such topics as youth gangs in schools, youth gang homicides, risk and protective factors for gang membership, drug trafficking, illegal gun carrying, and programs and strategies. Some of these studies have been published in *Crime and Delinquency, Criminology,* and the *Journal of Research in Crime and Delinquency.*

David M. Kennedy is Senior Researcher at the Program in Criminal Justice Policy and Management, Kennedy School of Government, Harvard University. He has written and consulted extensively in the areas of community and problem-solving policing, police corruption, and neighborhood revitalization. He is the coauthor of a seminal work on community policing, *Beyond 911: A New Era for Policing,* and numerous articles on police management, illicit drug markets, illicit firearms markets, youth violence, and deterrence theory. He has advised the Justice Department; the Department of the Treasury; the Bureau of Alcohol, Tobacco, and Firearms; the Office of National Drug Control Policy; and the White House on these issues. He directed the Boston Gun Project, a groundbreaking problem-solving policing exercise aimed at serious youth violence. Its chief intervention, Operation Ceasefire, won the Ford Foundation Innovations in Government award, the Herman Goldstein International Award for Problem Oriented Policing, and the International Association of Chiefs of Police Webber Seavey Award.

Malcolm W. Klein is Professor Emeritus at the University of Southern California and an independent consultant on street gang issues. He is also holder of four prestigious awards from the Criminal Justice Association of California, the Western Society of Criminology, and the American Society of Criminology, and is a fellow of four national professional societies in sociology, psychology, and criminology. He has served as a consultant to scores of local, state, national, and international private and public agencies and commissions, has been visiting professor in Sweden and Spain, and has lectured at several dozen major universities here and abroad. His research has been supported by 60 grants and contracts from major foundations and from government agencies in the United States and Europe. His research is reported in almost 100 articles and invited chapters, and in 14 books, including *The American Street Gang.* He is continuing his research under several grants and has initiated a series of undertakings on gangs in Europe with a number of international colleagues. A consultant or expert witness in more than 100 court cases involving gang matters, he continues to be engaged in court cases and is frequently featured in local and national media coverage of gang crime.

Janet L. Lauritsen is Associate Professor of criminology and criminal justice at the University of Missouri-St. Louis and a member of the National Consortium on Violence Research. She has spent the past 3 years investigating the contribution of individual, family, and community factors to the risk for violent victimization by combining data from the Census Bureau with National Crime Victimization Survey records.

Cheryl Maxson is an assistant professor in the Department of Criminology, Law and Society at the University of California's Irvine campus. She is coeditor of *The Eurogang Paradox: Gangs and Youth Groups in the U.S. and Europe* (2001) and *The Modern Gang Reader* (1995, 2001) and coauthor of *Responding to Troubled Youth* (1997). Her articles, chapters, and policy reports concern street gangs, status offenders, youth violence, juvenile justice legislation, drug sales, community policing, and community treatment of juvenile offenders. Currently funded research projects include identifying risk and protective factors for joining gangs and for violence, describing patterns of adolescent violence in Los Angeles, assessing the impact of civil gang injunctions on communities, and evaluating the effectiveness of a juvenile probation program.

James W. Meeker received his J.D. and Ph.D. in sociology from the State University of New York at Buffalo. While working on his dissertation, he served as a personal judicial clerk at the Fourth Appellate Division of the Supreme Court of New York. He joined the faculty at the University of California, Irvine, in 1981. Currently he is a professor in the department of Criminology, Law and Society and is Associate Dean for the School of Social Ecology. He is also the director of the Orange County Gang Incident Tracking System, a cooperative effort between UCI and the Orange County Chiefs' and Sheriff's Association. He serves on the board of directors for the Public Law Society of Orange County and is a member of the California Commission on Access to Justice. His research interests include the sociology of law, criminology, and applied research methodology and statistics with particular emphasis on policy analysis. Currently he is working on the application of Geographic Information Systems to the analysis of gang incidents and to the analysis of legal needs and the delivery of legal services by legal aid organizations. He has published in the areas of gangs, procedural justice, access to justice for the poor, legal services delivery mechanisms, domestic violence, the impact of criminological research on policy, and prosecutorial strategies against organized crime.

Jody Miller is Assistant Professor of Criminology and Criminal Justice at the University of Missouri-St. Louis. Her monograph on young women and gangs, *One of the Guys: Girls, Gangs and Gender,* was published in 2001. She is currently completing a study of the commercial sex industry in Sri Lanka, funded in part by a Fulbright Senior Scholar Award. In addition, she is a member of the National Consortium on Violence Research, through which she is currently researching (with Norman White) violence against urban African American adolescent girls. She has published research on young women's involvement in gangs and street crime in *Criminology, Justice Quarterly, Journal of Research in Crime and Delinquency,* and *Social Problems.* She is the 2001 winner of the American Society of Criminology's Young Scholar Award.

John P. Moore is the director of the National Youth Gang Center, Institute for Intergovernmental Research (IIR), in Tallahassee, Florida. He joined IIR in 1987 and worked with state and local law enforcement agencies coordinating Department of Justice-funded intelligence, narcotics enforcement, and training programs. Immediately prior to joining IIR, he was director of the Mid-States Organized Crime Information Center. He is a graduate of the F.B.I. National Academy and a member of the Advisory Board of the National Alliance of Gang Investigators Associations.

Dana Peterson is a doctoral student in Criminal Justice at the University of Nebraska at Omaha. Her present research interests include gangs and youth violence, families and delinquency, and sex and gender issues in crime.

Kent H. Shafer is commander of the Strategic Response Bureau (SRB) of the Columbus (Ohio) Division of Police, overseeing community-oriented policing and problem-solving activities. He is also charged with investigative and enforcement responsibility for gang, career criminal, and related street crime activities. His previous assignments include narcotics investigations and the anti-gang unit. He is a graduate of the F.B.I. National Academy, has undergraduate degrees in electronics engineering and business administration, and is currently a graduate student at Ohio State University's School of Public Policy and Management. His research and writing interests include gangs, community-oriented policing, and police organizational reform. He is the recipient of the Washington Times Foundation National Service Award for his design and development of the Division's Mission Aligned Policing Philosophy.

James F. Short, Jr., is Professor Emeritus, Washington State University. He was Director of Research (with Marvin Wolfgang) of the National Commission on the Causes and Prevention of Violence (1968-1969). He has been a member of the National Research Council (National Academy of Sciences) Committee on Law and Justice, and that committee's Panel on the Understanding and Control of Violent Behavior. Currently he is a member of the NRC Committee to Review Research on School Violence. He served as editor of the *American Sociological Review* and as president of the American Sociological Association, the Pacific Sociological Society, and the American Society of Criminology. His most recent book is *Poverty, Ethnicity, and Violent Crime*. He is a member of the Academic Advisory Council of the National Campaign Against Youth Violence and of advisory committees for the National Consortium on Violence Research and the National Youth Gang Center. His honors include the Edwin H. Sutherland Award (ASC), the Bruce Smith Award (Academy of Criminal Justice Sciences), the Paul W. Tappan Award (Western Society of Criminology), and the Guardsmark Wolfgang Award for Distinguished Achievement in Criminology. The American Sociological Association's Section on Crime, Law, and Deviance has created in his honor the James F. Short, Jr., Best Article Award.

Terrance J. Taylor is currently a doctoral student in the Department of Criminal Justice at the University of Nebraska at Omaha. His research interests include criminological theory, juvenile delinquency and victimization, research methodology, and policing.

George E. Tita is an Assistant Professor in the Department of Criminology, Law and Society at the University of California, Irvine. His interests include the study of interpersonal violence with a focus on homicide, urban street gangs, and the community context of crime. His methodological expertise includes both qualitative and quantitative approaches, with a strong interest in mapping and spatial analysis. His work in these areas has appeared in several academic journals, book chapters, and policy reports. He also serves as a consultant with the RAND Criminal Justice Unit where he is co-PI of an NIJ-funded gun violence reduction program in the Boyle Heights neighborhood of the City of Los Angeles. He is also a member of the National Consortium on Violence Research (NCOVR), a research and training center specializing in violence research.

Kenneth S. Trump is president of National School Safety and Security Services, a Cleveland-based firm specializing in school security and crisis preparedness training and consulting. He served more than 7 years with the Division of Safety and Security for the Cleveland Public Schools, the last 3 as founding supervisor of its Youth Gang Unit. He then served as assistant director of a federally funded gang project in three southwest Cleveland suburbs, where he was also director of security for the ninth largest Ohio public school system. Since 1997, he has trained and consulted full-time for schools and law enforcement officials in over 30 states. He is the author of two books and more than 30 articles on school security, crisis preparedness, and gang issues. His work on school security and crisis issues is frequently cited in the national media. In 1999, he testified before the U.S. Senate Committee on Health, Education, Labor, and Pensions at its school safety hearing.

James Diego Vigil is Professor of Criminology, Law and Society at the University of California, Irvine. He previously served as Professor of Anthropology at University of California, Los Angeles; Professor of Anthropology at the University of Southern California; Visiting Professor of Education, Harvard University; and held other faculty positions. He received his Ph.D. in anthropology from UCLA. As an urban anthropologist focusing on Mexican Americans, he has conducted research on ethnohis- tory, education, culture change and acculturation, and adolescent and youth issues, especially street gangs. This work has resulted in such publications as *From Indians to Chicanos: The Dynamics of Mexican American Culture* (2nd ed., 1998), *Personas Mexicanas: Chicano Highschoolers in a Changing Los Angeles* (1997), and *Barrio Gangs* (1988), and articles in journals such as *Harvard Educational Review, Hispanic Journal of the Behavioral Sciences, Human Organization, Social Problems, Aztlan,* and *Ethos.* His new book, *A Rainbow of Gangs,* takes a cross-cultural look at the street gangs of Los Angeles and will be published in early 2002.

Bryan Vila is Associate Professor of Criminal Justice at the University of Wyoming and Director of the Wyoming State Criminal Justice Statistical Analysis Center. He was previously Assistant (later Associate) Professor at the University of California, Irvine, and Director of the UCI Focused Research Group on Orange County Street Gangs. Before he became an academic, he spent 17 years in law enforcement, including 9 years as a street cop and supervisor with the Los Angeles County Sheriff's Department—including a stint as Gang Sergeant at East Los Angeles Sheriff's Station. He also served for 6 years as a police chief helping the emerging nations of Micronesia develop innovative law enforcement strategies, and 2 years in Washington, D.C., as a federal law enforcement officer working on policy issues. His newest book, *Tired Cops: The Importance of Managing Police Fatigue,* was published in late 2000. He also has published two recent books with Cynthia Morris, *The Role of Police in American Society* (1999) and *Capital Punishment in the United States: A Documentary History* (1997).

Monica L. Whitlock is a Project Director at University of Southern California's Social Science Research Institute. Her research investigates risk and protective factors for joining gangs, with a focus on refining the definition and measurement of protection. Her current research focuses on identifying family and school-based causes and interventions with youth at risk of joining delinquent peer groups. She has coauthored various reports with Cheryl Maxson and Malcolm W. Klein concerning risk factors for joining gangs.

Steve C. Yun finished his medical studies in June of 2000 and is now a practicing physician at St. Joseph's Hospital in Orange, California. With degrees in anthropology (from the University of Wisconsin–Madison) and medicine (from the University of Southern California), he completed his residency at UCLA. While completing his medical training, he continued to conduct ethnographic fieldwork with James Diego Vigil and was coauthor of several articles and book chapters addressing Vietnamese youth. His interest in street gangs as an anthropologist will resume when he returns to graduate school to earn a doctoral degree.

Sheldon X. Zhang received his Ph.D. in sociology from the University of Southern California. He is Associate Professor in the Sociology Department at California State University, San Marcos. He research areas include Chinese organized crime, Asian gangs, juvenile corrections, and program evaluation. He is currently leading a 2-year federal project investigating the social organization of organized Chinese human smuggling activities across the Pacific.